ANIMALIA AMERICANA

CRITICAL PERSPECTIVES ON ANIMALS: THEORY, CULTURE, SCIENCE, AND LAW

CRITICAL PERSPECTIVES ON ANIMALS: THEORY, CULTURE, SCIENCE, AND LAW

Series Editors: Gary L. Francione and Gary Steiner

The emerging interdisciplinary field of animal studies seeks to shed light on the nature of animal experience and the moral status of animals in ways that overcome the limitations of traditional approaches to animals. Recent work on animals has been characterized by an increasing recognition of the importance of crossing disciplinary boundaries and exploring the affinities as well as the differences among the approaches of fields such as philosophy, law, sociology, political theory, ethology, and literary studies to questions pertaining to animals. This recognition has brought with it an openness to a rethinking of the very terms of critical inquiry and of traditional assumptions about human being and its relationship to the animal world. The books published in this series seek to contribute to contemporary reflections on the basic terms and methods of critical inquiry, to do so by focusing on fundamental questions arising out of the relationships and confrontations between humans and nonhuman animals, and ultimately to enrich our appreciation of the nature and ethical significance of nonhuman animals by providing a forum for the interdisciplinary exploration of questions and problems that have traditionally been confined within narrowly circumscribed disciplinary boundaries.

ANIMALIA AMERICANA

Animal Representations and Biopolitical Subjectivity

COLLEEN GLENNEY BOGGS

Columbia University Press   New York

Columbia University Press
Publishers Since 1893
New York   Chichester, West Sussex
cup.columbia.edu
Copyright © 2013 Colleen Glenney Boggs

Library of Congress Cataloging-in-Publication Data
Boggs, Colleen Glenney.
Animalia Americana : animal representations and biopolitical
subjectivity / Colleen Glenney Boggs
p. cm. — (Critical perspectives on animals: theory, culture, science, and law)
Includes bibliographical references and index.
ISBN 978-0-231-16122-0 (cloth : acid-free paper) —
ISBN 978-0-231-16123-7 (pbk. : acid-free paper) —
ISBN 978-0-231-53194-8 (e-book)
1.   American literature—History and criticism.   2.   Animals in literature.
3.   Subjectivity in literature.   4.   Human-animal relationships—United States.
I.   Title.

PS169.A54B64   2013
810.9'362—dc23   2012019970

∞

Columbia University Press books are printed on
permanent and durable acid-free paper.
This book is printed on paper with recycled content.
Printed in the United States of America

c 10 9 8 7 6 5 4 3 2 1
p 10 9 8 7 6 5 4 3 2 1

Jacket Design by Noah Arlow

Author photo by Eli Burak, college photographer, Dartmouth College.
Used with permission.

References to websites (URLs) were accurate at the time of writing.
Neither the author nor Columbia University Press is responsible for
URLs that may have expired or changed since the manuscript was prepared.

For Sean Reed Boggs
Best brother, best friend

CONTENTS

ILLUSTRATIONS

ACKNOWLEDGMENTS

In writing this book, I was fortunate to have tremendously insightful and generous interlocutors to engage with my work: Neel Ahuja, Sandy Alexandre, Anthony Bogues, Hamilton Carroll, Russ Castronovo, Marianne DeKoven, Elizabeth Maddock Dillon, Donatella Izzo, Lindgren Johnson, Cindy Katz, Eric Lott, Michael Lundblad, Laurie Shannon, Ramón Soto-Crespo, John Stauffer, Jordan Stein, Eleonora Stoppino, Rei Terada, Cary Wolfe, and Elizabeth Young made my thinking sharper. I owe a particular debt to Bill Brown, Tim Dean, and Peter Travis. At Dartmouth, I have generous colleagues: Amy Allen, Lisa Baldez, Aimee Bahng, Michael Blumenauer, Leslie Butler, Michael Chaney, Mary Coffey, Soyica Colbert, Kate Conley, Jonathan Crewe, Mona Domosh, George Edmondson, Marty Favor, Veronika Füchtner, Cecilia Gaposchkin, Gretchen Gerzina, Lenore Grenoble, Christopher MacEvitt, Annabel Martin, Andrew McCann, Patricia McKee, Klaus Milich, Klaus Mladek, Monika Otter, Kristin O'Rourke, Donald Eugene Pease, Adrian Randolph, Ivy Schweitzer, George Trumbull, Barbara Will, and Melissa Zeiger—thank you! I am grateful to Darsie Riccio and Isabel Weatherdon for their significant contributions to the ease and efficiency with which I could work.

The Summer Institute for American Studies has been vital to bringing this book into existence: that's where ideas became talks and talks became chapters. I thank Don Pease for bringing this amazing intellectual environment into existence year after year and for inviting me to participate. To him, the codirectors, plenary speakers, and especially my seminar participants, thank you for holding me to high standards, offering constructive criticism, and giving me the opportunity to think about my work in dialogue with your scholarship. Thanks also to audiences at Brown's Pembroke Center, the Modern Language Association convention, and the American Studies Association conventions for their feedback on earlier versions.

The American Philosophical Society funded my work with a year-long sabbatical fellowship, and Dartmouth College gave me leave from teaching during the tenure of this award. This time to research, write, and think was and is much appreciated. At Dartmouth College, I held a faculty fellowship through the Leslie Humanities Center in 2007–2008, and a Curtis Welling Fellowship in 2008–2009 supported my research.

The Leslie Humanities Center—which I now direct—funded a manuscript review: Amy Allen, Jonathan Crewe, Marianne DeKoven, Andrew McCann, Don Pease, Adrian Randolph, Ivy Schweitzer, and Cary Wolfe read the manuscript in its entirety and provided insightful feedback that made it a better book. The Leslie Center's Humanities Institute on "States of Emergency" that Klaus Mladek and George Edmondson codirected in 2009 crucially enhanced my thinking about biopolitics, and I am grateful to the co-organizers as well as to the participants and presenters for their rigorous intellectual contributions to my work.

Many thanks to Wendy Lochner, Christine Mortlock, Christine Dunbar, Anne McCoy, Kathryn Jorge, and Noah Arlow at Columbia University Press, the probing readers whose reports offered crucial guidance for the final stages of revision, and copyeditor Annie Barva.

Thanks to Marylène Altieri and Sarah Hutcheon at the Schlesinger Library, Radcliffe; to Paul Erickson at the American Antiquarian Society; as well as to Hazen Allen, Susan Bibeau, Laura Braunstein, Bill Fontaine, Jay Satterfield (who first said to me, "Millie"), and Susan Simon for library and computing support at Dartmouth. Thanks to my brother, Sean Reed Boggs, for helping with some of the images. Thanks also to my research assistants, Andrea Olinger and Aurora Wells, as well as to the students in my course "Of Nags, Bitches, and Shrews: Women and Animals in Western Literature."

I am grateful to John Stauffer for his generosity in sharing with me his transcription of Frederick Douglass's "Pictures" lecture and for helping me locate Douglass's description of his encounter with the dog in his speech "Farewell to the British People."

An earlier version of chapter 1 appeared as "American Bestiality: Sex, Animals, and the Construction of Subjectivity," *Cultural Critique* 76, no. 3 (Fall 2010): 98–125, Copyright © 2010 Regents of the University of Minnesota. Chapter 4 has appeared in two previous versions. It is adapted from my essay "Emily Dickinson's Animal Pedagogies," *PMLA* 124, no. 2 (March 2009): 533–541, and is reprinted here by permission of the copyright holder, the Modern Language Association of America. It was also published as "Animals and the Formation of Liberal Subjectivity in Nineteenth-Century American Literature," in Russ Castronovo, ed., *The Oxford Handbook of Nineteenth-Century American Literature*, 197–216 (Oxford: Oxford University Press, 2012). Citations from Emily Dickinson's poems are reprinted by permission of the publishers and the Trustees of Amherst College from *The Poems of Emily Dickinson*, edited by Ralph W. Franklin (Cambridge, Mass: Belknap Press of Harvard University Press), Copyright © 1998, 1999 by the President and Fellows of Harvard College, Copyright © 1951, 1955, 1979, 1983 by the President and Fellows of Harvard College. Citations from Emily Dickinson's letters are reprinted by permission of the publishers of *The Letters of Emily Dickinson*, edited by Thomas H. Johnson (Cambridge, Mass: Belknap Press of Harvard University Press), Copyright © 1958, 1987 by the President and Fellows of Harvard College; 1914, 1924, 1932, 1942 by Martha Dickinson Bianchi; 1952 by Alfred Leete Hampson; 1960 by Mary L. Hampson. The image reproductions from Frederick Douglass's work appear courtesy of the Dartmouth College Library. I thank the American Antiquarian Society for the picture of Carlo. The photo of Barbara Bush and her dog Millie from the cover of *Life* magazine appears here courtesy of the photographer, William Wegman; LIFE® is a registered trademark and used here by permission of The Picture Collection, Inc. Thanks to all these presses, institutions, and people for giving permission for this work to appear here.

While I wrote this book, my children were in excellent hands at the Dartmouth College Child Care Center: thanks to Terri Crane, Denise Ayers, Lori-Jane Higgins, Susan Quimby, Jennifer Boudro, Teresa Hahn, Terri Hollis, Bobbie-Lynn Stone, Ray Garcia, Tatyana Bills, Raquel Fluette, Karen Gray, Kristin Cole, Sunnie McPhedres, Jeffrey Robbins, Amy Potter, Terry Chase, and many others for their support of my work and my family.

Personal friends sustain me: Fina Cañas Barouch, Cathy Boies, Martha Bohrer, Silke Deitmar, Pat Murray, thank you and Danke!

A number of real and imaginary animals accompanied me in the process of thinking and writing. Our cats, Kaya and Peevish, are highly anthropomorphized, and—thank goodness!—highly resistant to that anthropomorphism. They continue to teach me about alterity. The link between children and animals that I draw here goes back much further, however, to my childhood dog, Watson (1979–1995). In his own inimitable way, he remains my Carlo.

My greatest debt goes to my family: Brian, Noah and Liam, my mother as well as my father, the memory of my grandmother, Annemarie Klemme. Sean Reed Boggs is the best brother I could have.

ANIMALIA AMERICANA

INTRODUCTION

On April 14, 2009, President Barack Obama made good on a campaign promise: his daughters Malia and Sasha got a dog, as he had said they would if he won the election. After months of public speculation,[1] revolving mainly around the kind of dog the Obamas would get to accommodate their daughters' allergies and around the manner in which they would acquire that dog, the first family introduced Bo, a purebred Portuguese waterdog and present from Senator Ted Kennedy, to the White House press corps.[2] Reporting for the *Washington Times*, Christina Bellantoni captured the occasion in footage now available on YouTube: "The White House Press Corps got a rare glimpse of the first family as they got to know the first dog of the United States. . . . We were herded out to the White House South Lawn, where we usually watch *Marine One* take off and land. They had wranglers there to make sure we didn't get out of hand."[3] Billing the occasion as private and intimate, the narration also captures its public and political dimensions: although the "glimpse" of the "family" is "rare," they are the "first" family, and they walk their dog—the "first dog of the United States"—on the White House South Lawn. As Bellantoni emphasized, that lawn is usually the staging ground for the president's role as commander in chief in that it is the landing place for his military helicopter, *Marine One*. Although the "first dog's" introduction to the American public on the ground where the president most commonly makes visible U.S. global military power may seem coincidental, this apparently frivolous occasion reveals a key mechanism of biopolitics (a term I will define presently) by which forms of power as seemingly disparate as state authority and familial intimacy get conjoined and worked out via animal representations.

But which animals are we talking about when the press corps is "herded" onto the lawn and disciplined by (presumably cattle) "wranglers" so as to behave appropriately? The literal animal, Bo, here receives company from figurative animals, the bovine White House Press Corps. The lines between the figurative and the literal as well as between different species blur in the course of the report. If the press corps becomes animalized, the "first dog" becomes humanized: one reporter asks, as one would of a new child's arrival in a family, "Is it a boy or a girl?" The dog's sex matters and is definitively identified by the president, who proclaims: "A boy." Although the answer to that question is straightforward, it seems more difficult to discern whether the boy is a dog: a discussion ensues of the dog's seemingly natural (or at least of his breed's cultivated) characteristics. Sasha informs the reporters that her Portuguese waterdog can't swim, and the president explains that, although the breed has webbed feet, these dogs have to be taught to swim. The fact that the dog is in need of pedagogy to perform his own doghood appropriately and is subject to discipline is brought home by the reporters' asking whether he has had an "accident" yet, and by the president didactically informing them that everyone in the family will have to take turns walking the dog: "We want to make sure that we're responsible dog owners, and we hope everyone is, too." Here, again, a shift occurs, by which it is not only the dog who must be taught to perform his species correctly, but also his human caregivers who have to be taught their responsibilities. In the location where military force usually gets staged, we see a different social ordering take place. What both of these scenes share, I argue, is that they reveal animal representations to be a complex site where the construction of subjectivity occurs by affective means and pedagogical methods that hinge on the literal relationship to animals and on their figurative representation. The president's concluding comment in the video sums up these affective dimensions and the way they complicate our understanding of relationships and subjectivities: invoking President Harry Truman's lament that the only way one can have a friend in Washington is to get a dog, President Obama says that he finally got a friend. Bo is no longer the child one would associate with the question about the new arrival's sex; Bo is now both utterly canine—inhabiting the role of "man's best friend"—and superhuman—being the president's only friend where all interhuman relationships fail. How do we begin to sort out these different roles, relationships, and meanings, and what significance do we want to attach to the relationship between the seemingly important (the White House, the president, U.S. military power) and the seemingly trivial (the family pooch)? What is the cultural and political work of animal representations? To address these questions, and to recognize their significance, we need to bring American studies in dialogue with critical animal studies.

"The Question of the Animal": Animal Rights, Animal Studies, and Posthumanism

Our tools for theorizing and historicizing the relationship between animal representations and subject formation have recently multiplied.[4] Animals are everywhere these days. Legal scholars, political theorists, cultural critics, historians, anthropologists, religion scholars, sociologists, and literary critics have undertaken a rigorous examination of "the question of the animal" in its relation to their respective fields.[5] Their efforts press beyond disciplinary boundaries in the sense that a field conceptualized as "animal studies" is in the process of articulating its rationale. At its core, animal studies asks what happens when we include other species in our understanding of subjectivity. Different answers to this question have led to the development of two divergent and seemingly incompatible strands of animal studies: the branch grounded in the social sciences that emerged out of the animal rights movement and the branch that developed in the humanities out of post-structuralist theory, especially in response to the work Jacques Derrida published shortly before his death in 2004.[6] Whereas the animal rights movement argues that our understanding of subjectivity needs to include animals, post-structuralist analysis uses animals to deconstruct our notions of subjectivity. One strand of animal studies has a firm investment in the subject, whereas the other has an equally firm investment in erasing the subject.[7] This book places the two approaches in dialogue with each other and argues that the way we read subjectivity depends on the way we represent the relationship between human beings and animals.

The current concern with animal rights emerged in the 1970s out of a reconsideration of liberal subjectivity. Modeling itself on nineteenth-century utilitarian philosophy and twentieth-century movements for racial and gender equality, animal rights advocacy grew out of Peter Singer's *Animal Liberation*, published in the late 1970s.[8] In Singer's account, animals are part of liberalism's progressive telos: they are the last step in a history that has increasingly abolished discrimination based on physical differences. Arguing that "speciesism" (that is, a bias in favor of one's own species and against members of other species) parallels racism and sexism in making the body a site of discrimination, Singer insisted that the time had come to recognize animals as liberal subjects.[9] Reviving Jeremy Bentham's argument that animals are sentient beings whose suffering matters, he grounded their claim to ethical consideration in the body: pointing out that bodily difference had long been the grounds for discriminating against animals, he argued that they had a similar capacity to suffer pain and that therefore they needed to be included in a utilitarian model of society premised on minimizing suffering.[10] Although Singer's book did not itself advocate for animal rights and in many ways is incompatible with the rights model subsequently developed by Tom Regan and others, it was nevertheless received as a call for increased legal representation for animals and sparked a debate over subjectivity that continues today.[11]

As the position statements compiled in the recent volume *Animal Rights: Current Debates and New Directions* make clear,[12] this inclusion of animals in liberal subjectivity has ignited a fierce discussion over the relationship between representation and embodiment, and has raised the question whether species is a marker of alterity akin to or different from race and sexuality. In arguing that rights are exclusively reserved for human beings, scholars opposed to the inclusion of animals in legal models of subjectivity, such as Richard Posner and Richard Epstein, have deliberately embraced the speciesism of which their opponents, such as Steven Wise and Peter Singer, accuse them. Espousing a Darwinian position that differentiates human beings from all other animals, Richard Epstein writes: "We have to separate ourselves from (the rest of) nature from which we evolved."[13] Claiming that "membership in the human species is not a morally irrelevant fact, as the race and gender of human beings have come to seem," Richard Posner insists that animals are not to be classified as subjects, but as property.[14] Animals, says Epstein, should "be treated as objects of human ownership," not as "bearers of independent rights."[15] For Epstein and Posner, the conditions of embodiment are not conterminous with the conditions of representation; on the contrary, by their account, being fully embodied means being barred from the abstractions on which legal representation depends.

Different as the advocates and opponents of animal rights seem from one another, they ultimately share in the same logic of binary thinking. Both sides of the debate pragmatically take for granted that "the law divides the physical universe into persons and things,"[16] though they disagree whether the binary division between subjects and objects should correspond to the division between human beings and animals. Each side of the rights debate is invested in the liberal subject, either by guarding against the notion that animals can participate in a model of subjectivity based on reason and the proprietorship of one's own person or by arguing for the inclusion of animals in the liberal subject's rights, thereby reinstating the fundamental underpinning of the liberal subject—namely, its claim to universality—by expanding its reach; their disagreement over the parameters of that subject does not challenge but on the contrary reaffirms the liberal subject's importance. What is missing on both sides is an understanding of the ways in which the liberal subject already depends at its core—as I argue—on a relationship with animals that undercuts this binary and that reveals "the animal" as well as "the human" to be "a linguistic, cultural, and sociopolitical construct of comparatively recent date."[17] We need to understand the history of that construct because we cannot otherwise account for the structural position that animals have in opposition to humans or for the way that relationship straddles the subject/object divide and functions as a mechanism of violence on the one hand and a means of alterity on the other.

Post-structuralism enables us to read animals as an immanent other that founds and confounds the liberal subject. Animals represent an alterity that underwrites the formation of the subject as its disavowed point of origin and unassimilable trace. Post-structuralist animal studies challenge the "schema of the knowing subject and its anthropocentric underpinnings."[18] This shift away from the "knowing" or reasoning subject puts post-structuralism in unexpected alliance with the animal rights movement in its emphasis on feeling.[19] The validity of this claim—that post-structuralism theorizes feeling—is not self-evident. Post-structuralism's relationship to feeling was largely ignored or dismissed before Rei Terada's landmark 2001 publication *Feeling in Theory: Emotion After the "Death of the Subject."* Terada does not merely argue that post-structuralism opens up a space for considerations of feeling. She also demonstrates that post-structuralism has a notion of affect at its core, and that it develops a theory of subjectivity via an understanding of what it means to feel for others. Taking issue with the ideological gesture that "casts emotion as proof of the human subject," post-structuralist critics—as Terada has demonstrated—map affect as the "common ground of the physiological and the psychological," where "emotions emerge only through acts of interpretation and identification by means of which we feel *for others*."[20] As Jacques Derrida's last works powerfully demonstrated, those "others" need not always already be human. By examining specific representations of animals, abjected as beasts and sentimentalized as pets, my work tests the boundaries of who or what can count as an "other" that we feel "for" and what forms such "feeling" takes in the context of a particular history of subject formation. As I argue, the subject is not self-sufficient but relies on affective relationships that cross the species line.

Feeling is a particularly ambivalent site for the engagement with animals.[21] One recurring and dominant strand of argumentation about the relationship between human beings and animals points to the "emotional contradictions" by which "pets and wildlife evoke deep positive feelings, but domestic animals feeding the consumer market are a morally troubling reality."[22] Gary Francione has argued that "when it comes to non-humans, we exhibit what can best be described as moral schizophrenia. We say one thing about how non-humans should be treated, and do quite another."[23] Such statements suggest there are two poles to our affective engagement with animals: that of "positive feelings" and that of violence; by transmuting those structures of feeling into political terms, we might begin to map them onto the division between *bios* and *zoē* as well as between affirmative and thanatological biopolitics, terms that I take up later. These seemingly contradictory attitudes toward animals serve an important function. They make affect the mechanism for claims to ontological difference. Human and nonhuman are themselves mutable categories whose definitions are worked out in these affective relationships.

Charting the "emergence of the 'animal question'" through these different schools of thought, Kari Weil has suggested that we need to focus "on three trends or moments in literary and critical theory for which the animal becomes a test or limit case: the linguistic turn, a counterlinguistic or affective turn, and the ethical turn."[24] My book sets those three strands in dialogue with one another: locating animals at the core of language inevitably means confronting its limit, its outside, its enabling and negating conditions. That confrontation is one where language and reason emerge but also unravel. I do not see this attention to language necessitating a counterlinguistic turn, nor would I equate the counterlinguistic with the affective; instead, I locate the linguistic and the affective in dialogue with one another as the terrain on which subjectivity gets worked out via intertwined symbolizations and embodiments. One of the relationships that I constantly trace is the relationship between language and affect, a relationship that does not presume a binarization between the human and the animal. The attempts to intervene in and control those shifts in various ways are what I understand as constituting the "ethical turn." Weil helpfully defines the relationship of animals studies to the ethical turn, which she defines as "a concern with and for alterity, especially insofar as alterity brings us to the limits of our own self-certainty and certainty about the world."[25] But what kind of alterity we encounter in animals is already determined by a complex set of expectations about that encounter: Lorraine Daston and Gregg Mitman caution that "before either animal individuality or subjectivity can be imagined, an animal must be singled out as a promising prospect for anthropomorphism."[26] I want to shift the terms here and suggest that "an animal must be singled out as a promising prospect" for a *relationship*. That relationship can certainly be anthropomorphic, but it can also function, in Weil's formulation, as an affect-based " 'critical anthropomorphism' in the sense that we open ourselves to touch and be touched by others as fellow subjects and may imagine their pain, pleasure, and need in anthropomorphic terms but must stop short of believing that we can know their experience."[27]

But if human and animal themselves emerge as relational and shifting categories, what justifies describing the field that engages with them as " 'animal' studies," and what are the methodological implications and limitations of that approach? The bifurcation in animal studies between the rights approach and the post-structuralist approach has recently occasioned the question how the emerging field might otherwise be described and whether *animal studies* is an adequate term. Cary Wolfe cautions against the use of the terms *animal studies* and *human–animal studies* because they allow for the continuity of anthropocentrism: "Indeed, one of the hallmarks of humanism—and even more specifically that kind of humanism called liberalism—is its penchant for that kind of pluralism, in which the sphere of attention and consideration (intellectual or ethical) is broadened and extended to previously marginalized groups, but without in the least destabilizing or throwing into radical question the schema of the human who undertakes such pluralization. In that event, pluralism becomes *incorporation*, and the projects of humanism (intellectually) and liberalism (politically) are extended, and indeed extended in a rather classic sort of way."[28] Michael Lundblad has suggested that we replace the term *animal studies* with *animality studies* to embark on scholarly inquiries that explore "how constructions of the animal have shifted historically in relation to the human and how discourses of human and nonhuman animality have produced various identity categories within the human."[29] Although I find the term *animality* useful in a number of ways that will become evident, I am wary of letting go entirely of the term *animal.* The importance of retaining the latter stems from three factors. First, "animality" is not a single construct but operates on a spectrum where "the animal" is one position. Second, the term *animality* risks foreclosing difference by turning back to "categories within the human" (a critique I also extend to the terms *creature* and *creaturely* when I discuss them in chapter 5); I want to make sure to hold on to a notion of animal alterity and, for that matter, to see such alterity's importance for rethinking subject formation.[30] And third, "animality" is a useful theoretical concept but not a term that we should anachronistically impose on the historical materials I examine.

The approach that has emerged with the greatest force as an alternative to "animal studies" is posthumanism, which sees itself as a critique not just of liberalism and the kinds of humanist scholarship it enables, but of the very premises about species distinctions that underlie them.[31] Popularized by N. Katherine Hayles's 1999 book *How We Became Posthuman: Virtual Bodies in Cybernetics, Literature, and Informatics,* the term challenged Enlightenment models of subjectivity by reflecting on modern technologies' ability to mimic core traits of the human.[32] Posthumanism grew out of an interest in the role that technology plays for unsettling our understandings of such binaries as culture and nature, biology and technology. What I draw from posthumanism is a commitment to seeing the connections between seemingly disparate entities and an attentiveness to embodiment.

The cultural importance of embodiment and the relationship between the body and discourse has been long and well established by scholars engaging with Michel Foucault's work, and has not been limited to posthumanism. To cite but one example, Peter Stallybrass and Allon White write: "The body cannot be thought separately from the social formation, the symbolic topography, and the constitution of the subject. The body is neither a purely natural given nor is it merely a textual metaphor, it is a privileged operator for the transcoding of these other areas."[33] This passage crucially makes the body a nodal point for subject formation and provocatively unsettles the binaries that had separated the natural from the textual and privileged the latter. Important as this attention to the body has been for critiquing models of subjectivity based on reason and universality by drawing attention to embodiment and particularity, what is striking about this passage and paradigmatic of many discussions of "the body" is its implicit definition of "the body" as the human body. How might other bodies unsettle that association? What happens to this critical approach when "the body" becomes "bodies" in the plural?

Posthumanism offers answers to these questions and critiques scholars' ongoing equation of "the body" with the human. For instance, in her discussion of the Turing test (which assesses a machine's ability to show intelligent behavior), Hayles argues: "What embodiment secures is not the distinction between male and female or between humans who can think and machines which cannot. Rather, embodiment makes clear that thought is a much broader cognitive function depending for its specificities on the embodied form enacting it. This realization, with all its exfoliating implications, is so broad in its effects and so deep in its consequences that it is transforming the liberal subject, regarded as the model of the human since the Enlightenment, into the posthuman."[34]

Useful as I find this approach, I ultimately depart from posthumanism in three crucial and connected ways: whereas posthumanism is interested in the challenges technology poses for our definitions of its constituent term *human*, I am interested in the challenges that cross-species relationships pose for that term.[35] This interest shifts my attention from notions of a "post" to the concept of "inter," as in "intersubjective," "interrelated," "interactive," "interspecies," and even "intercourse."[36] It also positions me differently in relation to the liberal subject: instead of critiquing liberalism from the outside by imagining posthumanism as an alternative, I want to read at least a certain kind of posthumanism as being intrinsic to a certain logic of liberalism. To that end, I read animals as integral to liberalism, as a structuring force that destabilizes the liberal subject at its core. This emphasis on the liberal subject also redirects my attention from such macroconcerns as computing technology (Hayles) and systems theory (Wolfe) to the microlevel of relationships and the ways in which political structures get enacted and resisted on the level of interactions in such seemingly mundane acts as petting a dog.

The Absent Animal: Theorizing Biopolitics and Biopower in Relation to Species

Within the field of posthumanist inquiry, a dichotomy has arisen (which in certain ways replicates the bifurcation in animal studies) between an approach based on embodiment and one concerned primarily with semiotics or, more broadly speaking, information technologies.[37] In thinking about subjectivity as a discourse formation along Foucauldian lines—that is, as something that occupies a shifting nexus of power—I bring these symbolic dimensions and bodily registers into contact with each other. But the terrain of inquiry then necessitates another set of considerations: Anat Pick has recently mapped a move in the work of Cora Diamond and Jacques Derrida *"from rights to lives."*[38] The shift in terminology suggests that we need to bring animal studies and posthumanism in conversation with inquiries into the way biopolitics operates in that biopolitics at its core aggregates to itself the power to define whose "lives" matter.

Michel Foucault coined the terms *biopolitics* and *biopower* but never fully elaborated on them in his work. As Michael Donnelly has observed, Foucault "wrote comparatively little" about "such regulatory controls," especially when we consider that "it is the population or species-body, emerging as a field of intervention and then as the ultimate end of government, which leads Foucault to conceptualize that new cluster of power relations, beyond the juridical framework of sovereignty, which he describes as the 'governmentalisation of the State.'"[39] Foucault identified two vectors of biopower: one, the *"anatomo-politics of the human body,"* which were "ensured by the procedures of power that characterized the *disciplines"*; and two, *"a biopolitics of the population."*[40] These two aspects of biopower position it between disciplinarity and governmentality. They reconcile the central tension in political philosophy between the individual (Locke) and the collective (Hobbes) model of subject formation in the modern state.[41] In Foucault's theorization, the collective and the individual produce each other: in order for the body to be marked as *human*, an understanding of *population* as species must be in place.

But this tautology by which human and population (as well as population and human) define one another as the proper terrain of the political is itself a conceit of biopower's operation and comes at the deliberate exclusion of the nonhuman from the realm of political representation. Animals are integral in two ways to a full understanding of biopolitics. First, the "anatomo-politics" of the modern state does not limit its reach to human bodies but also exercises power over animal bodies; and second, the differentiation between human beings and animals is the fundamental mechanism by which biopolitics exerts power. This fluidity by which affect determines ontology is not a failure of biopolitics, but its operative core: as Nicole Shukin has argued, biopower hinges on the "production of species difference as a strategically ambivalent rather than absolute line, allowing for the contradictory power to both dissolve and reinscribe borders between humans and animals."[42] Affect is historically produced and regulated, and this affective ambivalence is central to the process by which subject formation occurs in the biopolitical state.[43]

Biopolitical theory and animal studies have markedly different critical genealogies and have, to date, had little to say to each other. As Cary Wolfe has recently pointed out, animal studies has largely ignored the political frame that biopolitics offers, and biopolitical theorists have largely ignored the question of how animals might figure into theorizations of sovereign power (with the result that these theorists themselves run the risk of replicating the model of sovereign politics they set out to analyze and critique).[44] Both fields have had virtually no engagement with gender and sexuality.[45] This book fills that gap and advances our understanding of the crucial role animals play for the psychosexual formation of biopolitical subjectivity.[46]

Whereas animal studies has largely been an American phenomenon (and that is not to dismiss the vibrant interest currently under way in Australia, Germany, and elsewhere), biopolitical theory has been developed primarily in Europe, especially in French and Italian philosophy. But biopolitical theory has recently entered the American academy with a vengeance.[47] The sudden but massive scrutiny that biopolitical theory, especially the work of Giorgio Agamben, has received in the past decade can be explained by American academics' renewed interest in understanding the exercises of sovereign power. Two particular focal points have been, one, the use of the rule of exception to expand presidential executive power and, two, the rhetoric of American exceptionalism, both driven by the American response to the terrorist attacks of September 11, 2001. At its inception, American studies focused on exceptionalism. Although that focus initially took a celebratory form in the symbol–myth–image school's readings of American culture as a coherent enterprise of encountering new intellectual and geographic territories, that reading and its concomitant assumptions about subjectivity came under scrutiny in the late 1970s, when exceptionalism itself became an object of criticism rather than a field-defining paradigm.[48] The work especially of Giorgio Agamben on the use of exception in relation to sovereignty has thus fallen on fertile ground. But a larger dialogue among American studies, biopolitical theory, and animal studies has yet to emerge, and this book maps some of the ways in which we might imagine that conversation unfolding.

In response to Foucault's theory of biopower, two major schools of thought have developed: one, represented chiefly by Giorgio Agamben, sees biopower as a negative force tied to death, whereas the other, as represented by Michael Hardt, Antonio Negri, and Roberto Esposito, emphasizes an affirmative version of biopower. What emerges from this discussion, as I argue, is a larger issue by which the question of what counts as life and who exerts power over life hinges on a complex system of representations. It is in the struggle over defining biopower that the figurative and the literal, the political and the scientific, encounter each other at the intersection that modernity tries to negate (more on that later). Even when animals function figuratively, those figurations are often more messy than we might suspect. Susan McHugh argues that

> the ideals of intersubjective relations . . . effectively unsettle habits of mind that otherwise render intimacies within and across other species insignificant, and along the way model approaches to gaining and sustaining more meaningful engagements. Together they begin to explain why, in lieu of definitively identifying individual agents as subjects, questions about the narrative functions of animals and animality lead directly to concerns about populations, that is, the possibilities for nonsubjective agency forms required of whole ways of life, and so lead to open-ended engagements with the biopolitics of life itself. . . .

[F]amiliar household pets like cats and dogs serve on the front lines of people's everyday attempts to work out these problems.[49]

Animal representations form the nexus where biopolitical relationships get worked out. My book argues that we need to focus specifically on American literature as a key site for that negotiation. To develop an understanding of the important functions animal representations take on in the struggle over biopower, I draw on two key scholarly interventions into theorizations of biopower and animal studies—one by Andrew Benjamin in his analysis of Maurice Blanchot's philosophy and the other by Alice Kuzniar, who works out a theory of productive abjection in her work on animal representations.

According to Giorgio Agamben, the power to differentiate between life forms is key to the exercise of sovereign power in the modern state. Revitalizing categories first introduced by Aristotle, Agamben argues that life is divided between *bios*, which refers to life in its political forms, and *zoē*, a physiological life that is excluded from but foundational to the political order. Foucault was the first to remark on how the sign of the animal emerged, in Shukin's description, as the "threshold of biological modernity, marking a shift to 'untamed ontology' or 'life itself' as the new object of power."[50] For Agamben, sovereignty is the exercise of determining which life forms count as *bios*. To make that determination, the sovereign must remove himself from *bios*: he inhabits an exceptional position that mirrors the *homo sacer* (sacred man) of Roman law and the wolf-man of Germanic law—that is, the form of life that is placed outside of the law.

It is important to note three problems with Agamben's model: his absent treatment of gender, his monolithic account of history, and his Eurocentric views of race. First, Agamben reads Aristotle selectively in that he sets aside Aristotle's examination—in his writings on natural history as well as in his writings on politics—of sexual difference. Agamben thereby arrives at a theory of biopower that ignores gender as a category of analysis (thus going against the Foucauldian grain) and that is implicitly masculine. Second, Agamben privileges his version of Aristotelian philosophy as the dominant and only model for understanding political power and Western attitudes to life. Writing about the moral status of animals, Gary Steiner proposes that a flexibility of categories marks "Homeric and pre-Socratic thought." That flexibility, says Steiner, is not simply replaced by Aristotelian determinations but presents an ongoing challenge to them that makes Western philosophy's relationship to animals far more complicated and less monolithic than many scholars have suggested: "Some aspects of that early openness persist in Western thought and conflict with the dominant line of thought."[51] Agamben posits the Aristotelian model of power as a transhistoric monolith for organizing biopower. Dominick LaCapra has taken Agamben to task for "an insufficiently situated version of transhistorical, structural, or existential trauma that, in Agamben's account, may well induce an evasion or misconstruction of specific historical, social and political problems, including the status and use of the animal in society."[52] And third, Agamben's model remains Eurocentric by not taking into account the global and imperial mappings on which biopower depends. The mirroring of the sovereign and the wolf-man is refracted: explaining how the exclusion from *bios* is racialized and territorialized, Achille Mbembe argues that we must understand biopolitics as a fundamental mechanism of colonialism, founded in slavery and operational today in an array of global conflicts.[53] In the colonial context, biopolitics operates by producing race as a category of alterity. Barred from political life, these racialized, nonwhite "others" experience biopolitics as "necropolitics"—that is, as an exercise of power that hinges on what has been problematized as a social death. Necropolitics is a condition for "the deathly logic of citizenship that sentenced women and slaves to excessive and lethal embodiment" in order to "reanimate the lifeless citizen, hinting that *his* abstract identity and legal authority always rests on memories, corporeal residues, and other material contexts, no matter how completely disavowed or forgotten they seem."[54] As Ann Laura Stoler writes, "Domains of the intimate . . . are strategic for exploring two related but often discretely understood sources of colonial control: one that works through the requisition of *bodies*—those of both colonials and colonized—and a second that molds new 'structures of feeling'—new habits of heart and mind that enable those categories of difference and subject formation."[55] Biopolitics, states Anthony Bogues, has to "trap both the imagination and desire" in its quest to "shape, control, and make human life in its own image."[56] That task makes literature both central to and excluded from its operations, as I argue at greater length in subsequent chapters. The reliance on imagination and desire places representation and affect at the core of biopower's operation. Biopower depends on regulating representation and affect precisely because imagination and desire make it possible to oppose the "death drive of imperial power" and its totalizing aspirations.[57] But what form can that opposition take?[58]

The question is complicated by the collusion between death and desire that developed in the nineteenth century, as Philippe Ariès has documented.[59] This dimension of desire is all but absent from current accounts of biopower's operation. I make it key to my analysis: I examine different practices and representations of animal love to understand how the affective engagement with animals functions as a site of biopolitical regulation as well as resistance. I read two moments in the seventeenth century as being central to the emergence of a specifically American biopolitics: the criminalization of bestiality at Plymouth Plantation and the related development—in the wake of John Locke's *Thoughts on Education* (1693)—of animal pedagogy, a term Kelly Oliver defines as "discourses" that use animals to "teach us to be human."[60] Instead of charting a telos by which the disciplining of bodies gives way to other forms of governmentality, I read these two strands of animal love as being "organized around a radical and irreducible incoherence," as Eve Sedgwick puts it, and as generating what she calls "overlapping, contradictory, and conflictual definitional forces" that create a "performative space of contradiction."[61] This book examines how the double legacy of animal love (that is, bestiality and "puppy love" as conjoined discourses) gets worked out in American literature's engagement with animals in order to explicate an iconography that haunts our current understandings of subjectivity and that links colonialism with neoliberalism, particularly in its strategies of infantilization and its depictions of children and animals as subjects in the making.

Whereas Agamben's work focuses mainly on the thanatological drift in biopolitics, Roberto Esposito has tried to counter that focus with a model of affirmative biopolitics, which he arrives at via a reworking of Michael Hardt and Antonio Negri's model of the multitude that resists empire. In an interview conducted by Timothy Campbell, Esposito usefully sums up the differences between these models and the importance of his intervention:

> Where Agamben accentuates the negative, even tragic tonality of the biopolitical phenomenon in a strongly dehistoricizing modality—one that pays tribute to Heidegger, Schmitt, and Benjamin—Negri, on the contrary, insists on the productive, expansive, or more precisely vital element of the biopolitical dynamic. . . . Indeed, Negri imagines that biopolitics can contribute to the reconstruction of a revolutionary horizon in the heart of empire, and in so doing, he absolutely accentuates the moment of resistance to power, in opposition to the letter of the

Foucauldian text. For my own part, I don't radicalize one of the two semantic polarities of biopolitics to the detriment of the other. Instead I have tried to move the terms of the debate by providing a different interpretive key that is capable of reading them together, while accounting for the antinomical relation between them. All done without renouncing the historical dimension, as Agamben does, and without immediately collapsing the philosophical prospective into a political one, as Negri does.[62]

For Esposito, there is no *zoē* separate from *bios*. Perceiving resistance against the death drive as located in positions that are not exterior to power, he sees power in conflict with forces that are not always already abjected and that are more closely aligned with Foucault's original view of biopower as productive. The model that emerges in Esposito is far messier than the one we get in Agamben. Instead of seeing biopolitics in relation to a symmetry between sovereignty and *homo sacer*, Esposito locates biopolitics in bodies, forces, technologies, disciplines, and institutions that are constitutive of biopolitics but that also map a terrain of power relations that is much more complicated than a model premised on state sovereignty. Arguing that the modalities of *bios* cannot be inscribed in the borders of the conscious subject and therefore cannot be limited to persons, Esposito's work opens up a larger terrain of thinking about power. Although Agamben's contribution lies in showing how the anthropological apparatus needs a remainder (one he variously frames as the *homo sacer* or the animal or the wolf-man) that needs to be excluded from the operations of power that depend on it, thinking about the affirmative dimensions of biopower opens up the possibility of seeing animals in a position that need not always be abjected. There are two interconnected ways of examining that double operation: one in relation to affect—for instance, in the model Alice Kuzniar works out (via the theorizations of Julia Kristeva) in arguing for melancholia as a site where abjection becomes productive of new representational possibilities—and a second in relation to language, as we see in the work of Andrew Benjamin, to whom I now turn.

Animal representations provide a way of rethinking the equation of biopolitics with thanatopolitics. In his work on Maurice Blanchot, Andrew Benjamin gives an account of how such a rethinking might be possible and of the crucial role that literature plays in the process. Taking as his point of departure the "question of human being" and challenging "an eventual equation of that question with death," Benjamin affords a central role to animals in thinking biopolitics beyond thanatopolitics. The challenge for this undertaking lies in the fact that, seemingly, "the propriety of human being demands either the exclusion or the death of the animal." But death itself takes on complicated and multiple meanings in this context. Pointing out that "it is vital to note that the place of the animal within much philosophical and literary writing is positioned by a death that is no mere death," Benjamin confronts the difficulty of accounting philosophically "for a radically different situation—one in which the particularity of human being was not dependent on forms of privation and sacrifice." For Benjamin, that situation raises fundamental questions: "What would be the effect on being human—and thus the thinking of that being philosophically—if the maintained animal were allowed? If, that is, the 'without relation' gave way to a fundamentally different form of relationality?" For Benjamin, that "different form of relationality" emerges through animals' ability to figure a "distance that both joins and separates," a distance that "cannot be thought outside its founding relation to death," but that functions as a "between" and as such "identifies a form of commonality, the common as the co-presence of ethos and place in addition to death, brings community to the fore. More importantly, it positions the question of community such that it eschews a relation given by sameness and allows for the introduction of a sense of alterity. Rather than merely being the other to the same, alterity in this context is defined in terms of founding 'irreciprocity.' "[63] This figuration fundamentally unsettles a dichotomy between the human and the animal and enables us to think beyond the structures of the dyad sovereign/*homo sacer*. The multiplication of death that takes place via the animal's sacrificial position as a structuring device of human being also introduces a fundamental plurality to the very notion of subjectivity, a plurality that cannot be thought of separately from its relation to animals. Allowing for the "maintained animal" to have an ongoing relevance multiplies its presence. Thinking about "real" animals and "real" human beings also requires taking into account figurative animals and figurative human beings—and vice versa. Instead of functioning as a delimitation that consolidates ontological differences and circumscribes the realm of the properly symbolic, "the maintained animal" opens them up.

In that proliferation, a collapse of these categories themselves takes place, as Benjamin explains:

For Blanchot, the point at which literary language and thus writing takes place, is encapsulated in the moment when it becomes possible to say (more accurately, to write, and thus never to say!), "When I speak death speaks in me" (Quand je parle la mort parle en moi). "When" here is both a singular utterance and announces an action, thus indicating the moment that should have been absorbed into the "I" who speaks while yielding that "I," for there cannot be pure particularity here. This impossibility is not due to the presence of an original plurality, but to the fact that the death in question, the one that "speaks in me," is already doubled. The "I" in whom death speaks is there, and only there, as the result of a death that makes that "I" possible. There is therefore what can be described as a "death of possibility"—namely, the unannounced sacrificial death within death's now doubled presence. The animal dies in order that there be alterity. In more general terms, the force of the questions "who and what dies?" springs from their necessary relation to both literature and writing. . . . It is clear that the relationship constructed by death's emphatic presence—the presence in which the dying of the other always occurs—defines particularity and intimacy.[64]

Emily Dickinson captures this complicated philosophical statement in one line (as I explain in chapter 4): "there was a fly buzzed when I died." In Benjamin's view, the fundamental relation between the "I" and an alterity that is not simply another "I" but a structuring and interconnected part of that "I" connects "death and the logic of sacrifice—death's double presence—as that which founds community." This reading of death as enabling an affirmative biopolitics is a fundamental departure from Agamben: for Agamben, the operative logic of thanatopolitics is its destruction of both subjectivity and community. In Benjamin's reading of Blanchot, the opposite holds true: that it is the proliferation of death and the structure of animal death that "founds community." But the difficulty then becomes how to think of that community in relation to animals: if "community occurs with the sacrifice of the animal," then how would it be possible to inscribe animals within that community in any meaningful way? "The reiteration of the logic of sacrifice," after all, "continues to position the animal's inclusion as predicated upon the necessary and productive nature of its death." For Benjamin, the answer lies with language or, more specifically, with an "Adamic naming in relation to the animal," where naming "affirms relation."[65] Such naming "preserves the animal" "within a space that will always be contested, and where the endlessness of the naming has as its correlate the inevitable endlessness of the 'nameless unspoken language'" that I associate especially with voice in the chapters to come. Writing, says Benjamin, then becomes the way in which we can imagine an alternative biopolitics that does justice to animals: "Both the endless naming and the nameless unspoken language operate within domains and relations in which one neither exhausts nor masters the other. Both continue within their difference. The animal will have been maintained. Writing will continue. There is another relation to the other."[66] My book explores what that other relation might look like and how American literature negotiates its relationship to biopolitics and subjectivity via animal representations.

American (Animal) Literature and
the Politics of Countermodernity

I am interested in tracing the cultural work that animal representations do, first, as the other in a set of binaries that are constitutive of the subject and, second, as the middle ground that enables and unsettles that binarization. On the one hand, animals function as the absolute other of the human subject; they are the negatively defined nonhuman. On the other hand, animals serve as mediators between the subject and its others. A problematic double articulation emerges of what we mean by "animal": ("the") animal is the binary opposite of ("the") human. But animals, especially when figured as pets, also function as a middle ground between sets of binaries that oppose the subject and the object, the human and the nonhuman, the psychological and the physiological, the real and the symbolic. In that sense, animal representations are mediators; they perform what Jacques Rancière calls a "process of subjectivization that bridges the interval between two forms" of existence.[67] Animal representations mark the limit of the subject and reveal the mechanisms of its functioning. But even beyond that, "representations" mark a paradox: whereas in political contexts representation suggests the ability to be recognized by a subject in the political system and to participate in it, in the context of literature *representation* is a more generic term for depiction. In speaking about "animal representations," I am gesturing toward a set of tensions: in political contexts, animals cannot have representation; in literary contexts, they can be represented, though it is questionable even there whether they can participate in any meaningful way in that representation. And yet I want to suggest that it is on the grounds of such representations that the terms of animals' exclusion become legible—that animals achieve a representation of their exclusion from representation and that here at minimum a critique of and at best an alternative to this exclusion becomes possible.

This approach presents a challenge to the way animal studies has been configured as a field: as Christine Kenyon-Jones points out, a "literary approach" has until recently been "at odds with many other cultural studies of animals, which have deliberately excluded art and literature from their discussions."[68] This reluctance has been based on a suspicion that "canonical art and literature . . . has little connection with real creatures," according to Harriet Ritvo.[69] I explore and question that assumption by asking how literature grapples with the meaning of "real" animals and the possibilities as well as limitations for their depiction. Instead of seeing representation as a hindrance to an engagement with animals, as Erica Fudge worried it might be for historians,[70] I suggest that animal representations on the contrary provide an important opportunity to inquire into the bigger mystery: not why we have constructions of animality, but the fact that the construct animal gets to inhabit a position of the ontologically real.

I selected the case studies that form the focus of my analysis on the basis that they are ones in which the writers imagine their texts as spaces of engagement, where language is not a medium for representing animals, but a grounds for encountering them. That makes literature the site where the relationship with animals is worked out—where it is not an already formed subject that enters into the articulation of its intimate connections, but where the expression of relationships fundamentally confront us with questions of subjectivity. Literature is not a point of separation or distinction, but a means of encounter, and it is in literature that we confront the irreducible alterity of animals that is the basis for a relationship beyond anthropomorphism. As Laura Brown has argued, "Neither alterity nor anthropomorphism, in itself, can account for the versatility and complex nature of the imaginary animal." Whereas the "opposing claims that see the animal either through the lens of anthropomorphism or [through the lens] of alterity have largely shaped the critical understanding of animal-kind," it is possible to move beyond that duality: "literature provides an alternative model."[71] My aim is to understand what that model has to offer us for the American context and vice versa.

Taking up the question of "the animal" in relationship to literature might be seen as replicating a central problem: that animals are being represented in language and that language is always already a human construct. I find Susan McHugh's reflections particularly helpful in addressing this issue: arguing that "the problems of metaphor especially point to the danger of arriving at the same old conclusions, namely that animals are only literary as human subjects," she suggests that "putting the relationship between these forms of literary criticism and historical methodologies under scrutiny disturbs the sedimentation of these patterns of reading literary animals in western humanist traditions, and the interdisciplinary methods of animal studies prove particularly useful in launching this critique" because such "readings of animal representations inform and are informed by axiological and other 'unnatural' histories."[72] McHugh, then, presents use with two challenges that I take up: one, seeing animal representations as a way of producing alternative "histories" and, two, thinking about what animal representations have to offer us for our readings of American literature.

Countermodernity

Animals are a recent invention. In his landmark two-volume publication *Man and the Natural World,* Keith Thomas traced changing attitudes toward animals.[73] Initially an undifferentiated part of nature that was subject to conquest and exploitation, animals only gradually gained recognition as distinct from a broader natural landscape. By about 1800, animals had attained a special status (one unevenly distributed among different animals) as being able to enter into fellowship with human beings. Thomas links these changes to empirical methods of science and pays particular attention to new descriptions of the natural world that no longer relied primarily on analogies with human beings and on symbolic meanings.[74] He pays particular attention to the work of Comte de Buffon and Carolus Linnaeus for developing biological taxonomies that established a physical likeness between human beings and animals.[75] However, Thomas not only examines philosophical changes but also thinks about changing social parameters and in particular links changes in attitudes toward animals to urbanization, which he associates with the reduction of human beings' exposure to animals and with the simultaneous rise of pet keeping.[76] The meaning of the term *pet* changed in the process: initially referring to lambs—that is, to domesticated farm animals—it came to mean any animal kept for enjoyment as opposed to utility. In the American context, farm animals are largely a neglected category, with the scholarly focus being on "wild animals" or on "pets" in the term's later meaning.

Mary Allen's 1983 publication *Animals in American Literature*, is among the first—and up until recently, among the only—books to examine the presence of "literal animals" in American literature. Allen argues that "it was during the Darwinian awakening that the first great blossoming of American literature took place," and she connects the two. For Allen, the focus in American literature is on "*wild* animals."[77] By contrast, Jennifer Mason's *Civilized Creatures: Urban Animals, Sentimental Culture, and American Literature, 1850–1900*, published twenty-two years later, explores the role of urbanization and pets in (roughly) the same time period. The difference between Allen's and Mason's books is instructive for the way literary analyses of animals have developed over the past twenty years: whereas Allen sees animals as "realistic" in that they are "wild, terrestrial beings," Mason wants to locate the realism of animals in urban setting and creatures, where a melding between nature and culture has already taken place, and argues that we need to read animals beyond "America's affair with the frontier."[78] What both Allen and Mason share and what I in turn share with them is a resistance against claims such as Steve Baker's that "the animal is the first thing to be ruled out of modernism's bounds."[79] On the contrary, to understand modernism requires understanding the emergence of biopower in relation to animals. Whereas Mason speaks of the "domesticated/wild animal divide,"[80] I question the notion of a divide and think about the way in which these concepts both crucially enable one another and remain highly volatile categories. That volatility becomes evident, for instance, in the intrusion of Edgar Allen Poe's orangutan into the inner sanctum of the domestic, the room with no exit, where domesticity is the ultimate confine that nevertheless is penetrated by the orangutan, that oxymoronic creature, the soldier's wild pet.

In "Looking at Animals," John Berger argues that for the medieval peasant it was possible to love *and* kill the animals he raised. As Berger puts it, "Animals came from over the horizon. They belonged *there* and *here*. Likewise, they were mortal and immortal. . . . This—maybe the first existential dualism—was reflected in the treatment of animals. They were subjected *and* worshipped, bred *and* sacrificed. Today the vestiges of this dualism remain among those who live intimately with, and depend upon, animals. A peasant becomes fond of his pig and is glad to salt away its pork. What is significant, and is so difficult for the urban stranger to understand, is that the two statements in that sentence are connected by an *and* and not by a *but*."[81] Whereas for Berger this "*and*" disappears with the removal of animals from our daily lives and their replacement by the attenuated creatures that are pets, I trace how it persists at the core of subject formation and especially in relation to affect. Philip Armstrong argues that "first—like the conceptualization of humanity, inhumanity, rationality and other terms fundamental to Enlightenment modernity—the culture of sensibility cannot be understood without reference to human–animal interactions. . . . Second, early eighteenth-century manifestations of sympathetic engagement between humans and other animals proved to be remarkably varied."[82] Jonathan Lamb has identified a spectrum of sympathetic relationships between human beings and animals that emerged in the eighteenth century. Troping on William Hogarth's image sequence "Four Stages of Cruelty" (1751), which depicts scenes of animal abuse, Lamb traces "four stages of likeness" that provide a "schematic account of sympathy." First, "physiological similarities" provide the basis for recognizing "the symptoms of our own emotions in others." Second, those commonalities "raise questions of the rights belonging to those with whom we sympathise"; and third, a "more oblique degree of resemblance" arises "by means of imagination or figurative expressions." Finally, sympathy erases all differences and "proclaims the identity of the subject and object."[83] Lamb charts how these stages get worked out in *Gulliver's Travels* and thereby links animal representations to the biopolitics of the early modern colonial enterprise.

My selection of case studies follows a cultural logic that Laura Brown usefully explains:

> The experience of nonhuman animals was dramatically reshaped by two major and related historical phenomena that coincided in this period [the seventeenth century]: . . . [T]he globalizing context of mercantile capitalism, through travel, trade, and exploration . . . gave rise to an explosion of popular and scientific speculation about the relationship between humans and nonhuman animals that threw European thought into "turmoil," . . . [raising] problems of ontology

and [disrupting] accepted ideas of human identity or genealogy. At the same time, the cultural practice of pet keeping arose in the commercial, bourgeois society of eighteenth-century England, creating the companion animal as an antidote to the alienation and commodification of modern urban life. . . . Together these two historical innovations in human–animal contact generated a vital imaginative power that fundamentally shaped the idea and the roles of nonhuman animals as they are represented in the literature of the modern period.[84]

Animals are not only a recent invention; they are an invention that goes hand in hand with the emergence of colonial modernity. Brown's work participates—as does my own—in current investigations into the way in which animals are the grounds on which colonial and domestic power relations get negotiated. This enterprise goes back to Harriet Ritvo and Donna Haraway's work from the 1980s.[85] And yet such "zoocriticism, understood here in the context of intersections between animal studies and postcolonialism, is still in its infancy."[86] As Carrie Rohman has argued, we need to analyze the "animalizing of disenfranchised groups and the concomitant humanizing of imperialist power." Useful as I find Rohman's analysis, I disagree with her when she says that animality is "displac[ed] onto marginalized groups" via a mechanism of "scapegoating." She argues that "the vigorous reentrenchment of Western sovereignty through the primarily racialized displacement of animality away from the European subject . . . reveals how deeply the animal threatened a destabilization of that subject."[87] Of course, a passage like this needs to be read against the larger work of her book, which carefully reflects on what we might mean by "the subject" and locates animals and animality as integral to the subject's fragmentations. Yet at moments like this Rohman's writing risks suggesting that there is such as thing as "the" subject, that such a subject is stable, and that animals threaten its stability. What interests me is an instability that lies at the core of subjectivity and that strategically gets worked out by biopower. In my account, there is no subject that predates the relationship with animals—subjectivity emerges in and remains unhinged by cross-species encounters.

Central to my work, then, is the claim that "the human" and "the animal" are shifting and acquired constructs, and my chapters uncover a variety of ways in which this acquisition operates. Since the founding of the Great Ape Project in 1993, much work has been done to "prove that a variety of animal species possess the basic capabilities deemed necessary for subjectivity: self-consciousness, rational agency, the capacity to learn and transmit language."[88] My focus is not on understanding animals' shared humanity or uncovering "how animals made us human," to invoke Paul Shepard's title, which Temple Grandin repeats almost verbatim in her most recent work,[89] because I have no interest in an evolutionary account of human–animal relations or in tracing biological points of overlap via affective neuroscience. Although there are a few moments when I reference evolution—for instance, in my engagement with Donna Haraway's work on "companion species" that have coevolved—I am tracing a different set of embodied relations and relational paradigms than the ones suggested by evolutionary theory.[90]

Instead of mapping a history of human–animal ontology, I produce a genealogy of human–animal sexuality—a topic that remains taboo even in recent criticism. In tracing that genealogy, I am trying to retell the story of modern subject formation. The usual narrative goes like this (as Harriet Ritvo sums it up): "The publication of Charles Darwin's *On the Origin of Species* in 1859 is usually considered to mark the beginning of a new era in the study of life. . . . [C]ertainly for those who were persuaded by it, Darwin's theory of evolution by natural selection . . . eliminated the unbridgeable gulf that divided reasoning human being from irrational brute" and "dethroned humankind almost implicitly."[91] According to such accounts, the year 1859 marks a caesura by which the understanding of animals shifted from one of categorical difference to one of gradated kinship. But as Ritvo has shown in her own correction of the narrative she is summarizing, the history of human–animal relations is messier than this neat taxonomy would suggest, especially because of the ongoing relevance of the early modern period.

Scholars of the early modern period have documented what René Girard refers to as a "crisis of distinctions" in regard to human–animal relations,[92] where, according to Fudge, the human as a "category begins to collapse into absurdity."[93] One account of modernity insists, as Eileen Crist explains, that Cartesian philosophy resolved these ambiguities and that they did not resurface until the emergence of Darwin's evolutionary theory.[94] With the notable exception of Philip Armstrong's work, the field of animal studies itself has by and large replicated that periodization.[95] A strange bifurcation has emerged in how we define modernity, one that focuses on either the twentieth century (Eric Santner and Beatrice Hanssen, who study German texts) or the early modern period (Bruce Boehrer, Erica Fudge, and Laurie Shannon, who focus on British literature) but does not create a dialogue between these models of modernity and largely elides the American nineteenth century.[96] For that matter, some accounts of the field of animal studies explicitly perform that elision: in her introduction to *Renaissance Beasts*, Erica Fudge sides with Peter Harrison when she writes that "the seventeenth century is linked to the twentieth by the sheer volume of discussion in both about the place of animals. The early modern and the modern share a fixation on them that marks both periods as crucial to developments in the understanding of human relationships with animals and also marks animals as vital figures that historians of all kinds must take notice of if we are to offer a full assessment of that past and if we are to fully understand our own interests in the present."[97] I find the idea of using modernism to link the early modern period with twentieth-century modernity compelling and have framed my book accordingly, but the bulk of my work focuses on the nineteenth century elided by these accounts of modernity and considers this century the crucial ground on which notions of biopolitics and liberal subjectivity get worked out via animal representations.

Bruno Latour has questioned our current taxonomizing of modernity by demonstrating modernity's own crises of taxonomizing. He has described a disavowed conjunction between the representation of things and the representation of subjects.[98] I locate that conjunction in a range of animal representations in popular, canonical, mainstream, and obscure works. Those works tell a different tale of human–animal relations than the one that has emerged from the history of philosophy and history of science perspectives. Armstrong has developed this view for the context of an imperial modernity that grew out of Britain's empire. Arguing that a "reconceptualization of agency" can "facilitate a mode of analysis that does not reduce the animal to a blank screen for the projection of human meaning, and might offer productive new ways of accounting for the material influence of the non-human animal upon humans, and *vice versa*," he insists that a feature of "Enlightenment modernity" is "the formative role played by human–animal relations. Whether as a concept (*animality*) or as a brute reality (*actual animals*), non-humans play a constitutive role in the preoccupation of the modern enterprise: its relentless mobility (spatial, social, economic and epistemological), its development of commodity culture, its promotion of new scientific paradigms and its determination to reconceptualize the human." Tracing that history back to British writers' engagement with Descartes, whose work first appeared in a popular translation in 1694, Armstrong argues that English writers "scrutinized it sceptically and, more often than not, rejected it." He sees eighteenth-century English literature as deconstructing "man" as well as the "crucial companion term, 'animal.'" Central for that undertaking is John Locke, who "reverses Descartes' method—the separation of rationality from the body, the abandonment of the latter to the realm of animality and the location of humanity in the former—by welding body and mind back together" so that "the development and testing of novel ways to manage the relationship between human and non-human life became the defining labour of modernity." Armstrong argues that out of this engagement emerged "two competing structures of feeling at work in the eighteenth century, namely the intellectual detachment of projectors (both scientific and capitalist) . . . and the exorbitant sympathetic identification embodied by Gulliver, who experiences being treated as an animal and eventually aligns himself so completely with the virtues of an equine species that he can no longer bear the company of humans."[99] The forms of writing on which I focus are ones in which questions of who and what counts as a subject takes center stage as the object of inquiry: slave narratives, lyric poetry, animal autobiography, and confessional writing (a category into which both William Bradford's *Of Plymouth Plantation* and Edgar Allan Poe's "The Black Cat" fit in different ways). Like Latour, Armstrong, and McHugh, I believe that it is important to get "out from under the master narratives of evolution, ecology, and more pervasively of disciplines," as McHugh puts it, and that doing so "requires this understanding that stories can (and indeed always) do more than represent selves at the expense of others."[100]

But how do we engage with "others" responsibly? Instead of asking how, whether, and when animals should be included in existing models of subjectivity, I argue that they already underlie the core of that subjectivity—that definitions of self-consciousness, rational agency, the capacity to use language are foundationally underwritten by an understanding of "the human" as emerging in relation to "the animal" and that we need to go the other direction and envision viable forms of alterity that are neither appropriative nor oppressive. The danger in this approach lies in using animals for purposes that remain anthropocentric. Keenly aware of that problem, I believe that my work on the contrary unsettles anthropocentrism at its core by demonstrating that there can be no centering of the human because the human is a relational category that cannot be separated from the animal. This view does not, however, negate a power differential that lies in that core, and I remain attentive throughout to the question how that power gets played out and played against. The case studies that I chose concern writers who recognize the dual cooptation of a power structure that uses not only violence (a model I develop via Agamben) but also affect (which I historicize via Locke and theorize through Foucault's legacy in the works of Rei Terada and others) to structure "the human" in its relation to "the animal." What interests me is not the distinction between human beings and animals, but their complex and shifting relationship to one another. That relationship has the human and the animal as constantly changing coordinates. Tracing those shifts and their implications for the limitations and possibilities of complex subjectivities lies at the center of this project. I focus on the terrain where questions of species—human, animal—get worked out at the intersections with race and gender.

The "animal turn" may raise a concern about the reinscription of "the human" as an operative concept that gender studies, critical race theory, and post-structuralism have critiqued in their different ways. Whereas the larger field of animal studies works on the level of philosophical abstraction, weighing "the human" in relation to "the animal," I agree with Donna Landry's trenchant assessment of these debates when she writes that "cultural specificity is more compelling than . . . philosophical concern with 'the animal'" and that "we need to interrogate the significance of the various 'social, cultural, economic, political and environmental contexts' that gave shape to particular relationships between humans and animals, and to particular representations of animals, in specific times and places."[101] Animals are often referenced as a universal category, but this book develops an understanding of the specific cultural work that animals and animality (terms that call for repeated definitions and reconsiderations) do in the context of American literature.

American (Animal) Literature

Scholarship that emerged in the 1990s demonstrated that nationalism depends on affective structures that make up a "*love of country*," whether that is "an eroticized nationalism" or the "commerce between eros and nation" runs "in the other direction," for instance by producing homophobia.[102] Borrowing from Anne McClintock's claim about gender, this book argues that "theories of nationalism have tended to ignore *species* as a category constitutive of nationalism itself" and that "nationalism is constituted from the very beginning as [an animal] discourse, and cannot be understood without a theory of [species] power."[103] In this quote, I replaced the word *gender* with the words *animal* and *species*, but that rewriting on my part itself will need to come under scrutiny for raising the question whether species erases gender and under what circumstances one can serve as a substitute for the other. For now, I turn my attention to another matter: What is the relation between species and nation, and how might an understanding of American literature shed light on that question?

American literary studies has until recently fallen into a trap that Walter Benjamin noted in his essay on the tenth anniversary of Franz Kafka's death: the trap that "it is possible to read Kafka's animal stories for quite a while without realising that they are not about human beings at all."[104] I do not want to follow Benjamin and say that American animal stories are not about human beings "at all" but rather to suggest two things: one, that animals are animals in American literature and that we have not adequately accounted for them as such; and two, that accounting for them as such will change how we read that literature. Carrie Rohman worries that "historicist readings have proven inadequate to the task of illuminating the complexities of the subject's relation to animality within and beyond symbolic codes."[105] Cary Wolfe similarly has recently taken to task "current U.S. literary and cultural studies and their ruling disciplinary norms, which are, at the current moment historicist," and has objected that this approach "takes for granted and reproduces a specific picture of the knowing subject that undercuts the putative historicist commitment to the materiality, heterogeneity, and externality of historical forces: a subject that is clearly . . . an ideological expression of liberalism."[106] I take up these provocations to ask what a historicist approach might look like that does not take for granted that it knows the knowing subject and that tries to understand the complexities of liberalism's ideological constructions.

Anyone writing on animals in nineteenth-century American literature owes a debt to Jennifer Mason, and this book certainly participates in her query into "the dynamic relationship between people's lived relations with animals and the multiple, species-specific and often markedly affective discourses relating to these animals" as "essential for understanding the contest for power in the human social order" as it is "played out in literary texts."

Mason focuses on a distinct period, from 1850 to 1900, which she identifies as one in which Americans reflected on "their affinities with animals" in relation to "the built environment," especially with respect to increasing urbanization. Mason's periodization (like Mary Allen's, which traces its account from the 1850s forward) coincides with the way American literature was initially canonized—that is, with F. O. Matthiessen's argument that a distinctly *American* literature emerged in the 1850s. This focus leads Mason to conclude that "we are the inheritors of beliefs about the importance of emotional connection to animals generated in the nineteenth century" but also of "repressions sustaining current narratives about animal politics and animals' significance to American literary and cultural history."[107] I find Mason's work tremendously compelling and engage with her specific contributions throughout my own work. But my work challenges hers in two important ways: by insisting that we need to look at a much longer genealogy (as I explained earlier) and by resisting the repressive hypothesis that Mason develops and looking at the tremendous proliferation of discourses that the affective relationship with animals has generated.

For the discussion of American literature's relationship to animals, Mary Allen's inaugural work precluded a discussion of sexuality, which the field has by and large continued to follow—although recent interest in the connections between Darwinian and Freudian theory seems to be pointing to a change.[108] Allen wrote that "in American literature animals offer a type of purity that rarely conflicts with violence but does require chastity. Their most peculiar characteristic is the avoidance of sexual activity—even the absence of desire. Virility is assumed in most cases, but mating is as much to be avoided by the animal as by the human character. . . . Animals are generally beyond sexual activity. . . . With animals, the American writer might have released Puritan inhibition and shown lust without guilt. But that did not happen."[109]

I question these assumptions and locate animals and sexuality at the very core of an investigation that goes back to some of the earliest records of human–animal interaction in New England: bestiality trials. This book traces a history of human–animal sexuality through the connected permutations of bestiality and puppy love to understand how subjectivity depends on sexualized animal bodies and affective pet relations. The scholarly literature on such relations uses the larger rubric of zoophilia to capture various permutations ranging from the violent (zoosadism) to the nonviolent.[110]

The term *zoophilia* was coined by Richard von Krafft-Ebing in 1894 and has encompassed a range of practices; for instance, "sometimes a general love of animals *without* any sexual interest has been called zoophilia."[111] Although the term *bestiality* has long been a catch-all for cross-species affective relations, a more differentiated discussion has emerged recently among social scientists (psychologists, anthropologists, criminologists) whose data "support the existence of another phenomenon closely related to bestiality—zoophilia—where the key feature, in addition to sexual interactions, is a strong emotional involvement with the animal."[112] Although I tie much of that discussion to my analysis of bestiality, I do not see the term *bestiality* as functioning as a "singular and reductive signifier"[113] for a variety of affective relations between human and nonhuman animals. Instead, I see bestiality as pointing to a spectrum of affective relationships that are subject to different forms of scrutiny and control and that are, most important, at the very core of the way subjectivity emerges in pedagogical and cultural contexts.

Even among scholars invested in examining affective relationships with animals, the subject of bestiality remains taboo. Alice Kuzniar has critiqued the work of Kathleen Kete, Harriet Ritvo, John Berger, Marc Shell, Yi-fu Tuan, and even Marjorie Garber for distancing itself "from the seriousness of pet love." Kuzniar's work goes a long way toward impressing on us that seriousness and working out a complex model of alternative intimacy. But for all her own complicated and compelling insights into the topic, she persists in defining "pet love" as everything except bestiality: the term *bestiality* is not listed in the index to her book, and, by my count, she mentions it only three times (on pages 10, 109 and 130). There might of course be a very good reason for this—namely, a principled definition of bestiality as a violently unequal relationship that cannot encompass a viable notion of "love." But even and especially if that is the case, we need to examine the complex cultural negotiations by which differentiations between bestiality and "pet love" operate so that we can consider what they reveal about biopower. We may still, then, pause and puzzle over a moment in Kuzniar that seems out of keeping with her careful analysis of shame and abjection and that turns her focus away from melancholia to dog love as a form of *jouissance*: "Those who have an ardor for dogs know that such passion is unavailable and inaccessible elsewhere: it opens up the subject in unique ways that, precisely because independent of gender and sexuality, are liberating."[114] There are many things in this statement with which I agree: the idea of dog love as pointing to an affect "unavailable and inaccessible elsewhere" resonates with arguments I develop here, as does the emphasis on the way this affect opens up our understandings of subjectivity. But my focus on animal love as a site where raced sexuality gets negotiated takes issue with the idea that dog love is "independent of gender and sexuality" and that this independence would necessarily be "liberating." As I demonstrate, the affective relationship to animals is a site where gender and sexuality get worked out and worked through. Because that negotiation depends on mechanisms of racialization and othering, the "liberating" qualities we might see here are ones we want to qualify carefully.

Such caution applies particularly to the context of animal love as a queer relation, which several writers are currently celebrating. Again, Alice Kuzniar's work provides an important reference point. She writes that "one of the major repercussions of pet love is that it reorients companionship and kinship away from the normative strictures of heterosexual coupling and the traditional family."[115] For Kuzniar, that reorientation has the potential of continuing and furthering the work of queer studies that interrogates the binaries that arise from inflexible gender and sexual identity categories: "Our affective life with its fluctuating sensual needs, devotions and obsessions can be complex and inconsistent in ways that call into question self-definitions based primarily on sexual preference. Object choice as in the case of the pet can complicate, as does the fetish, a simplistic adherence to male–female or hetero–homosexual binaries when defining one's intimate self. In other words, to admit that one's object choice might not always be restricted to one's own species means to loosen the power granted sexual identity categories to socially regulate the individual."[116] For reasons that become obvious in my book's frame (its first and final chapters), I particularly like Kuzniar's claim that dog love is "queer beyond queer!" and her justification of that claim via a reading of animal affect as a triangulated relationship.[117] Although I certainly explore the liberating potential she and others ascribe to cross-species affection, I am wary of embracing too readily any celebratory optimism. For one thing, the larger history that I chart demonstrates how animal love is not simply a move "away from the normative strictures of heterosexual coupling and the traditional family" but also deeply inscribed at their core, as becomes evident in the fact that the first family must show its normalcy and normativity by being dog lovers. Moreover, the ability to celebrate dog love as liberating strangely depends on the object choice's not being flexible in the sense that the object is defined as a dog and that this definition is given fixed ontological meaning. But if we grapple with the way biopower constructs and unsettles the human/animal binary and think about overlapping territories, one thing that opens up and requires careful consideration is a domain of animality whose complicated sociocultural history is deeply rooted in colonialism, slavery, and sexism. It seems to me, then, that for the American context, we need to understand that history and the instrumentalization of animals and animality that produced that history before we can decide on the mechanisms and conditions that would turn animal love into an alternative to the very system it has helped put in place.

Here, then, is also a point where I want to be very cautious of the current embrace—my own included—of posthumanist theories that see species boundary crossing as part of a liberating narrative, whether sexual or otherwise. There is a history by which species blurring and boundary crossing has been at the very heart of race- and gender-based violence, and it seems vitally important to me to parce out that history if we are to pursue this line of inquiry. My turn to literature is meant to provide a model for a particularly important methodology for such engagement. Because literary representations of animals always implicitly if not explicitly raise the question of whether the animal is to be taken literally or figuratively (with the Puritans intriguingly collapsing the two, as I discuss in chapter 1), animal representations crucially confront readers with the complex terrain of epistemology and ontology, of representation and symbolization.

Chapter Summaries

As I explain in chapter 1, bestiality and its criminalization offer one model for the emergence of subjectivity under biopolitics that continues to haunt us, as the abuse of prisoners at Abu Ghraib made clear. Bestiality is a site for the development of what Foucault calls *homo juridicus*—that is, the legal subject that hinges on its relation to animals. The criminalization of bestiality provides a specific instance in which the law emerges via the regulation of physical bodies, where representation is worked out via embodiment, and where animals are a fundamental relay between the two. The criminalization of bestiality is a hallmark of modernity: according to Richard Bulliet, the sexual interaction with animals is a staple of normal development for adolescent men in "domestic" society; its criminalization marks the entry into

a "postdomestic" society in which the spatial and epistemological separation between human beings and animals takes place. An upsurge in the legal
prosecution of bestiality occurred in the 1640s and led to some of the earliest
legal regulations in Plymouth Plantation. Drawing from the punishment for
bestiality outlined in Leviticus, the colonists made bestiality a capital crime
for which both the human perpetrator and his animal victims were put to
death. In criminalizing bestiality, the law drew a line between human beings
and animals by prohibiting sexual intercourse between them. Sexual practices defined and divided species. The law established a distinction between
human beings and animals. But cases of bestiality also revealed that distinction to be fungible: the existence of the law testified to its transgression.[118]

In cases of bestiality, colonial law did not merely separate *bios* from *zoē*;
because animals themselves became subject to the law that put them to
death, they participated in *bios*. Conversely, the accused was recognized as
bios before the law, but his crime relegated him to the category of *zoē* in
that he was stripped of his legal rights and put to death. Because human
beings and animals suffered the same fate in convictions of bestiality, their
affective engagement proved to be ontologically transformative; the very categories that the law meant to establish as absolute turned out to depend on
a mobile system of representation. In discussions of bestiality, a strange category emerged, of the beastly as an excessive form of animal being. Bestiality
extended beyond human interaction with the animal body; it also produced
an animalization of human bodies. Bestiality, then, was not only a literal,
physiological act but also a symbolic, representational register that informed
the exercise of biopower. The animalization of human bodies hinged on representational practices that mapped species onto a grid.[119] That grid served
two purposes: it enabled connections between species while also positing
binary oppositions, and it created a structural position of bestial abjection
but also used animals to elicit and mediate affect. That mediation under-
wrote the second aspect of biopolitical subject formation—the pedagogical
discourse that made kindness to animals crucial for the formation of the
liberal subject. Tracing this strand of biopolitics to John Locke's educational
writings, I understand the "liberal" subject as a subset of the "biopolitical"
subject—that is, as one way in which subjectivity gets figured and functions
in the biopolitical state. The use of animals for didactic purposes reaches
back to antiquity and Aesop's animal fables. Whereas the fable tradition
used animals as stand-ins for human beings, it was not interested in animals

as such. Locke's widely read *Thoughts on Education* (1693) made animals themselves central to children's education and enabled them to have both a symbolic and literal presence in literature. Locke suggested that we gain our humanity by performing acts of kindness to animals and located subject formation in the relationship among different species. He asked that "children should from the beginning be bred up in Abhorrence of *killing*, or tormenting any living creature.... And indeed, I think People should be accustomed, from their Cradles, to be tender to all sensible creatures."[120] Emotional and physical feelings are coupled in Locke's prohibition against torment and his call for tenderness. Animals function as the "other" *and* as the ground from which liberal subject formation becomes possible.

My reading of Edgar Allan Poe's crime fiction brings the legal and pedagogical formations I have been outlining in dialogue with each other and locates the subject's fissures in the fraught relationship to animal representation. In referring to representation, my primary aim is not to reanimate the philosophical discussion of (anti)representationalism,[121] but to engage Latour's observation that from the development of modernity in the seventeenth century forward, "the representation of things through the intermediary of the laboratory is forever dissociated from the representation of citizens through the intermediary of the social contract" and that this separation hinders us from establishing any "direct relations between the representation of nonhumans and the representation of humans, between the artificiality of facts and the artificiality of the Body Politic." According to Latour, "the word 'representation' is the same," but the conditions of modernity render "any likeness between the two senses of the word unthinkable."[122] As shown in chapter 3, Poe's work is an exercise in the unthinkable; his animal representations locate us in the terrain where American literature negotiates between the two uses of representation and shows that their function as synonyms and opposites is key to the way biopolitics operates. Exploring the tension between alterity and identity, Poe's fiction develops a hermeneutics that reads the "symbolic order" in relation to the bodily, the abject, and the animalized. By affording that bodily register its own legibility, Poe develops grounds for understanding the mechanisms by which subjectivity produces itself via an engagement with the beastly and provides a means for engaging critically with that production. Examining animals' extralegal position, these texts demonstrate that animals generate and confound the relation between the literal and the figurative. They occupy a position in which abjection becomes a site for subject formation. Although animals function within texts to provide a sense of the real that the text can reference and distinguish itself from, they in fact point to the traces of the real that remain embedded in the representational. Conversely, animals themselves are already highly mediated. They generate a process of destabilization: the figurative points to the real, and the real asserts itself as figurative. So animals are always both: they are the embodied core of literature, and literature is the symbolic core of embodiment.

In the context of American literary studies, the theoretical discourse of biopolitics has a particular provenance in the issue of slavery. In chapter 2 on Frederick Douglass's work, I examine how the animal(ized) other can respond to these structures of abjection despite his and her exclusion from the symbolic order. By casting the abuse that Aunt Hester endures as a scene fraught with animal imagery, Douglass shows how race and gender are contingent on species and how that contingency reveals them to be social constructs rather than ontological realities. Douglass reads the category of the beastly along the lines that I propose in chapter 1, as the failed attempt to polarize human *bios* and animal *zoē*. But his method for doing so shifts our understanding of the beastly. Instead of establishing the differentiation between the sovereign and the wolf-man, the beastly functions in Douglass's reading as the site of an emergent liberal subject formation that reveals the animal origins of biopolitics. Douglass's work rejects the mechanization of animals and instead emphasizes animals' and human beings' shared sensibility; put in theoretical terms, Douglass's writing challenges Agamben's reading of biopower as an effect of sovereignty by advancing a Foucauldian model of subjectivity. Douglass initially portrays Hester as inhabiting the position that Agamben calls "bare life." Yet Douglass accomplishes a rereading of Hester's expendable, consumable flesh as itself the locus of an alternative gender and discourse formation. Understanding pain as a discursive register, Douglass suggests that the beastly not only founds the juridical subject *homo juridicus* but also produces the interest-bearing subject that Michel Foucault calls *homo oeconomicus*. Foucault initially develops his notion of *homo oeconomicus* through a reading of David Hume that makes the desire to avoid pain the irreducible measure of self-interest. This emphasis on pain establishes the individual and collective body as the locus of meaning: although the avoidance of pain marks the individual's irreducible self-interest, that avoidance also functions as the base line for an interest that all members of society share. Douglass examines such interest as a basis for extralegal subjectivity: removed from the discursive register of the law and situated in the bodily register of sentiment, this interest enables a redescription of subjectivity that hinges on embodiment.

In chapters 4 and 5, I examine how the scene of bestiality gets rewritten as one of "puppy love" with the rise of sentimentalism in the nineteenth century and its permutations in the twentieth century. Framing my discussion of Emily Dickinson in relation to affect theory, I demonstrate how Dickinson might advance our understanding of liberal subjectivity beyond its current parameters. Because affect studies produces "a new ontology of the human or, rather, an ontology of the human that is constantly open and renewed," it generates a space for inquiry that presses us beyond the explicitly humanist framework of liberal subject formation.[123] What particularly interests me is Dickinson's use of that framework to radically rethink the parameters and representational modes of subject formation: engaging with the pedagogical and literary models that became a staple of childhood education in the nineteenth century, Dickinson stretches our understanding of literary representation beyond symbolization by rethinking orthography as a confrontation with literal animals. Deliberately invoking Lockean pedagogy, Dickinson adopts the persona of a child. That persona enables her to reject the telos of Lockean pedagogy—namely, the separation of the human being from the animal. Placing herself in a position of ambiguity, where the human and the animal are conjoined and not yet separated, Dickinson engages the parameters of liberal subject formation to envision an alternative. Affect theory and liberalism open a space for radical alterity, but they too easily foreclose that space by reinscribing affect in an ontologically defined frame that distinguishes human beings from animals. At stake in that foreclosure is the production of a particular notion of subjectivity as one marked by an individuality independent of others and clearly demarcated by the separation of reasoning from embodiment. Looking at animals gives us a different account of the subject as relational and contingent on an alterity that cannot easily be reinscribed in the registers of either abstract rationality or embodied affectivity. Through the literal and figurative presence of animals, we see new possibilities for subjectivity and poetry emerge in Dickinson's work.

Chapter 5 allows me to return to the questions I was asking about "Bo Obama" and presidential pets. In my opening comments, I largely focused on Barack Obama and set aside the role that his daughters play in the staging and framing of affective biopower. This chapter takes up the conflation of pets with children by examining the genre of animal autobiography—that is, of autobiographies written from the perspective of an animal. Concluding that animal representations locate a queerness at the very heart of liberal subject formation, I take up the case study of *Millie's Book, as Dictated to Barbara Bush* to argue that animal autobiographies participate in and unsettle the heterosexual matrix (that is, in Judith Butler's definition, the link between sexual norms and power) they are meant to affirm. As "things" with which we engage affectively, pets suffer from a double animation—as commodities and as creatures—that situates them at the core of modern biopolitics. In fact, they become exemplary "things" in the sense that they realize the central fantasy of commodity culture, the fantasy that things have a life of their own beyond their relationship with the desiring subject. I examine the genre of "animal autobiography" to understand how our affective engagement with pets gives rise to an embodied intersubjectivity that emerges between the subject and the object. I look at objectification as a mechanism of biopower, but also at another genealogy by which animals can be more or other than a commodity and can reshape the subject via object relations. If object relations structure our sense of subjectivity, then the pet—as a creature and as a commodity—occupies a physical and figurative position beyond and at the very core of our subjectivity; it both exemplifies and unsettles liberal subject formation.

This book argues that animals are central to the way in which we are taught to perform our humanity and that species is crucial to the regulation of subjects in the biopolitical state. Biopolitics thrives on the mutability of the line between human beings and animals. The constant renegotiation of the species line via means of representation produces an excess that is never fully regulated. Animals are embedded as and at the core of subjectivity. Figures of radical alterity and the embodiment of biopolitics, animals are simultaneously exceptional of and exemplary for the biopolitical subject. Animal representations reveal the structuring force of a species imagination through which our culture's deepest investments are made available and distorted.[124] Examining the figurative treatment of animal(ized) others reveals the mechanisms of ambivalence that establish and undercut the stabilization of the symbolic economy. Animals produce a hyperrepresentation that lacks the stability it is meant to produce. The liberal subject at its core, then, hinges on its relationship to real and imagined animals that obscure and create the distinction between the real and the representational. Animal representations locate us between the symbolic and the real; they function as one pole of a binary and as the relay between the representational (*bios*) and the physical (*zoē*) that the modern state creates.

1

AMERICAN BESTIALITY

Sex, Animals, and the Construction of Subjectivity

(PLYMOUTH PLANTATION, ABU GHRAIB)

On March 21, 2006, a U.S. Army dog handler was convicted of charges brought against him in conjunction with the abuse of prisoners at Abu Ghraib in Iraq. Sergeant Michael J. Smith, age twenty-four, was found guilty of six out of thirteen indictments. Smith expressed remorse for only one of those convictions, his conviction for indecency. That conviction stemmed from Smith's "directing his dog to lick peanut butter off the genitals of a male [American] soldier and the breasts of a female [American] soldier." Smith said: "It was foolish, stupid and juvenile. There is nothing I could do to take it back. If I could, I would."[1] Smith expressed remorse for having his dog engage in sexual acts with his fellow soldiers. What made this one charge among the many for which he was convicted legible to Smith as an offense? Smith apologized for the one act that involved other Americans and for an offense that situates his case within a practice that is foundational to the social order itself—the practice of constructing subjectivity by dividing human beings from animals. His reference to his acts as "juvenile" marks them as a rite of passage into adult maturity; his apology itself performs a learning process by which he came to recognize subjects (those fellow beings who have legal standing in the courts and interpersonal recognition from acts such as apologies) by distinguishing them from animals (those nonsubjects that lack legal and discursive representation). There was no mention of the Iraqi detainees or of the dog.

My pointing out that second absence will seem ludicrous in and of itself, and my linking the dog with the detainees might come across as offensive: of course Smith did not apologize to the dog. After all, we reserve rights and apologies exclusively for human beings because only they count as subjects in our system of language-based political representation. Representational subjectivity sets human beings apart from all other living creatures—it lies at the core of our secular notion that human beings are special, that there is such a thing as human exceptionalism. I borrow the term *human exceptionalism* from Kay Anderson, who uses it to describe the belief that each human being is fundamentally different from all animals.[2] That belief has its strategic purposes in allowing us to conceptualize human rights as a category of legal, ethical, and symbolic representation that extends subjectivity beyond state boundaries. But I worry that human exceptionalism actually enables the abuses it critiques because it sets up a dichotomy between human beings who have representational subjectivity and animals who lack it.[3] Smith's apology exemplifies this problem. He defined representational subjectivity ontologically and tautologically: one has rights by virtue of being human, and one is human by virtue of having rights. By that definition, animals lack rights because they are animals, but those who lack rights, such as the abused detainees, are all too easily animalized. Human and animal are categories that lay claim to utter ontological fixity, but are highly fungible. Any creature who is not deemed human becomes subject to abuse without recourse to standards that would mark such an injury as wrong: Smith never apologized to the detainees he brutalized; like the dog, they remained nonsubjects to him, beyond recognition. Human exceptionalism ultimately does not protect human beings from abjection but enables abuse by creating a position of animality that is structurally opposed to humanity.

What complicates the matter is the fact that animality and humanity are neither dichotomous nor separable, but deeply inscribed in one another. Animality is not simply outside of the social order and its mechanisms of subjectification; it is foundational to it. In current critical discourse, the meaning of animality is still being worked out, but Dominick LaCapra provides a useful working definition when he describes animality as two things: the structural opposite of humanity and a quality that animals and humans share.[4] What interests me is the question how these positions get worked out in the uneven terrain between the figurative and the literal—that is, in the terrain that I am trying to conceptualize as "animal representations." In the example with which I began and that I develop more fully toward the end of this chapter, the positions of humanity and animality multiply because we are not dealing simply with binaries (human/animal), but with a triangulated relationship between the soldier, the guard dog, and the detainee or fellow soldier. That triangulation places the categories of humanity and animality, of "the" human and "the" animal, in shifting relation to one another, where those shifts are a mechanism of biopower but also generate possibilities for disrupting its operation.

By reexamining Michel Foucault's notion of biopower as a key mechanism of sovereignty in the state of exception, Giorgio Agamben has made a similar argument—which I draw on for its ability to explain the violence and structure of biopower but which I also critique for its limited understanding of biopower as merely violent and structural. Agamben has argued that an abject position of "bare life" stands outside religious and social law and functions as the disavowed counterpart to the equally unlawful position of the sovereign.[5] He identifies "bare life" with the figure of the *homo sacer*, the "sacred man" who "may be killed and yet not sacrificed" under Roman law, and likens that figure to the "wolf-man" of Germanic law.[6] He identifies that wolf-man as "the man who has been banned from the city" but who remains "in the collective unconscious as a hybrid of human and animal, divided between the forest and the city."[7] Although Agamben avails himself of psychoanalytic vocabulary when he refers to the "unconscious" and is gender specific in his accounts of "man," his discussion by and large remains devoid of any analysis that would explain the role this wolf-man's sexual presence plays for the formation of gendered subjectivity. Agamben produces a version of Aristotle that replicates some of the latter's exclusions of women from the polis without reflecting on the complexities that exclusion raises for an account of the sovereign's other(s). He does, however, reflect on the wolf-man's relation to discourse formation, specifically the challenge the wolf-man poses for imagining alternative forms of representation: he argues that the wolf-man "is not a piece of animal nature without any relation to law and the city. It is, rather, a threshold of indistinction and of passage between animal and man, *physis* and *nomos*, exclusion and inclusion."[8] For Agamben, this threshold marks the zone in which the sovereign can exercise power. But the same can be said for domesticated animals (especially pets and particularly dogs)—that they inhabit a "threshold of indistinction" in which they function as both animal and man (not just in the form of man's best friend, but via the association of sodomy with bestiality that I discuss later) and where we see the emergent and collapsed distinction between *physis* and *nomos*. A dog's ability to inhabit the role of the wolf-man maps the drama of sovereignty onto the mundane territory of pet keeping, where affect determines subject positions. Because domesticated animals such as dogs can take on the function of the wolf-man, there is a doubling of the hybridized figure that impacts the "collective unconscious" in that it produces an effect of uncanny recognition between human beings and animals. Agamben's analysis ultimately privileges the human side of that hybridity in insisting on the human origins of the wolf-man and in reading (to quote the title of one of his other books) "the open," the space of indeterminacy between human beings and animals, as a (if not "the") human condition, thereby negating animal subjectivity. He sees the wolf-man as the result of a particular political relationship and relegates animals to a separate category, that of an "animal nature without any relation to law and the city."[9] This claim is problematic in that it runs the risk of reproducing the category it aims to critique—namely, the category of *zoē*. However, I suggest that it also opens the possibility for alternative subject and discourse formations in that it posits an elsewhere, an outside to the totalizing aspirations of biopower. In this chapter, I attempt to understand the double function of the wolf-man—the animalized human and the humanized animal (terms I develop later)—as creating a position of animality that underwrites and unsettles the modern formation of representational subjectivity.[10] What becomes clear in the process is, in Derrida's key intervention into biopolitical theory, "not that political man is still animal but that the animal is already political."[11]

To develop this analysis, I begin with an originary moment for the development of modern biopower and the mechanisms of differentiation: the criminalization of bestiality.[12] In the commentary on Abu Ghraib, virtually all critics have ignored this dimension of the abuse. One case in point is Jasbir Puar's work, which provides a complex and provocative reading of the gender politics displayed in the abuse but glosses over the role of animals

and animality. Writing that the abuse "vividly reveals that sexuality constitutes a central and crucial component of the machinic assemblage that is
American patriotism," Puar outlines how "the use of sexuality—in this case,
to physically punish and humiliate—is not tangential, unusual, or reflective
of an extreme case, especially given continuities between representational,
legislative, and consumerist practices." Recognizing the role that depicting
detainees as animalistic plays for the abuse, Puar quotes testimony by one of
the prisoner guards at Abu Ghraib:

> "I saw two naked detainees, one masturbating to another kneeling with
> its mouth open. . . . I saw [Staff Sergeant] Frederick walking towards
> me, and he said, 'Look what these animals do when you leave them
> alone for two seconds.' I heard PFC England shout out, 'He's getting
> hard.'" Note how the mouth of the Iraqi prisoner, the one in fact kneel-
> ing in the submissible position, is referred to not as "his" or "hers," but
> "its." The use of the word "animals" signals both the cause of the torture
> and its effect. Identity is performatively constituted by the very evi-
> dence—here, getting a hard-on—that is said to be its results. (Because
> you are an animal you got a hard-on; because you got a hard-on you
> are an animal).[13]

Important as these insights are, Puar separates her reading of sexed animality
from the actual animals that were present and instrumentalized as part of the
abuse, surprisingly writing that "not all the torture was labeled or understood
as sexual, and thus the odd acts—threatening dogs, for example—need to
retain their idiosyncrasy." Outlining how "state of exception discourses doubly foster claims to exceptionalism," Puar explains that these practices cast
"the violence of the United States" as "an exceptional event, antithetical to
Americanness." By extension, she argues, "U.S. subjects emerge as morally,
culturally, and politically exceptional through the production of the victims as repressed, barbaric, closed, uncouth, even homophobic, grounding
claims of sexual exceptionalism that hinge on the normativization of certain
US. feminist and homosexual subjects."[14] Compelling as this account is for
recognizing some of the regulatory mechanisms in place and for demonstrating the centrality of sexuality for the formation of subjectivities, it is
complicit with human exceptionalism in that it takes animals out of the picture. My point here is not simply that animals are being overlooked, but that

overlooking animals leaves us with an incomplete understanding of the way biopower operates in constructing subjectivity.

I take seriously the charges brought against Smith for involving his dog in sexual acts. The criminalization of bestiality provides an instance in which the *homo sacer* and the sovereign directly encounter one another via the figure of the pet. In that encounter, we see suspended the differentiation between subjects and nonsubjects that underlies the symbolic order and its concomitant forms of representation. The regulation of sexual relations between species marks a moment where symbolic representation is disrupted and emergent, where the metaphoric and the metamorphic conjoin and become differentiated, where the categories of the human subject and the animal object come into play. To flesh out that claim requires rethinking representation itself. In this chapter, I begin my book's larger enterprise of developing the concept of animal representation, by which I mean a nexus between the symbolic depiction, physical presence, and political significance that one model of modernity wants to spread out over different species, but that merges and emerges in human–animal relations.

Alfonso Lingis and Midas Dekkers have argued for the pervasiveness of bestiality by insisting that it underlies all acts of love: in making love even to a fellow human, we are always encountering an animal or animalized other.[15] Useful as their arguments may be for allowing us to reflect on the alterity of love, they do not help us to see the power differential at play in acts of bestiality, nor do they enable us to understand fully the complex literal and symbolic meanings of bestiality.[16] Bestiality and its criminalization offer a model for the emergence of subjectivity in the biopolitical state. According to Richard Bulliet, the encounter with animals is a hallmark of "domestic" society from which our "postdomestic" society has become removed. He differentiates the two terms on the basis of people's encounter with animals: whereas human beings used to come in contact with domestic animals on a daily basis, they now have no relationship to animals other than as pets and never encounter the animals who produce their food and clothing as well as their medicine and cosmetics. Paying particular attention to children's development, he argues that in domestic society children were exposed regularly to animal sex in the sense of witnessing animals having sex with each other and of witnessing acts of bestiality. Although "domestic societies around the world have generally had a scornful attitude toward engaging in sexual intercourse with animals," he quotes Havelock Ellis to justify his claim that these societies "have also recognized that it happens—and not all that infrequently." Bulliet points out that these acts of bestiality primarily involve men and that they are in that sense gendered. In postdomestic societies, the actual intercourse between men and animals "appears to be rare," but with the decline in literal acts of bestiality comes a shift "to luridly fantasizing about it." In fact, Bulliet argues, an intensification takes place: "By hiding the animal sex that in the domestic era was an inescapable component of life, and thereby keeping children 'innocent' until their first adolescent encounters with pornographic images, postdomesticity encourages expressions of sexuality that put fantasy in the place of carnal reality."[17] The criminalization of bestiality functions as a transitional moment from domestic to postdomestic society and its concomitant literal and figurative relationships to animal sex: it inaugurates the regulation of the affective relationship with animals.[18] Whereas that regulation initially occurs via the law, the law ultimately functions as a mode of textuality that conjoins with other forms of representation to play out the production of biopolitical subjectivity via punitive and affective means that straddle the relationship between the body and discourse.

Scholars have long recognized the connection between the body and discourse. Focusing on the early American period to which I turn in a moment, Janet Moore Lindman and Michele Lise Tarter, for instance, write:

> Bodies are maps for reading the past through lived experience, metaphorical expression, and precepts of representation. They tell us about . . . formations of subjectivity and identity. Yet, as living, breathing, ingesting, performing entities, bodies afford a specificity of lived experience that has been devalued and all but erased in western philosophical traditions. . . . Cultural reevaluation of the human frame reveals the historical importance of sentience and materiality in early American societies, and consequently leads us to a more complete story of the past. Bodies . . . are never unmediated; they are related but not reducible to cultural concepts of differentiation, identity, status and power. . . . Encompassing both the physical and the symbolic, it [the body] is, therefore, fully enmeshed in the social relations of power.[19]

Useful as this formulation is for thinking about the recalcitrant meanings of materiality, it is also symptomatic of the way in which scholars theorize "bodies" as synonymous with "the human frame." That association is in many ways perplexing: If the critical force of turning to the body has stemmed from, in Judith Butler's formulation, the fact that "thinking the body as constructed demands a rethinking of the meaning of construction itself," why does some version of "the human" underwrite that enterprise, even when that enterprise is—in a formulation that aligns Butler with Agamben—attentive to "a domain of unthinkable, abject, unlivable bodies"?[20] If we shift our attention to bodies, and especially if we consider the body as producing a "movement of boundaries, a movement of boundary itself," and a "resistance to fixing the subject,"[21] why maintain this implicit focus on "the human"? What happens when we include animal bodies in our considerations? What would it mean to examine "a radical rearticulation of the symbolic horizon in which bodies come to matter at all"[22] if we allow for those bodies to be other than human?

In this chapter, I inquire into the biopolitical function of animal representations in two seemingly disparate historical and geographical moments: the criminalization of bestiality at Plymouth Plantation and the bestialization of prisoners at Abu Ghraib.[23] Taking seriously the commentators who have related the abuses at Abu Ghraib to a larger register of American racial (Patricia Williams) and gendered (Susan Sontag) iconography,[24] I argue that we must understand the crucial role that animal representations play for the production and negation of biopolitical subjectivity as and at the founding of a legal order premised on colonial violence. I understand bestiality through its historical definition as a synonym for *sodomy* and as the performance of human–animal sexual relations. As these uses imply, the term *bestiality* refers to a sexual act in which one party of the encounter is an animal or is portrayed as an animal (that is, the way sex between men is characterized as sodomy in ways that are undifferentiated from bestiality). This blurring of the literal and the figurative in the conjoint discourse around sodomy and bestiality interests me in that it opens the question how we are to understand the relationship between bodies and subjectivity to begin with. In the historic documents I discuss, bestiality refers to a specific sex act, but also to a supposedly innate quality that the parties involved in that act share—that is, the term *beastly* functions as a synonym for the current critical term *animality* in that both describe a quality that humans and animals share and where there is a concerted discussion of what that means for understanding subjectivity. Although I retain the use of the term *bestiality* for sex acts that cross species lines, I adopt the term *animality* to discuss the structural and representational position that bestiality produces. Recent scholarship has tried to differentiate between "animal" and "animality" by charting a distinction between nonhuman animals and a quality they share with human beings.[25] In my use of the term, *animality* collapses the distinctions between humans and animals but also calls into question how we distinguish between species as an ontological or epistemological—and performative—category. *Animality* is a floating signifier, and one of my chief interests in this chapter lies in charting its mobility, the way in which it moves between, as LaCapra explains, functioning as the structural opposite of humanity and serving as a quality that animals and humans share.[26] Animality refers to the structural position that is the opposite of humanity. Because a human being can also inhabit this structural position, animality is not limited to literal animals. Although the opposition between human and animal is meant literally, it functions figuratively: in using the term *animality*, I refer to the fact that a human being can occupy "the animal's" structural position. The fact that animals or animalized human beings can inhabit the position of animality unsettles the distinction it is meant to establish and collapses the differentiation between the literal and the figurative.

This "collapse" is immanent to the historical materials I discuss. Anne Kibbey argues that "the threats and acts of physical harm, the symbolism of physical identity, and the rationale of iconoclastic violence against people as images—all these aspects of prejudice were informed by a concept of figuration that was qualitatively different from what we usually take 'figurative' to mean in literary thought." She explains that

> Puritanism relied on the classical concept of *figura*, an idea that initially had nothing to do with language. In its earliest usage *figura* meant a dynamic material shape, and often a living corporeal shape such as the figure of a face or a human body. This ancient concept of figuration has a modern equivalent in our sense of the human bodily form or appearance as a "figure." For the Puritans, the concept of *figura* was a means of interpreting the human shape, whether as artistic image or as living form, and it comprehended both nonviolent and violent interpretations of human beings. Among its most important qualities, the classic concept of *figura* as it meant material shape defied the conventional metaphoric opposition between "figurative" and "literal." The configuration or shape was simply there, and its defining property was the dynamic materiality of its form.[27]

This association between the figurative and the literal might also explain why not only physical acts of but also jokes about—that is, figurative acts of—bestiality were punishable in the past.[28] Bestiality is more than a peculiar historic remnant in the operations of American biopower; it is the origin of modern biopolitical subject formation, and, as such, it confounds our understandings of that modernity. As Jens Rydström has argued, "Bestiality was never incorporated into modernity."[29] I want to read that statement so as to suggest that bestiality operates as a paradigmatic instance of animal representation—that is, as a practice where the separation of representation as a political or cultural enterprise breaks down. A contemporary theorization that ties the notion of the *figura* to a way of rethinking modernity emerges in Richard Nash's "notion of a 'material/semiotic actor,'" which he borrows "from those contributions to science studies (notably those of Donna Haraway and Bruno Latour) that seek a productive analysis of nature/culture that does not originate with an a priori separation of the human and the world."[30] Not only does the figurative intrude on the literal, but the literal also intrudes on the figurative in that biopower instrumentalizes animals to differentiate between the structural positions of humanity and animality. Animals such as guard dogs can inhabit the position of animality, but they can also take on a mediating function between the structural position of humanity and the position of animality. I locate the birth of the biopolitical subject in that mediation.

"Man with Beasts and Other Creatures": Bestiality and the Birth of American Biopolitics

A peculiar epidemic swept through the New England colonies in the 1640s.[31] Several young men were brought to court and convicted on charges of bestiality, leading Governors John Winthrop and William Bradford as well as a number of other prominent men to fear that a larger pattern was emerging in the young colonies.[32] Given the historical record, this concern seems to have been exaggerated: Roger Thompson has argued that cases of bestiality were "statistically insignificant" in local courts.[33] Why, then, did these isolated cases give rise to such concern, and why did the crime "not to be named" generate such sustained discussion? The small number of cases brought to trial belies the frequency with which acts of bestiality occurred. Bestiality seems "to have been wide-spread," but the broader population regarded the practice as "commonplace" and resisted its criminalization.[34] The discrepancy between the frequency with which bestiality occurred and with which it was brought to trial points to an "underlying disjunction between official ideology and popular responses"[35] and suggests that the contact between human beings and animals was contested ground for biopower's operation. Because early Americans understood bestiality as a specific sex act *and* as the reflection of innate qualities, its criminalization was part of a mechanism to distinguish natural from civic order and served to legislate that distinction. The distinction hinged on a specific understanding of ethnic subjectivity that depicted racial differences as species distinctions. At stake in the criminalization of bestiality was the production of gendered subjectivity and ethnic citizenship.

In analyses of sexed and gendered subjectivity, bestiality has remained absent as a meaningful concept in its own right and has garnered attention mainly because of its association with sodomy—that is, with same-sex acts. The association between bestiality and sodomy emerged in the European Middle Ages and produced an intensification of the punishments for such transgression. Tracing the "history of bestiality" from prehistory to the present, Hani Miletski argues that a change occurred in the European Middle Ages, whereby "equating homosexuality with bestiality not only increased the penalty, but it communicated a change in the way people looked at animals. Instead of being an irrelevant object, the animal became a participant as in the equivalent of a homosexual encounter, and it became important to kill the animal, in order to erase any memory of the act."[36]

Jonathan Ned Katz and Jonathan Goldberg have argued that the colonial persecution of bestiality was a founding moment for the oppression of gays, that it established a precedent for subsequent laws denying the right to practice sodomy and that it revealed "the tacit limits to the American version of liberalism."[37] They point out that in the historic record the terms *bestiality* and *sodomy* often function as synonyms for one another. The authors themselves do not differentiate between the terms in the sense that they do not reflect on human–animal sex but read references to bestiality as animalizing gay men and dehumanizing same-sex encounters.

Work has recently emerged that tries to understand not only the links that the historic record established between bestiality and sodomy, but also the way they became differentiated from one another. In his comprehensive historical survey of the Swedish regulation of sexual practices, Jens Ryd-ström provides a profound reassessment of the history of sexuality as one that must include bestiality.[38] Charting the development "from sinner to citizen, namely, the transition from the sodomitic to the homosexual paradigm," Rydström argues that "in Sweden, as elsewhere in the Christian world, same-sex sexuality and sexual intercourse with animals were conceptually connected as two aspects of the sodomitic sin, or the crime against nature." Although the archival record is particularly rich (bestiality was explicitly outlawed "in all Swedish law books, from the thirteenth century until 1944"), scholarly discussion on the topic has been remarkably absent: "not many authors have discussed the phenomenon of bestiality, fewer still [the exceptions Rydström names are John Murrin and William Monter] have compared it to same-sex sexuality, and no one has discussed it in a twentieth-century context." He argues that "in order to fully understand what lies behind some of the peculiarities of modern discourse on homosexuality, it is necessary to analyze its connection to bestiality and the factors that lay behind the disappearance of this connection from the collective mind in the middle of the twentieth century. Also, the disappearance of bestiality, as compared to the rise of homosexuality, provides a challenging example of the contingency of sexual categories." Rydström's focus ultimately points to the "normative mechanisms that increasingly establish heterosexuality as a dominant structure and punish . . . sexual behavior outside heterosexuality." Yet there is a surprising blind spot in Rydström's study. Although he carefully charts the way in which "the discourses concerning male same-sex sexuality have since antiquity been structured around difference" such as age and class, he on the one hand reads bestiality as undifferentiated when he points to "the conceptual conflation of sex with animals and same-sex sexuality which was made by the historical actors under study" but on the other hand says that "the analysis of *bestiality* does not concentrate on the difference between the sexual partners. The difference between man and animal can be considered as given. (The similarity would perhaps be more interesting to think about)." That parenthetical caveat seems important to consider: What would it mean to think of the difference between man and animal as not simply a given and how might we make this difference a subject of analysis? The persistence and focus of Swedish law on bestiality would certainly warrant these questions: "Of the 'three sodomitic sins,' only bestiality had been continuously and explicitly outlawed since the medieval laws," giving bestiality a special status among the prohibited sexual acts with which it is associated. Swedish laws "did not outlaw same-sex sexuality for many hundreds of years, but only bestiality," thus giving this practice particular status among the "crimes against society"—that is, a "crime against property and a crime against morality."[39]

Defined by penetration, bestiality was closely tied to masculinity, but because that masculinity was not associated exclusively with human beings, bestiality has particularly interesting meanings in relation to women and lesbianism. Katz documents a legal case brought in Georgia in 1939 that tested whether women could be convicted of sodomy for same-sex acts. The judge ruled on the "question whether the crime of sodomy, as defined by our law, can be accomplished between two women," finding that "by Code . . . sodomy is defined as 'the carnal knowledge and connection against the order of nature, by man with man, or in the same unnatural manner with woman.' Wharton, in his Criminal Law . . . lays down the rule that 'the crime of sodomy proper can not be accomplished between two women, though the crime of bestiality may be.' We have no reason to believe that our law-makers in defining the crime of sodomy intended to give it any different meaning."[40] As Katz documents, sodomy was a male phenomenon in that it required an act of penetration, but bestiality could include women:

> A strict penetrative concept did, curiously, allow colonial lawmakers to imagine intercourse between women and animals (male animals were apparently inferred). It is ironic that colonial legislators, who hardly ever prohibited carnal relations between women (and never explicitly) did often explicitly penalize copulation of women with beasts. That the intercourse of women and (male) animals received much explicit statutory recognition indicates the social dominance of a strict penetrative concept. When illicit intercourse was defined primarily by reference to a male organ it was of only secondary import whether that virile member was attached to man or beast. The colonists' concern about the interpenetration of humans and beasts was no doubt linked to their belief that interspecies intercourse could result in the birth of part-human, part-bestial creature. And their concern about human–animal contacts was also no doubt linked to the temptations and probable prevalence of bestiality in an agricultural economy commonly utilizing animals for many other services.[41]

The persecution of women for bestiality often took the form of witch trials. The relationship between witches and animals was threefold: (1) witches were said to attack the livestock of others; (2) they were seen as transforming themselves into animals; and (3) they had animals as familiars. Their relationship to animals thus placed the animals on a scale from pure object (livestock that they attacked) to an impermissible subjectivity. The boundary between the human and the animal was blurred, as John Putnam Demos points out: "There is, in sum, a kind of paradox here. Prevailing belief ascribed to witches a particular animus against infants and small children. Moreover, a parallel belief declared that witches might directly intervene in the nursing process—for example, by causing acute soreness in the breasts . . . or by inhibiting lactation itself. . . . Yet witches, too, had small creatures under their personal care. They, too, undertook to nurture and protect such creatures, and even to 'give them suck.' The witch with her imp was a figure—albeit a distorted one—for human motherhood."[42] As I discuss at greater length in subsequent chapters, the relationship between human beings and animals thus involves issues of gendering that revolve precisely around the ambiguous status of animals as children and in turn of children as animals, which the focus on lactation demonstrates.

Rydström's study includes many theorizations that make his work useful beyond Sweden's historic archive. In *Of Plymouth Plantation 1620–1647*, one of the American urtexts (which is also a key nineteenth-century text by virtue of the full manuscript's recovery in 1856), William Bradford describes the trial of sixteen-year-old Thomas Granger. Accused of a "horrible case of bestiality," Granger was convicted of having had sexual intercourse with a mare, a cow, two goats, five sheep, two calves, and a turkey.[43]

For a transgression to count as bestiality, a specific definition of sex—namely, intercourse—had to be met.[44] Moreover, that intercourse had to be established discursively: although the birth of deformed animals with features resembling the defendant sometimes gave rise to suspicions of bestiality, to meet the standards of proof the judicial system required either a confession or the testimony of two independent witnesses.[45] This requirement interestingly expanded the practice of bestiality from the specific act of penetration to a larger social context. In mapping different kinds of bestiality, Gieri Bolliger and Antoine F. Goetschel distinguish between five "sexual acts between human beings and animals": "genital acts, oral–genital acts, masturbation, 'frotteruism' (rubbing of genitalia or the entire body on the animal), and voyeurism (observation by third parties during sexual interactions with animals)."[46] The requirements for legal trial proliferated acts of bestiality in that they relied not only on the physical act of penetration but also on voyeurism. Giving equal weight to verbal testimony (the confession) and eyewitnesses, the criminalization of bestiality inscribed a public quality in the act. In Granger's case, such standards of public testimony were evidently met: following the punishment for such offences dictated by Leviticus 20.15, the animals were put to death in front of Granger before he himself was executed.[47] Considering the animal carcasses to be unclean, the settlers destroyed them and did not use the meat or skins they could have yielded.[48]

Elaborating on the reasons for such harsh punishment in relation to another case, Samuel Danforth explained a few years later in *The Cry of Sodom Enquired Into* (1674): "*Bestiality*, or *Buggery*, [occurs] when any prostitute themselves to a *Beast*. This is an *accursed* thing ... it turneth a man into a bruit Beast. He that joyneth himself to a Beast, is one flesh with a Beast. ... This horrid wickedness pollutes the very Beast, and makes it more unclean and beastly than it was, and unworthy to live amongst Beasts, and therefore the Lord to show his detestation of such Vilany, hath appointed the Beast it self to be slain."[49] This passage suggests that the line between human beings and animals is absolute, but that it is possible for individuals to move from one category to the other: bestiality "turneth a man into a bruit Beast."[50] Sex determines an individual's standing and functions as a source of transformation, but bestiality does not simply produce a conversion from one state of being to another: it creates a joint corporeality by which man becomes "one flesh with a Beast," a hybridity we might associate with the wolf-man. This hybridity affects not only man, but also the beast, which it "pollutes" and makes "more unclean and beastly" than it was. The beast goes from merely being an animal to having a highly charged quality of animality—beastliness in historical parlance—that the sexual relationship with a human being generates. The language escalates into the hysterical—the beast verbally proliferates, and its *degree* of beastliness increases. This notion that beastliness is not an absolute but has varying degrees reflects a deep uneasiness about the distinction between human beings and animals. By criminalizing a crossing of the species barrier, the law tries to establish and naturalize ontological categories that it simultaneously reveals to be highly unstable.

The law does not simply apply to a subject that exists a priori; it constructs the humanity of that subject (or his lack thereof).[51] As Susan Stabile has demonstrated, "In the eighteenth century, biological sex was understood as a fluid category indivisible into the binaries of male and female. 'To be a man or a woman was to hold a social rank, a place in society, to assume a cultural role,' argues historian Thomas Lacleur, 'not to *be* organically one or the other of two incommensurable sexes.' The discourse of evangelical religion thus configured sex as a sociological rather than ontological category."[52] The law also configured species as a social category: by demanding that human beings ought not to engage in sexual acts with animals, it regulated the boundary between human beings and animals. This act of prohibition defined the difference between human beings and animals as simultaneously absolute and fungible.[53] Although it maintained that human beings and animals are absolutely different from one another and therefore ought not copulate, it acknowledged that such copulation occurs. As John Canup has argued, "There can be no more vivid testimony to the contemporary belief in the possibility of dissolving the boundaries between humans and animals through sexual communication."[54] In the colonial case, sex itself took on the power to be ontologically transformative: it removed Granger's humanity and attributed to him an animality that he shared with his victims. That transformation occurred via Granger's relationship to the law. By engaging in a sexual encounter with an animal, he forfeited his rights and the law's protections; he inhabited the same relation to the law as the animals with whom he was sexually involved and suffered the same death as they. Excluded from legal subjectivity, animals are nevertheless subject to the law's punitive reach. That punitive reach defines those condemned to death by law as animals: animals function as a category of legal death from which the law temporarily and conditionally exempts human beings. Granger witnessed the death of the animals with whom he had had intercourse as a metonymic act in which his own execution was inscribed. In losing his legal subjectivity, his right to life and liberty, Granger became subject to the law, victim to its punitive powers, and inhabited the position of animality from which the law temporarily exempted those to whom it granted legal subjectivity.

Far from being a peripheral legal matter, these cases of bestiality point us to the pivotal role that animal sex plays as the primal scene of biopolitics, through which individual subjectivity and collective social structures develop.[55] What these legal cases reveal about gender-discourse formation has recently sparked a debate among scholars of early American literature. Richard Godbeer has documented that three categories were crucial for Puritan distinctions between different sexual transgressions: marital status, sex, and species. Sexual transgression figured into an attempt to understand and produce the category of "the natural" itself, an endeavor that was compli-cated by the understanding that since the fall from grace, the natural had become a morally compromised category.[56] Godbeer argues that sexual sin was a "manifestation of human depravity" and emphasizes the spiritual dimension by claiming that "the basic issue was moral rather than sexual orientation." He documents that Puritan theology integrated acts of sexual transgression "into a larger moral drama" by reading them as the result of the "innate corruption of fallen humanity."[57]

Whereas Godbeer reads sexuality as standing in service to a discourse of morality, David Halperin insists that we see the emergence of sexual identi-ties in these documents. Rereading Foucault's famous distinction between the sodomite and the homosexual, Halperin argues that "the current doctrine that holds that sexual acts were unconnected to sexual identities in European discourses before the nineteenth century is mistaken in at least two different respects. First, sexual acts could be interpreted as representative components of an individual's sexual morphology. Second, sexual acts could be inter-preted as representative expressions of an individual's sexual subjectivity."[58] Bestiality participated in the gendering of subjectivity.[59] Because penetration had to occur, bestiality was tied to masculinity, though that masculinity did not have to be human.[60] Bestiality was thus a key concern when it came to the production of sex and gender.

Mapping the production of gender onto the formation of social struc-tures, Sigmund Freud explores the link between bestiality and masculinity in *Totem and Taboo*. Collapsing the Puritan distinction between natural and unnatural sexual transgressions, he links bestiality and incest to explain the disavowed foundations of heteronormative patriarchy. On the surface, the prohibition against bestiality and the prohibition against incest may seem to follow diametrically opposed logics—the first being a prohibition against straying too far from the range of sexually acceptable partners, the second being a warning against not straying far enough. Certainly, critical discourse dating back to Aquinas has argued for and upheld such distinctions and mapped the two into differential relationship with one another.[61] However, Freud departs from this line of interpretation. Arguing that a totem is "as a rule an animal" that "is the common ancestor of the clan," he points to an act of cross-species miscegenation that inaugurates human social formation. He asks: "How ... did they ["primitive" men] come to make the fact of their being descended from one animal or another the basis of their social obligations and, as we shall see presently, of their sexual restrictions?" Observing that "almost every place where we find totems we also find a law against persons of the same totem having sexual relations with one another and consequently against their marrying," Freud speculates that "the most ancient and important taboo prohibitions are the two basic laws of totemism: not to kill the totem animal and to avoid sexual intercourse with members of the totem clan of the opposite sex. These, then, must be the oldest and most powerful of human desires." Freud further explores this conjunction between the desire to kill the totem animal and to have intercourse with members of the totem clan: seemingly digressing into a discussion of children's animal phobias (a topic that also preoccupied him elsewhere—for instance, in the case of the "Wolf-Man" that he documented in *History of Infantile Neurosis*), he concludes that children "displace some of their feelings [of fear] from their father on to an animal." The payoff of this analysis for Freud lies in his comparison between children and "primitive" men, which enables him to suggest that "the totem animal is in reality a substitute for the father," that is, a kind of wolf-man.[62] Freud explains early social formation as contingent on the figure of the animal and its ability to regulate heteronormative social relations; the totem animal both predates and originates the formation of the social and symbolic order.[63] As Kalpana Shesadri-Crooks has concluded, "We must read the murder of the father as the moment not only of the institution of the prohibitions against murder and incest, but of the very notion of the human, of the separation between human and animal, and of their interrelation."[64]

The subjectivity that was being negotiated in colonial trials of bestiality is then directly tied to what Judith Butler has called the "heterosexual matrix," which she also refers to as the "matrix of gender" and the "matrix of power."[65] Butler argues that compulsory heterosexuality defines who counts as a subject. At stake is not just the "strategic aim of maintaining gender within its binary frame," but the fact that this aim itself serves to "found and consolidate the subject."[66] As concerned as she is about the effects that these mechanisms of power have on subject formation, she ultimately shares with the order she critiques an assumption that subjectivity is always already human. Taking Butler's argument a step further by challenging that assumption, we can recognize that the subject produced by compulsory heterosexuality under the rules of patriarchy is doubly man and mankind—there is a dual operation here of androcentrism and anthropocentrism: when it comes to bestiality, the discourse of species and the construction of gender conjoin to create a notion of subjectivity that mandates physical behavior for the construction of the human. Butler has described physical behavior not just in terms of normative heterosexuality, but also in terms of gender performance—that is, as the daily acts through which we conform to social expectations of how our bodies ought to signify.[67] Useful as her argument is for deontologizing gender, it runs the risk of reontologizing species in that it is implicitly humans and humans only who perform gender and participate in this social construct. The exclusion of animals from the matrix of gender relegates them to a realm of nonperformative embodiment that is hypersexualized precisely because it is denied gendered status and figured as nonrepresentational physicality.

In the context of early American literature, the stakes of charting the precise location of bestiality on a map of moral and criminal standards lay in determining the relation between subjectivity and governmentality. Michael Warner has documented that "the Puritan rhetoric of Sodom had begun as a language about polity and discipline" and that it was "linked primarily to the topic of national judgment."[68] Puritan theologians explicitly linked the discourse of species to the discourse of liberty. John Winthrop warned in 1645 against forms of "liberty" that made men "grow more evil, and in time to be worse than brute beasts." He argued that there

is a twofold liberty, natural (I mean as our nature is now corrupt) and civil or federal. The first is common to man with beasts and other creatures. By this, man, as he stands in relation to man simply, hath liberty to do what he lists; it is a liberty to evil as well as to good. This liberty is incompatible and inconsistent with authority, and cannot endure the least restraint of the most just authority. The exercise and maintaining of this liberty makes men grow evil, and in time to be worse than brute beasts; omnes sumus licentia deteriores. This is that great enemy of truth and peace, that wild beast, which all the ordinances of God are bent against, to restrain and subdue it. The other kind of liberty I call civil or federal, it may also be termed moral, in reference to the covenant between God and man, in the moral law, and the politic covenants and constitutions, amongst men themselves. This liberty is the proper end and object of authority, and cannot subsist without it; and it is a liberty to that only which is good, just, and honest. This liberty you are to stand for, with the hazard (not only of your goods, but) of your lives, if need be. Whatsoever crosseth this, is not authority, but a distemper thereof. This liberty is maintained and exercised in a way of subjection to authority; it is of the same kind of liberty wherewith Christ hath made us free.[69]

In Agamben's interpretation of biopower, it operates by distinguishing "natural" (*zoē*) from "civil" (*bios*) liberty. Animals participate in the natural form of liberty, but Winthrop banishes them from the civil form; that is, he creates a distinction between animals' bare physiological life (*zoē*) and human beings' political life (*bios*). That *bios* is fragile and contingent and has life itself for its object and its means: those included in civil liberty need to "hazard" their "lives" to uphold the social order that they participate in. The liberty they achieve is that of "subjection to authority," which the reference to Christ makes both spiritual and bodily. Although this distinction seems to invoke the Great Chain of Being, in which differences are mapped hierarchically, Winthrop concerns himself with the mobility rather than the fixity of these different positions. The exercise of natural liberty does not merely liken men to beasts but makes them "worse than brute beasts."[70] For Winthrop, that excess is both external and internal to men. The improper exercise of liberty exposes the "wild beast"—that is, an internal quality brought out by the improper exercise of liberty. According to this naturalizing discourse, beastliness is an internal quality that man shares with animals and other creatures; beastliness is also a relation to the law. It is only in relation to the proper kind of liberty—namely, the subjection to authority—that this beastlike quality is restrained and that a full humanization occurs. The subjection to a specific kind of authority produces both liberty and the human subject.

Yet the binary division Winthrop establishes between man and animal turns out to be gradated: not only does he differentiate between men and beasts, but he also creates an enigmatic category of "other creatures." For Winthrop, this category is both external and internal. He produces a complicated doubling by which the beast figures as a way of demarcating racial distinction but also represents a quality of the self. He establishes a racial hierarchy by which he differentiates the white settlers from the animals and indigenous peoples they encounter.[71] His distinction is based on species as well as ethnicity; his strange specification invokes Native Americans, as an earlier passage makes clear.[72] He reflects on members leaving the colony and thereby "depriving themselves of . . . those civil liberties which they enjoyed there" by going "into a wilderness, where are nothing but wild beasts and beastlike men."[73] The distinction between "beasts" and "beastlike men" functions similarly to the distinction between "beasts" and "other creatures." For Winthrop, Native Americans inhabit a middle ground between men and beasts—that is, a category of similitude in which they are "beastlike" despite being "men." They function as wolf-men who mark the threshold of subjectivity in its relation to the biopolitical state. As "beastlike men," they take on the role of the *homo sacer* or wolf-man in relation to the colony. The prohibitions against bestiality thus also regulate sexual intercourse with "beastlike" Native Americans.[74]

But Winthrop also includes the settlers themselves in his reference to "other creatures": their exercise of natural liberty makes them "worse than brute beasts" and creates an animality in excess of the natural liberty that nonhuman animals and racial others exercise. Although "other creatures" are removed from the social order, they are also an immanent other that calls forth technologies of self-discipline.

That was certainly Cotton Mather's view when he wrote: "We are all of us compounded of those two things, *the Man* and *the Beast*."[75] For Mather, the wolf-man is the biopolitical subject per se. Beasts take on the function of the other than human—that is, as the binary opposite of the human. They mark an ultimate alterity and evoke fears of miscegenation.[76] Mather's and Winthrop's accounts double the role of the wolf-man. The wolf-man takes on a specific ethnic and racial dimension in that Native Americans function as these figures of hybridity. They stand outside the exercise of civil power but are also the objects that civil power tries to control: the wolf-man also marks an internal condition in that the colonists do not just regulate the hybridity of others but are themselves hybrid.

In Cotton Mather's description of Thomas Hooker, the relationship to animals in general and dogs in particular becomes a complex image not only of self-discipline, but also of discipline more generally. Mather describes Hooker as "a Man of a Cholerick Disposition . . . yet he had ordinarily as much Government of his Choler as a Man has of a Mastiff dog in a chain; he *could let out his Dog, and pull in his Dog, as he pleased*."[77] Punning on the terms *collar* and *choler*, Mather describes Hooker's "choler" as something that he himself exercised "government" over. That kind of "government" is a technology both of self-mastery and of mastering alterity. Mather creates a simile that likens the "government of his choler" to the control "a Man has of a Mastiff dog in a chain."[78] But the simile breaks down in his use of the pun. The "choler" functions as a "collar," a disciplining mechanism that collapses the distinction between man and mastiff, master and servant; the binaries the simile sets up break down via the pun and are modulated not by their binary opposition to each other but by the practice of controlling pleasure—of exercising liberty (*"let out"*) and restraint (*"pull in"*) precisely *"as he pleased."* This passage then conjoins and confounds government and pleasure around the establishment and collapse of binary oppositions between the human and the animal, where the animal serves as an intermediary that modulates the binaries it deconstructs.

This double articulation of animality relocates the drama of sovereignty on the terrain of human–animal relationships. As Canup argues, just as bestiality "blurred the inner boundary between man and beast, so it also weakened the comfortable external dichotomy of civilization and wilderness. The occurrence of bestiality within the area of English culture suggested that while the colonists might conquer the wilderness as a physical presence, its moral influences were less easy to combat. And if the curse of wilderness had taken root in the colonists and their culture, no scapegoat could possibly draw off all the corruption they would generate."[79]

That inability to externalize the beast fully and remove it from man meant that bestiality presented a particular challenge to the biopolitical order. If in fact it is not possible to dichotomize and excise alterity, then the thanatological drift of biopolitics is disrupted in that the very practice that nominally produces bare life is also tied to the subject's internal structures, especially because those structures are sexed and gendered. That opens up the possibility for an "affirmative biopolitics" by which animals and animality are not only a mechanism of biopolitical control, but also the locus for alternative subject and discourse formations. As Timothy Campbell explains, Roberto Esposito argues that we can only reverse the thanatopolitical dimensions of biopolitics by "developing another semantics in which no fundamental norm exists from which the others can be derived."[80] Such new semantics hinge on rereading subjectivity. Abandoning our notion of the individual, argues Timothy Campbell in his explication of Esposito's work, will shift our attention "to producing a multiplicity of norms within the sphere of law." The result will be that "norms for individuals will give way to individualizing norms that respect the fact that the human body 'lives in an infinite series of relations with the bodies of others,'" in which "the radical toleration of life-forms that epitomizes Esposito's reading of contemporary biopolitics is therefore based on the conviction that every life is inscribed in *bios*."[81] But the questions become how those life forms violently removed from *bios* are or remain legible as *bios* and what kinds of relationship one can enter into with them when confronted with the violence of sovereign power.

From Rights to Rites: Reading Outside the Law

The engagement with animals is a particularly fecund site for thinking through these issues because reading *zoē* as *bios* forms the locus of animal studies' resistance against thanatopolitics. In the 1798 work *Introduction to the Principles of Morals and Legislation*, the text that has retrospectively become foundational to the branch of animal studies that emerged out of the engagement with questions of legality and rights, Jeremy Bentham worries that

> the day has been, I grieve to say in many places it is not yet past, in which the greater part of the species, under the denomination of slaves, have been treated by the law exactly upon the same footing, as, in England for example, the inferior races of animals are still. The day *may* come, when the rest of the animal creation may acquire those rights which never could have been withholden from them but by the hand of tyranny. The French have already discovered that the blackness of the skin is no reason why a human being should be abandoned without redress to the caprice of a tormentor. It may come one day to be recognized, that the number of legs, the villosity of the skin, or the termination of the *os sacrum*, are reasons equally insufficient for abandoning a sensitive being to the same fate. What else is it that should trace the insuperable line? Is it the faculty of reason, or, perhaps, the faculty of discourse? But a full-grown horse or dog, is beyond comparison a more rational, as well as a more conversible animal, than an infant of a day, or a week, or even a month, old. But suppose the case were otherwise, what would it avail? The question is not, Can they *reason*? Nor, Can they *talk*? But, Can they *suffer*?[82]

Taking issue with the law's limitations, Bentham calls for nothing short of a political and semantic revolution. Through his references to the recent

French overthrow of "tyranny," he envisions a utopian state in which the wrongful withholding of rights from animals and animalized beings will be redressed. He challenges Christian theologians' belief in a Great Chain of Being that justifies the submission of "animal creation" to abusive practices of dominion on the basis of a hierarchical distinction between "inferior races" and superior species. He also rejects rationalist philosophers' notion that human beings and animals are fundamentally different from one another and that an absolute "faculty of reason" and "faculty of discourse" separate all human beings from all animals. He points out that some animals are "more rational" and "more conversible" than some human beings. Recognizing that such comparative terms still place animals and those likened to them at a disadvantage, he redefines the very grounds of rights bearing when he argues that subjectivity can be located in feeling—that is, in the physical capacity to suffer.[83] Pitting participation in the symbolic order (the capacity to *talk*) against an embodied experience (the ability to *suffer*), Bentham calls attention to the power that figuration has to create a nonfigurative category of abjection into which the physically "other" can be lumped.[84] Like Esposito, he calls for another semantics when he insists that the body itself has a legibility and meaning in excess of the symbolic order.

This semantics of suffering, however, risks reproducing the essentialism it sets out to critique. Peter Singer self-consciously modeled his call for "animal liberation" on Bentham's claims.[85] Grounding his appeal for animal liberation in the belief that subjectivity and responsibility emerge where there is actual or possible suffering, he argues that the interests of human beings do not necessarily outweigh those of animals and that both need to be measured against the greater good. By using suffering as a measure for legal and ethical subjectivity, he locates ethics in naturalism: as Cary Wolfe has pointed out, Singer anchors "the contingency of the social contract" on "noncontingent natural ground." To avoid such essentialism, Wolfe insists that we shift our attention from animal rights to what he calls "animal rites." Taking humanism as a starting point for the development of what Esposito characterizes as a multiplicity of norms, Wolfe argues that we need to expand our categories for subjectivity and rights bearing across species boundaries when certain criteria are met: "When our generally agreed-on markers for ethical consideration are observed in species other than *Homo Sapiens* [*sic*], we are obliged to take them into account equally and to respect them accordingly."[86] This approach hopes to deconstruct the

humanism from which it departs without resorting to essentialist categories.[87] But, as always, the devil is in the details.

Rejecting ontological claims, Donna Haraway argues in her most recent
publications that we need to understand subjectivity as a relational category
that emerges in the interaction between human beings and companion animals
such as dogs. Eroding the very ground for human exceptionalism, she states
that "dogs are about the inescapable, contradictory story of relationships—
co-constitutive relationships in which none of the partners pre-exist the
relating, and the relating is never done once and for all."[88]

Gilles Deleuze and Félix Guattari have taken issue with the sentimental
investment that people have in "individuated animals," especially pets, claiming that they take on an "Oedipal" status and are the subject of "narcissistic
contemplation."[89] Haraway tries to redress these problems by insisting that
love is about alterity. Like Esposito, she shifts our attention from notions of
individual subjectivity as an a priori given to an understanding of subjectivity as a relational category that emerges in the encounter between different
beings. Trying to replace the violent abuses of bestiality with mutually affirming "acts of love," Haraway imagines a subjectivity that emerges from and
generates an ever-widening social fabric, a global politics based on affect: she
argues that "acts of love like training . . . breed acts of love like caring about
and for other concatenated, emergent worlds."[90] Conceived in that way, love
for an animal can become the prototype for loving others as others. Loving others calls into question one's own subjectivity precisely because we are
never sure if that love will be reciprocated. Loving an animal is the ultimate
kind of such other-love because it opens us up to the alterity of the other and
the possibility that the reciprocity we hope for will not follow. Such love is
not the expression of a self-replicating or self-sustaining emotion, but, quite
the contrary, it makes emotion the very hallmark of subjectivity. It is in the
loving encounter with animals that the possibility emerges for a subjectivity
that is deeply relational and nonviolent.

Compelling as I find Haraway's argument, I worry about three things.
First, her notion of "love" already seems to depend on an idealization of
affection as the antidote to violence. Second, her identification of companion species relies on a literalism by which a dog is always a dog. Yet from its
inception in Bentham's writing, animal studies has recognized the fact that
animality (just like humanity) is first and foremost a figurative relation to the
symbolic order. Third, I worry about the pastoral strain that runs through

Haraway's manifesto and about the positions of exclusion that the companion-species relationship creates. Focusing on the relationship between shepherds and sheep dogs, we can indeed see the symbiosis between companion species at work as it finds expression in emotional and discursive registers. But what about the similarly symbiotic relationship between a soldier and a guard dog? As I demonstrate by revisiting the case of Abu Ghraib with which I began this chapter, the bond or symbiotic relationship between the dog and the soldier becomes the very grounds of aggression against abjected others, creating a third position, that of the detainee who is relegated to a position of animality that is excluded from legal rights, but whose exclusion we can critique via the discourse of animal rites.

The Dog in the Picture: Animal Representation at Abu Ghraib

At Abu Ghraib prison, guards acted out the drama of sovereignty as a drama of animal representation. One principal mode for disciplining prisoners was treating and depicting them as animals.[91] To that purpose, the guards availed themselves of a host of devices, including dog leashes, guard dogs, real and imaginary sex acts. These sex acts drew on bestiality as part of their "postdomestic" visual repertoire.[92] The guards not only used photography to document the abuse but turned representation into its own form of abuse: guards deliberately made prisoners aware that photos were being taken and threatened to release the photos in order to shame prisoners into cooperation.[93] But photographic representation was not just a means of abuse; it also served to affirm the guards' own subjectivity: the initial audience for these photos were the perpetrators of the violence, who understood themselves to be acting on behalf of and for the good of the larger national community.[94] It is striking that they photographed not only their victims, but also themselves in the act of victimizing others. By inscribing themselves in the photographic representations of their actions, they tried to generate solidarity between themselves and their fellow American viewers, who were "meant to identify with the proud torturers in the context of the defense of a political and cultural hierarchy."[95] When the photos were leaked to a larger audience, however, the spectatorship shifted from people who participated in the abuse and the brutal assertion of sovereignty to an audience that critiqued those practices and whose members were formed, via that critique, as liberal subjects. Instead of identifying with the torturers, this audience condemned their actions and reacted with sympathy to the victims of the abuse and to their suffering.

According to Anne McClintock, this shift in identification came about because the photographs conjoined the two formerly separate functions of the camera that Susan Sontag and John Berger identified: its capacity to function "as an instrument of state surveillance" and its capacity to function "as a means of private pleasure and spectacle for the masses." The collision of these two representational discourses, McClintock argues, "threatened to rupture the function of state surveillance and plunge the administration into crisis."[96] But the leak of the photographs did not fundamentally disrupt the biopolitical order; on the contrary, because the legal fallout impacted only the Americans involved in these acts but not their victims, the law corroborated the division between humanity and animality that the guards had enacted: the detainees continued to be excluded from legal representation.

In their response to the photos of prisoner abuse at Abu Ghraib, scholars, journalists, and politicians focused on two issues: the images' relation to pornography and their relation to lynching. As W. J. T. Mitchell pointed out at the time, "Most of the furor over the photographs of torture . . . has centered on the pornographic pictures."[97] Right-wing politicians joined forces with Slavoj Žižek in reading the abuse as the result of pornography; they argued, as Frank Rich summed it up in his column's title, that "it was the porn that made them do it."[98] Pointing to the accounts of sodomy that accompanied the photographs, Dora Apel saw the images as "indulging a covert form of homoerotic gratification through the subjugated bodies of black men."[99] These commentaries cumulatively suggest that the images were shocking because of their familiarity and their construction of "an American family album of racist, pornographic iconography."[100] Summing up the relation of these images to a larger visual repertoire, McClintock argues that they are "continuous with a long imperial archive of colonial and racist cruelty. They belong to a well-established, imperial regime of discipline and punishment in which colonized people were for centuries depicted by the West as historically 'primitive,' as animalized, as sexually deviant: the men feminized, homosexualized, or hypersexualized; . . . [This] long-standing and tenacious imperial narrative of racial 'degeneration' [was] at the very moment of its redeployment . . . once more elided in the storm of moral agitation about pornography."[101]

Although that elision might be true for the larger popular discussion of the images, scholars have insistently drawn attention to the racial dimension, especially by focusing on the similarity between the modes of representation employed in these images and those employed in lynching photos.[102] What has been missing, however, is an understanding of the role that species violence plays not just as another dimension of abuse, but also as the underlying mechanism by which violence becomes racialized and gendered. As Carrie Rohman has pointed out, "The coherence of the imperialist subject, like that of the Freudian subject, often rests upon the abjection of animality."[103]

Images of bestiality and practices of bestialization lie at the crux of colonial violence and legal formation; they reveal the underlying "pornography of the law" and inscribe animality at its founding.[104] Resurgent in the abuse at Abu Ghraib and the response to it was the implicit association of sodomy with bestiality—that is, the link between being "animalized," "sexually deviant," and "homosexualized."[105] The popular press repeatedly associated sexual violence with a crossing of the species line—for instance, in headlines such as "Abu Ghraib: Inmates Raped, Ridden Like Animals, and Forced to Eat Pork."[106] In the many assessments that have by now been published on this abuse, the commentators usually reference the use of animal imagery in the abuse but fail to provide an account of its functions as an aspect of torture. For that matter, many of the writers themselves take over this imagery in a strange move that not only fails to perform an analytic function but also recycles this imagery. One of the few commentators to address this animalization directly is Judith Butler. Arguing that "there is something more in this degradation [at Abu Ghraib] that calls to be read," she identifies that excess as "a reduction of these human beings to animal status, where the animal is figured as out of control, in need of total restraint"—like Mather's "choler" in need of a collar. For Butler, "the bestialization of the human in this way has little, if anything, to do with actual animals, since it is a figure of the animal against which the human is defined."[107] Useful as these observations are, Butler's conclusion is too hasty in that it overlooks the importance of animals and animal representations for unsettling "an established ontology" and producing what she describes as "an insurrection at the level of ontology, a critical opening up of the questions, What is real? Whose lives are real? How might reality be remade? Those who are unreal have, in a sense, already suffered the violence of derealization. What, then, is the relation between violence and those lives considered as 'unreal'? Does violence effect that unreality? Does violence take place on the condition of that unreality?"[108]

In the encounter with animals, we see suspended the differentiation between subjects and nonsubjects that underlies the symbolic order and its concomitant forms of representation. As Deborah Morse and Martin Danahay have argued, bestiality suggests "acts that take people out of the realm of the 'human' but that also bring animals within the matrix of human desire, sin and transgression."[109]

The images out of Abu Ghraib become legible in a new way when we think about them in relation to bestiality and bestialization, on which they trope incessantly.[110] In figure 1.1, we see Lynndie England in U.S. Army fatigues holding an Iraqi prisoner on a dog leash. England had been well prepared for the military's use of animal imagery in the service of violence. In her civilian life, she had worked at the aptly named Pilgrim's Pride chicken-processing plant in Moorefield, West Virginia. When People for the Ethical Treatment of Animals conducted an undercover investigation at that plant, it caught on video workers "stomping on chickens, kicking them, and violently slamming them against floors and walls. Workers also ripped the animals' beaks off, twisted their heads off, spat tobacco into their eyes and mouths, spray-painted their faces, and squeezed their bodies so hard that the birds expelled feces—all while the chickens were still alive."[111]

Compared to this description and other photos from Abu Ghraib, the extreme physical violence seems muted in the photo of England and the leashed detainee, but the picture nevertheless indicates the range of representational devices that supplement physical violence. The photo establishes a visual hierarchy: the soldier stands looking down on the detainee, whose face is on the level of her combat boots. Stripped naked, he is relegated to a hypersexualized position of sheer physicality. The dog leash establishes his animalized position and functions as an instrument of control wielded by England within a disciplinary regime that exercises (il)legality via punishments and abjection.[112] But England's position in this image is downright illegible: she is ambiguously gendered; she seems to be actively giving and passively following orders; she is using as an instrument of torture a device that also serves to connect people with pets; she occupies the position of the sovereign issuing the ban by creating a wolf-man while apparently participating in the bourgeois rite of dog walking; she is asserting her subjectivity by enacting a ritual of bestialization that will make her subject to the law from which she

FIGURE I.I Lynndie England holding Iraqi detainee on dog leash at Abu Ghraib prison, 2003. Photograph courtesy of Wikimedia Commons

temporarily removes herself; and she seems to be revealing the underlying order of the law—namely, the differentiation between human beings and animals—by violating the law by treating a human being as an animal.

The difficulties of reading this image stem from the stakes of this encounter: the image is working out the differentiations between subjects and nonsubjects that underlie the symbolic order and its concomitant forms of representation. Bestialization marks a moment where representation is both inoperative and emergent, where the metaphoric and the literal conjoin and become differentiated. In that sense, this picture is both illegible and overdetermined: we can read this image as a simile (the detainee is being treated *like* a dog) or as a metaphor (England has leashed a dog), and thus our reading practice already establishes our complicity with or our critique of the abuse. The image can stand in for the definition of metaphor that the *Concise Oxford Dictionary of Literary Terms* provides: "The most important and widespread figure of speech, in which one thing, idea, or action is referred to by a word or expression normally denoting another thing, idea, or action, so as to suggest some common quality shared by the two. In metaphor, this resemblance is assumed as an imaginary identity rather than directly stated as a comparison: referring to a man as *that pig*, or saying *he is a pig* is metaphorical, whereas *he is like a pig* is a simile."[113] Using the visual iconography of the leash to suggest a common quality between the detainee and a dog, this stated resemblance inaugurates an "imaginary identity" between the objects of comparison. Although this association serves denigrating purposes, we know that metaphor also doubles back on itself via a process Henry Louis Gates has identified as "signifyin."[114] We perform such an act of reversal by reading the image as an act of "brutality"—that is, by judging the soldier and not her victim as a "brute." Troping on tropes reassigns metaphors but ultimately perpetuates their denigrating violence: reversing who counts as a brute does not critique the category of brutality as such. Instead of focusing on the reversibility of metaphor, I want to puzzle over the slippages of animal similes that lay claim to being metaphors; in other words, I want to examine how our reading of "the animal" itself establishes and unsettles the distinction between the physical and the symbolic, the body and its representations, the metaphoric and the metamorphic.

Jonathan Elmer and Cary Wolfe have mapped out the complex subject positions that emerge in this play between the metamorphic and the metaphoric. Tracing a "species grid," they identify four positions in the relationship between animals and human beings: the animalized animal, the humanized human, the humanized animal, and the animalized human.[115] The animalized animal is denied any subjectivity, any protection from suffering; "it" (not he or she) is abjected, exploited, abused, destroyed. As Granger's case at Plymouth Plantation demonstrates, the putting to death of that animalized animal is not only sanctioned by but requisite for the legal system: it divides the permissible violence against nonsubjects from the nonpermissible violence against subjects. The counterpoint to the animalized animal is the humanized human, a being who defines his humanity via his ability to exert total domination over the animalized animal and who achieves humanity by acts of brutality and destruction. Although the humanized human negates the importance of the animalized animal, that negation establishes his identity. At the very moment of differentiation, a relationship exists: human and animal identities depend on one another, and the humanized human's *brutality* metaphorically likens him to the violence and the lack of subjectivity he attributes to the *brute*, the animalized animal. The metamorphic violence of these associations becomes evident in the use to which metaphor is put in creating the two remaining subject positions, the position of the animalized human and the humanized animal. The use of metaphor to liken a human being to an animal creates the position of the animalized human, who is treated to the same kind of abject suffering as the animalized animal.

To see the species grid in play and to understand the representational violence it enacts, I turn to another photo (figure 1.2) that captured the abuses committed by army sergeant Michael J. Smith, with whom I began this chapter. The soldier's standing depends on a careful orchestration of positions on the species grid. Smith assumes the place of the humanized human in his domination of the guard dog and the detainee; he looms over them, while they inhabit the same lowly level in this image's spatial hierarchy. In his role as the humanized human, Smith dominates the humanized animal, the dog Marco, and the animalized human, the Iraqi detainee whose name, to the best of my knowledge, is not listed on any of the English-language Web sites that discuss this picture. That anonymity, the lack of a name, is itself indicative of the abjection enacted here, which places the detainee outside of the symbolic order. The detainee is confronted by both the dog and the soldier—by companion species at work, in Donna Haraway's terminology. The encounter with companion species places him not only in the position of the animalized human, but creates an excess by which he becomes the animalized animal: excluded from human–animal bonds, he figures as the other other of sheer alterity. The positions we see reenacted here are the ones Winthrop detailed when he distinguished between "man . . . beasts and other creatures": the Iraqi detainee is put in the position of the "other creatures" via his confrontation with the "beasts" and "man." He is racialized as a "beastlike man," a wolf-man who is "worse than brute beasts." This image produces the detainee as the excess of the political order. But that political order manifests itself in the bond between the soldier and the guard dog and therein creates a wolf-man figure that is not externalized but immanent to the structures of power. Instead of the wolf-man functioning as the figure of inclusive exclusion, we see a doubling of that figure. What this image suggests, then, is that the relationships of representation—symbolic and political—are worked out not just in regard to positions of animality, but to animals: what differentiates the soldier from the detainee is their respective relationship to the dog Marco. Cynically exploiting the widely held Sunni and Shi‘a Muslim

FIGURE I.2 Army sergeant Michael J. Smith baiting guard dog to frighten Iraqi detainee into defecating, Abu Ghraib prison, 2003. The dog is Marco, a four-year-old black Belgian shepherd, a military working dog. Photograph courtesy of Wikimedia Commons

attitude toward dogs as unclean animals, the very construction of the dog as a companion species already speaks to a particular cultural position; it simultaneously tries to capitalize on and to disregard other cultural attitudes toward dogs.[116] Confronting an unclean animal enforces the detainee's utter abjection. In the process, however, the image opens up fissures in which the mechanisms of sovereign authority become legible.

This image also adds something important to our understanding of those representational practices: it demonstrates how animals can be instrumentalized to enact state violence and to produce animality. The detainee is not only animalized but hyperanimalized in contrast to the guard dog. A problematic double articulation emerges of what we mean by "animal": ("the") animal is the binary opposite of ("the") human. But animals also function as a middle ground between sets of binaries that oppose the subject and the object: the human and the nonhuman, the psychological and the physiological, the real and the symbolic. The binaries constitutive of the subject break down where "the animal" functions as mediator between the subject and its others. The animal is not excluded from the social and political order but, on the contrary, is the nexus where forms of violent and affective power as well as positions of subjectification and abjection are worked out. Animal representations mark the limit of the subject and reveal the mechanisms of its functioning. In the process (and this will be the focus of the upcoming chapters), they open up possibilities for alternative ways of thinking about subjectivity and its relationship to representation.

The dog's presence facilitates the detainee's removal from the symbolic order and that order's concomitant forms of legal, social and verbal subjectivity. It also opens the possibility for a different kind of representational regime to arise. The position of the humanized animal, like the position of the animalized human, is precarious. In the military's scheme of valuation, military working dogs are animate objects that attain temporary fetish status but are destroyed when they lose their use value—that is, their ability to regulate and mediate the violence of disciplinary regimes.[117] The dog Marco is serving the disciplinary regime by doing the work of interpellation that Louis Althusser associates with the operation of "ideology and ideological state apparatuses."[118] Althusser argues that the ideological state apparatus functions by interpellating subjects. The example he gives for the way interpellation works is hailing: if somebody calls in the street, each person feels addressed and turns around—each person is interpellated as the specific subject whom the authoritative call addresses. But what happens when the prisoner is interpellated by the dog's growling or barking?[119] What happens when the response that this interpellation is meant to elicit is physical, bodily, visceral, anal? When the interpellation does not turn the prisoner into an accused, but into a detainee who will be held indefinitely without charges or due process? Is he interpellated as a subject? Can he be interpellated as a nonsubject?

The use of the guard dog for the animalization of the detainee challenges "the one boundary separating human and animal, a boundary that has been very jealously guarded by theologians, philosophers, and lawmakers: speech and discourse as the preserve of man."[120] The dog in this image takes on an intermediary position: he simultaneously serves the purpose of abjecting the detainee and calls attention to the process by which such abjection occurs.

The dog takes on a discursive function in bestializing the detainee. But that discursive function collapses the distinctions it is meant to draw between the symbolic, representational, human subject, on the one hand, and the real, nonrepresentational animal, on the other. Returning to Butler's question, we can see that "what is real" depends on the position one occupies in relation to the animal and specifically in relation to the animal's voice.

In a reading that conjoins Althusser and Agamben, Mladen Dolar thinks about voice in relation to the positions of the sovereign and the *homo sacer* or *bios* and *zoē*. Thinking about the voice's ability to interpellate, he argues that "*the voice is structurally in the same position as sovereignty*, which means that it can suspend the validity of the law and inaugurate the state of emergency. The voice stands at the point of reception which threatens to become the rule, where it suddenly displays its profound complicity with the bare life, *zoe* [*sic*]." For Dolar, "the emergency is the emergence of the voice in the commanding position, where its concealed existence suddenly becomes overwhelming and devastating. The voice is precisely at the unlocatable spot in the interior and the exterior of the law at the same time, and hence a permanent threat of a state of emergency." But he argues that the voice's unlocatable position places it in between seeming opposites and ultimately gives rise to a function that is different from the power to proclaim the state of emergency and that opens alternatives to the structures of power conceived as sovereignty: "The paradoxical topology of the voice as essentially between-the-two that we have been pursuing all along can be prolonged here to the relation between *phone* and *logos* as well as *zoe* and *bios*." What that means for a reading of Althusser is that

if one wants to become a subject, recognition and obedience are never quite enough; in addition to and apart from these, one has to respond to the "mere voice" which is just an opening, a pure enunciation compelling a response, an act, a dislocation of the imposing voices of domination. If in the first case one turns into a subject precisely by assuming the form of the autonomous "I," disavowing its heteronomic origin, so that ideological domination and autonomous subjectivity work hand in hand, as Althusser has forcefully shown, then in the second case one becomes a subject only by fidelity to the "foreign kernel" of the voice which cannot be appropriated by the self, thus by following precisely the heteronomic break in which one cannot recognize oneself. The ideological interpellation can never quite silence this other voice, and the distance between the two voices opens the space of the political.[121]

The interpellation by a guard dog undercuts the very premises of interpellation in that it unhinges subjectivity from symbolic representation. It creates an excess that serves biopolitical structures of violence. But it also creates an excess from which we can imagine alternative forms of representation and subjectivity.

Understanding that excess involves examining a more expansive register of representation that takes us beyond the visual and the verbal to the aural and the physical, to an engagement with the role animal sounds play as an alternate discourse—in Hester's cry at the core of Frederick Douglass's *Narrative* (chapter 2), in the garbled language of "The Murder's in the Rue Morgue" (chapter 3), in Emily Dickinson's reflections on noise (chapter 4), and in the voices of animal autobiography (chapter 5).[122] Those alternative forms of representation preoccupy me in the chapters that follow as I grapple with the ways in which American literature depicts animals to describe, support, critique, and unsettle the constructions of subjectivity on which biopower hinges.

To understand fully that process requires tracing not only the thanatopolitics on which much of this chapter has focused, but also the affirmative biopolitics to which the relationship with animals gives rise. It means bringing bestiality and bestialization in dialogue with the affective modes of animal love fostered by Lockean pedagogy and Benthamite sensibility. As my emphasis on bestiality as a disavowed foundation and an ongoing practice of American biopower has made clear, it is in the relation to animals that the social order establishes and reproduces itself. It seems to me, then, that the key for negotiating between these enmeshed practices is hermeneutic. The hermeneutics I am calling for are ones that read the "symbolic order" in relation to its other—that is, in relation to the bodily, the abject, the animalized that it produces at its founding. By affording that bodily register its own legibility, we achieve two things: we come to understand how biopolitics produces subjectivity via a process of bestialization, and we gain a means for engaging critically with that production.

BESTIALITY REVISITED

The Primal Scene of Biopower

(FREDERICK DOUGLASS)

In the context of American literary studies, the theoretical discourse of biopolitics has a particular provenance in the issue of slavery. In his landmark 1982 publication *Slavery and Social Death: A Comparative Study*, Orlando Patterson establishes a division similar to Giorgio Agamben's distinction between *bios* and *zoē* when he argues that slavery functioned as "a substitute for death" and that the slave became a "social nonperson" who had "no socially recognized existence outside of his master."[1] For Patterson, social death was orchestrated via the slave's "natal alienation" or removal from family structures that would bestow birthrights on him and embed him in a familial and social genealogy. This alienation crucially rested on the master's "control of symbolic instruments," which "may be seen as the cultural counterpart to the physical instruments used to control the slave's body." Like Agamben, Patterson reads the relationship between the different forms of life that the master and the slave can lay claim to as paradigmatic of the modern social order. Rejecting the argument that slavery is an aberration to the ideals developed by liberalism, he insists: "Slavery is associated not only with the development of advanced economies, but also with the emergence of several of the most profoundly cherished ideals and beliefs in the Western tradition. The idea of freedom and the concept of property were both intimately bound up with the rise of slavery, their very antithesis."[2]

This argument resonates with Michel Foucault's understanding of biopolitics as emerging from liberalism and also marks a significant departure from Agamben's appropriation of the term *biopolitics*. Foucault first developed a sustained analysis of biopolitics in part 5 of *History of Sexuality*, volume 1, and in a series of lectures before the Collège de France that have only recently become available in English translation.[3] He demonstrated that biopower emerges in a society where political power no longer limits itself to regulating death through the power of punishment (as Agamben and Patterson suggest) but expands to administering life itself.[4] Whereas Agamben grounds his argument about biopolitics in a reading of the law and its relation to sovereignty, Foucault differentiates between sovereignty and biopower. In the newly translated lectures Foucault gave before the Collège de France, he argues that biopower is "absolutely incompatible with relations of sovereignty" in that "this new mechanism of power applies primarily to bodies and what they do rather than to the land and what it produces."[5] He reflects on the shift from sovereignty to biopower as one marked by a turn from "a *symbolics of blood* to an *analytics of sexuality*," though he acknowledges that the passage from one to the other "did not come about . . . without overlappings, interactions, and echoes," so that "the preoccupation with blood and the law has for nearly two centuries haunted the administration of sexuality."[6]

According to Foucault, the analytics of sexuality hinged on two distinct readings of the body—one that examined the body as a machine regulated by disciplines and another that focused on the species body administered by a system of governmentality. The nexus between the two was sex, which was a means of "access both to the life of the body and the life of the species" and which mediated between the representational structures of the social and the individual.[7] For Foucault, a shift from a model of power based on sovereignty to one based on biopower correlates with the differentiation between *homo juridicus* and *homo oeconomicus*. He argues that the shift to biopower came with a new understanding of the subject as defined by interests that exceeded the legal definition of subjectivity. In *The Birth of Biopolitics*, Foucault links this rise of biopower to the rise of liberal capitalism, which he traces back to Locke (on whom I focus in chapter 4) and Hume:

> What English empiricism introduces—let's say, roughly, with Locke—and doubtless for the first time in Western philosophy, is a subject who is not so much defined by his freedom, or by the opposition of soul and body, or by the presence of a source or core of concupiscence marked to a greater or lesser degree by the Fall or sin, but who appears in the form of a subject of individual choices which are both irreducible and non-transferable. What do I mean by irreducible? I will take Hume's very simple and frequently cited passage, which says: What type of question is it, and what irreducible element can you arrive at when you analyze an individual's choices and ask why he did one thing rather than another? Well, he says: "You ask someone, 'Why do you exercise?' He will reply, 'I exercise because I desire health.'; You go on to ask him, 'Why do you desire health?' He will reply, 'Because I prefer health to illness.' Then you go on to ask him, 'Why do you prefer health to illness?' He will reply, 'Because illness is painful and so I don't want to fall ill.' And if you ask him why is illness painful, then at that point he will have the right not to answer, because the question has no meaning." The painful or non-painful nature of the thing is in itself a reason for the choice beyond which you cannot go. The choice between painful and non-painful is a sort of irreducible that does not refer to any judgment, reasoning, or calculation. It is a sort of regressive end point in the analysis. Second, this type of choice is non-transferable.[8]

Foucault initially develops his notion of *homo oeconomicus* by a reading of Hume that makes the desire to avoid pain the irreducible measure of self-interest. This emphasis on pain establishes the individual and collective body as the locus of meaning: although the avoidance of pain marks the individual's irreducible self-interest, it also functions as the baseline for an interest that all members of society share. In reading pain as "a reason" that does not "refer to . . . reasoning," Foucault uses "bare life" as the locus for the emergence of a subjectivity in excess of the law. He distinguishes between *homo juridicus* and *homo oeconomicus* and argues that "the subject of right and the subject of interest are not governed by the same logic" because the former "is integrated into the system of other subjects of right by a dialectic of the renunciation of his own rights or their transfer to someone else," whereas the latter "is integrated into the system of which he is a part, into the economic domain, not by a transfer, subtraction, or dialectic of renunciation, but by a dialectic of spontaneous multiplication."[9] That dialectic of spontaneous multiplication is the key mechanism of biopolitics, which exercises its power through the proliferation of knowledge-discourse formations. For Foucault, that discourse remains tied to and grounded in the body: as he points out, "bio-power was without question an indispensable element in the development of capitalism; the latter would not have been possible without the *controlled insertion of bodies* into the machinery of production and the adjustment of the phenomena of population to economic processes."[10] And yet this second claim also seems to call into question the link between liberal subject formation and biopolitics in the sense that it remains unclear how and whether the "controlled insertion of bodies into the machinery of production" allows for an economic being to emerge as a subject.

Foucault addresses this question by arguing that subject formation is not this social system's primary aim, but its by-product. The individual is not the origin but "one of the first effects of power."[11] As Patricia Ticineto Clough explains, he argues that in biopolitics the focus is not on the individual body, but on "a politics of population."[12] For Foucault, that population is the human population. But what happens when we engage with the desire to avoid pain more broadly as a desire shared by human beings and animals? What happens when we include animals in concerns over population and politics? After all, the focus on population makes species central to "the mechanisms of the state."[13] Within this economy of production, an understanding of animals as sentient beings opens up the possibility for a larger systemic critique. It becomes possible to read the structures of commoditization as producing *homo oeconomicus* in an expanded sense as a self-interested subject whose subjectivity is not tied to species boundaries. Both animal husbandry and slavery are premised on the physical exploitation of unfree bodies and on the harnessing of their reproductive capacities for the generation of biological capital. This statement needs to undergo careful reevaluation so as not to generate an unexamined equivalence. What I want to point out for now is that, as Nicole Shukin has recently argued, "the animal sign, not unlike the racial stereotype theorized by Homi Bhabha, is a site of '*productive ambivalence*' enabling vacillations between economic and symbolic logics of power."[14] Slaves and animals jointly inhabit an ambiguous position in which the shift from discipline to biopolitics is not linear and in which the vectors of individuality *and* collectivity are negotiated. To understand the challenges and possibilities of that negotiation, I turn to the way nineteenth-century statesman Frederick Douglass reflects on animals as a means to explain and disrupt the relationship between racial stereotypes and "the animal sign."

Frederick Douglass's engagement with animals and animality in relation to American biopolitics is graphically illustrated in his second autobiography, *My Bondage and My Freedom*, published in 1855. He divides the story of his life into two parts. Each part, "Life as a Slave" and "Life as a Freeman," is introduced by an elaborate woodcut (figures 2.1 and 2.2) that depicts, as Lisa Brawley points out, "the generic iconography of white nationalism" rather than specific scenes from the book.[15] All of the images in the first woodcut portray slavery in relation to animals and animality; the second woodcut defines the freeman's life by his ability to pursue economic prosperity. The two woodcuts jointly perform a shift from the slave as an object of economic exchange to his participation in the liberal economy. Crucial to that shift is the slave's relationship to animals and animality. The first woodcut explains slavery as contingent on a complex set of animal metaphors. In "Life as a Slave," the central vignette's depiction of an auction puts animals and slaves in an economically analogous position as chattel. The top vignette shows the iconic figure of the runaway slave being hunted by dogs and by men on horses. This vignette hovers above a set of flags to suggest that the runaway slave epitomizes American biopolitics, which uses animals to produce slaves' animality: working together as "companion species," men, horses, and dogs turn the runaway slave into prey, an animal barred from affective bonds.

The slave's animality becomes particularly clear in the one image that, to our modern viewing, does not seem to involve animals—the vignette of slaves dancing, to the right of center. As one of the most sought-after engravers of the time, the woodcut's creator Nathaniel Orr had made a name for himself by illustrating "many standard, mid-century minstrel productions,"[16] and this vignette invokes the minstrel stage. The text makes clear that the image is profoundly engaged with slaves' animality. Douglass describes how, "freed from all restraint, the slave-boy can be, in his life and conduct, a genuine boy, doing whatever his boyish nature suggests; enacting, by turns, all the strange antics and freaks of horses, dogs, pigs, and barn-door fowls, without in any manner compromising his dignity, or incurring reproach of any sort. He literally runs wild."[17]

FIGURE 2.1 Frontispiece from the "Life as a Slave" section of Frederick Douglass's *My Bondage and My Freedom* (New York: Miller, Orton & Mulligan, 1855). Courtesy of Dartmouth College Library

FIGURE 2.2 Frontispiece from the "Life as a Freedman" section of Frederick Douglass's *My Bondage and My Freedom* (New York: Miller, Orton & Mulligan, 1855). Courtesy of Dartmouth College Library

Experiencing what John Winthrop described as the "natural" liberty of animals, Douglass found himself excluded from "civil or federal" liberty by his animal status.[18] But his subtle prose already undercuts Winthrop's division by creating a verbal resonance between the child who "runs wild" and the runaway who traverses the wild to escape slavery. In describing how the slave child "runs wild," he links the slave's "natural liberty" to the runaway slave's desire for "civil or federal" liberty, thus collapsing the distinctions by redeploying their naturalizing discourse.

Throughout his work, Douglass uses animals and animality not only to reveal the logic of slavery, but to envision alternative forms of subjectivity. In philosophical terms, his work rejects the Aristotelian association of slaves with animals and the Cartesian classification of animals as machines. Instead, he emphasizes animals' and human beings' shared sensibility. Put in theoretical terms, Douglass's writing challenges Agamben's reading of biopower as an effect of sovereignty by advancing a Foucauldian model that separates the two from each other. By casting the abuse Aunt Hester endures, recounted in *Narrative of the Life of Frederick Douglass*, as a scene of bestiality, Douglass shows how race and gender are contingent on species and how that contingency reveals them to be social constructs rather than ontological realities. He reads bestiality along the lines I proposed in chapter 1, as the failed attempt to polarize human *bios* and animal *zoē*. Instead of establishing the differentiation between the sovereign and the *homo sacer*, bestiality functions in Douglass's reading as the site of an emergent liberal subject formation that reveals the animal origins of biopolitics. For Douglass, bestiality is the primal scene of biopower. But the question, then, becomes how or whether it is possible to critique the structures of abjection from the position of animality. Sharing with theorists of affect an understanding of pain as a discursive register, Douglass suggests that bestiality not only founds the juridical subject *homo juridicus* but produces the interest-bearing subject Foucault calls "*homo oeconomicus*."

Hester's Bondage

To understand how biopower operates, we need to examine how the analogy between slaves and animals functions. The analogy between race and species depends on a specific discourse that revolves around the question how meaning making occurs. In one of the most troubling passages of *Democracy in America* (1835–1840), Alexis de Tocqueville speculates whether one might not say "that the European is to men of other races what man is to the animals? He makes them serve his convenience, and when he cannot bend them to his will he destroys them. In one blow oppression has deprived the descendants of the Africans of almost all the privileges of humanity."[19] De Tocqueville is summing up some of the most egregiously racist practices and theories of slavery. At the time of his writing, efforts to distinguish blacks from whites culminated in a denial of their shared human origins. Josiah Clark Nott (1804–1873), George Robert Gliddon (1809–1857), Jean Louis Rodolphe Agassiz (1807–1873), and Samuel George Morton (1799–1851) founded the American school of ethnology when they argued that polygenesis, or multiple acts of genesis, had occurred and that blacks were a separate species from white men.[20] Although polygenesists generally did not claim outright that blacks were not human, they suggested that blacks had a degree of animality that whites lacked.[21]

Such racist discourse emerged in response to what Kay Anderson has called a crisis in "human exceptionalism": because of scientific advances, the category of the human needed to be accounted for in new ways.[22] Linguistic capacity had long been considered an exclusive marker of humanity, but new scientific discoveries and philosophical arguments were challenging the notion that language was an absolute dividing line between human beings and animals—it was no longer clear whether language could, as René Descartes had insisted, "be taken as a real specific difference between men and dumb animals."[23] Scientific racists exploited these discoveries by placing slaves in a liminal category that likened them to animals and differentiated both from whites. Arguing that slaves and animals shared the same linguistic capacities, they recoded "human exceptionalism" as white exceptionalism. Dr. Samuel Cartwright (1793–1863) argued that the slave's anatomical oral structure demonstrated his relationship to animals and his lack of white humanity. Cartwright developed the theory that blacks were "prognathous," a term he explained to be "derived from *pro*, before, and *gnathos*, the jaws, indicating that the muzzle or mouth is anterior to the brain. The lower animals, according to Cuvier, are distinguished from the European and Mongol man by the mouth and face projecting further forward in the profile than the brain."[24] This pre-Darwinian vocabulary motivates a discourse of species to establish categorical yet fungible distinctions that map living beings into hierarchical relation. Granting that blacks and animals shared a limited form of linguistic capacity, Cartwright distinguished the abstract language of slavery's symbolic order from a physiognomic language produced by and embodied in the "muzzle" of blacks and animals. This association presented African American authors with a special challenge because proving linguistic capacity was insufficient for protesting their condition.

My claim here flies in the face of roughly thirty years of commentary on African American writing that has emphasized the acquisition of language and literacy as a key liberatory tool but that has treated other discursive registers with caution for fear of replicating the reduction of slaves to the conditions of their embodiment. That caution is certainly well advised. The kind of difference posited by Cartwright and others might make one never again want to think of race in conjunction with animals for fear of replicating this denigration and perpetuating what Marjorie Spiegel has referred to as the "dreaded comparison" between human and animal slavery.[25] Yet precisely the racist connotations of much animal iconography raise the question why animal imagery recurs with such frequency and urgency in African American writing.

Dwight McBride has recently argued that a "return to the body, to physicality, seems to take us back to a place where one can say something about slave experience that is not just discursive and not just about narration and representational politics."[26] Frederick Douglass recoded the association of slaves with animals that was set up by scientific racism. By engaging with domesticated animals, he critiqued the position of liminal humanity that slaves and animals jointly occupied within the Southern plantocracy's classificatory blending of Aristotelian ontology and Cartesian epistemology. Abandoning the discourse of rationality and reason that these philosophies had established as the mark of humanity, he drew on a sentimental engagement with pain and sexuality as he redefined the body as the locus of a physical language that exceeded slavery's symbolic order. Instead of reading the slave as inarticulate zoē, Douglass appropriated the logic of biopower to make sex and affect themselves the sites of liberal subject formation. By depicting instances in which slaves were sexually abused as scenes of bestiality, Douglass revealed slavery to be a discourse constructed in relation to the very thing it negates—the body as a locus of meaning. Douglass raised these questions by invoking a specific practice that tested the relation between bodily narration and engendered subjectivity: bestiality. Although slaves and animals were categorically denied legal standing and gendered subjectivity, bestiality created a nexus between slavery's symbolic order and the realm of the bodily.

Through the writings of Sigmund Freud and Jacques Lacan, we have come to understand that subjectivity is fractured at the mirror stage and by the entry into the symbolic order. As a consequence, subjectivity is never whole or self-sufficient, but inherently relational: it emerges from the relation between self and other. Underlying their accounts are two fundamental assumptions: (1) that both the self and the other are human; and (2) that humanity is discursive. But what kind of subjectivity emerges where the "other" is an animal or an animalized being, and where discourse is embodied?

Douglass's first challenge in imagining slave subjectivity consisted in producing gender as a category applicable to slaves. As beings forcefully denied social standing, slaves were hypersexed and ungendered in slavery's symbolic economy. Treating slaves as hypersexed served slaveholders' desire to animalize them. In his autobiographies, Douglass describes the analogy slaveholders drew between slave owning and animal husbandry when he points out that Covey bought a slave woman "for *a breeder*" and when he argues that "the grand aim of slavery, . . . always and everywhere, is to reduce man to a level with the brute."[27] Emphasizing the reproductive body allowed slave owners to deny slaves' gendered subjectivity: thinking of slaves as bodies and naturalizing their reproductive role served to remove them from the social construction of gender.

This practice of describing slaves as sexed but not gendered dated back to Aristotle's justification of slavery, which provided American slavery's "most enduring" intellectual basis.[28] The denial of slaves' gender established an androcentric and anthropocentric social order. In describing the body politic, Aristotle argues that the male is "superior" to the female and that, in turn, "the female is distinguished by nature from the slave" and the animals.[29] He establishes two mutually reinforcing hierarchies: because of the male's and mankind's superior status, androcentrism and anthropocentrism go hand in hand. Yet if the male is categorically superior to the female, and the female is categorically superior to the slave, where in this hierarchy would we place male slaves or, for that matter, female slaves?[30] Aristotle erases the category of slave gender. By removing masculinity from femininity and from slavery, he implies that the male slave is at best feminized, if he is gendered at all. The ability of anthropocentrism and androcentrism to function in conjunction with each other thus depends on the negation of the slave's gendered subjectivity.

The negation of slave's gendered subjectivity makes Hester's treatment by Colonel Anthony illegible: under slavery's symbolic order, the scene is not readable as the rape it describes.[31] Because rape was defined as "the forcible carnal knowledge of a female against her will and without her consent," it was inapplicable to slaves, who were denied the very ability to have a will and give consent and hence to exercise "reasonable resistance."[32] Douglass's answer to this problem shifts the focus from an emphasis on "reasonable resistance" to a reading of pained physicality. As Sabine Sielke has demonstrated, although "the slave system does not recognize the rape of the enslaved," that rape becomes legible through the "rhetorical analogy between rape and torture."[33]

Douglass draws on that analogy with torture in his descriptions of Hester's abuse at Colonel Anthony's hands. An act of supposed sexual transgression inaugurates Hester's punishment: Colonel Anthony whips her for spending time with her boyfriend, Ned Roberts. Colonel Anthony sexualizes and animalizes Hester when he calls her a "d—d b—h."[34] His word choice is crucial: by calling Hester a bitch, he turns her into a female dog and negates her humanity. Yet his reference to Hester as a dog enables Douglass to recode what happens in this scene: unable to portray the violation of a slave woman as a rape under slavery's symbolic order, Douglass casts this scene in terms that make it legible as another kind of sex crime. By calling Hester a dog, Colonel Anthony shifts from the register of rape to the register of bestiality.[35]

Bestiality becomes the site from which Douglass can construct slaves' gender. According to the *Oxford English Dictionary*, bestiality refers to

1. The nature or qualities of a beast; want of intelligence, irrationality, stupidity, brutality. . . .
2. Indulgence in the instincts of a beast; brutal lust; *concr.* a disgusting vice, a beastly practice. . . .
   b. Filthy language, obscenity. . . .
3. Unnatural connexion with a beast. *Obs.* [which the example from the King James Bible associates with "Sodomie"][36]

Douglass runs the gamut of these definitions when he describes Hester's punishment. In accordance with the first definition, Colonel Anthony animalizes her and puts her in the position of a brute. In calling Hester a "d—d b—h," he engages in "filthy language." His pleasure in the violence enacted upon Hester marks his own "indulgence in the instincts of a beast," and his following his "brutal lust" in stripping her and penetrating her flesh with his whip performs an "unnatural connection with a beast."[37] This connection is apparent not only because Hester and Colonel Anthony are associated with animals, but because Douglass thinks of bestiality as a synonym for sodomy: he repeatedly draws attention to the fact that Colonel Anthony attacks Hester's back, thus invoking the use of his whip as performing an anal penetration.

When Douglass stages the flogging of Aunt Hester, he describes his initiation into the horrors of slavery as a scene of animal abuse. Colonel Anthony treats Hester as mere flesh when he strings her up like a carcass suspended from a meat hook: he "stripped her ... leaving her neck, shoulders, and back, entirely naked."[38] The stripping works in two registers here: on the one hand there is the taking away of the clothes, but on the other there is the allusion to his stripping off of her flesh itself through the use of his whip. Devoid of the clothing that physically marks her as human, Hester is reduced to a state of nakedness that is simultaneously animalized and hyperhuman- ized: because human beings are the only animals that wear clothing, being stripped of clothing is tantamount to being deprived of a marker of human- ity; yet, by the same token, because human beings are the only animals that are naked, being stripped also returns Hester to a state of primal humanity.[39] Hester inhabits what Louis Marin has called the "clinamen," a categorical intersection between such seemingly incompatible rubrics as the human and the animal, "verbality and orality, the instinct for self-preservation and the linguistic drive."[40]

One way to read this scene is via a logic of shame and victimization to which Hester is subjected, but which Douglass's reflections on her animaliza- tion disrupt in a way that critiques the violence enacted. Two texts are useful in this regard: Alice Kuzniar's *Melancholia's Dog* and Anat Pick's recent book *Creaturely Poetics*. Carefully distinguishing between different kinds of shame and in particular pointing out that "empathetic failure can be the result of the denial of shame," Kuzniar argues that "shame blurs the divide" between human beings and animals "in the very act of constructing it."[41] Douglass's text carefully maps out a triangulated relationship among Colonel Anthony, Hester, and Douglass himself. Whereas Colonel Anthony represents "empa- thetic failure," Douglass demonstrates how a shame that blurs the divide between human beings and animals can be the very basis for, as Kuzniar puts it a kind of "vicarious shame [that] offers the potential for productive social interaction."[42] For Pick, that vicarious shame revolves around a recognition that moves away from an emphasis on victimization—which risks replicating the imbalance inherent in shaming—to an emphasis on shared vulnerability. She argues that such "vulnerability offers a fundamental challenge to liberal humanism, both in terms of the rejection of the notion of rights and in a radical critique of subjectivity."[43] For Pick, the crucial distinction lies in the fact that victimization activates a set of humanitarian sympathies that ultimately support a human-centered understanding of the subject. Vulnerability, in contrast to victimization, produces an intersubjectivity that calls forth attention and enables what Pick describes as an ethical stance toward suffering that does not automatically reinscribe the human as the measure of that suffering. Yet her model of vulnerability departs from Douglass's concerns in that she imagines attentiveness as something that moves us beyond reading; for Douglass, reading remains central to the enterprise of figuring and critiquing vulnerability.

Douglass explores Hester's nakedness as a linguistic state. In this animalized yet primal state of humanity, Hester's words and supplications fail to move her tormentor, and Douglass describes how her voice itself becomes inscribed in her torture: "No words, no tears, no prayers from his gory victim, seemed to move his iron heart from its bloody purpose. The louder she screamed, the harder he whipped, and where the blood ran fastest, there he whipped longest. He would whip her to make her scream, and whip her to make her hush. . . . It was the most terrible spectacle. I wish I could commit to paper the feelings with which I beheld it."[44] Critics such as John Carlos Rowe have focused on Douglass's gaze,[45] but what interests me is the role that voice and hearing play in his description. Douglass stages his acoustic relation to this scene by pointing out that he has "often been awakened at the dawn of day by the most heart-rending shrieks of an own [that is, biologically related] aunt of mine."[46] His awakening to the horrors of slavery occurs through his relationship to Hester's voice, and he uses this whipping scene to theorize a slave language that is located in the pained body and that exceeds the symbolic order of slavery.

In this flogging, what Foucault calls the *"symbolics of blood* and *analytics of sexuality"* encounter and confound one another, and what emerges, according to Tobias Menely, is a "somatically legible subject."[47] Blood marks both the slave master's "purpose" and his victim's actual flesh; it functions as a symbolic as well as a literal marker that refers to the slave master's ability to control life itself.[48] In fact, the tie of the blood to reproduction is further highlighted by Douglass's use of narrative perspective: he describes himself as a child witnessing this scene and makes himself the offspring of such abuse when he argues that this violation marked his entry into slavery. Having already told us that his father was most likely a slave master, he casts this scene as one that establishes his own figurative as well as literal origins. The scene of bestiality he witnesses functions for him as the primal scene of slavery.[49]

The excess portrayed here initially seems to mark Hester's abjection: the more Hester uses her voice, "the louder she screamed," the more Colonel Anthony controls her physical body, "the harder he whipped." Through his actions, he tries to control her voice: he whips her "to make her scream" and to "make her hush" and turns her voice into an effect of his own brutal action. He produces her expressions as "prognathous"—that is, as animalistic and lacking in reason.[50] Hester's voice becomes hyperembodied in that it is directly responsive to the pain his whip inflicts. That hyperembodiment serves Colonel Anthony as a justification for his actions: by turning Hester's language into a bodily effect—an effect of his whipping and her pain—he denies her the disembodied reason and rationality that René Descartes used to distinguish human beings from animals.[51] According to Descartes, the "animal . . . lacks reason." That lack of reason manifests itself in relation to language: animals "are incapable of arranging various words together and forming an utterance from them in order to make their thoughts understood."[52] Colonel Anthony turns Hester into an instinctive, mechanical animal, responsive to external stimuli but devoid of reason. He negates her individual subjectivity and performs what Foucault refers to as a "controlled insertion of bodies into the machinery of production" that serves "the adjustment of the phenomena of population to economic processes."[53] Colonel Anthony reminds Hester that her physical labor in both the sense of work and the sense of childbirth belongs to him and that he controls her individual body as well as her reproductive and hence biopolitical body.

For Colonel Anthony, Hester's embodied voice is not a marker of her pained humanity—her very expressions of pain justify his treatment of her in that they mark her as an animal whose suffering is of no account. According to Colonel Anthony but also to our current critical accounts of language, Hester's pain negates her ability to articulate her humanity. Elaine Scarry has argued that "physical pain does not simply resist language, but actively destroys it" because it is only when "the body is comfortable, when it has ceased to be an obsessive object of perception and concern, that consciousness develops other objects."[54] Scarry's argument draws on Freud's and Lacan's notions that subjectivity depends on a differentiation between subject and object that forms the basis for subjectivity and the entry into the symbolic order of abstract language. In his late work, Jacques Derrida questions the assumption underlying such arguments—that the self and the other are a priori human and linguistically determined. As I discuss more fully in chapter 5, he criticizes Lacan for portraying animals in "the most dogmatically traditional manner, fixed within Cartesian fixity," and for "refusing the animal language." Faulting Lacan for depicting the animal "within the imaginary and unable to accede to the symbolic," he calls into question whether "what calls itself human has the right to rigorously attribute to man, which means therefore to attribute to himself, what he refuses the animal, and whether he can ever possess the *pure, rigorous, indivisible* concept, as such, of that attribution."[55]

Douglass's answer to this question is a resounding no, especially because the categories of the human and the animal are fungible. Douglass works out his argument by obscuring who inhabits the category of the human and the animal. He depicts Colonel Anthony, in the act of animalizing Hester, in a way that calls into question who the Cartesian animal is in this scene. The colonel is utterly unmoved by Hester's "words . . . tears . . . prayers," and language itself fails to have an effect on this mechanized being whose actions are guided by his "iron heart" and who is "not a humane slaveholder."[56] By mechanizing Colonel Anthony, Douglass animalizes him: according to Descartes, machines and animals are alike because "the laws of mechanics . . . are identical with the laws of nature."[57] Rather than indicating that Hester's utterance is animalistic and incomprehensible, he suggests that the master is animalistic and lacks understanding so that the efficacy of Hester's expression is lost on him.

Douglass undermines the racism of slavery's epistemic categorization of animalized humanity by including whites in it. He denies Colonel Anthony the very position of white exceptionalism that his cruelty to Hester is meant to establish. He casts the master in an animalized position and demonstrates Hester's inherent humanity. His manipulation of Cartesian philosophy points to the fungibility of the human and the animal as ontological categories. Signifyin', Douglass reverses the racist trope of the "*prognathous*" slave in his portrayal of Covey: "When he [Covey] spoke, it was from the corner of his mouth, and in a sort of light growl, like a dog, when an attempt is made to take a bone from him."[58] He locates Covey's animality in the language that is meant to distinguish him from animalized slaves. By drawing on animal similes, he demonstrates that slavery's symbolic order originates from the animality and physicality that it negates.

However, these strategies run the danger of merely reascribing and not fundamentally critiquing the abjection inherent in the discursive construction of slavery. Instead of focusing on the reversibility of metaphor, Douglass puzzles over recoding the significance of animality as such. To this end, he revisits the body as a site from which to challenge slavery's symbolic order. When he portrays Hester's pain and Colonel Anthony's pleasure, he creates a site of animality by which the body itself matters. By reporting on his own horrified response to the sounds and sights of Hester's abuse, he develops the possibility of establishing what by the logic of slavery amounts to a "cross-species identification."[59] He accomplishes this goal by shifting the focus from reason to sentiment.

Although we have come to associate this shift with the rise of sentimentality in the nineteenth century, it is already inherent in Aristotle's discussion of slavery. Although Aristotle dogmatically argues in *The Politics* that "he is a slave by nature who is capable of belonging to another . . . and who participates in reason only to the extent of perceiving it, but does not have it," his writings on the soul undercut the categorical distinctions that he draws here.[60] Whereas Descartes justifies his association of animals with machines by separating the soul from the body, Aristotle contends that the soul "cannot be separated from the body." For Aristotle, plants, animals, and human beings are on a continuum: they all share certain capacities of soul, such as "nutrition, appetency, sensation, locomotion and understanding." Although Descartes denies animals meaningful sentience, for Aristotle, "it is sensation primarily which constitutes the animal." Not only is sensation the distinguishing feature of animals, but "where sensation is found, there is pleasure and pain, and that which causes pleasure and pain; and, where these are, there also is desire, desire being appetite for what is pleasurable."[61] Aristotle does not draw the conclusion that human beings and animals are therefore alike, but an emphasis on gradated rather than absolute categories enabled David Hume to conclude that animal actions "proceed from a reasoning, that is not in itself different, nor founded on different principles, from that which appears in human nature."[62] Douglass makes a similar point when he says, "Reason is said to be not the exclusive possession of men. Dogs and elephants are said to possess it."[63] He turns pained animality into the site for a sympathetic identification. He demonstrates in the cruel modulations of Hester's cries the slave's animalistic position of—and here I borrow from Emmanuel Lévinas, to whom I turn more fully in a moment—having a *voice* but of being denied by her tormentor the capacity to have *language*. Hester's plight epitomizes the position of slaves and animals as "beings entrapped in their species," who are, "despite all their vocabulary, beings without language."[64]

Douglass describes his own position as a slave author in similar terms. Recounting the division of property that occurred after his master's death, he says, "I have no language to express the high excitement and deep anxiety which were felt among us poor slaves during this time. Our fate for life was now to be decided. We had no more voice in that decision than the brutes among whom we were ranked. A single word from the white men was enough—against all our wishes, prayers and entreaties."[65] Douglass finds himself without "language" to describe the emotional extremes of his feeling—the "high excitement" and the "deep anxiety." He likens his state of emotionally intense yet silenced suffering to the experience of "the brutes" among whom slaves were counted. By the logic of slavery, slaves and brutes are qualitatively the same, as Douglass makes clear by setting up a comparison that gives both slaves and brutes equal voice. That voice stands in marked contrast to the language of "white men," for whom a "single word" suffices to annihilate all verbal expression from slaves.

But Mladen Dolar's work offers a different reading of what this seeming failure of language means and theorizes voice in a manner that is helpful for understanding the significance of Hester's screams. Dolar's reflections on voice are particularly helpful for understanding how Hester's voice is both embodied and linguistic and how it challenges biopolitics as such. He distinguishes between three different uses of voice: (1) as the vehicle of meaning; (2) as the source of aesthetic appreciation; and (3) as an "object voice" that does not become subservient to either of the other two functions—that is, it does not take second rank to the message or become "an object of fetish relevance." He argues that "presymbolic uses of the voice," such as the scream, may seem to be external to structure, but on the contrary epitomize "the signifying gesture precisely by not signifying anything in particular." That claim enables Dolar to reevaluate the relationship between phoneme and logos and to map it onto and take it beyond the relationship of *zoē* to *bios*. Arguing that the "object voice" is "not external to linguistics" and produces a "rupture at the core of self-presence," he bases these claims on the realization that the voice is "the link which ties the signifier to the body. It indicates that the signifier, however purely logical and differential, must have a point of origin and emission in the body." Hence, it is the voice that "ties language to the body," but in a paradoxical way in that the voice belongs to neither—it is not "part of linguistics," and it is not "part of the body" but instead "floats." That analysis of the object voice that floats enables Dolar to reread Aristotle's definition of man as a political animal endowed with speech in distinction from the mere voice of other animals. Dolar argues that "at the bottom of this" distinction between speech and voice, phone and logos, lies "the opposition between two forms of life: *zoē* and *bios*." Rejecting the "partition of voice" that Aristotle thus creates, Dolar argues that voice is "not simply an element external to speech" but "persists" at the core of language, "making it possible and constantly haunting it by the impossibility of symbolizing it." He clarifies that he does not see this object voice as a precultural state, but as "sustaining and troubling" logos.[66]

By demonstrating that Hester specifically and slaves in general suffer in spite of or rather because of the inefficacy of their pleas, Douglass creates a means of sentimental identification that tests the limits of discursivity. For Douglass, language—and, in the *Narrative*, literacy—is not an alternative to embodiment; they go hand in hand and perform the "dialectic of spontaneous multiplication" that Foucault associates with the emergence of biopolitics.[67] The body is the locus for a language that precedes and exceeds Lacanian notions of the symbolic order. In *Bodies That Matter*, Judith Butler makes a similar claim when she points out that "there is an 'outside' to what is constructed by discourse, but this is not an absolute 'outside,' an ontological thereness that exceeds or counters the boundaries of discourse; as a constitutive 'outside,' it is that which can only be thought—when it can—in relation to that discourse, at and as its most tenuous borders."[68]

In his treatise *Origin of Languages* (1771), Johann Gottfried Herder explores those "tenuous borders" when he invokes but departs from Cartesian philosophy's emphasis on mechanization. He argues that an inquiry into the origin of languages "does not lead to a divine but—quite on the contrary—to an animal origin." Herder explains that in the sufferer the call for sympathy is not a conscious choice but a natural impulse. It is part of a "mechanics of sentient bodies." What Herder exactly means by the phrase "mechanics of sentient bodies," which echoes Descartes, is somewhat enigmatic, but he explains that calling out in pain in search of sympathy is an instinctive, not a reasoned act. The call for sympathy occurs even when no "sympathy from outside" can be expected—it is an act that the sufferer performs regardless of the response he or she will receive. But because such a call "can arouse other beings of equally delicate build"—that is, of an equally sensitized disposition—sympathy also reflects the innate quality of the sympathizer.[69]

By portraying Hester's voice as an instinctual response to her pain, Douglass associates her calls with a "mechanics of sentient bodies." But, for Douglass, these calls demonstrate rather than negate her innate need for sympathy: Hester's animalism—that is, her instinctive call—forms the linguistic basis on which Douglass and his readers can sympathize with her. Her calls mark her as an interest-bearing subject: as Foucault had suggested in his reading of Hume, *homo oeconomicus* emerges where an irreducible interest in avoiding pain occurs. That irreducible interest simultaneously marks the individual as a subject yet also makes that subjectivity an effect of power in the sense that it emerges from a commonly held and commonly shared response to suffering. Douglass accomplishes an expansion of that suffering's significance—no longer merely significant for human beings, such suffering also extends to those beings marked as animals.

For Douglass, sympathizing with those who suffer reveals man's "best and most interesting side . . . the side which is better pleased with feeling than reason."[70] By portraying his own horrified reaction, he argues that anyone of "equally delicate build" will differentiate themselves from the unfeeling Colonel Anthony and will respond sympathetically to Hester's call. In a marked departure from Cartesian rationalism, he motivates the discourse of sentimentality to argue for suffering as the locus (as Foucault would have it)—not the antithesis (as Agamben would insist)—of subjectivity. Douglass describes the effect of Hester's cries as "heart-rending" and opposes his own affective response to his master's cruel pleasure in the same scene. For him, the "spectacle" he witnesses is about "the feelings" it awakens in him. He reacts to the scene with a sense of sympathetic identification that validates Hester's suffering.

By drawing on the body in pain, Douglass establishes a comprehensive understanding of humanity that is deeply relational. As Timothy Morton has pointed out, "'Humanity' in the [nineteenth-century] period denotes both the non-sacred (non-Judaeo-Christian) study of culture (for example, classical literature), and sensibility or affection. The play on 'humane' is very important in certain contemporary animal rights texts. . . . Expressions of kindness amongst animals show that 'humanity' is a quality possessed equally by all animals, in a sense; but in particular, it links culture (defined as human frailty) to nature. To be humane is to be refined and to accord with nature."[71]

Both a natural and a cultivated sympathy, humanity was not what humans had a priori by virtue of being human, but what they acquired through their encounter with animals, as I explain at greater length. Humanity was not a hermetically sealed form of identity, but a form of subjectivity that emerged through an engagement with nonhuman alterity. Deeply relational, humanity marked a relationship that established and exceeded the category of the human; it shifts the focus, in theoretical terms, from biopolitics to *zoopolitics*, a term I borrow from Nicole Shukin. She has recently taken issue with the idea that "human social life (as the subject of biopolitics) can be abstracted from the lives of nonhuman others (the domain of zoopolitics). Zoopolitics, instead, suggests an inescapable contiguity or bleed between *bios* and *zoē*, between a politics of human social life and a politics of animality that extends to other species."[72]

This "bleed" between *bios* and *zoē* has a particular literary provenance in the beast fable. One of the most popular literary genres of nineteenth-century America, the beast fable "had from its origins functioned as a self-protective mode of communication . . . by a slave addressing the Master society."[73] Beginning in 1777 with the first American edition of Aesop,[74] fables gained popularity in both the Northern and Southern states as didactic texts for children and for language instruction; they were also centrally tied to Locke's educational philosophy and practices of child rearing and subject formation. Yet Aesop also provided a particularly poignant reference point for African American writers in that he was himself portrayed as being of African descent and enslaved. American editions from 1798 onward often reprinted *The Life of Aesop* alongside the fables,[75] and Aesop (who was a black author—his name was understood to derive from Ethiopia, his place of birth) gained status as a representative man in works such as Samuel Goodrich's *Famous Men of Ancient Times* (1843).[76]

Aesop's *Life* begins with an account of his accession to language, specifically to an embodied language that occurs at the "tenuous border" where Butler sees the "ontological thereness" function as a "constitutive outside" to slavery's symbolic order.[77] Originally a deformed slave without linguistic capacity, Aesop finds a means of justifying himself when his master falsely accuses him of stealing figs. By vomiting up the contents of his stomach and occasioning the true perpetrators of the theft to do the same, Aesop manages to produce not "a narrative body, but bodily narration." That bodily narration forms the origin of the fable in that it creates a "language ... [that] will be the supplement of gestures and of the body."[78] This act of bodily narration initiates the fable, which incessantly restages its physical origins and collapses the distinction between the body and discourse. Such bodily narration subverts slavery's symbolic order. As Louis Marin has argued, the fable operates on the logic of "the production of a body that tells a story, and in so doing, the body inverts the effects of the representational discourse. . . . [T]his bodily narration deconstructs the verbal story that explicitly claims to be true."[79]

This notion that a body can tell a story and that this body need not be human is not limited to the fables of antiquity; it underlies the very notion of literary character that developed in the early modern period, as Bruce Boehrer's recent work has shown. Arguing that "animal character" is "crucial to the development of notions of literary character in general," Boehrer suggests that we need to reassess the relevance not only of species, but of species mixing that underwrites "earlier notions of literary personhood." Explaining that Descartes grants "humanity exclusive access to consciousness via the ability 'to use words or other signs . . . to declare our thought to others'" and in the process "creates a new purpose for literary activity—that of drawing and redrawing the species boundary through the elaboration of literary character as defined by the revelation in words of a distinctive personal interiority," Boehrer points out that earlier writers such as Shakespeare instead had a "pre-Cartesian" understanding of both human–animal relations and literary representation. He sees that alternative understanding "elaborated in the Aristotelian and Theophrastan tradition of nature writing and animal writing that dominated western philosophy from classical times well into the early modern period,"[80] a classical tradition that remained central to the curriculum in institutions of American higher education well into the twentieth century and was circulated by Shakespeare's popularity in the nineteenth-century United States.[81] Douglass seems to illustrate Boehrer's point that "we can understand the notion of character in Aristotle and Theophrastus as a complex of ethical qualities or predispositions . . . shared by human and nonhuman animals alike to a greater or lesser extent, related to the body in both a causal and an expressive manner, and susceptible to classification just as are the physical qualities that distinguish one class or species of being from another."[82]

By engaging with the body—animalized, deprived of language, and in pain—Douglass reminds his readers that writing is itself a physical act when he tells them that his "feet have been so cracked with the frost, that the pen with which I am writing might be laid in the gashes."[83] He insists that the metaphorical body of his slave narrative and his literal body as a slave are inseparable from one another. His language supplements his gestures and his body. Restaging his acoustic relationship to Hester's cries as a relationship to slave expression more broadly, Douglass draws on this strategy when he writes:

> I did not, when a slave, understand the deep meaning of those rude and apparently incoherent songs [of the slave]. I was myself within the circle; so that I neither saw nor heard as those without might see and hear. They told a tale of woe which was then altogether beyond my feeble comprehension; they were tones loud, long, and deep; they breathed the prayer and complaint of souls boiling over with the bitterest anguish. Every tone was a testimony against slavery, and a prayer to God for deliverance from chains. The hearing of those wild notes always depressed my spirit, and filled me with ineffable sadness. I have frequently found myself in tears while hearing them. The mere recurrence of those songs, even now, afflicts me; and while I am writing these lines, an expression of feeling has already found its way down my cheek. To those songs can I trace my first glimmering conception of the dehumanizing character of slavery. I can never get rid of that conception. Those songs still follow me, to deepen my hatred of slavery, and quicken my sympathies for my brethren in bonds. . . . The songs of the slave represent the sorrows of his heart; and he is relieved by them, only as an aching heart is relieved by its tears.[84]

Confronted with his inability to "understand" in a reasoned manner what he sees as the "deep meaning" of the slave songs, Douglass develops an alternative, physical mode of expression and comprehension. The songs themselves are "breathed"—that is, they are examples of a physical mode of expression. Their effect on Douglass is physical as well in that the "sadness" they occasion in him expresses itself in the body—in his "tears," which form an "expression of feeling" where words fail him. By experiencing the limits of abstract language and the power of embodied sentiment, Douglass understands the means by which slavery's emphasis on rationality and negation of bodily narration operate: because slavery's symbolic order denies the body's affective and expressive qualities, it is "dehumanizing." For Douglass, humanity lies in understanding the physical expression of bodily narration.

Douglass's Freedom

One of Douglass's key strategies for achieving the recognition of the relationship between humanity and the body is by rethinking the position of animality in which slavery places him. He understands that animals serve to enact the animalization on which slavery depends, but that animals also disrupt that figuration. In his second autobiography, *My Bondage and My Freedom*, the engraving representing "life as a slave" (figure 2.1) contains what Michael Chaney has described as a "popular set piece of antislavery iconography, the slavecatcher's hounds in vicious pursuit of the pitiable runaway."[85] Such pieces typically show a slave about to be attacked by a dog who is charging in advance of a slaveholder on horseback.

Such slave-hunting dogs were apparently commercially profitable, as advertisements for their services attest. Dated January 29, 1856, one such advertisement read: "LOOK OUT. The undersigned would announce to the public generally, that he has a splendid lot of well broke NEGRO DOGS, And will attend at any reasonable distance, to the catching of runaways, at the lowest possible rates. All those having slaves in the woods will do well to address W. D. GILBERT, Franklin, Simpson co. Ky. [N.B. Please post this up in a conspicuous place.]"[86] This advertisement reflects the use and the double meaning of animal imagery in the practices and the iconography of slavery. Framed as an announcement to the "public generally," it defines that public as white and slaveholding. The top portion shows a hand pointing at a sequence of four iconic runaway salves. The layout links the runaway slave depicted in the top portion to the "NEGRO DOGS" of the central text in that the capitalized text functions as a caption for the image of the runaway slave. The advertisement works on two levels. It promotes the hire of dogs for the capture of slaves, but it also labels the runaway slaves as "NEGRO DOGS": the expression functions as a label for the images, and bestializes the escaped slaves, creating a racial slur that defines them as "NEGRO DOGS." By the logic of this advertisement, animals are both an instrument for the capture of slaves and an instrument for slaves' animalization. The advertisement gives the slave a heightened degree of animality in that it portrays him as inhabiting "the woods"—that is, as being wild and removed from civilization. By contrast, the dogs themselves are "well broke": they have a degree of training that more closely aligns them with the commercial interests of the "public generally" than with the "runaways" whom they will capture for "the lowest possible rates." Those rates are payable to "the undersigned," the named person "W. D. Gilbert," who establishes his subject position by arrogating to himself the means of representation (signing) and economic exchange (payable rates for services rendered). The positions we see enacted here recapitulate the ones Winthrop detailed when he distinguished between "man . . . beasts and other creatures": the slave is put in the position of the "other creatures" via his confrontation with the "beasts" and "man." He is racialized as a "beastlike man," a wolf-man who is "worse than brute beasts."

In this advertisement and in the "Life as a Slave" woodcut's depiction of slave hunting (figure 2.1), the slaveowner dominates the humanized animal (the slave-hunting dog) and the animalized human (the slave). The slave is confronted by both the dog and the rider—by companion species at work. The encounter with companion species places him not only in the position of the animalized human but creates an excess by which he becomes the animalized animal: excluded from human–animal bonds, he figures as the other other of sheer alterity.

This image demonstrates how animals can be instrumentalized to enact state violence and to produce animality. The slave is not only animalized but hyperanimalized in contrast to the dog. A problematic double articulation emerges of what we mean by "animal": ("the") animal is the binary opposite of ("the") human. But the binaries constitutive of the subject break down where "the animal" functions as mediator between the subject and its others. The dog's presence facilitates the slave's removal from the symbolic order and from that order's concomitant forms of legal, social, and verbal subjectivity. It also opens the possibility for a different kind of representational regime to arise. The dog takes on a discursive function in bestializing the slave. But that discursive function collapses the distinctions it is meant to draw between the symbolic, representational, human subject, on the one hand, and the real, nonrepresentational animal, on the other.

How can we theorize the collapse of these distinctions and imagine an alternative biopolitics? Emmanuel Lévinas provides an account that I want to read as imaging an affirmative biopolitics from within the thanatopolitics that Agamben associates with the logic of the camp. In one of the oddest and most complex accounts Lévinas published, "The Name of a Dog, or Natural Rights," he deconstructs Western attitudes toward animality when he describes his experience in a Nazi detention camp.[87] Lévinas and his fellow Jewish detainees found themselves in the position of animalized humans whose treatment at the hands of their captors "stripped us of our human skin" and placed them in a "subhuman" position. Despite the "small inner murmur" that kept affirming their "essence as thinking creatures," they found themselves "no longer part of the world."[88] Lévinas's wording here invokes and challenges Martin Heidegger's argument that "the animal is *poor in world*" whereas "man is *world-forming*."[89] Rejecting such ontological difference or, to be more precise, such different relations to ontology, Lévinas indicates that the distinction between human beings and animals is not absolute but relational, that their position in regard to the world is not ontological but situational.[90]

Describing himself and his fellow detainees as "beings entrapped in their species; despite all their vocabulary, beings without language," Lévinas explores the implications of that realization by examining the parameters of intelligibility.[91] Although David Clark reads Lévinas as ultimately subscribing to the notion that linguistic capacity separates human beings from animals and that only the human subject can bear proper witness,[92] the distinction Lévinas draws between vocabulary and language bears further investigation. Mapping Ferdinand de Saussure's differentiation between *parole* and *langue* onto the prisoners and guards, respectively, Lévinas indicates that he and his fellow detainees were capable of individual expression but were barred from having that expression signified in the structural contexts they inhabited. Expanding on this point, he writes that "racism is not a biological concept; anti-Semitism is the archetype of all internment. Social aggression, itself, merely imitates this model. It shuts people away in a class, deprives them of expression and condemns them to being 'signifiers without a signified' and from there to violence and fighting."[93]

Arguing that racism's ontology is discursively constructed, Lévinas demonstrates that metaphor (the use of archetypal referents) creates metamorphic positions. Instead of language being an absolute human capacity, Lévinas argues that it is possible for human beings to be deprived "of expression" and relegated to a position of nonsignification. That position of nonsignification places the detainee in the literal position of animality, where he meets with "violence."

Lévinas does not merely document that violence but also posits an alternative model of communication—something along the lines of what Alice Kuzniar calls "interspecial communication."[94] If Lévinas himself did not have any experience with German guard dogs, surely he was aware by the time of his writing in 1975 that they were used in detention camps. Yet Lévinas invokes the dog in a different capacity, as a creature that does not do the bidding of state interpellation and violence, but one that performs a different kind of subject formation by giving the body itself a discursive register with which to critique the model of abjection practiced by the Nazis. Lévinas describes the detainees' encounter with a dog whom they named Bobby who visited the camp: "He would appear at morning assembly and was waiting for us as we returned, jumping up and down and barking in delight. For him, there was no doubt that we were men." Introducing a dog early in his piece as "someone who disrupts society's games (or Society itself)," Lévinas finds his subjectivity affirmed—or rather newly constructed—in the encounter with Bobby.[95] While the prisoners endured forced labor, their relationship to Bobby occurred outside the camp's structures of domination and beyond the working relationship Haraway associates with companion species. However, this figure also seems to reinscribe some of the central notions of subjectivity: as a free agent, the dog seems to occupy the position of the humanized animal in the species grid, and through his acts of seeming volition to reaffirm the humanity of the animalized human. It is not clear that the animal is able to function here in a role as an animal other.[96]

Developing as his basic philosophical premise the notion that the face-to-face encounter with the other makes the human human, Lévinas struggles with the question whether animals can be included in his model of relational, ethical subjectivity. In an interview he gave in 1986, he responds directly to the question whether animals have a face. Affirming that "one cannot entirely refuse the face of an animal," he ambiguously argues that his "entire philosophy" hinges on the idea that for human beings "there is something more important than my life, and that is the life of the other. That is unreasonable. Man is an unreasonable animal." At the very moment of differentiation, then, Lévinas concludes indecisively: he argues for man's exceptional ethical capacity yet calls man an "animal." Rejecting an inscription of human beings in a model of animality, he asserts that they are in the exceptional position of creatures for whom the maxim does not hold that "the aim of being is being itself."[97] But his description of Bobby belies the exceptionalism he claims to endorse: risking his life to seek human companionship (Bobby was eventually "chased . . . away" by the "sentinels"), Bobby engaged in the unreasonable act that for Lévinas defines ethical subjectivity.

Recognizing such emotional intersubjectivity—and the privileged role that the body plays in it—enables us to expand our understanding of discursive registers. Lévinas talks about the guards being epistemologically and ontologically confused—unlike the dog Bobby, they "doubt[ed] that we were men." Dogs have a different kind of knowledge that is located in their own bodies: they know by "barking in delight" that the prisoners are men. As a different kind of social knowledge, "barking in delight" becomes Lévinas's countermodel to the symbolic order: the dog's recognition of a fellow being undid other human beings' withholding of that recognition. Lévinas's encounter with the dog marks his humanity yet at the same time makes humanity subject to recognition by animals. In the relationship with animals, on the liminal ground of humanized animality and animalized humanity, a form of subjectivity emerges that is relational and removed from the violence of the symbolic order. That subjectivity is not human as much as it is humane: it is in his sympathetic engagement with the animal that Lévinas renounces the violence inherent in the symbolic order. It is in the dog's "barking in delight" that Lévinas sees himself as a man. In the encounter between the detained Lévinas and the dog Bobby, we see suspended the differentiation between subjects and nonsubjects that underlies the symbolic order and its concomitant forms of representation.

Douglass stages a similar encounter, but his use of humor in doing so enables him to avoid the pitfall of instrumentalizing animals that Lévinas falls into. In the relationship between the human being and the animal, Douglass imagines subjectivity to become recognizable and meaningful. He makes the body the basis for a relational subjectivity that he locates in the encounter between human beings and animals. He often sounds as though he were categorically distinguishing human beings from animals. Although he says that animals have language and reason, he insists that only men have the capacity for imagination. For instance, in his address "Pictures," he argues that "man is the only picture-making animal in the world." However, his phrasing in making these distinctions is revealing: even though he categorically differentiates "picture-making" human beings from animals, he inscribes both in the category of the "animal." He describes in "Farewell to the British People" (1847) how slavery's symbolic order denies him subjectivity, but he also indicates that the relationship to animals makes the recognition of his subjectivity possible:

> Why, sir, the Americans do not know that I am a man. They talk of me as a box of goods; they speak of me in connexion with sheep, horses, and cattle. But here, how different! Why, sir, the very dogs of old England know that I am a man! (Cheers) I was in Beckenham for a few days, and while at a meeting there, a dog actually came up to the platform, put his paws on the front of it, and gave me a smile of recognition as a man. (Laughter) The Americans would do well to learn wisdom upon this subject from the very dogs of Old England; for these animals, by instinct, know that I am a man; but the Americans somehow or other do not seem to have attained to the same degree of knowledge.[98]

Douglass talks about Americans being epistemologically and ontologically confused—unlike the dogs of England, they do not "know" that Douglass is a "man." Dogs have a different kind of knowledge that is located in their own bodies: they know by "instinct" that Douglass is a man.[99] Limited entirely to a gestural register of expression, "with neither ethics nor *logos*," says Lévinas, "the dog will attest to the dignity of its person. This is what the friend of man means. There is a transcendence in the animal!"[100] The dog's bodily knowledge enables his recognition of Douglass's embodied voice as being different from "sheep, horses, and cattle." Instinct becomes Douglass's countermodel for social knowledge: he laments that the Americans have not "attained to the same degree of knowledge" as the dog acting on his instinct. Douglass's encounter with the dog marks his humanity and at the same time makes humanity subject to recognition by the animal. In the relationship with the animal, on the liminal ground of humanized animality and animalized humanity, a form of subjectivity emerges that is relational and removed from the violence of slavery. It is in his sympathetic engagement with the animal that Douglass reverses the violence inherent in slavery's symbolic order.

As a rewriting of American biopower, this scene is tremendously powerful: understanding how the instrumentalization of animals produces slave's animality, Douglass envisions an affective relationship that makes the encounter with an animal the site of an affirmative subjectivity. In allowing himself to encounter an animal affectively, he places himself in the position of the liberal subject that emerges from the relationship with animals. In Lévinas, that relationship is coded hierarchically in that the dog is not admitted to the same kind of subjectivity that he enables and produces. However, Douglass's use of humor allows him to envision at least the possibility of a radically different kind of subjectivity, one that—like his descriptions of Hester—reads animality as producing a subjectivity premised on alterity. In eliciting "laughter" from his audience, he is creating a verbal expression that is nonlinguistic. Producing in his listeners a response that is not symbolic but instead vocal, bodily, aural, he places them in the same position as the dog who, in Lévinas, barks with delight and who, in Douglass, smiles. Turning Covey's "light growl" and the guard dogs' interpellation into the happy barking of the smiling dog, Douglass does not abandon the discourse of animality as much as recode it. He places his audience in the dog's position in that the smile of recognition now becomes reflected and refracted in their laughter. Turning animality into a shared but affirmative biopolitical site, he opens the possibility for producing a subjectivity that collapses the binaries between "the human" and "the animal" and that generates alternative subject-discourse formations.

In this chapter, I have examined what possibilities arise for an alternative discourse when Douglass appropriates the logic of biopower to make sex and affect themselves the sites of subject formation by crossing species lines. Turning to the specifically American context of slavery that makes bestiality a biopolitical site, this chapter has demonstrated how the abuses of bestiality for Douglass function as a way to imagine alternative modes of representation that shift our attention from the subject of rights to the subject of interest. By depicting instances in which slaves are sexually abused as scenes of bestiality, Douglass reveals slavery to be a discourse constructed in relation to the very thing it negates: the body as a locus of meaning. Denied human identity under slavery's symbolic order, Douglass makes the body the basis for a relational subjectivity that he locates in the encounter between human beings and animals. He suggests that the wrongs of slavery occur outside the realm of reasoned discourse and are visited upon the suffering body. By validating that suffering even when—or, rather, because—it seems to occur beyond reason or language, he treats the pained body as the locus of an embodied language that bespeaks the cruelty endemic to slavery's symbolic order. By shifting from the *homo juridicus* to *homo oeconomicus*, he invests the body with discursive capacity and challenges us to rethink the parameters of subjectivity—a challenge that the next chapter takes up in relation to the work of Edgar Allan Poe. This turn from *homo juridicus* to *homo oeconomicus* raises the larger question how affect and commodification impact liberal subject formation. I have begun to address that question in this chapter but also develop it further in chapters 4 and 5, when I examine how the scene of bestiality gets rewritten as one of "puppy love" with the rise of sentimentalism in the nineteenth century and its permutations in the twentieth century.

3

ANIMALS AND THE
LETTER OF THE LAW

(EDGAR ALLAN POE)

In the previous chapters, I looked at cases of bestiality and bestialization to understand how biopower establishes and reproduces itself in relation to animals. I began to develop a hermeneutics that reads the symbolic order in relation to the animal bodies on which it depends at its founding. By affording those animal bodies their own legibility and by listening to animal voices, we gain a means for understanding the interdependence of human and animal subjectivity and for reassessing how American literature engages with and critiques biopower. To develop this argument, I now turn to Edgar Allan Poe's writing, which uses animals to link *ratiocination*, the abstract reasoning that undergirds symbolic discourse, with an alternative register of embodied meaning-making that founds and undercuts it. Poe's stories locate us at the (dis)joint between rights discourse and post-structuralism that I have identified as lying at the crux of animal studies: they inquire into the criminal justice system's codifications and erasures of subjectivity. In Poe's texts, animals unsettle the abstractions on which legal representation depends; they generate and confound the relation between the literal and the figurative. Poe's animal representations mark the "common ground of the physiological and the psychological" and draw attention to the fact that affect is the mechanism for establishing ontological categories.[1]

Poe's stories engage with the history Bruno Latour outlines when he claims that, from the development of modernity in the seventeenth century forward, "the representation of things through the intermediary of the laboratory is forever dissociated from the representation of citizens through the intermediary of the social contract" and that this separation hinders us from establishing any "direct relations between the representation of nonhumans and the representation of humans, between the artificiality of facts and the artificiality of the Body Politic." According to Latour, "the word 'representation' is the same," but the conditions of modernity render "any likeness between the two senses of the word unthinkable."[2] Poe's work is an exercise in the unthinkable; his animal representations locate us in the terrain where American literature negotiates between the two uses of representation and shows that their function as synonyms and opposites is central to the way biopolitics operates.

Key to that inquiry is his invention of two new genres: in writing tales of ratiocination, Poe simultaneously generated the genre of detective fiction and became "the inaugural true crime writer."[3] Participating equally in (detective) fiction and (true-crime) nonfiction, his works pit the imaginary and the empirical against each other. Franco Moretti maps that confrontation onto the relationship between the detective and the criminal, where the latter "has created a situation of semantic ambiguity, thus questioning the usual forms of human communication and human interaction. In this way, he has composed an audacious *poetic work*. The detective, on the other hand, must dispel the entropy, the cultural equiprobability that is produced by and is a relevant aspect of the crime: he will have to reinstate the univocal links between signifiers and signifieds. In this way, he must carry out a scientific operation."[4] Detective fiction is a key genre for exploring those two contradictory modes of representation in their relation to subjectivity. The genre takes the illegal taking of life as its point of departure: the inaugurating event is the death of the murder victim.[5] That death, says Moretti, precipitates a "return to the beginning";[6] that is, it inaugurates a process by which the narration tries to recover its own precipitating event and by which the criminal justice system keeps having to return to an act of its own negation and violation. That search for the narrative's own origins also includes a search for the origins of a narrative of subjectivity, which detective fiction simultaneously negates and inaugurates. On the one hand, detective fiction is premised, as Moretti puts it, on "the individualistic ethic of 'classic' bourgeois culture"—that is, on *homo oeconomicus* as the outcome of a particular liberal history of subject formation. On the other hand, that liberal subject is under several forms of erasure in detective fiction, which pits "the individual (in the guise of the criminal)" against "the social organism (in the guise of the detective)" and thereby creates a tension between a society "conceived of as a 'contract' between *independent entities*" and one imagined "as an organism or social *body*." That social body is established through a recursive set of individual deaths that amount, as Moretti has argued, to the death of individualism: "For the stereotypes to live, the individual must die, and then die a second time in the guise of the criminal." Moreover, the detective "sacrifices his individuality to his work . . . [and] prefigures and legitimates the sacrifices of the other individuality—the criminal's."[7] Detective fiction produces a set of social deaths; it does not merely stage the mechanisms of biopower but is deeply complicit with them.

But Poe's detective fiction plays with and resists the larger genre's complicities. If detective fiction ascribes "the individualistic ethic . . . to the criminal," Poe questions that ethic in the "Murders in the Rue Morgue" by making the criminal—that is, by Moretti's definition, the author of a "poetic work"— an animal.[8] Associating individuality and *poesis* with animals, Poe's fiction develops a practice and a theory of animal representation that not only critiques biopower's operations but imagines the negation of subjectivity as the grounds for new representative and representational possibilities.

"If Indeed a Murder Has Been Committed at All": Locating Subjectivity

In Edgar Allan Poe's "The Murders in the Rue Morgue" (1841, 1845), the newspaper account of the unfolding police investigation concludes: "A murder so mysterious, and so perplexing in all its particulars, was never before committed in Paris—if indeed a murder has been committed at all."[9] In the context of the newspaper report, this aside makes no sense: How can there be a doubt that "a murder has been committed" when we have just heard of one corpse having been thrust up a chimney and the other having been decapitated? The end of the sentence undermines its beginning, which declared "a murder" to have been committed, and creates a moment of doubt whose object is the validity of Poe's own account, his own true crime report on "the murders in the Rue Morgue."[10] This moment of textual contradiction not only strikes at the core of the newspaper's query but undermines the interpretative validity of the framing narrative—Edgar Allan Poe's story "The Murders in the Rue Morgue." That rupture in sense-making places the question "if indeed a murder has been committed at all" at the center of Poe's work.

The presence of two victims is not refuted. How and under what circumstances would a murder *not* have been committed? The newspaper's aside anticipates the story's resolution: it asks whether the actions of the Ourang-Outang (as spelled in Poe's story) who killed the two women can be considered "murder." In the context of the police investigation that frames the newspaper account, the answer to that question must meet certain judicial criteria to qualify as "criminal homicide with malice aforethought."[11] The definition of murder calls for a specific capacity: not only the capacity for thought, but also the capacity for a temporally forward-looking (afore) thought that carries a moral component (malice). Moreover, for homicide to be "criminal" implies that a legal subject carries it out. The newspaper calls into question whether the mystery at the heart of the tale is solved and solvable. Although Detective C. Auguste Dupin's investigation ultimately makes clear *how* the murders were committed, the question *whether* murder was committed remains unanswered. The judicial system never brings anyone to justice for the deaths, and, in that sense, these deaths remain outside of the purview of criminal prosecution that would make them murders. The question the story raises and fails to resolve is precisely "*Who* dunnit?"—that is, whether the Ourang-Outang has the forethought, the moral capacity, and the legal standing required to commit murder.

Poe's story raises a fundamental question about subjectivity and about our ability to interpret and "read" that subjectivity. Unhinging verbal representation from the ability to capture and express the subject adequately, Poe indicates that we must look elsewhere; we must *also* examine the body to understand subjectivity, and this understanding will be physically mediated.[12] In the 1845 version of his story published in *Tales*, Poe explains that "the mental features discoursed of as analytical are, in themselves, but little susceptible of analysis. We appreciate them only in their effects."[13] The 1845 text, on which most scholars have based their work on Poe's tale, later gives a clue how we are to read "effects" when it refers to "phrenologists" in distinguishing analytical power from ingenuity.[14] That reference to phrenology, the now discredited "science" of mapping cognitive and moral abilities onto the body, is far more pronounced in the originally published version of the tale, which included an additional paragraph that preceded the one just quoted: "It is not improbable that a few farther steps in phrenological science will lead to a belief in the existence, if not the actual discovery and location of an organ of *analysis*."[15]

Although this emphasis on analysis seems to draw attention to Dupin's role in the story, Poe in fact links the detective early on to the Ourang-Outang when he writes: "As the strong man exults in his physical ability, delighting in such exercises as call his muscles into action, so glories the analyst in that moral activity which *disentangles*."[16] On the most basic level, the simile establishes a link between someone of physical strength and someone of analytic strength. But Poe presses beyond that analogy: the story repeatedly describes the murderer by his strength, and in that sense the "strong man" invoked here refers to the murderer.[17] Thus, the sentence constructs a parallel between the murderer and the detective. But Poe complicates that parallel further yet. When the murderer turns out to be an Ourang-Outang, this initial reference to a "strong *man*" would seem to be misleading in that the murderer is strong but not a man. Poe uses that seeming misdirection to frame his narrative in relation to fundamental questions regarding human and animal subjectivity. In Poe's time, a synonym for the word *Ourang-Outang* was *wild man*.[18] In the discourse that emerged in eighteenth-century naturalism, that wild man was both a colonial subject and a figure of liminal humanity/animality (what Agamben might call a "wolf-man" and what is here configured as an ape-man). The very thing that the story seemingly reveals to be true—that the murderer is "strong" without being a "man"—is called into question by this synonym. Poe seems to confound our ability to *disentangle* the bodily from the analytic in this opening. Instead of separating the analytical subject, Dupin, from the object of analysis, the Ourang-Outang, Poe places them in proximity to one another. The question the story's unresolved inquiry into murder then raises is not solely a question about the murderer's specific identity, but a question about subjectivity as such.[19]

It is, of course, nothing new to suggest that Poe's stories reveal a deep interest in and deep anxiety about matters of subjectivity. Scholarly interest in Poe has centered on this issue, though between the two major schools of Poe criticism—the psychoanalytical and the historicist—there has been much disagreement about the appropriate terms in which this investigation should be framed. The psychoanalytic school of reading Poe has by and large privileged an approach that reads his work as highly symbolic and has rejected literal readings even among its own ranks. For instance, one of the founders of this psychoanalytic approach to Poe, Marie Bonaparte, in the late 1940s read "The Murders in the Rue Morgue" as a particularly violent Oedipal triangle in which the Ourang-Outang represented the male infant.[20] Her work has been criticized for depending "on a style of anatomical literalization now out of fashion, discredited in an era in which psychoanalytic critics rightfully prefer textual and rhetorical criticism to readings that, as [Peter] Brooks notes, mistakenly choose as their objects of analysis 'the author, the reader, or the fictive persons of the text.'"[21] The work of Jacques Lacan especially has privileged a reading of the letter in Poe's stories—that is, a privileging of the symbolic order and the slippage of the signifier, on the one hand, and an insistence on the inaccessibility of the real and imaginary, on the other.[22] Dissatisfied with this emphasis on individual subjectivity (however fragmented and mediated), historicist scholars have integrated Poe into the antebellum literary, cultural, and historical landscape. Reintroducing both the body and the body politic to his work, they have succeeded especially in capturing Poe's complicated racial politics. Arguing that Poe's notions of subjectivity depend on a racial unconscious, critics such as Toni Morrison have documented the centrality of slavery to Poe's works.[23]

As much as they differ from one another, these critical assessments of Poe share a fundamental approach to the question I am raising here in that they both read the Ourang-Outang as symbolic—of the infant and his primitive impulses, on the one hand, and as an index of Poe's own or his era's racist association of African Americans with apes, on the other.[24] In both contexts, the question I am asking about animals' relation to subjectivity is a critical heresy that risks being hopelessly literal and therefore at best naive, at worst complicit with the racism to which such literal reading has all too often been in service. Keenly aware of these dangers, I hope nevertheless to take up the question that I have located as being at the heart of Poe's enterprise: the question of the animal in its bearing on our understanding of subjectivity and of reading as not only a symbolic act, but also a corporeal process. Although I have so far been focusing on "The Murders in the Rue Morgue" and will anchor much of my discussion in that text, animals are in fact present in and central to virtually all of Poe's works; a brief catalog includes the title characters in "The Black Cat," "Hop-Frog; or, The Eight Chained Ourang-Outangs," "The Gold-Bug," and "The Raven." Indeed, Poe's most famous work, "The Raven," centers on an animal that by his own account he chose as a "*non*-reasoning creature capable of speech,"[25] a figure for the conundrum that psychoanalytic criticism confronts in letting go of notions of linguistic intentionality but brushes aside in insisting that the subject is always verbal and the verbal subject always already human. Poe asks us to question those certainties and to inquire anew into the relationships between verbal representation and subjectivity with all their ethical and legal repercussions.

Human(e) Rearing

In characterizing Edgar Allan Poe, T. S. Eliot described him as having suffered an "arrested" development.[26] As Jonathan Elmer has argued, Eliot reads Poe as "both childish and sick, sick *because* childish."[27] Dismissive as these comments sound, they give us a vantage point into Poe's fascination with childhood as a scene of self-making and unmaking, a fascination that puts him in dialogue with John Locke's educational theories in their emphasis on children's relationship to animals. Although Poe rarely describes children per se in his works, he often stages an inquiry into childish behavior and children's development. Central to that inquiry are the relationship between children and animals and the role that relationship plays for the formation of subjectivity.

The most sustained example of this interest occurs in "The Black Cat," which stages the protagonist's evolution and devolution through his relationship to animals:

> From my infancy I was noted for the docility and humanity of my disposition. My tenderness of heart was even more conspicuous as to make me the jest of my companions. I was especially fond of animals, and was indulged by my parents with a great variety of pets. With these I spent most of my time, and never was so happy as when feeding and caressing them. This peculiarity of character grew with my growth, and, in my manhood, I derived from it one of my principal sources of

pleasure. To those who have cherished an affection for a faithful and sagacious dog, I need hardly be at the trouble of explaining the nature or the intensity of the gratification thus derivable. There is something in the unselfish and self-sacrificing love of a brute, which goes directly to the heart of him who has had frequent occasion to test the paltry friendship and gossamer fidelity of mere *Man*.

I married early, and was happy to find in my wife a disposition not uncongenial with my own. Observing my partiality for domestic pets, she lost no opportunity for procuring those of the most agreeable kind. We had birds, gold-fish, a fine dog, rabbits, a small monkey, and *a cat*.[28]

This passage pivots between two ways of framing the affective relation to animals: the frame of bestiality that I outlined in the previous chapters and the frame of Lockean pedagogy that I explore here and in subsequent chapters. Poe depicts a scene of bestiality in these two paragraphs. Although he initially seems to be invoking merely an emotional connection that ties the speaker's "tenderness of heart" to the "love of a brute," the passage constructs this affection in relation to bestiality by tying it to the speaker's growing "manhood" and to the (incomplete) transfer of his (physical) affection to his wife. Poe emphasizes that the speaker relates directly to the animals' bodies—he enjoys "feeding and caressing them." Instead of abandoning this connection, the speaker intensifies his relationship to animals, and they become one of his "principal sources of pleasure" as he enters a stage of sexual maturity and develops into "manhood"; he derives intense "gratification" from his relationship to animals. Although this gratification seems to lead him to his marriage, he does not (fully) transfer his affections to his wife. She sets out to find any "opportunity for procuring" for him a range of "domestic pets" of a "most agreeable kind" and thus perpetuates his relationship to animals.

But the passage also invokes the assumption prevalent in nineteenth-century children's literature that we learn to be human by being taught how to be humane. John Locke's widely read *Thoughts on Education* (1693) made animals themselves central to children's education. As I discuss more fully in the next chapter, Locke suggests that we gain our humanity by performing acts of kindness to animals, and he locates subjectivity in the relationship among different species. Animals function as the "other" *and* as the ground from which subjectivity becomes possible. In this passage, Poe constructs not only an aberrant subject by invoking bestiality, but also an exemplary subject in his use of sentimental pedagogy. We find out that the speaker was "noted" from "infancy" for his "humanity" and that this "humanity" manifested itself in his relationship to animals. Mocked for his "tenderness of heart" by his human companions, he finds better companions in the animals that his parents (and later his wife) procure for him. His "character" thus develops in relation to its emotional ties to animals, whose friendship and fidelity exceeds that of "mere *Man*." Animals lie at the crux of his construction of manhood and model for him a superhuman way of constructing humanity. Poe's narrator stages for us a scene of Lockean pedagogy, but one that goes awry because he maintains a literal love of animals and fails to undergo the expected process of symbolic transference.

Poe's relationship to Locke has been well documented,[29] but even if Poe had not directly engaged with Locke's educational writings, they would have been available to him in their popularization by the didactic children's literature of his time. Poe may have gotten the idea for his particular story from books such as *The Fire, or, Never Despair. With the History and Adventures of a Cat* (1812).[30] The book combines the account of a family that prevails through the destruction of their home by fire and an animal autobiography—a first-person account narrated by an animal who recalls her trials and tribulations before finding loving human caregivers (see chapter 5 for a fuller discussion of this genre). A typical excerpt from this children's literature appears in *The Hare; Or, Hunting Incompatible with Humanity: Written as a Stimulus to Youth Towards a Proper Treatment of Animals* (1802): when the titular animal is rescued from imminent death, he reflects that "the humanity of the son was only equaled by the humanity of the father; and seeing this, I learned whence the youth had derived his merciful temper. What a blessing is a virtuous education!"[31] Poe's narrator seems in his childhood to have perfected the lessons learned by this educational literature. He exhibits to a heightened degree the kindness to animals that is a marker of humanity and whose transference to his wife enables the child to move from the parental home to the formation of his own family.

But Poe's account explores the tensions and the fissures in the assumptions that kindness toward animals is commensurate with kindness to human beings and that both are markers of humanity. Indeed, such didactic tracts' reliance on the animal's first-person perspective already raises a question of speakerly subjectivity and how the transmission between an animal and human subject occurs and is mediated. That question is further complicated by the tension in these accounts between humanity as an inheritance by which the "humanity" and "merciful temper" of the son derives from that of the father and a humanity that is portrayed at times as a familial, biological inheritance and at other times as the imprinting of education on the child.

At stake in the relationship to animals is a moral education that determines the individual's ability to participate in society as a subject. Redirecting Puritan concerns with bestiality into the pedagogical enterprise of regulating affect, books such as the widely popular *The Rotchfords; or the Friendly Counsellor: Designed for the Instruction and Amusement of the Youth of Both Sexes* (1801) link these lessons of kindness to animals with an evangelical desire to "inculcate the benevolent religion of Christianity, and teach the youthful heart to reflect upon the importance of each word and action." Reprimanding his son for having beaten up a boy who was tormenting birds, Mr. Rotchford explains that "mercy ought indeed to be shewn towards every *beast* and *insect* that has *life*, yet are not the human species exempted from sharing it, and to *injure* one of your fellow creatures, for the sake of defending a bird, can certainly by no means be right. . . . To *check our own* impetuosity, *Charles*, is one of the first, as well as most necessary duties; and till we can enough *conquer ourselves*, to be guided by the dictates of *reason* and *prudence*, we are very ill qualified (however *good* our *intentions* may be) to set up for the correctors of others."[32]

Kindness to animals is the very origin of reason—from which Poe's narrator has removed himself by his violent actions that precede the telling of his tale. By virtue of this logic, Poe's narrator is indeed what he most vehemently denies—mad.[33] However, he creates a tension between his statement that he is not mad and the unreasonable violence to which he confesses.[34] One way of understanding that tension is via the post-structuralist distinction between the content (the *énoncé*) and the act of speaking (*énonciation*)—that is, between intentionality and iterability and the production of the subject via its entry into and its splitting in language. But Poe's story questions the assumptions that go into this line of argumentation—the assumptions of the signifier's slippage and the inaccessibility of materiality. In "The Black Cat," Poe develops that line of questioning by the open narrative frame of his story: "For the most wild, yet most homely narrative which I am about to pen, I neither expect nor solicit belief. Mad indeed would I be to expect it, in a case where my very senses reject their own evidence. Yet mad I am not—and very surely do I not dream. But to-morrow I die, and to-day I would unburden my soul. My immediate purpose is to place before the world, plainly, succinctly, and without comment, a series of mere household events. In their consequences, these events have terrified—have tortured—have destroyed me."[35]

The repeated inversion of the sentence structure ("Mad indeed would I be" as opposed to "I would be mad" and "Yet mad I am not" instead of "I am not mad") relegates the subject to a subordinate position that anticipates physical death. The narrator draws attention to the bodily act of narration—to his act of speaking: he is "about to pen" his "narrative," but instead we get a verbal statement. That verbal statement begins with a reference to "the most wild," which is only later clarified by its referent "narrative." That narrative is described via a parallel construction that links "the most wild" with the "most homely." Juxtaposing the wild with the homely breaks down what should (by John Winthrop's logic, as I discussed in chapter 1) be a division between nature and domesticity (Poe again emphasizes an association between the home and the word *homely* by referring to "household events").[36] That juxtaposition between two seeming opposites creates a crisis of understanding: the narrator explains that he can "neither expect nor solicit belief" and then justifies that statement by pointing not to abstract cognition, but to "my very senses," which "reject their own evidence." Here, Poe invokes an important understanding of the term *sense*: its double reference to cognitive and physical ways of understanding. The paragraph underscores this emphasis on the physical: the narrator draws attention to the somatic effects that these events have had in terrifying and torturing him, and his assertion that they have "destroyed" him makes them anticipate and enact his pending execution.

The story's conclusion further highlights that physical, somatic effect. The story does not return to its opening frame, to the prison cell confession, but instead revisits the scene of the murder's revelation: "Of my thoughts it is folly to speak. Swooning, I staggered to the opposite wall. For one instant the party upon the stairs remained motionless, through extremity of terror and of awe. In the next, a dozen stout arms were toiling at the wall. It fell bodily. The corpse, already greatly decayed and clotted with gore, stood erect before the eyes of the spectators. Upon its head, with red extended mouth and solitary eyes of fire, sat the hideous beast whose craft had seduced me into murder, and whose informing voice had consigned me to the hangman. I had walled the monster up within the tomb!"[37]

The narrator begins with the inadequacy of thought and of speech—it has become "folly" to "speak" one's "thoughts." His expressive register has shifted to the physical act of "swooning" and staggering.[38] The "folly" of speech affects not only the narrator, but also the spectators (and by extension the readers), who experience the "extremity of terror and of awe" as a somatic effect: they "remained motionless."[39] Moreover, the narrator next refers to these spectators metonymically, as "a dozen stout arms." Those arms tear down the wall and are themselves implicated when it "fell" by their "bodily" strength and in its falling it reveals the "erect" body of the narrator's dead wife. That body is emphatically described as physical matter, "greatly decayed and clotted with gore." Although the "spectators" can read this body that stands "before the eyes," their visual testimony is underscored and amplified by the "solitary eyes of fire" and the "red extended mouth" of the "beast." That beast has come to occupy the seat of cognition and reason—the head—and from there speaks with the "informing voice" that condemns the narrator "to the hangman." The cat's vocal testimony, not the narrator's own confession to the crime, convicts the killer. That confession is secondary to this scene of revelation and through the story's open-ended frame remains inadequate; the physical referents and the animal's "informing voice" form the conclusion of this story and the narrator's culpability. The animal not only is an extension of the physical evidence against the narrator but provides an alternative form of vocal testimony that is more authoritative than his own narration. This point bears emphasis: the story does not align the animal with the physical and the human with the verbal but, on the contrary, shows the intermingling and interdependence of both across the species line. Poe does not engage here, as Joan Dayan has suggested in another context, with the "precise and methodical transactions in which he revealed the threshold separating humanity from animality";[40] instead, he examines the permeability of that threshold. The animal relays the relationship between the verbal and the physical, the linguistic and the bodily, rationality and matter; it lies at the crux of these different reading practices, enabling and confounding both.

Reading the Body

What reading practice, then, does this relationship call for? One way in which this question has been answered is through the recovery of the details of Poe's historical context, especially his fascination with animal magnetism and phrenology. Both practices were interested in making the body the locus of interpretation and shared "in the conviction that mind and body were interrelated, that via the mind changes could be effected in the functions of the body, and that between metaphysics and physics there was no gap."[41] Poe capitalized on the profitability of both practices when he published "Mesmeric Revelations" (1845) in the *American Phrenological Journal*, though he later retracted the text as a hoax.[42] But Poe's serious engagement with these practices is evident—for instance, in his favorable review of Mrs. Miles's *Phrenology and the Moral Influence of Phrenology: Arranged for General Study, and the Purposes of Education, from the First Published Works of Gall and Spurzheim, to the Latest Discoveries of the Present Period* (1836). Writing in the *Southern Literary Messenger* in March 1836, Poe argued that phrenology had "assumed the majesty of a science" and that its most "salutary" use "is that of *self-examination and self-knowledge*."[43] Recapping Miles's argument, Poe explained that

the faculties are divided into *Instinctive Propensities and Sentiments* and *Intellectual Faculties*. The Instinctive Propensities and sentiments are subdivided into *Domestic Affections*, embracing Amativeness, Philoprogenitiveness, Inhabitiveness, and Attachment—*Preservative Faculties*, embracing Combativeness, Destructiveness, and Gustativeness—*Prudential Sentiments,* embracing Acquisitiveness, Secretiveness, and Cautionness—*Regulating Powers*, including Self-Esteem, Love of Approbation, Conscientiousness, and Firmness—*Imaginative Faculties*, containing Hope, Ideality and Marvelousness—and *Moral Sentiments*, under which head come Benevolence, Veneration, and Imitation. The *Intellectual Faculties* are divided into *Observing Faculties*, viz: Individuality, Form, Size, Weight, Color, Order, and Number—*Scientific Faculties*, viz: Constructiveness, Locality, Time, and Tune—*Reflecting Faculties*, viz: Eventuality, Comparison, Causality and Wit—and lastly, the *Subservient Faculty*, which is Language.[44]

In invoking the "homely" narrative of "household" events, Poe opens "The Black Cat" by invoking the domestic affections, but he also warns us that they are paired with the "wild" preservative faculties. The instinctive propensities and sentiments are also the locus of subjectivity, especially in regard to the regulating powers, and the site of the imaginative faculties, in which the poet's supreme quality, "ideality," is located. Whereas psychoanalytic and post-structuralist criticism has privileged language, for phrenologists language functions as the "subservient faculty" and is located in the intellectual faculties, which are distinct from the instinctive propensities and sentiments.

Mapping these qualities onto their supposed physical manifestations, nineteenth-century phrenologists developed an elaborate system of racial categorization, in which the term *race* designated different species as well as distinctions within them—that is, the categorization of the so-called races of man.[45] Engaging in comparative anatomy, the most egregious examples of this practice performed a racial comparison that invariably attributed superior qualities to whites over blacks.[46] This practice of interpretation was also extended to texts; indeed, it might count as a professional embarrassment that one of the origins of literary criticism lies in phrenology. Taking literally the physical descriptions of characters, phrenologists used them as a basis for making character judgments. Phrenologists paid particular attention to Shakespearean characters, most notably Iago from *Othello*. The character was invoked as an example of phrenology's standing as an accurate science. Writing in the *American Phrenological Journal*, "L.N.F."—Lorenzo Niles Fowler, the coeditor of the journal with his brother, Orson Squire Fowler—delighted in two articles from the *Edinburgh Phrenological Journal* in which a phrenologist had performed a reading on the character Iago and had then passed on his sketch as if it were of a "*real*, and even of a *living*, character" to another phrenologist, who had arrived at the same interpretive results.[47] This practice of literary interpretation not only attaches a premium to reading the body as text but also allows for a reading of the text as body.

Poe was familiar with the Fowlers, and it is quite likely that he drew inspiration for "The Black Cat" from their phrenological literary analysis.[48] In an 1839 follow-up article that further expanded phrenological readings of Iago, "A. Wren" quoted the passage from Shakespeare's text where Iago admonishes Roderigo: "Come, be a man. Drown thyself? Drown cats and blind puppies. . . . If thou wilt needs damn thyself, do it a more delicate way than drowning . . . seek thou rather to be hanged in compassing thy joy, than to be drowned."[49] Whereas Shakespeare's character argues for a distinction between the proper modes of animal and human death, the larger phrenological debate continuously blurred the boundaries between the human and the animal. In the same article, for instance, we hear about Iago that "his intellect was quite considerable, but it wrought in the service of the selfish and animal feelings. . . . To refinement of feeling and elevated sentiments he was a comparative stranger; and hence his attachments to the other sex, though strong, were merely *animal* and *selfish*."[50] Used here as an adjective, *animal* becomes a quality proper to human beings and, moreover, one that functions synonymously with *selfish* in defining a key quality of subjectivity—namely, the self-interest of *homo oeconomicus*. The same applies to animals as well and precisely around the issue of expression and language. In a later lecture, Lorenzo Niles Fowler argued that "animals have their language: even the cat and dog express their peculiar states of mind by the intonations of their voices. Man has more language than animals. He can modulate his voice so as to express every variety of emotion. The voice, under the action of the base of the brain, will be strong and harsh."[51]

Fowler separates animal and human languages from one another by degree, not by kind. Those differences by degree enable and unsettle categorizations by species, race, gender, and (dis)ability. As Joan Dayan has reminded us, "animality . . . emerges for most nineteenth-century phrenologists, theologians, and anthropologists in those beings who are classified as both human and beast: lunatics, women, primates, black men, and children. . . . Poe's reconstructions depend upon experiences that trade on unspeakable slippages between men and women, humans and animals, life and death."[52] In other words, he confronts us with hybrids such as the wolf-man (in "The Gold-Bug") and the ape-man (in "The Murders in the Rue Morgue").

There are many instances where Poe replicates the racist trope of using animal imagery to describe slaves.[53] For instance, in "The Gold-Bug," he describes the slave Jupiter's demeanor as "dogged" and attributes to him a "dogged air of deliberation." However, he also draws our attention to the logic that enables this racism—the logic that wants to turn a simile (a slave is like a dog) into a metaphor (the slave is dogged)—and removes that metaphor from the symbolic realm into the real (the slave is a dog). Poe in fact points out the rhetorical strategies and the logic of racism by including a dog that these descriptions themselves mark as a literal dog in counterdistinction from the symbolizations of doggedness. Here is the context of the phrase I just quoted: "We dug very steadily for two hours. Little was said; and our chief embarrassment lay in the yelpings of the dog, who took exceeding interest in our proceedings. He, at length, became so obstreperous that we grew fearful of his giving the alarm to some stragglers in the vicinity . . . . The noise was, at length, very effectually silenced by Jupiter, who, getting out of the hole with a dogged air of deliberation, tied the brute's mouth up with one of his suspenders, and then returned, with a grave chuckle, to his task."[54]

This passage participates in several cultural assumptions yet delights in their reversal. The link between slaves and domestic animals was a commonplace—in the Virginia debates on slavery, for instance, slaves were habitually referred to as "pets."[55] Poe aligns Jupiter with that association by referring to him as "dogged." But the fact that he is "dogged" in tying up a dog's mouth is important. The dog's presence marks as an image the reference to Jupiter as "dogged"; Jupiter is symbolically but not literally "dogged," as the contrast with the dog establishes. The dog disrupts the symbolism to which it also gives rise. Animals draw our attention to the symbolic order's functioning—that is, to its processes of symbolization. But Poe insistently returns us to animal voices and noises as discursive registers in excess of that symbolic order. That point is brought home by the fact that Jupiter marks his silencing of the dog with "a grave chuckle" as he and his companions continue working. If Jupiter is animalized here, then it is only in the sense that the animal cannot and will not be silenced—if he is animalized, then it is in a way that would undermine the metaphor. Instead of perpetuating slavery's symbolization of slaves as animals, this scene disrupts those processes of symbolization by imagining animal voices as an alternative discursive register that will not be silenced but that perpetuates itself and gives rise to nonlinguistic forms of communication. The dog's silencing marks a shift from linguistic to other forms of communication. The passage reveals to us the real constraints that define Jupiter not—or at least not only—as a sliding signifier, but as a slave. For Poe, the relation to animals gives rise to a mode of understanding that exceeds processes of symbolization.

Again, "The Gold-Bug" provides an important example. Much has been made of Poe's interest in cryptography and his boast of being able to solve any soluble cryptogram.[56] But two of the chief examples for Poe's staging of ratiocination—"The Gold-Bug" and "The Murders in the Rue Morgue"— disrupt the course of reasoned, linguistic analysis via the presence of animals. Legrand, in recounting how he solved the mystery of the treasure's location, recalls that "without the intervention of the dog at the precise moment in which he appeared, I should never have become aware of the death's head, and so never the possessor of the treasure." The animal is not only central to the discovery of the invisible ink, but the writing itself revolves around the figure of the animal: Legrand's deciphering of the legend hinges on his understanding "the figure of what I at first supposed to be a goat," which on "closer scrutiny" turned out to be "intended for a kid." That kid turns out to be a referent for Captain Kidd; Legrand recounts that he "at once looked upon the figure of the animal as a kind of punning or hieroglyphical signature. I say signature, because its position upon the vellum suggested this idea."[57] Poe establishes a circular reference here to the animal, the person, and the signature. The intervention and interpretation of the animal lie at the core of the reading processes and subject formations Poe stages in his stories.

The Letters and Bodies of the Law

I return now to the specific circumstances that frame the linguistic and physical reading process in many of Poe's stories, among them "The Black Cat" and "The Murders in the Rue Morgue." Poe draws on the figure of the animal to ask whether the letter of the law depends on a category of the unlawful that it abjects as *zoē* excluded from *bios* or whether the letter of the law and *zoē* are always already implicated in one another so that the very distinction between *zoē* and *bios* becomes nonsensical. His answer to this question hinges on the animal's ability to relay both.

To explain that relay, I need to step back from the use of the term *animal* or *the animal* and ask what these terms designate. The binary *human/animal* is itself vexed, as several scholars have pointed out, in that the term *animal* becomes the catchall for creatures as different as the elephant and the snake.[58] A helpful way of speaking about "animals" without replicating the human/animal binary and without repeating structures of abjection may be achieved by drawing a key analytic move from "thing theory" (with which I engage more extensively in chapter 5). In defining this theory, Bill Brown argues that "things" are not the same as objects and do not preexist the conditions of our encounter with them; they are "objects asserting themselves as things."[59] We may likewise—very cautiously—define Poe's understanding of "animal theory" as life asserting itself as animal. The caution here comes from the fact that I do not want my argument about Poe to replicate, as I have been saying, the structures of abjection that attach to the notion of "bare life." What I am trying to work toward in my reading of Poe is a way of critiquing those structures via Derridean notions of otherness that can function as a viable critique to the biopolitics of bare life outlined by Agamben. I am also interested in invoking thing theory here for the way in which attributing agency to animals—"asserting themselves"—blurs the subject/object dyad. In this way of thinking about assertion as a physical and a verbal act, subject and object cease being ontological categories and become performative. The danger remains that it is possible to perform or to be performed as an object, but the performance structure itself makes the object relational, not categorical. The animal becomes a relational agent by this definition and can enter into ad hoc relationships where individuality and subjectivity become possible. The human conversely emerges in this relationship not as the opposite of the animal, but as the result of the relationship to another designated as "animal." The production of "human" subjectivity is then contingent on the relation to "the animal," where both share the same shifting terrain.

Poe's clearest exploration of this argument occurs in "The Murders in the Rue Morgue." His story does not just present a conundrum of agency; it interrogates the limits the law imposes on notions of subjectivity. One way of reading subjectivity in this story is via a clear hierarchy (along lines of gender and race), mapped onto structures of embodiment on the one end of the spectrum and onto structures of symbolization on the other. The women in this story are purely corpses and, for that matter, are anomalous in the Poe canon: whereas many of his dead women find an afterlife as (poetic) subjects, the women here are utterly inanimate, physical matter. The position of (re)animated embodiment is occupied by the figure of the animal, the Ourang-Outang, and his excessive physical strength. At the top of this hierarchical reading, we can then place Dupin, whose ratiocination apparently allows him to occupy the preeminent position of symbolization—that is, of someone who can both produce and decode symbols, who is both a reader and a writer.

The reading I just presented works seamlessly with the way Poe's own theorization of poetic composition is usually excerpted: he is often quoted as saying that "the death . . . of a beautiful woman is, unquestionably, the most poetical topic in the world—and equally is it beyond doubt that the lips best suited for such topic are those of a bereaved lover."[60] But the story also subverts that reading and that way of thinking about and hierarchizing the body and language, the abject real and the abstract symbolic. Poe prefaces his comment by explaining how he alighted on the figure of the Raven to achieve his desired "effect . . . of Beauty" and the "*tone* of its highest manifestation": "Here, then, immediately arose the idea of a *non*-reasoning creature capable of speech; and, very naturally, a parrot, in the first instance, suggested itself, but was superseded forthwith by a Raven, as equally capable of speech, and infinitely more in keeping with the intended *tone* of melancholy."[61]

The idea of a creature that is nonreasoning yet articulate stages one of Poe's favorite themes: the theme of "in-sanity" as a removal from social structures. Poe unhinges reason from speech, and abstracts tone, a physical quality of poetry, and affect (melancholy) as the somatic origins and aims of literary work. To understand Poe's theorization, it is helpful to invoke Jean-Luc Nancy's discussion of the "corpus." Arguing that the "*ontology of the body* is ontology itself," Nancy insists that "*Bodies don't take place in discourse or in matter. They don't inhabit 'mind' or 'body.' They take place at the limit, qua limit*: limit—external border, the fracture and intersection of anything foreign in a continuum of sense, a continuum of matter."[62] For Poe, that limit and continuum mark the threshold where animals and animality encounter one another.

Nancy explains that "sense" is precisely where making sense of something becomes possible and impossible in that "sense making" only partially accounts for sense and vice versa. The second newspaper account of the investigation in "Murders" consists largely of interviews with witnesses. Those witnesses are markedly not eyewitnesses, but earwitnesses. Each testifies to having *heard*, not seen, the crime as it occurred, thus highlighting Poe's interest in language as *tonal*. Yet each fails to recognize, to witness tonally, because each attempts to witness linguistically. Although the witnesses hear the same sounds, they seem to interpret them differently. What only Dupin recognizes is that, in fact, they all interpret these acoustic events uniformly: they disagree on *which* language was spoken, but they agree that what they heard was a language and that it was a language with which they were not familiar. They all hear the same sounds and share the same sensory perceptions; what distinguishes them from each other is the sense making they perform—that is, the way in which they try to examine cognitively the bodily data they have received. It is that sense making that ultimately obscures their sense perception. Their mistake lies in wanting to ascribe that language to a national frame, which reinscribes *all* language in a human frame. Dupin can break with that frame of reference because of his more expansive understanding of language and his ability to recognize an otherness that is not readily recoded as a similarity, but that can entertain the limit or fracture produced by the senses and sense making. Although the earwitnesses' senses are correct, their sense making is incorrect—Poe stages a misattachment of the sound to the symbolic structure, and that misapplication for him marks the crisis of symbolization as such.

The way in which this alternative practice of reading the body challenges our notions of subjectivity and especially human subjectivity has recently been the subject of several articles that investigate Poe in relationship to the "posthuman." These articles take up N. Katharine Hayles's critique of post-humanist inquiry for having "systematically downplayed or erased" embodiment "in the cybernetic construction of the posthuman in ways that have not occurred in other critiques of the liberal humanist subject, especially in feminist and postcolonial theories."[63] Poe scholars have located their inquiry into his "posthumanism" precisely by examining his understandings of embodiment, particularly as they occur in his invention of what we might consider to be science fiction "cyborg" characters. James Berkley has argued that the way Poe deconstructs the liberal humanist subject makes him the "first great author of reification" precisely because he emphasizes "language's ability to circulate . . . forms that are curiously detachable, even prosthetic, with regard to individual agency."[64] Matthew Taylor similarly argues through a reading of Poe's "Eureka" that his version of posthumanism is neither celebratory nor anthropocentric and that he creates an ahuman universe by collapsing selves and worlds into a single term—*bodies*.[65]

What is missing from this discussion is a consideration of the way Poe sees bodies as not always-already human. What happens to arguments about Poe's posthumanism when we read his animals? To address this question, it might be helpful to follow Taylor's lead and to situate Poe's interest in bodies in relation to his study of a "science" affiliated with phrenology—mesmerism, also known as "animal magnetism."[66] This practice studied the "influence mutuelle entre les corps célestes, la terre, & les corps animés"—the mutual influence of heavenly bodies, the earth, and animated bodies, which the movement's founder, Anton Mesmer, elsewhere refers to as a "corps animal," an animal body.[67] Poe repeatedly invokes the scene of mesmeric trance to (re)produce this slippage between animated bodies and animal bodies. For instance, the raven makes his entry: "while I nodded, nearly napping, suddenly there came a tapping, / As of some one gently rapping, rapping at my chamber door."[68] This scene places the raven at the center of a practice that relied on states of trance and on interpreting rapping noises; it produces an odd replacement in which the communion with the transcendent realm turns out to be a communion with the animal.[69] That animal simultaneously stands in for the lover and the lost love; it becomes a liminal figure that unsettles the division between life and death. The raven becomes the figure for the corpus itself—that is, for "the absolute contradiction of not being able to be a *body* without being the body *of a spirit*, which disembodies it."[70] For Poe, literature, especially poetry, creates that paradox. Writing in "The Poetic Principle," he divorces Poetry from Truth and argues that "taste informs us of the beautiful." For Poe, taste is a literal, physical quality, as he makes clear when he refers to the "sense of the Beautiful" as an "immortal instinct," which "administers . . . the manifold forms, and sounds, and colours, and odours, and sentiments" that "oral and written repetition" of nature accomplishes.[71] These definitions expand aesthetic experience to encompass sensory experience; Poe's work meditates on the conditions under which sensory experience is produced and instantiates a significant expansion of the aesthetic from the sublime to the abject. Indeed, the "death of a beautiful woman" then becomes "unquestionably, the most poetical topic in the world" precisely because it combines the corporeal (death, the woman's body) with the aesthetic (beautiful).[72] Punning on the French (the language in which "Murders in the Rue Morgue" presumably takes place and with which Poe was well familiar from childhood), Poe's stories often read the term *corps animés* literally as "animated corpses." The animated corpse is most often that of a woman, but in "The Murders in the Rue Morgue" and "The Black Cat" animals take on the role of animated corpses.

Given Poe's rejection of "the heresy of *The Didactic*,"[73] we should reread what he is setting out to accomplish in the so-called tales of ratiocination. Writing to Philip P. Cooke in 1846, Poe expressed his concern at Evert Duyckinck's selection of tales to publish. He complained that the focus on tales of ratiocination and the emphasis on analytic stories did not adequately represent his "mind in its various phases," and he included a copy of the "Philosophy of Composition" as a corrective. Poe's tales themselves immanently include this critique and this desire to integrate, as his letter points out, ratiocination into a larger "*whole*" that locates its aesthetic enterprise in relation to the body.[74]

As Doris Falk has pointed out, Dupin is in a state of mesmeric trance as he investigates the murders in the Rue Morgue; that is, he is in a state of communion with the *corps animés*.[75] Although most critics privilege Dupin's reading of the newspaper, Poe insists throughout his story that Dupin's reading practice is also bodily and embodied.[76] Poe's tales engage in a "relentless literalism, . . . [a] desire to demetaphorize, which often involves the reinvigoration of formerly dead metaphors."[77] In the opening of the tale, Poe places Dupin in a "time-eaten" mansion, where he indulges the "wild fervor . . . of his imagination" and follows his "wild whims," venturing out only at night "amid the wild lights and shadows" of the city to experience the "mental excitement" they afford. This emphasis on consumption and lack of emotional restraint animalizes Dupin, as does the incantatory evocation of his "wild" actions. Moreover, his sequestration resembles that of the victims, Madame and Mademoiselle L'Espanaye, but also that of the Ourang-Outang, whom the soldier kept "securely confined" till he could recover from a "wound in the foot."[78]

These forms of sequestration share an important element: each is linked to a removal from symbolic circulation. The Ourang-Outang is a commodity temporarily removed from the marketplace; upon recovering him, the soldier hopes to (and eventually does) sell him. The L'Espanayes trade in the circulation of physical signs—Madame L'Espanaye is reputed to have "told fortunes"—but they remove themselves from symbolic circulation: they hoard money and have just withdrawn their savings from the economic system altogether. Dupin presents an even more extreme form of this lack of economic symbolization and circulation: he is from "an illustrious family" that "had been reduced to such poverty that the energy of his character succumbed beneath it, and he ceased to bestir himself in the world, or to care for the retrieval of his fortunes." Unlike Madam L'Espanaye, who still "told" fortunes, Dupin has removed himself from such symbolic modes of signification; the realm of meaning making in which he engages is that of "counterfeit[ing]," in which he and his companion "busied our souls in dreams—reading, writing, or conversing."[79] This encounter with the unconscious is not, as it is for Lacan, an encounter with language and vice versa; it is a "making animal" of the two protagonists. Poe underscores this point by describing Dupin's analytic abilities as giving him an "intimate knowledge" of men, who, "in respect to himself, wore windows in their bosoms." They offer him the same mode of access, the window, that the Ourang-Outang turns out to have found in entering the home of the L'Espanayes. The most important doubling, however—between Dupin and the Ourang-Outang—occurs in the explanation of analytic method: "the analyst throws himself into the spirit of his opponent, identifies himself therewith."[80] To solve the mystery, Dupin has to identify with the Ourang-Outang, which ultimately means that the crime committed is not solved but rather repeated in the act of analysis. The crime's repetition is the process of law enforcement itself, which, however, will always remain incomplete because the body is related to writing but is not itself part of the symbolic order that links the letter to the letter of the law; it produces a language that is subjected by and yet is not subject to the law precisely because of the strategy of doubling, which always leaves room for extralegal excess.

For Lacan, the very condition of subjectivity is fracture, but for him that fracture creates a disassociation from the body, which in the mirror stage can be seen as whole, the Ideal-I, only in projection. Poe experiments with forms of subjectivity that experience fracture as physically imminent and in the process doubles the systems of signification at his disposal. That doubling achieves two goals: on the one hand, it illustrates how a process of law and of law making can occur, and, on the other, it marks an excess that cannot be subsumed to that law, even though it occupies the position of its disavowed origin and supplement. That extralegal position is precisely the position of animality. The question whether that animality is literally or figuratively an animal—that is, whether it is an Ourang-Outang or a rebellious slave—becomes available only in light of Poe's argumentation. At the site of the animal, the literal and the symbolic become possible and are confounded. This use of the figure of the animal makes it available for racist iconography, but it also reveals the mechanisms for such racism and such iconography, all the while opening up alternative forms of subjectivity and representation. In the encounter with animals, the letter and the letter of the law become (un)hinged.

4

ANIMALS, AFFECT, AND THE FORMATION OF LIBERAL SUBJECTIVITY

(EMILY DICKINSON)

My reading of Edgar Allan Poe's crime fiction locates the subject's fissures in the fraught relationship to animal representation. Exploring the tension between alterity and identity, his fiction develops a hermeneutics that reads the "symbolic order" in relation to the bodily, the abject, and the animalized. By affording that bodily register its own legibility, he develops grounds for understanding the mechanisms by which subjectivity produces itself via an engagement with the beastly and provides a means for engaging critically with that production. In this chapter and the next, I take up an issue I raised in the previous chapter's discussion of "The Black Cat": how the scene of bestiality gets rewritten as one of "puppy love" with the rise of sentimentalism in the nineteenth century and its permutations in the twentieth century. I focus in particular on the role that theories of childhood education play for understandings of subjectivity and on the way in which infantilization—as a practice, as a strategy—maps animal relations onto psychological and commoditized object relations.

Framing my discussion of Emily Dickinson in relation to post-structuralist affect theory, I demonstrate how she might advance our understanding of liberal subjectivity beyond its current parameters.[1] Post-structuralist affect theory and liberalism open a space for radical alterity, but they too easily foreclose that space by reinscribing affect in an ontologically defined frame that distinguishes human beings from animals. At stake in that foreclosure is the production of a particular notion of subjectivity as a subjectivity marked by an individuality independent of others and clearly demarcated by the separation of reasoning from embodiment. Looking at animals gives us a different account of the subject, as relational and contingent on an alterity that cannot easily be reinscribed in the registers of either abstract rationality or embodied affectivity. Through Dickinson's experimentations with animal representations, we see new possibilities for subjectivity and poetry emerge in her work. Engaging with the pedagogical and literary models that became a staple of childhood education in the nineteenth century, Emily Dickinson stretches our understanding of literary representation beyond symbolization by rethinking orthography as a confrontation with literal animals. Deliberately invoking Lockean pedagogy, she adopts the persona of a child. That persona enables her to reject the telos of Lockean pedagogy—the separation of the human being from the animal. Placing herself in a position of ambiguity, where the human and the animal are conjoined and not yet separated, Dickinson engages the parameters of liberal subject formation to envision an alternative.

The Liberal Imagination and Post-structuralist Affect Theory

In 1950, Lionel Trilling published a collection of his essays under the title *The Liberal Imagination*. In two essays that frame his reflections on topics ranging across nineteenth- and twentieth-century literature, he outlines his definition of liberalism as well as his understanding of the role that literary criticism plays in bringing that liberalism to fruition. For Trilling, liberalism's potential and its shortfalls hinge on its ability to engage both ideas and emotions (or sentiments, which he uses as a synonym) and to keep both in dynamic relation to one another. For models of how such balance might work, he repeatedly turns to examples of nineteenth-century writers for whom the stakes of balancing ideas and emotions—and of engaging with literature—were political. By *politics*, Trilling means the "wide sense of the word"—that is, "the politics of culture, the organization of human life toward some end or other, toward the modification of sentiments, which is to say the quality of human life." Although this statement echoes the scope and vagueness of his earlier claim that liberalism is "a large tendency rather than a concise body of doctrine," it also makes a programmatic claim about literary criticism itself: that its domain is properly the political, where the political is understood as emerging at the intersection of emotions and ideas.[2]

Trilling's assessment of the political has met—as has the larger postwar discourse celebrating liberalism—with a wide range of appropriations and dismissals over the years since the volume's publication.[3] Without positing a causal relationship between Trilling's work and later scholarly developments, we might nevertheless read his remarks on the role of the emotions and their connections to politics as a prescient commentary on the engagement that the scholarly field of nineteenth-century American literary studies has with figuring out how sentiment, emotion, intimacy, and affect produce and unravel subjects, liberal and otherwise.[4] The methodologies of this enterprise have been eclectically borrowed from feminism, gender studies, queer studies, post-structuralism, new historicism, and cultural studies, but scholars have recently begun to identify this field of inquiry as its own theoretical school and to speak of "the affective turn" in American literary studies, as the title of a 2007 collection of essays on the topic proclaims.[5]

Writing in the preface to this volume, Michael Hardt argues that "affects refer equally to the body and the mind" and place reason and passion "together on a continuum." As a consequence, affect studies produces "a new ontology of the human or, rather, an ontology of the human that is constantly open and renewed."[6] Hardt's comment begs the question what anchors that new ontology in relation to "the human." Although his claim echoes Trilling's emphasis on the role that emotions play for the construction of "the nature of the human mind," "the organization of human life," and "the quality of human life,"[7] Hardt's concluding reference to a new ontology opens a space for inquiry that presses us beyond the explicitly humanist framework of liberal subject formation outlined by Trilling.

It is this ontological openness that I want to explore in order to understand how the affective relationship between human beings and animals founds and confounds the parameters of liberal subject formation. Beginning with an overview of what affect studies might teach us about nonhuman ontologies, I then situate key concerns of this current scholarly undertaking in relation to the historical origins of liberal humanism in John Locke's educational philosophy. Tracing the impact of his pedagogy on American literature, I demonstrate how liberal subject formation emerges from the relationship with animals. That relationship plays a key role in the development of literacy, which is the very staple of liberal subjectivity. As I demonstrate in my case study of Emily Dickinson, animals literally disrupt and figuratively challenge the parameters of representation on which liberal subjectivity is founded.

Although many scholars working in affect theory remain dedicated to an explicitly humanist enterprise, the logical outcome of their work opens the possibility for thinking about subjectivity in a more expansive register than one limited to existing notions of the human. In *Feeling in Theory*, Rei Terada argues that we need to rethink emotion as "nonsubjective." She explains that emotion is often cast "as a basis for naturalized social or moral consensus," but she also draws our attention to the fact that "such a gesture depends on an even more fundamental one that casts emotion as proof of the human subject." Terada wants to "free a credible concept of emotion from a less credible scheme of subjectivity . . . the effect of this exploration is to suggest that we would have no emotions if we *were* subjects."[8] She takes issue with how affect theory is willing to grant that "even nonsubjects have affects" but then distinguishes emotions as the realm of the human.[9] Terada rejects this differentiation and rewrites the critical nomenclature of affect theory so that it includes not only the psychological experiences of human beings, but also the physiological sensations of all living creatures. Terada's reconceptualization usefully eliminates one of the many binaries that result from the dichotomy between "the human" and "the animal": the dichotomy between emotion and affect.

The conflation of emotion and affect hinges on the fact that for Terada, "emotion is an interpretive act": "our emotions emerge only through acts of interpretation and identification by means of which we feel *for others*. . . . We are not ourselves without representations that mediate us, and it is through those representations that emotions get felt."[10] By refusing to specify that those "others" must always already be human, Terada opens the terrain that nineteenth-century literature tried to negotiate in imagining how affective bonds with animals had a constitutive effect on subjectivity. She also draws our attention to the role that representation plays for the process of affective engagement and subject formation. She argues that affect studies arose out of a reaction against "the things [that] 'linguistic' theories" supposedly cannot do, which is to "explain 'effects' of thinking, willing, and . . . feeling."[11] Terada's work brokers a relationship between language and feeling that does not subsume one to the other but instead shows their complicated, refracted connections to each other.

What we mean by representation and by the "linguistic" will get reshaped in the process of such an inquiry. Lauren Berlant argues in her landmark special issue on intimacy for *Critical Inquiry* that "to intimate is to communicate with the sparest of signs and gestures, and at its root intimacy has the quality of eloquence and brevity." By this account, intimacy functions as a relay between the body and representation, where both operate as discursive registers that we can understand only in relation to each other. How that understanding develops hinges on a particular set of "pedagogies." Intersubjectivity gets produced across uneven terrain, leading Berlant to ask: "How can we think about the ways attachments make people public, producing trans-personal identities and subjectivities, when those attachments come from within spaces as varied as those of domestic intimacy, state policy, and mass-mediated experiences of intensely disruptive crises?" For her, the answer lies in finding ways of reframing intimacy that engage and disable "a prevalent U.S. discourse on the proper relation between public and private, spaces traditionally associated with the gendered division of labor." The stakes of such an enterprise are high because "liberal society was founded on the migration of intimacy expectations between the public and the domestic." Berlant sees both a normative and a liberatory potential in reframing how we understand "liberal society": "While the fantasies associated with intimacy usually end up occupying the space of convention, in practice the drive toward it is a kind of wild thing that is not necessarily organized that way, or any way." Crucial for this enterprise of approaching the "wild thing" remains an inquiry into the linguistic: Berlant writes that it is "the linguistic instability in which fantasy is couched [that] leads to an inevitable failure to stabilize desire in identity." Reading that linguistic instability calls "for transformative analyses of the rhetorical and material conditions that enable hegemonic fantasies to thrive in the minds and on the bodies of subjects"; that is, they call for an engagement with the conventions of affect and with strategies for exploiting those conventions for the purpose of transforming them.[12]

Although this attention to the representational and the linguistic might seem to return us to the domain of the human, I want to suggest that it instead presents us with the possibility for reading the relationship with animals as integral to structures of a reconfigured subjectivity. Christopher Peterson has formulated the question at which we arrive: "How might our relationship to the 'radical alterity' of nonhuman animals contest, instead of simply reaffirm, our normative conceptions of intimacy? What might the alterity of nonhuman animals have to teach us about the alterity of those human animals with whom we imagine the most intimate kinship?"[13] I want to explore the affective relationship between human beings and animals and examine how that relationship is worked out in animal representations.

Locke, Animals, and the Formation of American Literature

These relationships are central to the text—and especially to its reception—credited with founding our understanding of liberal subject formation: John Locke's *Some Thoughts Concerning Education* (1693). This text has variously been recognized as inaugurating the fields of pedagogy, child psychology, children's literature, the sentimental novel, and American literature as such; it was "probably even more widely read and circulated than the *Two Treatises of Government*,"[14] and it "served in its various popularized forms as perhaps the most significant text of the Anglo-American Enlightenment."[15] Responding to a friend's request for advice on how to rear his son, Locke eschews physical punishment and makes affect central to a pedagogy that accounts equally for children's physical and mental well-being. What interests me here is the special status he affords animals in the didactic enterprise of enabling children to develop their capacities: the affective relationship to animals forms the nexus between the body and mind that is requisite for liberal subject formation, but it also challenges the very parameters of that subject formation.

At first glance, Locke's reflections seem to distinguish human beings as rational creatures from other beings who are driven by appetites and emotions. He emphasizes the importance not only of teaching children how to moderate and control their emotions but advocates modeling such control in disciplining them: "When I say therefore, that they [children] must be *treated as Rational Creatures*, I mean that you should make them sensible by the Mildness of your Carriage, and the Composure even in your Correction of them, that what you do is reasonable in you, and useful and necessary for them."[16] Locke defines children as "Rational Creatures" who recognize "what is reasonable" in their parents and who in turn come to act reasonably by the example set them. However, this emphasis on reason depends on the ability to make children "sensible" to the kinds of emotions their parents exercise when they demonstrate "mildness" and "composure" in their reactions. Children's ability to learn from their parents hinges on their ability to develop a kind of empathy with their parents: they recognize their own ability to reason in seeing what is "reasonable in" their parents and in turn reflect that reasonableness back on themselves by recognizing it in utilitarian terms as what is "useful and necessary for them." In the encounter with their parents, they come to recognize their own interests and to develop a sense of themselves as interest-bearing subjects. That recognition of their interests precedes their entry into full legal personhood and their social recognition as legal subjects.

Although children learn from watching their parents' reasonable behavior, their mode of education is practical, not abstract. Locke insists that in all aspects of learning "children are *not* to be *taught by Rules*, which will be always slipping out of their Memories. What you think necessary for them to do, settle in them by an indispensible Practice, as often as the Occasion returns; and if it be possible, make Occasions."[17] For Locke, learning occurred experientially, not abstractly.[18] Eschewing abstract "rules," he argues that memory formation occurs through practice and repetition. This practical education depends on children's experience of other people's actions but also involves guiding their own actions.[19] Locke sets up an analogy by which parents' treatment of their children mirrors children's treatment of animals; this analogy functions as a literal chain of creaturely hierarchy by which the more powerful exercise control over the less powerful and, as I explain more fully later, as a chain of metaphoric substitutions by which each component of the chain represents the other.

At stake in these carefully calibrated relationships is children's initiation into proper modes of governance. Pointing out that "children love *Liberty*," he says, "I now tell you, they love something more; and that is *Dominion*: And this is the first Original of most vicious Habits, that are ordinary and natural."[20] Here he infuses his reflections with a political vocabulary, in which the desirable "love" of liberty fights against an undesirable "love" of dominion.

Insisting that affects differ qualitatively, Locke also indicates that his key pedagogical strategy—practice—can produce results conducive or adverse to good social order. In using the explicitly biblical language of "dominion" and an invocation of "Original" sin ("vicious Habits"), he is working out what role "natural" inclinations play in forming children's political desires. For him, the "natural" here is the *product* of habits, not their *origin*.[21]

The relationship with animals is crucial to the process of redirecting children's love for dominion into a proper love of liberty that hinges on the mutual recognition of subjects' interests. In his advocacy of humane practices, Locke initially focuses on human beings themselves, not on their animal victims. He explains that "the Custom of Tormenting and Killing of Beasts, will, by Degrees, harden their [children's] Minds even towards Men; and they who delight in the Suffering and Destruction of inferiour Creatures, will not be apt to be very compassionate, or benign to those of their own kind. Our Practice takes Notice of this in the Exclusion of *Butchers* from Juries of Life and Death."[22] Locke argues that humane conduct to animals ensures that human beings will treat each other with compassion. In repeatedly exercising one kind of affect, delight in the suffering of animals, children lose the ability to engage in the bonds of sympathy that underlie civic society: like butchers, they become unfit to enter into the juridical process, which is based on a balance between reason and compassion. Even though Locke's emphasis is on the way human beings treat each other, his argument depends on the substitution of animals for human beings: being cruel to animals results in being cruel to other human beings; the two are not separate from one another but, on the contrary, lie on a continuum. The ability to identify affectively with other human beings and to enter into social and legal relations with them depends on an ability to exercise proper compassion to animals.

Kindness to animals produces "good Nature" in children. That good nature expresses itself not only in reasoned relationships, but in emotional and physical ones: Locke emphasizes that the children should be "tender"— that is, feeling, loving, caring—to all "sensible" creatures, or all beings who have the capacity for physical and emotional feeling. Locke spells out what he means by "sensible" when he reproaches children for putting "any thing in Pain, that is capable of it."[23] At this point in his reflections, animals are no longer simply stand-ins for human beings; their own capacity for feeling has become important. Yet recognizing that importance defies social conventions, which Locke critiques in comments that pave the way for anticruelty and animal welfare activism. For Locke, the enjoyment of another creature's pain is "a foreign and introduced Disposition, an Habit borrowed from Custom and Conversation. People teach Children to strike, and laugh, when they hurt, or see harm come to others ... By these Steps unnatural Cruelty is planted in us; and what Humanity abhors, Custom reconciles and recommends to us, by laying it in the way to Honours. Thus, by Fashion and Opinion, that comes to be a Pleasure, which in it self neither is, nor can be any. This ought carefully to be watched, and early remedied, so as to settle and cherish the contrary, and more natural Temper of Benignity and *Compassion* in the room of it."[24] Pitting humanity against custom, Locke comes close to abandoning his own precept that nature is the product and not the origin of education; he entertains the notion that human beings are innately good and that cruelty is the "unnatural" result of habits "planted in us." Yet he retreats from this approach by casting *natural* as a comparative term: he advocates establishing a "more natural Temper" in children that runs contrary to social habits and returns children to a sense of "benignity." The relationship with animals has the capacity to "instill Sentiments of Humanity, and to keep them lively in young Folks."[25] Humanity itself has here become a "sentiment," one that hinges on compassion for animals. Far from functioning as an ontological category, humanity is the product of an educational process that relies on the relationship to animals to elicit and direct emotions; in other words, the liberal subject emerges through its properly affective engagement with animals.

Locke's work produces two connected strands in its writing on animals: it engages with the corporeal relationship between human beings and animals, and it inscribes that relationship at and as the core of representation. Turning to the topic of how children learn to read, Locke suggests that adults ought "to teach Children the *Alphabet* by playing." Once that basic literacy has been accomplished, adults should provide a child with "some easy pleasant Book suited to his Capacity," for which Locke has a specific recommendation: "I think *Aesop's Fables* the best, which being Stories apt to delight and entertain a Child, and yet afford useful Reflections to a grown Man." Locke's recommendation takes on an even more specific tone when he suggests that "if his *Aesop has Pictures* in it, it will entertain him much the better, and encourage him to read, when it carries the increase of Knowledge with it. For such visible Objects Children hear talked of in vain, and without any satisfaction, whilst they have no Ideas of them; those Ideas being not to be had from Sounds; but from the Things themselves, or their Pictures. And therefore I think, as soon as he begins to spell, as many Pictures of Animals should be got him, as can be found, with the printed names to them, which at the same time will invite him to read, and afford him Matter of Enquiry."[26] Animals come to occupy a central position in the child's—and by extension the man's—literacy. Children are not able to translate "sounds" into a connection with "ideas"; they arrive at those ideas through a relationship to "Things themselves, or their Pictures." Things and pictures take on an interchangeable relationship that makes animals figuratively *and* literally present for children as they develop their literacy skills.

These claims establish two important trajectories for people's engagements with animals subsequent to Locke. First, they blur the distinction between human beings and animals; animals themselves increasingly become subjects. Instead of seeing animals as a vehicle for human relationships, the animals themselves begin to matter in their own right. Second, these engagements give rise to writing and reading practices centered on (animal) bodies. As scholars such as Karen Sánchez-Eppler have pointed out, sentimentalism makes "reading . . . a bodily act."[27] Reading becomes an act of encountering the bodies of others and of needing to come to terms with their proximity and alterity. This encounter with animal bodies challenges us to expand our understanding of the work sentimentalism can do for cross-species relations. Elizabeth Dillon has explained that sentimentalism creates a "shared humanity" because it links individuals via their capacity "to feel deeply" and "to suffer."[28] What happens when sentimentalism does not automatically link back to humanity but instead creates connections with animals that press us beyond the human and humanist pale?

This question is far from peripheral to our understanding of nineteenth-century literature. As Gillian Brown and others have documented, "Americans knew Locke's ideas not only from these books, but also, and more profoundly, from the popular pedagogical modes and texts inspired by Locke's thought. Whether or not they knew Locke's writings, early Americans assimilated Lockean liberalism as they grew up."[29] In Locke's writing, the relationship between human beings and animals provides a model for initiating and integrating children into the social fabric as liberal subjects. But in the hands of a writer such as Emily Dickinson, the relationship to animals also provides modes for resisting social orders and imagining alternative subjectivities. In the next section, I situate Dickinson's work in the context of the nineteenth-century engagement with Lockean notions of subject formation.[30] Dickinson's case is interesting to me because she successfully channels a larger social discourse and in the process questions its assumptions and methodologies. She reevaluates the relationship between physical bodies and abstract representation and is particularly attentive to the role that gender plays in the formation of subjectivity. Demonstrating a link between the social construction of species and the social construction of gender, she explores how relationships to animals can unsettle both constructions and can generate alternative forms of representation.

Emily Dickinson and the Discontents of Liberal Subjectivity

Carlo died—
E. Dickinson
Would you instruct me now?[31]

In 1866, Emily Dickinson ended a lapse of eighteen months in her correspondence with Colonel Thomas Wentworth Higginson by sending him three lines that connect the major concerns of her work: death, subjectivity, and the conditions of knowledge. When Higginson later published these lines among Dickinson's letters, he explained that the poet would on occasion include "an announcement of some event, vast to her small sphere as this," the death of her dog, who had been her companion for sixteen years. In feminizing and privatizing Dickinson's loss and measuring it biographically by the "small sphere" of her life, Higginson sets aside this particular poet's ability to "wade grief" and situates Dickinson's letter within the sentimental culture of pet keeping that had transfigured a predominantly agricultural practice (as noted in the introduction, the word *pet* initially referred to a lamb) into a staple of genteel domesticity and bourgeois subjectivity.[32] Far from participating uncritically in the roles and relationships Higginson projects onto her, Dickinson interrogates the formation and gendering of sentimental subjectivity by placing "Carlo died" in relation to the other two lines—the signature and the call for instruction. "E. Dickinson" refers ambiguously to Emily or to her father, Edward Dickinson. The signature pluralizes the subject; it doubles and ultimately obscures "E.'s" gender.[33] This ambiguous subject hinges on the animal's death as a scene of pedagogy: it stands in the liminal space between the announcement of Carlo's death and the request "Would you instruct me now?"

It is easy to overlook this question's relevance to and bearing on Carlo's death because the call for instruction is a constant refrain in Dickinson's correspondence with Higginson. If we trace that refrain, it becomes apparent that Dickinson consistently links the scene of pedagogy with the formation of subjectivity via the trope of the animal. In her introductory letter to Higginson, she asked him "to say if my Verse is alive? . . . Should you think it breathed—and had you the leisure to tell me, I should feel quick gratitude."[34] Dickinson portrays a liveness that animates her poetry and whose breathing produces the poet's own affective "quick[ening]." She more fully develops these connections when she responds to Higginson's request for a self-description: "You ask of my Companions Hills—Sir—and the Sundown—and a Dog—large as myself, that my Father bought me—They are better than Beings—because they know—but do not tell—and the noise in the Pool, at Noon—excels my Piano."[35] This composite portrait blends the animate and the inanimate, the object with the subject, to unhinge their epistemological meanings and ontological differentiation. But what exactly is the surplus that makes her "Companions . . . better than Beings"? In using the term *companion*, Dickinson draws on the same vocabulary that informs Donna Haraway's reading of human beings and dogs as "companion species" that stand "in obligatory, constitutive, historical, protean relationship" to one another.[36] Like Haraway, who argues that animals "are not about oneself. . . . They are not a projection,"[37] Dickinson abandons the normative reference to human subjectivity by making the dog "better than Beings" and placing the implied adjective of "Beings," *human*, under erasure.

That erasure should also give us pause from mapping Dickinson too readily in relation to Haraway and the growing number of feminist scholars who believe animal studies in general and "dog writing" in particular "to be a branch of feminist theory."[38] Dickinson's terse prose cautions us about patriarchy's vested interest in sentimentalizing women's relationship with animals and in making the way women perform their gender contingent on the way they perform their species. That contingency is exemplified in Thomas Wentworth Higginson's 1887 article "Women and Men: Children and Animals," where he insists that "the care given by the young girl [to her pet] was simply the anticipated tenderness of a mother for her child."[39] As with Locke's metaphors, casting the girl's relationship to the dog as analogous to the mother's relationship with her child infantilizes women (they are like girls), anthropo-morphizes animals (pets are like children), and animalizes children (children are like pets).

Early reviews picked up on Dickinson's interest in using infantilization as a strategy for exploring these oddly mutable subject positions; they described Dickinson's poetry as showing "the insight of the civilized adult combined with the simplicity of the savage child."[40] In describing the dog as something that "my Father bought me," Dickinson casts herself in the role of her parent's child—that is, in the role of the subject to be formed by Lockean education. She draws attention to the objectifying structures that underlie the senti-mental association of women and animals by pointing to Carlo's status as a commodity and gift. Her double reference to "myself" and "me" inscribes her subjectivity in this act of gift giving and places her in the precarious posi-tion that women share with fetish objects and anthropomorphized subjects: by dropping the preposition *for* in "bought me" and establishing a simile between the "dog" and "myself," Dickinson allows for the double possibility that Carlo and "me" were the objects her father "bought me." With this odd slippage between the dog and the daughter, the gift and the recipient, she sug-gests that women, children, and animals mediate the relationship between the object and the subject; they establish the boundaries along which human subject formation in distinction from nature becomes possible.

In staging her relationship to her dog, Dickinson performs and under-cuts these differentiations. Although her relationship with the dog her father bought her infantilizes her, Carlo allows her small stature to appear "large."[41] By drawing on the animal as a trope-reversing trope, Dickinson deconstructs the very processes and parameters of gendered subject formation. The name "Carlo" signifies the central role that dogs play in the literary construction of subjectivity. Dickinson named Carlo after two literary characters, St. John River's dog in *Jane Eyre* and Ik Marvell's dog in *Reveries of a Bachelor*.[42] The name is thus not only a referent for a real dog, but also a referent for the fictional representation of animals.

Fictional representations of animals have been popular in English-lan-guage literature since the Middle Ages: Caxton published his translation of Aesop's *Fables* in 1484, and Locke's suggestion that this was the "only Book almost" suited to children's education speaks to the work's popularity. Moreover, Locke's recommendation itself initiated an interest in integrating animal characters into the children's literature that emerged as a new genre in response to his writings.[43] Locke's reflections on animals' didactic importance fundamentally changed pedagogical strategies for educating children to become liberal subjects. In the late eighteenth century, animals began to take on a central function *as animals* in the instruction of children. Even fables were enlisted in this new endeavor, as the subtitle of Sarah Trimmer's vastly popular *Fabulous Histories* (1786) illustrates: the book was "designed for the instruction of children respecting their treatment of animals."[44] In fact, animals played an increasingly important role not just in moral education, but in children's initiation into language itself—as indicated by the example of *Aesop's Fables in French: With a Description of Fifty Animals Mentioned Therein and a French and English Dictionary of the Words Contained in the Work* (1852).[45]

Emily Dickinson's Carlo participated in this educational reform. In 1863, her uncle by marriage, Asa Bullard, published a book entitled *Dog Stories* that prominently featured a dog named Carlo. As the secretary and general agent of the Massachusetts Sabbath School Society, Bullard edited the *Sabbath School Visitor*, to which Edward Dickinson subscribed for his children beginning in 1837, and Bullard numbered among the relatives Dickinson knew best because she stayed with him and her aunt Lucretia when she visited Boston for eye surgery. In sketches that restage the constant warfare between his dog-loving niece Emily and her cat-loving sister Lavinia, Bullard depicts scenes that amount to Christian allegory: in his portrayal of Carlo, the "Faithful Dog" cannot be lured away by temptation to abandon his master's charge. In Bullard's account of "Little Charlie and Fido," the dog "appears to *know* about as much as *some* boys; and he is a great deal more ready than some are to do a favor, and more thankful for any act of kindness shown him." Indeed, dogs come to stand in for knowledge itself when Bullard describes how Carlo eventually clears a ditch because his master's voice has encouraged him: "Many children find their school duties hard to accomplish. Let the *kind* word of encouragement be given, and many of them, like the little dog Carlo, will surmount the difficulty and find their future course a joyous one."[46] Animals inhabit the same didactic position as the texts that represent them, and serve as mediators for liberal subjectivity: Bullard's admonition ties the "*kind* word" and animals to each other as jointly enabling scholarly accomplishments; it promises that the pursuit of learning will find "joyous" fulfillment in a "future course."

What situates Bullard's book in a larger context of nineteenth-century children's literature is that it does not just portray the animals' behavior as exemplary; it uses animals to teach children kindness, and draws on versification to do so:

I'll never hurt my little dog,
But stroke and pat his head;
I like to see him wag his tail,
I like to see him fed.
The coward wretch whose hand and heart
Can bear to torture aught below,
Is ever first to quail and start
From slightest pain or equal foe.[47]

These stories operate on the basis of what I call "didactic ontology," by which I mean the practice of teaching children how to be human by teaching them how to be humane. Animals take on a double role in this didactic literature: animals stand in for children—their behavior models for the child how to behave, and they are important as animals whose vulnerability and exposure to potential cruelty teaches children to be kind. Children relate to animals through a double sense of identification and separation: because the animal is like them, they are asked to extend kindness, but the kindness they extend makes them human stewards of animals and marks their separation from them. Animals remain the trace of children's own presocial being and become the supplement to liberal subjectivity. This relationship depends on the use of simile; in the passage I quoted earlier, Bullard writes that children should be aided in their schoolwork by the "*kind* word of encouragement," which will allow "many of them, like the little dog Carlo" to "surmount the difficulty." Whereas metaphor (as I discuss later) conflates the two positions that ontology wants to separate, the human and the animal, simile keeps them recognizably separate: it gestures at a *tertium comparationis*, a third entity that enables the comparison while maintaining the differentiation between the entities that are being compared. In this case, that third entity is the "*kind* word," which functions not only to encourage children but also to inscribe them in a linguistic structure that separates them from animals: it integrates them into the pedagogical setting and disciplines them into fulfilling their "school duties."

Dickinson reinvents this use of simile by making language itself the locus of an animal presence that does not separate human beings and animals, but rather integrates them. Dickinson's portrayal of her dog as "better than [human] Beings" echoes a key assertion of this literature: that the virtues of animals reflect on the moral shortcomings of human beings. But Dickinson undercuts that lesson by dropping the word *human* and confounding the parameters of didactic ontology where the human is the teleological outcome. Her insistence that her companions "know—but do not tell" indicates her resistance to the didactic interpretation of the animal. Dickinson silences the pedagogical voice and instead gives play to "the noise in the Pool, at Noon" which functions as a form of knowledge that does not express itself in telling, in human language, but in a musical mode of expression that "excels my Piano" in that, as "noise," it is an experiential and disordered form of natural expression.[48]

Dickinson stages and suspends the child's entry into an adult symbolic order that turns animals into dead metaphors by disavowing and historicizing their presence. Using the same metric form and rhyme pattern as Bullard, she performs a formal parody of this kind of animal writing in a poem from 1871:

A little Dog that wags his tail
And knows no other joy
Of such a little Dog am I
Reminded by a Boy

Who gambols all the living Day
Without an earthly cause
Because he is a little Boy
I honestly suppose—

The Cat that in the Corner dwells
Her martial Day forgot
The Mouse but a Tradition now
Of her desireless Lot

Another class remind me
Who neither please nor play
But not to make a "bit of noise"
Beseech each little Boy—[49]

Dickinson begins the poem sounding like the didactic literature she is imitating: she suggests that the boy is like the dog, but the moral lesson we expect to follow—that such likeness obliges him to a kindness that ultimately separates him from the dog—is missing. Indeed, if we look closely, the dog is not a stand-in for the boy; on the contrary, the boy is a stand-in for the dog in Dickinson's reversal of the trope. Dickinson's boy is allowed to inhabit a relationship to the dog that resists their didactic separation from one another. This resistance to didactic separation deepens when we contextualize this poem with its private circulation. In letters to her family, Dickinson habitually referred to herself as a boy—for instance, when she wrote to her nephew Ned: "Mother told me, when I was a boy, that I must turn over a new leaf. I call that the foliage admonition. Shall I commend it to you?"[50] Turning an admonition into a question, Dickinson here, as in the poem, undercuts the didactic message that "another class" wants to impart. Indeed, that resistance to "admonition" is a theme throughout her correspondence with Ned. In the letter that included an abridged version of this poem, Dickinson offset its purported didacticism by adding a postscript: "P.S.—Grandma characteristically hopes Neddy will be a good boy. Obtuse ambition of Grandma's!"[51] Far from reprimanding the boy, she allies herself with him against those adults who would silence him. Unlike the cat's dead "Tradition" of a "martial Day" that stands in opposition to the boy's "living Day," the boy is free to "know no other joy" than the expression of his own pleasure.

But in being asked "not to make a 'bit of noise,'" the boy is soon deprived of the ability to participate in "the noise in the Pool, at Noon"—that is, in the natural forms of expression that provide an alternative discourse to the language of pedagogy. Dickinson resists the didactic separation of children from animals; it is in their connection with one another that the possibility for poetic expression lies. Yet even in a poem like this one, that possibility is always deferred. Being "reminded" links memory to admonition. In portraying the little boy, the "I" of first-person liberal subjectivity can be "reminded" of the "little Dog" but is already part of the didactic structures that prohibit the subject's participation in that undifferentiated relationship between the boy and the dog.

Whereas her parodic poem identifies this problem, Dickinson reaches in other works for a "Phraseless Melody"[52] by reshaping her relationship to language—that is, by making poetry itself animate. Animals mark in Dickinson's work the liveness of a natural language beyond social silencing:

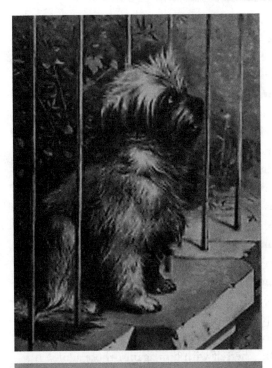

FIGURE 4.1 From Cousin Daisy's *The Picture Alphabet* (Philadelphia: J. B. Lippincott, 1879). Courtesy of the American Antiquarian Society

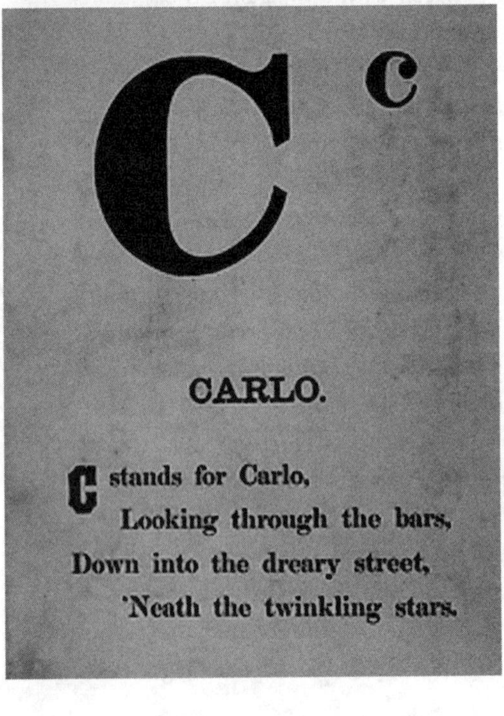

C c

CARLO.

C stands for Carlo,
Looking through the bars,
Down into the dreary street,
'Neath the twinkling stars.

FIGURE 4.2 From Cousin Daisy's *The Picture Alphabet* (Philadelphia: J. B. Lippincott, 1879). Courtesy of the American Antiquarian Society

Many a phrase has the English language—
I have heard but one—
Low as the laughter of the Cricket,
Loud, as the Thunder's Tongue—

Murmuring, like old Caspian Choirs,
When the Tide's a'lull—
Saying itself in new inflection—
Like a Whippowil—

Breaking in bright Orthography
On my simple sleep—
Thundering it's Prospective—
Till I stir, and weep—

Not for the Sorrow, done me—
But the push of Joy—
Say it again, Saxon!
Hush—Only to me!⁵³

Whereas Bullard maintained a differentiation between human beings and animals by using simile to establish a third entity, language, as the basis of comparison and distinction, Dickinson here makes language itself the locus for relating animal and human subjectivity. The "one" phrase withheld is figured in relation to "the laughter of the Cricket" and the "new inflection" of the "Whippowil." This utterance takes on the shape of "Orthography" in Dickinson's "simple sleep." Akira Lippit's work is useful for reading this poem: through an interpretation of Freud's dreamwork, Lippit locates "a kind of originary topography shared by human beings and animals" in which "the animal becomes intertwined with the trope, serving as its vehicle and substance."⁵⁴ Lippit coins the term *animetaphor* to describe the animal as both "an exemplary metaphor" and an "originary metaphor" and argues that animals function "as the unconscious of language, of *logos*." Following Jacques Derrida, he argues that *logos* "is engendered by a *zoon*, and can never entirely efface the traces of its origin. The genealogy of language . . . returns to a place outside of *logos*. The animal brings to language something that is not a part of language and remains within language as a foreign presence." The animal thus takes on the role of "a vital metaphor, that enters the world from a place outside of language," a "figure that is metamorphic rather than metaphoric."[55] Key to Dickinson's imagining of this metamorphic figure is her odd enjambment: "Like a Whippowil— / Breaking in bright Orthography" brings the "new inflection" of the phrase in conjunction with "the branch of knowledge which deals with letters and their combination to represent sounds and words."[56] Dickinson is literalizing one of Higginson's odder suggestions, that "kittens . . . about the house supply the smaller punctuation in the book of life; their little frisks and leaps and pats are the commas and semicolons and dashes, while the big dog puts in the colons and the periods."[57] Dickinson locates animal presence in orthography, in writing itself.

To achieve a vital poetry beyond the parameters of animal metaphors, Emily Dickinson deconstructs liberal subjectivity by alphabetizing her poetry. "Carlo" participated in the nineteenth-century vogue of animal alphabets that linked a letter with an image and with rhymed text to initiate children into literacy. In *The Picture Alphabet* (1879) by "Cousin Daisy," the picture of a scruffy dog looking through bars (figure 4.1) is accompanied by the rhyme: "C stands for Carlo, / Looking through the bars, / Down into the dreary street, / 'Neath the twinkling stars" (figure 4.2).[58] This kind of animal alphabet participated in the structures of liberal subjectivity. As Patricia Crain has documented, "By the beginning of the nineteenth century, alphabetization supplants rhetorical training, not only as a mode of communication but as a primary structuring of subjectivity." Alphabets function as an "androgyne, moving back and forth between text and image," and complicate the relationship between textual and physical representation. The extensive use of animals in these alphabets also indicates "that there are two kinds of utterances: a natural, irresistible, autonomic kind, which we share with the animals—an exhale, a cry of a baby, the communication between working man and working beast; and an artificial, learned kind—that of alphabetic, educated speech, which we draw from the animals, but which distinguishes us from them."[59] Dickinson aims to recapture the former utterance, that noise, in her use of animal orthography.

The animation of orthography reshapes the relationship between writing and subject formation. "Carlo" is an anomaly in Dickinson's references to animals in that he is one of only three named animals (Carlo, Chanticleer, Pussy). Even those animals are not named individually but generically; they participate in the larger animal orthography of Dickinson's poetic enterprise.

In fact, the sheer range and number of animals Dickinson mentions in her poems is astonishing: by my count, she lists more than seventy different animals and names at least one animal in 20 percent of her poems. In creating an animal orthography, Dickinson then strains beyond metaphor to an animetaphor that gives poetry itself an extrasocial liveness, as one of her most famous poems illustrates:

I heard a Fly buzz—when I died—
The Stillness in the Room
Was like the Stillness in the Air—
Between the Heaves of Storm—

The Eyes around—had wrung them dry—
And Breaths were gathering firm
For that last Onset—when the King
Be witnessed—in the Room—

I willed my Keepsakes—Signed away
What portion of me be
Assignable—and then it was
There interposed a Fly—

With Blue—uncertain—stumbling Buzz—
Between the light—and me—
And then the Windows failed—and then
I could not see to see—[60]

Having "signed away" that "portion of me" that is "Assignable," Dickinson relinquishes the scene of domestic confinement in the "room" and the social "witnessing" to harness the "Breaths" for her own postliberal subjectivity. The subject's death enables an animation of the poem itself: incessant buzzing and alliterative sounds invoke the impersonal fly whose intervention in the first line separates the "I" of liberal subjectivity from an undefined "I" that gains animation from the scene of death. Animals allow Dickinson to play one kind of death against another. The death of liberal subjectivity is the scene of an imagined overturning of the animal's figurative death and an entry into a poetic liveness.

Dickinson's letter to Higginson stages just such an animal orthography:

Carlo died—
E. Dickinson
Would you instruct me now?

Starting with C for "Carlo," moving to D for "died" and E for a signature, she replicates in her lines the progression of the alphabet. Adding another D for "Dickinson," she also symbolizes the rhyme scheme of the poems associated, as Bullard's verses illustrated, with children's education into a relationship with animals: CDED. Her concluding question to Higginson, whom she admired as a naturalist,[61] ironizes the didactic lessons that animals impart: she has, indeed, been well instructed. The fact that "Carlo died," then, poses a threat and opens up a possibility for Dickinson's enterprise. As Higginson put it, "A dog is itself a liberal education, with its example of fidelity, unwearied activity, cheerful sympathy, and love stronger than death."[62] In staging her carefully learned lessons of animal pedagogy, Dickinson portrays Carlo as a figure for liberal education. But she also takes his literal death to explore Higginson's promise in that the dog exceeds the parameters of liberal subject formation and provides a figure of liveness beyond social formation. The danger here is that this development naturalizes social formations; in turning to representation, Dickinson offsets the reemergence of ontology with an emphasis on orthography. Carlo's literal death opens the possibility for his orthographic liveness; through Carlo, "E. Dickinson's" subjectivity can again become an open-ended question.

I have been tracing an arc that links the ontological questions posed by current affect theory to Lockean origins and subsequent intellectual receptions of liberal subject formation. Post-structuralist affect theory and liberalism open a space for radical alterity. But they too easily foreclose that space by reinscribing affect in an ontologically defined frame that distinguishes between the human and its animal others. At stake in that foreclosure is the production of a particular notion of subjectivity as marked by an individuality independent of others and clearly demarcated by the separation of reasoning from embodiment. Looking at animals gives us a different account of the subject—as relational and contingent on an alterity that cannot easily be reinscribed in the registers of either abstract rationality or embodied affectivity.

Because that alterity is both physical *and* representational, it enables us to recognize that reading is a bodily act and that the body is a readerly act. These two modes of meaning making are contingent on but not reducible to each other; they function as one another's excess and *différance*. In the process, they unhinge the naturalizing discourse of ontology and point to ontology itself as a construct that emerges relationally. Through the literal and figurative presence of animals, we come to see a fundamental relationality that points to the contingencies of our being. It is in that relationality that new possibilities for subjectivity and poetry emerge.

5

RETHINKING LIBERAL SUBJECTIVITY
The Biopolitics of Animal Autobiography

(KATHARINE LEE BATES, BARBARA BUSH)

This final chapter takes up the conflation of pets with children to examine how biopower infantilizes and commoditizes the liberal subject as it maps the drama of sovereignty onto the mundane territory of pet keeping.[1] By examining the genre of animal autobiography, or biographies written from the perspective of an animal, I focus on texts that exemplify the slippage between commodification and subject formation, and I ask what happens to the animal voice when it finds expression in human language. Autobiographies in general produce writers as speakerly subjects and as objects for purchase. The conceit of the speaking and writing animal contributes to this commodification but also generates representational fissures through which a recognition and critique of biopolitical subjectivity become possible. The dog narrative is "a vital sub-genre" whose central premises "are fully evident by 1825," but it is "in the first two decades of the nineteenth century, that dog-protagonist narratives become a popular sub-genre,"[2] one whose popularity connects nineteenth-century explorations of liberal subjectivity with current practices of neoliberal subject formation. Through a case study of President George H. W. Bush's dog "Millie," I explore what happens when sovereign power and biopolitical governmentality encounter one another and the scene of bestiality gets rewritten as one of "puppy love." I return to the connections between bestiality and sodomy here, but in the context of women's writings to ask what functions of heteronormativity and what possibilities for queering arise in these affective relationships to animals. In bringing to a conclusion my attempt to rethink the "history of sexuality" as a "history of bestiality," I examine the gender politics of animal autobiography by situating *Millie's Book, as Dictated to Barbara Bush*, published in 1990, in relation to a broader genealogy of queer animal autobiography, focusing specifically on works by Katharine Lee Bates (the lesbian founder of American literary studies) and Virginia Woolf (whose biography of Elizabeth Barrett Browning's dog Flush was a best-seller in America). Demonstrating that animal autobiographies explore structures of objectification that—at times inadvertently—unsettle the biopolitics they are meant to affirm, I conclude that animal representations locate a queerness at the very heart of liberal subject formation.[3]

"Puppy Love" for Mother's Day

On the cover of its Mother's Day edition for May 1989, *Life* magazine featured a photograph of First Lady Barbara Bush with her dog, Millie, who had just given birth to six puppies, five of them female (figure 5.1).[4] The cover had beaten out, so publisher Kate Bonniwell informed her readers, two other options. One featured Ralph Lauren, who was profiled in this issue as a rags-to-riches entrepreneur and dedicated family man. Under the caption "America's Toughest Job: The Working Mother," the other alternate cover displayed a picture of Pat Menzel, who worked an astonishing 133 hours each week as a hairdresser and mother of two young sons. But the editors decided to go with the issue's "biggest coup," the "exclusive photo session at the White House with Barbara Bush, her dog Millie and newborn pups."[5] Winning out over other family themes, "Puppy Love by Barbara Bush" portrayed motherhood for *Life* magazine's readers.

The magazine's use of the first lady invoked and displaced the political aspirations of Mother's Day. In the United States, Mother's Day was first invented

MAY 1989/$2.95

LIFE

Puppy Love

by Barbara Bush

FIGURE 5.1 "Puppy Love." First Lady Barbara Bush with Millie and her puppies. Cover of *Life* magazine, Mother's Day edition, May 1989. Photograph by and courtesy of William Wegman. LIFE® used by permission of The Picture Collection, Inc.

when Julia Ward Howe proclaimed the holiday in 1870 and wrote the "Mother's Day Proclamation" as a call for peace and disarmament via women's political agency.[6] In response to the carnage and abject horrors of war, to which her "Battle Hymn of the Republic" had contributed, Howe called for women to

> Say firmly: "We will not have great questions decided by irrelevant agencies. Our husbands will not come to us, reeking with carnage, for caresses and applause. Our sons shall not be taken from us to unlearn all that we have been able to teach them of charity, mercy and patience. We, the women of one country, will be too tender of those of another country to allow our sons to be trained to injure theirs."[7]

Imagining a solidarity between women that hinged on affect to counterbalance the biopolitics of warfare and carnage, Howe insisted that women could develop relevant "agencies" via a politics of transnational gender solidarity. Her vision replaced the patriarchal family with a queer bond in that it withheld "caresses" from husbands and bestowed "tender[ness]" on other women. Secularizing religious vocabulary, Howe maintained that lessons of "charity, mercy and patience" needed to be reaffirmed by women's relationship to one another. That relationship had children for its objects and mediators, children who in the process became collectively mothered. The affective bond between women, so Howe hoped, would prevent their sons from "unlearning" what their mothers had aimed "to teach them" and would prevent them from entering an apprenticeship in which they were "trained to injure" others. Far from imagining that women would exercise this pedagogical and affective agency exclusively in the home, Howe called for Mother's Day as an opportunity for a "general congress of women" to assemble and to work toward a politics of disarmament and peace.[8] With such a day given additional urgency by the wars against Native Americans and the Franco–Prussian War, Howe tried to imagine women's affective agency as an affirmative biopolitics that could counter the thanatopolitics of domestic and international warfare.

Biopolitical Objects

These aspirations seem to have been lost in the commercialization of the holiday, but commoditization itself can tell us something about the exercise of neoliberal biopower and its figurations of subjectivity. Taking up Foucault's claim that biopower emerged when "political power had assigned itself the task of administering life,"[9] Gregory Tomso has pointed out that this administration of life founded liberal subjectivity on a paradox: liberal subjectivity was understood in terms of freedom, yet at the same time that freedom was grounded in a discourse of "natural" rights thought to be inherent in that liberal subject.[10] The joint between these seemingly competing ideological strands was capitalism, with its ability, on the one hand, to promise individual freedom and its capacity, on the other hand, to insert objectified bodies into the machinery of production.[11]

Commenting on the simultaneous historical emergence of biopolitics and consumer capitalism, Eric Santner has recently argued that the "creaturely" comes to occupy the center of "literary and philosophical elaborations of *human* life under conditions of modernity" because it "names the threshold where life becomes a matter of politics and politics comes to inform the very matter and materiality of life." Biopower blurs the distinction between subjects and objects; as Santner explains, "one might . . . speak of the birth of (the subject of) psychoanalysis out of the 'spirit' of the commodity."[12] Santner is engaging with arguments advanced by theorists of material culture who puzzle over the way in which the central division between use and exchange value cannot account for the structures of desire and affect that mark the relationship between subjects and objects in commodity culture. But Santner problematically follows the same trajectory as Giorgio Agamben in that he ultimately locates the creaturely within the human. In *The Open*, Agamben writes that the "decisive political conflict" is that "between the animality and the humanity *of man*" and analyzes a "central emptiness, the hiatus that—within man—separates man and animal."[13] What would it mean instead to see the relationship *between* man and animal as one that does not "separate" as much as connect them, and what would it mean to do so without letting go of the bodily and material dimensions of those relations and of the queer affections to which they give rise? Bill Brown has examined the key insight that Marxist and psychoanalytic theory share: that object relations are always-already subject relations. By developing what he calls "thing theory"—that is, an understanding of things' capacity to exceed the relation to both objects and subjects—he argues that "the story of objects asserting themselves as things . . . is the story of a changed relation to the human subject and thus the story of how the thing really names less an object than a particular subject–object relation."[14] Pointing to the "object's capacity to materialize identity," he argues that "this relation, hardly describable in the context of use or exchange, can be overwhelmingly aesthetic, deeply affective; it involves desire, pleasure, frustration, a kind of pain."[15] In this chapter, I try to understand how we might read the animal as a "thing" in a way that is not associated with—or at least not limited to—the denial of subjectivity but rather is productive of alternative subjectivities. If one of the conditions of biopolitics is not just the control over but also the commercialization of animal life, how might we locate alternative subjectivities at its very core in those processes of objectification?

For Donna Haraway, this alternative is precisely where Marxist paradigms need to be expanded. Asking, "What happens when the undead but always generative commodity becomes the living, breathing, rights-endowed, doggish bit of property sleeping on my bed?" she argues that the Marxist "doublet of exchange value and use value" is insufficient; the dog is where "value becomes flesh again, in spite of all the dematerializations and objectifications inherent in market valuation." Haraway asserts that we need to supplement the Marxist structure by adding to use and exchange value what she calls "encounter value"—that is, a recognition that "the human–animal companionate family is a key indicator for today's lively capital practices. . . . Kin and brand are tied in productive embrace as never before." She calls that embrace "biocapital" and argues that it emerged as "the crucial new kind of reproductive wealth in the late eighteenth and nineteenth centuries." For her, the term *biocapital* not only modifies Marx but also expands Foucault's understanding of biopower beyond his "own species chauvinism." That is, through her attention to biocapital, Haraway wants to expand Foucault's notion of biopower as a practice of regulating state subjects to a biopower that especially impacts creatures whom the state does not recognize as subjects. For her, encounter value stands in tension to the practices of biocapital in that it is the "underanalyzed axis of lively capital" that reveals to us the "face-to-face, body-to-body subject making across species" that forces us to expand our currently limited categories of subjectivity.[16] In the first chapter of my book, I mapped that "body-to body" relationship in a reading of bestiality, which I reexamined in chapter 2 via the "face-to-face" encounter that Douglass and Lévinas have with dogs. Taking up in chapter 3 the question of how animal love gets transmuted from criminalized bestiality to Lockean pedagogy, I then explored in chapter 4 how "subject making across species" occurs between the dog Carlo and the child Emily. In this chapter, I want to draw these strands of discussion back into dialogue with each other by reading queer bodies in relation to childhood as a form of social reproduction that resists biocapital by its excessive relation to animals.[17]

One way to accomplish that reconfiguration is via a renewed inquiry into relational subjectivity in general and object relations in particular. Pointing out that psychoanalysis by and large ignores the significance of objects, Bill Brown has recently wondered "what a theory of object relations could accomplish if . . . it turned its attention to things." Such an inquiry necessitates a reevaluation of what we might mean by objects in that, for most psychoanalysis, "the object, be it constituted through projection or introjection, is never not another human subject."[18] Yet the work of D. W. Winnicott on what he calls "transitional objects" forms a notable exception to this understanding of objects. Winnicott introduces the term to designate an "intermediate area of experience, between the thumb and the teddy bear, between the oral erotism and the true object-relationship, between primary creative activity and projection of what has already been introjected, between primary unawareness of indebtedness and the acknowledgment of indebtedness." He defines transitional objects as ones that "are not part of the infant's body yet are not fully recognized as belonging to external reality." He claims that there is "an intermediate area of *experiencing*, to which inner reality and external reality both contribute. It is an area that is not challenged, because no claim is made on its behalf except that it shall exist as a resting-place for the individual engaged in the perpetual human task of keeping inner and outer reality separate yet interrelated." Departing from his friend Melanie Klein's analysis, he argues that "sooner or later in an infant's development there comes a tendency on the part of the infant to weave other-than-me objects into the personal pattern. To some extent these objects stand for the breast, but it is not especially this point that is under discussion"; he insists that it is not the object's "symbolic value so much as its actuality" that interests him. Whereas for Klein the concept of the internal object takes on primary importance, for Winnicott the transitional object is neither an internal object nor an external object either; "the transitional object is never under magical control like the internal object, nor is it outside control as the real mother is." This intermediate area of experiencing, says Winnicott, is precisely where we need to rethink the relationship between the symbolic and the literal: "When symbolism is employed the infant is already clearly distinguishing between fantasy and fact, between inner objects and external objects, between primary creativity and perception. But the term transitional object, according to my suggestion, gives room for the process of becoming able to accept difference and similarity. I think there is use for a term for the root of symbolism in time, a term that describes the infant's journey from the purely subjective to objectivity; and it seems to me that the transitional object (piece of blanket, etc.) is what we see of this journey of progress towards experiencing." For Winnicott, this journey is developmental, but it lacks telos in that "this intermediate area of experience . . . throughout life is retained in the intense experiencing that belongs to the arts and to religion and to imaginative living, and to creative scientific work."[19] Whereas animals take on a teleological function in Locke, by Winnicott's account, animal *representations* become *the* transitional object par excellence in that they form the nexus between the different forms of life and the different forms of representation that modernity—and here again I am invoking Bruno Latour—seeks to separate. The transitional object calls into question the extent to which the child ever fully relinquishes her participation in the real and imaginary upon entering into the symbolic order.[20] It undercuts the trajectory of Lockean education and makes it possible to think of children—as Kathryn Bond Stockton has suggested—as growing sideways rather than growing up and thereby developing queer, alternative subjectivities that hinge on animals.[21] I want to suggest that animal autobiographies locate us at the nexus between these different ways of thinking about objects—as the "mere" objects of commodity culture or as the recalcitrant transitional objects that function as biopolitics' vexing and exhilarating surplus.

Biopolitical Commodities

The *Life* magazine cover featuring Barbara Bush and Millie invokes the political origins of Mother's Day by depicting the first lady, but it uses sentimental iconography to displace the lived reality and abject labor of the working-class mother. Instead of forging bonds with other human women, Barbara Bush shares the solidarity of motherhood with her dog, Millie. By describing mothers' affective agency as "puppy love," the cover situates Mother's Day in a saccharine commercialism that inscribes Howe's vision of antipatriarchal family politics within conservative consumerism.[22] Making motherhood revolve around the dog and her puppies places Millie in the service of an

overdetermined commercial iconography that aims—but ultimately fails—
to inscribe the photo in the heterosexual matrix that lies at the core of the
modern nation-state.[23]

Although the *Life* cover photo is easily legible as a celebrity image, it is
more difficult to discern what it and its title "Puppy Love" say about the relationships the photo depicts. The term *puppy love* is usually used figuratively
to describe that first burgeoning of romantic attraction between teenagers.
The term carries "contemptuous" overtones, as the *Oxford English Dictionary* informs us.[24] Perhaps the best-known use of the term is Paul Anka's 1959
hit "Puppy Love," in which he wistfully reflects on the dismissal with which
adults treat teenage affection.

Given these contexts, the use of the term *puppy love* as the title for *Life*'s
cover in May 1989 strangely codes the relationships depicted as romantic.
That raises the question of who exactly is experiencing "puppy love": Does
the term refer to the relationship between Millie and her puppies or to the
one between Barbara Bush and the dogs, or is it the viewer who is expected
to experience "puppy love" when confronting this image? Subjectivities
multiply and become unsettled in affective relationships with pets. A search
using the key word *puppy love* on Google Images renders, in addition to the
occasional pornographic picture that explicitly connects "puppy love" to
bestiality, images that show two puppies who presumably love one another
and whom the viewer is expected to love. The images' capacity to depict and
elicit affection collapses the distinction between identification and objectification; it puts the puppies in the precarious position of anthropomorphized
subjects and fetish objects. The puppies share with children that tenuous
subjectivity of animated objects.[25] Some of these photos replace one puppy
with a child, breaking down the divide between the literal puppy and the
figurative puppy. Functioning simultaneously as a stand-in for the puppy and
for the viewer, this child becomes a mediator for an affection that crosses
species barriers but also normalizes that boundary crossing by providing an
anthropomorphic center.

Because this image of puppy love describes a sentiment and inscribes the
viewer in the affect portrayed, it both infantilizes the viewer as a child and
animalizes her as a puppy, all the while placing her in the adult role of lover
and mother in relation to the animal. Placing Barbara Bush in the *Life* cover
picture makes visible this lover–mother role: looming over Millie, she represents a dog lover and a surrogate mother in her relationship to Millie and the

puppies, whose biological bond is highlighted by the fact that three of the six puppies are nursing. Coding the role of the lover–mother in terms of surrogacy and biology, around the two poles of the postmodern family, adoption, and reproduction, this image sets up a crisis of representation: although the photo participates in the symbolic ordering of family romance, it also disrupts the very process of symbolization that lies at the heart of the family.

Yet the cover tries to make the relationships it depicts conform to heteronormative social structures. The clearest explanation of "Puppy Love" as a descriptor of the photo lies in the song title's capacity to frame motherhood nostalgically; *Life* magazine's caption invokes that most wholesome of wholesome American decades, the 1950s, and places an iconic value on family. Reframing teenage romance as family romance, "puppy love" designates identities that are constructed relationally by sentimental means of depiction. But the reference to puppy love firmly inscribes the relationships depicted here within the structures of the heteronormative family. The article itself enhances the cover's romantic coding and compulsory heterosexuality: a photo showing Millie getting a "husbandly nuzzle from Tug III at his Kentucky farm" informs us that the "two were bred during inauguration week."[26] Note the use of the passive voice when it comes to the act of reproduction and the description of the dogs' relationship: the "husbandly nuzzle" indicates that marriage is not reserved for human beings and can occur in other species so long as marriage remains heterosexual. It is indeed hard to imagine how *Life*'s readers would have reacted to this article if it had drawn on the language of dog breeding to describe Millie as a bitch who was decked.

Yet even without such language, the article is complicit in the crude sexual commodification of Millie. The text wavers between portraying Millie as a subject and describing her as an object—that is, as someone who, on the one hand, could enter into the consensual relationship that is marriage but who, on the other hand, cannot actively exercise her own sexual agency and—the passive voice here is important—was "bred." The title of the article reads "Millie's Six-Pack" and puns on the names "Millie" and "Bush" by invoking the Miller Brewing Company and Anheuser-Busch. It commodifies Millie and her offspring by troping on the manliest of manly commodities, beer, and it strangely masculinizes Millie by attributing to her the "six pack" usually associated with body-building men and not postpartum women; it portrays Millie not only as a bitch, but also as a butch. Through its repeated attentions to Millie's body, the article and *Millie's Book, as Dictated to*

Barbara Bush try to work out a theory of sexuality via the discourse of species and vice versa.

Following up on the success of the *Life* article, *Millie's Book* appeared in 1990. Written from the dog's perspective and purportedly composed by Millie herself, *Millie's Book* made it to number 1 on the *New York Times* nonfiction best-seller list and raised nearly $900,000 to promote literacy.[27] Those sales figures meant that Millie, as the nonfiction book's author, earned roughly four times George Bush's salary as president and outdid by far the royalties he received later for his autobiography *Looking Forward* (1987).[28]

If biopolitics has a genre, it must surely be autobiography, which connects life (*bio-*) to writing (*-graphy*) and the self (*auto-*). Within the larger field of autobiography, animal autobiography forms a strange subgenre. Because autobiographies in general are preoccupied, as Sidonie Smith and Julia Watson have pointed out, with the "processes of subject formation," the legacy of defining animals as objects that cannot speak would seem to categorically exclude animals from participation in this genre.[29] And yet since the nineteenth century the conceit of writing animal autobiographies has been consistently popular.[30] One explanation for this popularity might lie in attempts to appropriate the voice of the animal by submitting it to language, but I want to suggest instead that the animal voice—however anthropomorphized—remains an alien presence within language and unsettles the subject formations in which it participates.

The popularity of animal autobiographies coincided with and responded to the historical rise of biopolitics. Animal autobiographies connect us with a larger literary genealogy of animal writing that, as Teresa Mangum points out, looks "backward to the late-eighteenth-century sentimental novel, a form which remained popular through the nineteenth century despite being criticized as a debased, emotionally exploitative, feminized form which sought to awaken sensibility and benevolence rather than reason." But animal autobiographies also "interweave sentimentality with the experiential, flawed view of human nature associated with realism."[31] As a genre, then, animal autobiography is interstitial in that it connects animals to sentimental and realist forms of writing and places them in dialogue with one another around a shared investigation of subjectivity.

Animal autobiographies take on two distinct forms. In the first, they are books written about an animal but from the perspective of a human being who makes the animal an essential reference point and partner in his or her own life story (John Grogan's *Marley and Me* is a recent example of this form). The animal in this context is the vehicle for an autobiography of the human subject. But the opposite also holds true—the human is a vehicle for our understanding of the animal subject; because of its emphasis on relationships, animal autobiography constantly confounds the subject–object divide. Animal autobiographies locate us in an intermediary terrain where it becomes possible to rethink who counts as a subject and to critique biopower. In *Dog Years: A Memoir*, for instance, Mark Doty gives an account of the years he spent with his dogs while nursing his partner as he died of AIDS. Doty's animal representations become a profound meditation on subjectivity in relation to the social negations of queer masculinity in the 1980s and enable a reflection on how to reaffirm life when confronted with its biological and political annihilation in the AIDS crisis. Animal autobiographies, then, do not simply reaffirm subjectivities but reinvent them via the relationships they represent. In the second form, animal autobiographies are books purportedly written from the animal's perspective about his or her own life; they usually function as a kind of bildungsroman that playfully engages the conventions of Lockean pedagogy. Again, this second form of animal autobiography productively blurs the boundary between subjects and objects by making literacy available to the animal and allowing him or her to participate in the kinds of authorial and linguistic subject formation we usually reserve for human beings.

Millie's Book begins with an account of how Millie came to live with the Bushes when their previous dog had died, and they were looking for a replacement. George Bush contacted the family's friend Will Farish to see if they could have one of the dogs whom "Bar had fallen in love" with on a recent visit. Farish asked "if a girl would be all right" even though the Bushes "had never had a female dog before." When Millie met the Bushes, "it was love at first sight. Both Bushes kissed me and I sat on Bar's lap all the way to Maine."[32] In these descriptions, Millie goes from being an object of evaluation and negotiation, whose female gender might hinder her from meeting the criteria requisite for "Bar" falling "in love" with her, to acquiring the status of a love object on whom the Bushes lavish expressions of physical affection. Yet this romantically coded encounter, which the book underscores by including photos of the Bushes kissing Millie, is undercut by Millie making "a confession that is difficult for me to make": in the evening, she recounts, Barbara Bush whispers to her, "You are *so* sweet, but you are *so* ugly. You have a pig's nose, you are bowlegged, and your eyes are yellow." Millie's response to this statement is to see it as a challenge for personal betterment: "I knew immediately that I was going to have to try harder."[33] Because Millie's agreeable temperament is not a matter of dispute, her attempts presumably are meant to be for physical self-betterment. In reflecting on her physical properties as subject to self-discipline, Millie occupies the central tension and fantasy of liberal subject formation: that biology itself is subject to discipline.

Throughout the book, Millie occupies a double status as pure object and object of affection, with the two roles at times reinforcing and at other times standing in tension with each other. The book's attempted humor revolves around the dog's anthropomorphizing herself when the narrative insists that, for all her aspirations, she remains a dog. But that sense, that she remains a dog, then also undercuts the book's own conceit—its anthropomorphizing depictions of Millie. Even in the act of negating her subjectivity—she is not a dog, she is a human; she is not a human, she is (only) a dog—the narrative inadvertently opens up a space for the alterity it negates.

The book stages a rivalry between Millie and Barbara Bush that revolves around who is the better wife and mother. Millie informs us that "the alarm goes off at 6 a.m. The Prez says that I go off a few minutes earlier by shaking my ears pretty hard in their faces."[34] Here, she is likened to an alarm clock, but an alarm clock that has physical, intimate contact with the Bushes; she is in fact describing herself as the third party in their marriage bed. Millie has an affective relationship with each of the Bushes individually and also serves as a mediator for their relationship to each other. Moreover, she facilitates their relationship to the public: recounting the beginnings of the 1988 presidential campaign, Millie remembers that "posing for *Vanity Fur*, the stylish fashion magazine, made me feel that I was giving my all for George."[35] Millie's comment establishes an intimacy between her and the president; she strangely participates in or even usurps the role of the wife. Millie functions as an extension as well as a stand-in for Barbara Bush, and her role as the supportive wife who selflessly gives her "all for George" models 1950s marital iconography.

Millie's role as spousal object is brought home to the reader when she underscores her own superior ability to fulfill her role as mother in competition with Barbara Bush. Recounting that Barbara Bush was unable to tell the female puppies from the male puppy, Millie scoffs: "To think that Bar thought she was going to help me when she couldn't tell a boy from a girl!" This insufficiency when confronted with biological needs and necessities again manifests itself when Barbara Bush turns her back while the puppies receive their first shots. Millie comments: "Please note the lady who thought that she could help deliver the pups! Makes me wonder what kind of mother she was." The culmination of these claims lies in Millie's own reading of her appearance on the cover of *Life*: "I could only conclude that I was their selection for 1989 Mother of the Year." These reflections are juxtaposed by Millie's own seeming recognition of her and her offspring's status as objects, not subjects. Reflecting on her special friendship with the Bushes' granddaughter Marshall, she recounts that "on her third birthday, I gave her a puppy . . . Ranger, my only son."[36] This passage creates a strange complicity between affect as a site for subject formation and affect as the site of objectification. Because of the "special friendship" that she shares with Marshall, Millie wants to exchange a bond of affection with the child. The gift that she gives is her own child, Ranger. In that exchange, the child Marshall becomes recognized as a subject, whereas Ranger is objectified as a gift.

The book integrates such an astonishing aside seamlessly into a narrative of Millie's motherhood by incorporating it into an account of family itself as the place where affective agency stands in service to biopolitical discipline. The meaning Millie attaches to family becomes evident when she tells us about her appearance, simultaneously with the *Life* cover, in the July 1989 issue of *The Washingtonian*, where she was featured as "Our Pick as the Ugliest Dog: Millie, the White House Mutt." Although this assessment of her as homely resonates—so Millie points out—with Barbara Bush's attitudes, Millie lists the many people who came to her defense by writing fan mail and other publicity pieces, such as the one released by the office of Senator Bob Dole, whose own dog Leader extolled Millie, saying that "as first dog, Millie has set a great example for millions of American dogs. She is raising a family, doesn't stray from the yard, and does her best to keep her master in line. It's just not right for her to be hounded like this."[37] The letter explicitly ties Millie's biological reproduction—the fact that she is raising a family—to her role as an "example" for the nation ("millions of American dogs"), for whom she models discipline in her own obedience to rules ("doesn't stray from the yard"), and her ability in turn to act as a disciplining agent who tries to "keep her master in line."

The biopolitical discipline Millie exercises hinges on her double performance in the narrative as physical object and linguistic subject. Her own response to *The Washingtonian* focuses, like Leader's, on her role as a mother but reads that role as the cause of the article. She argues that the picture included with the article "was taken the very afternoon of my delivery. Show me one woman who could pass that test, lying on her side absolutely 'booney wild' (family expression for undressed) on the day she delivered six babies!"[38] Tying her appearance to her recent delivery, Millie portrays herself as exemplary for all woman, who would be unable (according to this book's aesthetic standards) to "pass the test" of looking beautiful after giving birth. The comment suggests that the act of giving birth is a hindrance to the aesthetics of motherhood: the passage brings this point home by coding nakedness through the expression "booney wild"—that is, by emphasizing that the act of giving birth is uncivilized and undisciplined ("wild") labor that does not participate in the aesthetics of nudity or the discipline of representation. Yet the passage also exercises such aesthetic discipline through the inclusion of the peculiar aside: " 'booney wild' (family expression for undressed)." Portraying biological motherhood itself as an embarrassment, the invocation of a familial phrase shifts the attention to motherhood as a cultural construct. As a cultural construct, it takes on a privileged role in that it creates its own idiom for the description of biology.

This invocation also creates the illusion that the narrative itself is part of a multilayered translation, from familiar terms into the public idiom, from dog into human terminology, from the lived experience of the real into the terms of the symbolic order. With these references, the book insistently draws attention to Millie's own role as author and to the central conceit of dog authorship. Millie describes her schooling and her ongoing relationship to textual reception and production. Before being sent to live with the Bushes, Millie's previous "owner" "sent me to school to brush up on my manners." Although this comment places Millie in the context of a gender-specific setting, the finishing school, she highlights her relationship to literacy when she mentions what "the papers" reported on any given day and recounts that she received "more than my fair share" of mail once the puppies were born. In response to those letters, the White House mail room sent out a thank-you card, which "the babies and I signed also": the card had the White House at the top, the thank-you note in the middle, and seven paw prints, one large and six small, framed on either side by the signatures of Barbara Bush and George Bush at the bottom.[39] To the extent that a signature establishes authorial subjectivity, Millie repeatedly asserts herself in these contexts as the author of her own text; as its topic, she simultaneously occupies the position of the object under discussion.[40]

What truly bears underscoring in this context is the book's classification as nonfiction. The copyright for *Millie's Book* was taken out by the Barbara Bush Foundation for Family Literacy. This foundation linked literacy with so-called family values, as the book's opening mission statement makes clear: "The mission of The Barbara Bush Foundation for Family Literacy is: 1. To support the development of family literacy programs . . . 2. To break the intergenerational cycle of illiteracy . . . 3. To establish literacy as a value in every family in America." The book itself is not sure what to do with this frame or with its conceit of Millie's authorship. On the one hand, it consistently affords Millie literacy, yet she finds it necessary to reflect at the end: "One last thing I'd better make clear. I know the Bushes love me. They told me so. But they love people more, all people. So I have written this book and the proceeds will go to help people, all people. I hope it will strengthen families and family life in our great America. The Prez used to tease Bar and tell her that if she'd 'stick with him, he'd show her the world.' And he did. The Prez told me that if I'd stick with him, he'd show me my name in a THOUSAND POINTS OF LIGHT, and he did."[41] The phrase "thousand points of light" was one that Bush frequently used in speeches and thus firmly links Millie to the president's politics. It referred to community organizations throughout the United States, such as the Bush Literacy Foundation, which were working toward the improvement of American society. In arguing that Millie's name would be inscribed in a thousand points of light, the book is making Millie herself into a volunteer for literacy education and affording her a role in the betterment of American society. Her authorship then inscribes her firmly in the project of creating a society that affirms the superiority of the human: in the end, the dog takes on a secondary role to "people, all people." Millie's own text affirms the species hierarchy in which the dog underscores the superior status of human beings. That hierarchy emphasizes biology in its hierarchical ranking of species. Yet at the same time, it makes biology an insufficient condition. In writing, "I hope it will strengthen families and family life in our great America," Millie in fact performs an interesting shift. Up to this point, she has been portraying the way in which she herself strengthens the Bushes' family life, but she now substitutes her book—"it"—for herself. The dog and the book function as stand-ins for each other in shoring up American family life. This final move undercuts the very distinction that the narrative purports to uphold—between the real (the realm of the dog) and the symbolic (reserved for human beings); it places the dog and the book in interchangeable relation to one another and suggests that, to the extent that liberal subject formation hinges on literacy, it is firmly ensconced in its relationship to the animal other that lies at its core. The narrative's end undercuts the distinctions and hierarchies it wants to affirm.

Queering Biopolitics

But what are the consequences of that slippage for our understanding of animal autobiography as a site for alternative subject and family formations? Millie's multiple subject and object positions speak to the insufficiency of mapping her onto a Marxist matrix of use and exchange value. The instability of her positions hinges on the relationships into which she enters, with the other characters in her narrative and with the reader—that is, with the real and virtual others she encounters. For Donna Haraway, these moments of encounter between human beings and other species call for an examination—as I quoted earlier—of the "underanalyzed axis of lively capital" that reveals to us the "face-to-face, body-to-body subject making across species" that force us to expand our currently limited categories of subjectivity. In this section, then, I want to explore how animal autobiographies stage moments in which human beings and animals come face to face with each other and what that encounter tells us about expanded categories of subjectivity. Revisiting the kind of encounter with dogs that Emmanuel Lévinas and Frederick Douglass used to theorize race (chapter 2), I examine the face-to-face encounter with animals from the perspective of gender. What particularly intrigues me in this context is Michel Foucault's insight that biopolitics not only regulates gender and sexuality but also becomes the domain for the formation of queer subjectivities. I draw on queer-authored case studies to explore how animal autobiographies perform two kinds of affective queering: seeing the animal as a relay between same-sex partners and crossing the species boundary. These works also present a challenge to the current implicit focus on the human that underwrites queer theory and that has recently come under pressure—for instance, in Jeffrey Cohen's puzzlement that "a critical movement predicated upon the smashing of boundary should limit itself to the small contours of human form."[42]

Millie's relation to Barbara Bush replicates a pervasive and significant trope that developed in eighteenth-century literature: the trope of the lady and the lapdog. As Laura Brown has demonstrated, "The image of the lady and the lapdog arises as a widespread literary trope at the same time as companion animals become widely evident in the bourgeois household." In these depictions, "inter-species intimacies often substitute for human ones in precisely this way in the representation of pet keeping in the eighteenth century."[43] Teresa Mangum concludes that "the dog narrator's gender, whatever it is, rarely signifies as important. Thus the dog provides a comforting substitution for the domestic heroine when she perfidiously questions the characteristics of which she is constructed: modesty, affection, submission, and loyalty." Mangum's work isolates the figure of the old dog in particular as "the canine voice of authority,"[44] but we arrive at a different account when we examine the genre in relationship to children and children's literature and see the dog as participating in and representing childhood. As Kathryn Bond Stockton has argued, the dog "is the child's companion in queerness."[45] In the case studies on which I focus, the dog stands in for the "domestic heroine" at times, but also for the heroine's children; when the dog functions as a substitute for human beings, it often mediates more than one substitutive relation. Because of this ability to facilitate different substitutive relationships and in the process to mediate different forms of intimacy, the animal's sex and gender matter.

Millie's authorship inadvertently returns sentimentality to its roots in a politically engaged gender politics in that Millie's commercial success calls into question the very parameters of the patriarchal symbolic order and challenges our understanding of subject formation. For all the ways in which Millie is disciplined and performs her own disciplining as a heteronormative subject of biopower, what we have on the cover of *Life* is a queer family romance. In Barbara Bush's account of "puppy love," the referent for the affection and for the subjectivity the article constructs is doubled. We find out from Barbara Bush that she named her dog

after a very close friend of mine, Mildred Kerr—that is *not* c-u-r, but Kerr. [Millie] was trained to be a retriever, but she's become a lover, not a hunter. We bonded immediately. She never takes her eyes off me. I never had a girl dog before. I had boy dogs all my married life. George loves Millie, but she is attached to me. I spend more time with her. I walk her at six a.m. and feed her—kibble only. She gets White House table scraps when the President slips them to her. He gives her showers—how else do you wash your dog? Every week or two we climb right in the shower with our dog. We use dog shampoo. She has her own dog bed in our bedroom. She doesn't always choose to use it, but she has one.[46]

Millie plays the roles of both a child and a woman. In turning from a hunter into a lover, she fulfills the wish that Julia Ward Howe had expressed for children to learn affection instead of aggression. But Millie is not just in the role of a child; she is also the symbolic referent for another woman, Mildred Kerr. She is named for Barbara Bush's absent friend, whom she figuratively represents and whose "close[ness]" she literalizes via her daily physical proximity and intimate insertion into the Bushes' married life. Millie seems to occupy the position of a transitional object in that she facilitates relationships that distinguish between subjects and objects but is herself neither the one nor the other. As a real object and a figurative subject, she is in between. From that position, she unsettles established patterns of subject formation and their concomitant gender paradigms. In displacing George, Millie functions as the other woman with whom mothers enter into "tender" relationships by Howe's account. Much of that tenderness seems to hinge on the dog's ability to gaze—on the fact that "she never takes her eyes off" Barbara Bush, who in turn feels "bonded" and "attached" to the dog. The encounter with Millie opens up multiple venues for affection and intimacy that exceed the narrative of heteronormative subject formation.

But theorizing the relational subjectivity that arises in the encounter between human beings and animals presents us with a problem: not only are we confronted with the iconic, heterosexual overdetermination of popular culture, but the preeminent theorists of relational subjectivity, such as Jacques Lacan, place animals and forms of subjectivity that do not conform to heterosexist iconography outside of the symbolic order, beyond legibility. Lacan initially excluded animals categorically from the first stage of subject formation: he argued that the "experience" of the mirror stage "is a privileged one for man. Perhaps there is, after all, something of the kind in other animal species. That isn't a crucial issue for us. Let us not feign any hypotheses." In his later writings, he grudgingly afforded animals participation in the mirror stage, only to exclude them from the symbolic order. Writing in the seminar on Freud's ego theory, he argued that "living animal subjects are sensitive to the image of their own kind. This is an absolutely essential point, thanks to which the whole of living creation isn't an immense orgy. But the human being has a special relation with his own image—a relation of gap, or alienating tension. That is where the possibility of the order of presence and absence, that is of the symbolic order, comes in."[47] This claim already presupposes that animals mirror only animals and that humans mirror only humans; the mirror stage relies on the precondition that the subject already recognizes itself as itself. The mirror stage is tautological in that it presupposes the kind of subject formation it is meant to exemplify—namely, human subject formation.

But what happens if we let go of that tautology? What happens if we allow the animal and the human to mirror each other? What consequences does that carry for the mirror stage and for the symbolic order? Jacques Derrida's final work before his death, "L'animal autobiographique"—to which my account of "animal autobiography" is a critique as much as an homage—locates the autobiographical animal at the disavowed core of subject formation.[48] Promising that he will speak frankly—that is, speak of naked truths in conceptualizing the modern subject—Derrida arrives via a series of puns at a point where he imagines what it would mean to appear naked in front of a cat who "has its point of view regarding me. The point of view of the absolute other; and nothing will have ever done more to make me think through this absolute alterity of the neighbor than these moments when I see myself seen naked under the gaze of a cat."[49] Mapping the cat's gaze onto the very history of subjectivity that denies the cat a gaze, he inscribes animals within an autobiographical mode of writing that founds and confounds the parameters of representational subjectivity by rewriting the mirror scene as an encounter in which the animal reflects and refracts the human subject.[50] In fact, for Derrida, the mirrored gaze of the animal becomes the privileged site at which, according to Lacan, "a relation of gap, or alienating tension" arises.[51]

However, Donna Haraway reads Derrida as himself becoming complicit with a Lacanian indifference to animals: "Somehow in all his worrying and longing, the cat was never heard from again in the long essay." Haraway explains this failure by Derrida's nudity, suggesting that "shame trumped curiosity, and that does not bode well for an autre-mondialisation," a term by which she means a different way of looking at the world.[52] The very attempt to imagine alternative subjectivities seems to fail, then, because the animal other is ultimately subsumed to the structures of human subjectivity. Haraway faults Derrida for promising to produce the animal as the subject of its own autobiography but instead making it the vehicle for his autobiography, which ties her critique back to the topography of animal autobiography that I mapped earlier.

However, I want to propose a different way of reading Derrida in conjunction with a scene from *Flush*, Virginia Woolf's 1933 best-selling animal (auto) biography of Elizabeth Barrett Browning's spaniel.[53] Woolf explores the possibilities of creating a gaze that is not objectifying; here is her description of the first encounter between Flush and Elizabeth:

> For the first time she looked him in the face. For the first time Flush looked at the lady lying on the sofa. Each was surprised. Heavy curls hung down on either side of Miss Barrett's face; large bright eyes shone out; a large mouth smiled. Heavy ears hung down on either side of Flush's face; his eyes, too, were large and bright: his mouth was wide. There was a likeness between them. As they gazed at each other each felt: Here am I—and then each felt: But how different! Hers was the pale, worn face of an invalid, cut off from air, light, freedom. His was the warm ruddy face of a young animal; instinct with health and energy. Broken asunder, yet made in the same mould, could it be that each completed what was dormant in the other? She might have been—all that; and he—But no. Between them lay the widest gulf that can separate one being from another. She spoke. He was dumb. She was woman; he was dog. Thus closely united, thus immensely divided, they gazed at each other. Then with one bound Flush sprang on to the sofa and laid himself where he was to lie for ever after—on the rug at Miss Barrett's feet.[54]

Woolf imagines that each of them, the human and the animal, has a gaze and that there is reciprocity in looking: "each was surprised." Figuring that reciprocity as one of rupture ("surprise"), Woolf nevertheless begins constructing a likeness between the human and the animal: despite being different species, they share certain physical attributes such as their curls, their eyes, and their mouth. These shared attributes amount to "a likeness": they mirror one another. That mirroring establishes a moment of reciprocity that founds subjectivity; it is in the reciprocal moment when "they gazed at each other" that each comes to articulate a subject position: "here am I." What is truly remarkable about that "here" is its displacement: it is not clear if the thinking subject is present unto him- or herself—that is, if the thinking subject is a Cartesian subject—or if instead the subject appears only in projective relationship. The end of the scene seems to bear out the first reading of the encounter in establishing a Cartesian subject: positing a "gulf" that separates the speaking human from the "dumb" animal, the scene seems to reaffirm the differences it temporarily unsettled.[55] The very attempt to imagine alternative subjectivities thus seems to fail because the animal other is ultimately subsumed to the structures of human subjectivity.

Yet the second reading I proposed, that we see Woolf as creating a subject who appears only in projective relationship with the other, would turn this scene into an encounter that engenders relational subjectivities. Rei Terada has explained that emotion itself—the feeling evoked in this encounter—has an ambiguous status when it comes to subjectivity. Rejecting the notion that emotion serves "as proof of the human subject," Terada argues that Jacques Derrida and Paul de Man "free a credible concept of emotion from a less credible scheme of subjectivity. . . . [T]he effect of this exploration is to suggest that we would have no emotions if we *were* subjects" because "auto-affection, Derrida argues, is necessarily second-order, and its secondariness both obstructs epistemology and enables emotion. Experience is experience at all only because of the self-difference of self-representation. Thus experience and subjectivity are incompatible."[56] The emotion and subjectivity we see exchanged in the gaze between Barrett Browning and her dog constructs their emotion and their subjectivity via and in the place of the other. Although the passage seems to reinscribe difference as the difference of the other, it also points to the difference of the self. If the scene points to the difference of the self, then the difference of the other in fact becomes not so much a marker of separation or of the failure to imagine an "autre-mon-dialisation" as a marker of resisting the inscription of subjectivity in a narrative of self-sufficiency. By refusing to collapse difference, the relationship between the woman and the dog enables different forms of being to persist. The woman and her dog are in a double relationship to each other, "closely united, thus immensely divided" because each represents the divisions and fractures at the heart of subjectivity itself.

Yet we may wonder how that subjectivity is gendered and, specifically, what role the animal plays in the gendering of that subjectivity, especially given Derrida's emphasis on his nudity. Alice Kuzniar's discussion of *Flush* is useful here for insisting that the gaze between human beings and animals offers an alternative to the male gaze: "The dog is therewith not a convenient substitute for a male partner but quite the opposite—a compassionate antidote to the shame suffered in a male-dominated world."[57] Derrida experiments with that shame in turning the cat's gaze onto himself. But that reversal raises a further question: Does the sex of the gazing cat matter? Derrida's cat linguistically has a sex: usually speaking generically of "le chat" in the original French, Derrida also occasionally refers to "la chatte," especially when talking about other writers' cats.[58] He glosses over the difference between the male and the female cat when he argues that neither "le chat" nor "la chatte" can ever be naked and that nudity is the defining characteristic of "l'homme." But being naked in front of a cat is not just foundational for an awareness of species; it is foundational for the gendering of subjectivity. Derrida would certainly have been aware that, as Robert Darnton has documented, "the power of cats was concentrated on the most intimate aspect of domestic life: sex. *Le chat, la chatte, le minet* mean the same thing in French slang as 'pussy' does in English, and they have served as obscenities for centuries."[59] Confronted with the cat that has a sex even if it can never be naked, man becomes masculine. Seeing the cat's gaze, Derrida discovers his naked sex. That naked sex is a social construct in that it emerges in his relationship with the animal. As the foundational site for the construction of sexual identity, the cat's gaze collapses the distinction between sex and gender and inscribes both in the relationship between human beings and animals.

Jonathan Lamb situates animal autobiography in a broader field of writing that he refers to as the "it-narrative," in which material objects speak.[60] Usefully mapping animals into complex literary genealogies, this association nonetheless fails to capture the key function of the autobiographical animal: to force the "it" into sexual definition. The encounter with the cat is foundational to the very possibilities of sexed and sexual identity. For that matter, it is only via the animal's presence in the symbolic order that gendering can occur: after all, it is only in the third-person singular that we differentiate between "he," "she," and "it"; it becomes possible only in the third person to have binary categories of gender distinction but also the very indistinguishability, the "it," of a hybridity that straddles gender and species. In order for the "I" to write itself, it needs not only the fracture of the mirror stage, but the profoundly alien "it" of the pet and the animal's presence.

The hybrid "it" of the animal also opens a new representational space that dissociates subjectivity from the structures of the symbolic order. Asking if there is "in the history of discourse, indeed of the becoming-literature of discourse, an ancient form of autobiography immune from confession, an account of the self free from any sense of confession," Derrida understands animals as both the limit for and the grounds of subjectivity and writing.[61] His invocation of confession achieves two things: it situates autobiography in its own historical development, and it draws attention to the hermeneutic codes of the genre. Derrida summons a strand in the scholarly account of autobiography that sees the genre originating in "the prodigious *Confessions* of European history . . . [that] have formed our culture of subjectivity from Augustine to Rousseau."[62] As Linda Peterson has demonstrated, that form of autobiography establishes a close link between the notion of subjectivity and a particular hermeneutics: "The English autobiography derives from a Protestant tradition of religious introspection, one that is insistently hermeneutic. By 'hermeneutic,' I mean first that the autobiography from Bunyan to Gosse has placed in the foreground the act of self-interpretation: the autobiographer's interpretation of himself and his experience. Second, I mean that English autobiographers have traditionally appropriated their patterns and principles of interpretation from biblical hermeneutics (originally from biblical typology) and that they have done so self-consciously. One might even call autobiography a 'hermeneutic' genre."[63] Attentive to this hermeneutic aspect, Derrida is invoking confession to talk about two systems of coding: the divine and the human. In calling for an autobiography beyond confessional autobiography, in imagining a third thing, a *tertium quid*, above and beyond these parameters of selfhood, Derrida questions our assumption that subjectivity is always human and bound to the symbolic order; he opens up the possibility that the animal participates in subjectivity not just as a developmental stage, but as an ongoing presence.[64]

Women's autobiographies are particularly receptive to an exploration of animal presence. As Smith and Watson argue, "Crucially, the writing and theorizing of women's lives has often occurred in texts that place an emphasis on collective processes while questioning the sovereignty and universality of the solitary self."[65] Mary Mason has suggested that "the self-discovery of female identity seems to acknowledge the real presence and recognition of another consciousness, and the disclosure of female self is linked to the identification of some 'other.'"[66] Engaged in a process of making encounter meaningful and casting that encounter as one based on reciprocity instead of domination, women's autobiographies provide a fertile ground for exploring the encounter value Haraway associates with our relationship to animals.

For an illustration of the way in which we can then reimagine the site between human and divine codes and the effect this reading has on biopolitical discipline, I turn to an animal autobiography published in 1919 by Wellesley literature professor Katharine Lee Bates, who is best known today as a poet for having written the unofficial U.S. anthem, "America the Beautiful."[67] Bates's book *Sigurd Our Golden Collie* (1919) recounts the antics of the dog she adopted with her lover, economics professor Katharine Comen, whom she refers to in the book only as "Joy-of-Life." Pointing out that they did not choose Sigurd for his pedigree—that is, for his biological features—she insists that she selected the dog because "I want a friend. Njal [Sigurd's original name] has a soul." Ascribing to the dog the spirituality usually reserved for human beings in Judeo-Christian theology, she includes the dog in an order that is simultaneously human and divine. In describing Sigurd, she creates a deep sense of reciprocity that stands in defiance of order and discipline. Bates describes how, "now that we realized not only that we had adopted Sigurd but that Sigurd had adopted us, we entered into an ever deepening enjoyment of our dog." This sense of mutual adoption unsettles the relationship between the members of this family: it is no longer clear that Bates and Comen are the surrogate mothers and Sigurd the adopted child when a reversal of disciplinary roles takes place. Bates repeatedly emphasizes her and Comen's role as educators and the antidiscipline and counterpedagogy Sigurd brings to their lives: "Be it understood that we were teachers, writers, servants of causes, boards, committees, mere professional women, with too little leisure for the home we loved. Had our hurried days given opportunity for the fine art of mothering, we would have cherished a child instead of a collie, but Sigurd throve on neglect and saved us from turning into plaster images by making light of all our serious concerns. No academic dignities impressed his happy irreverence." Instead of portraying the home as a prime scene of biopolitical discipline, Bates portrays it as one where affection ("the home we loved") takes other forms. Although the dog inhabits a childlike role, she insists that the dog himself "throve on neglect" and in turn makes light of his caregivers' "academic dignities." The disciplining agency is profoundly unsettled by the dog's presence, and a reciprocity emerges by which the dog has as much of an impact on the women's lives as they have on his.

In fact, discipline itself gives way to a simulation of discipline: "Sigurd loved nothing better than make-believe discipline." The women become complicit in this staging of fictive discipline: "Apart from our enjoyment of his crimes, it was difficult to punish him, because his sunny spirit turned every fresh experience into fun."[68]

That excess becomes a mark of the text itself when Bates reflects on Sigurd's relationship to literature:

In pursuance of the theory that the immortal nonsense songs [of *Mother Goose*] were written by Oliver Goldsmith—this is what is known as Literary Research—I had obtained leave from a Boston librarian, . . . to take home for comparison with an accumulation of other texts a unique copy. . . . I carried the book home as carefully as if it had been a nest of humming-bird's eggs. As I used it that evening at my desk, I propped it up at a fair distance from any possible spatter of ink. Then I . . . turned to a good-night romp with the Volsung [Sigurd]. We tried several new games. He was a failure as Wolf at the Door, . . . nor did he shine as Mother Hubbard's dog. . . . So we practiced in secret for a few minutes on "a poetic recital" of Hickory Dickory Dock and then came forth to electrify the household. Taking a central seat, I repeated those talismanic syllables, at whose sound Sigurd jumped upon me, climbed up till his forepaws rested on the high top of the chair, in graphic illustration of the way the mouse ran up the clock, emitted an explosive bark when, shifting parts at a sudden pinch, he became for an instant the clock striking one, and then scrambled down with alacrity, a motion picture of the retreating mouse. This was no small intellectual exercise for a collie. . . . His mental energies had revived by morning and apparently he wanted to review his *Hickory Dickory Dock*, for he was in my study earlier than I and there . . . he must needs pick out *Mother Goose*, even that unique copy *de luxe*. When I came in, there was Sigurd outstretched on his favorite rug, beside my desk, with the book between his forepaws, ecstatically engaged in chewing off one corner. . . . We were too keenly concerned over the injury done to remember to punish him, but no further punishment than our obvious distress was needed. Never again would Sigurd touch a book or anything resembling a book. He had discovered, once for all, that he had no taste for literature.[69]

Bates stages her research as a quest for authorship: she is trying to determine a link between a text and an author—that is, between a literary object and its purported biographical, writerly subject. To establish that link, she pours over textual copies and tries to establish a literary comparison. These exercises are focused on the content of the books, but they also have to contend with the book's presence as a material, literal object. As an object, the book initially seems markedly different from its content: it shares none of the "immortal" qualities of the texts but is instead as fragile as "a nest of humming-bird's eggs." With this reference, Bates juxtaposes symbolic content and biophysical existence. But the text does not uphold as much as repeatedly confound their relationship. She goes on to describe how carefully she treats the book as object and how at the end of the day she turns to an enactment of the literary text—an exercise of giving the text biophysical reality. After a "poetic recital," Sigurd and Bates enact the story of Hickory Dickory Dock. Bates argues that this was a significant "intellectual exercise" for the dog.[70] But she resists inscribing Sigurd in the intellectual framework set by humans. Although he performs the text, he then chews up the book without any sense of its value as an object or as a text. For Sigurd, the book marks pure physical pleasure—he "ecstatically" chews on the cover. Sigurd himself emerges in this account as a real, literal animal who cannot be subsumed to symbolic representation. His chewing the book makes his literal, physical presence palpable—and yet it is a physical presence that Bates achieves by means of literary description. Through this portrayal, she creates for Sigurd an in-between position: he is a literal, physical, real dog who exceeds the parameters of literary and a linguistic representation, *and* he participates in the realm of the literary enterprise that is her own book. He functions as a transitional object in the sense that he makes possible the distinction between objects and subjects, but he himself does not fall exclusively into either realm.

Bates doubles the autobiographical subject: whereas the prose pieces of her work are written in her own first-person voice, she includes a poem written in Sigurd's voice.

SIGURD'S MEDIATIONS IN THE CHURCH-PORCH

The gaze of a dog is blind
To splendors of summit and sky,
Ocean and isle,

But never a painter shall find
The beautiful more than I
in my lady's smile.

The thought of a dog is dim.
Not even a wag he deigns
to the wisest book.
Philosophy dwells for him
In loving the law that reigns
In voice, in look.

The heart of a dog is meek.
He places his utter trust
In a mortal grace,
Contented his God to seek
In a creature framed of dust
With a dreaming face.

The human is our divine.
In the porch of the church, I pray
For a rustling dress,
For those dear, swift steps of thine,
Whose path is my perfect way
Of holiness.[71]

Speaking from a liminal position, on the "porch" of the church, the dog cannot enter into aesthetic relationships directly—he cannot see the "splendors of summit and sky." Instead, his gaze is directed toward a different kind of aesthetic, the encounter with the other. His appreciation of the "beautiful" in "my lady's smile" exceeds the parameters of human artistic appreciation—he finds more beauty in this encounter than "a painter" would. The second stanza compares this aesthetic appreciation to intellectual knowledge. Although the dog's thought is "dim" and he lacks interest in "the wisest book," he experiences an affective relationship to the "voice" and "look" of his beloved. That affective relationship takes on its own capacity to discipline: it is in affect, "in loving," that he experiences "law." That law is simultaneously secular and religious for him: he seeks a version of God in the beloved human who becomes his "divine." Through this relationship, the dog undergoes a transformation: the poem's first stanza begins with the reference to "a dog" but then shifts to allow the dog to voice his subjectivity in the first person, lyrical "I."

Speaking in the voice and from the perspective of the dog, the writer of the poem, Bates, is able to express a love that can be sanctified only by crossing species barriers and by reimagining the queer family through the heterosexist iconography of confessional autobiography. Yet the confession here shatters the very parameters of sacred confinement and places us closer to Derrida's fantasized position of a subjectivity that exceeds the symbolic as well as the divine order. The condemnations of dog love found in Leviticus and enacted at Plymouth Plantation have given way to a different form of "puppy love." Functioning simultaneously as a figure for closeted love and an icon of queer affection, the dog is both the stand-in for the beloved and the object of a shared affection. The dog is the lover and the beloved, the subject and the object of puppy love. Putting herself in the position of the dog who is gazing at her lover, Bates turns puppy love into a representational scheme that exceeds both the heterosexual matrix and the symbolic order. At one point, Bates recalls that she asked Sigurd, "Whose dog are you, Gold of Ophir?" and that "Sigurd, with an impartial flourish of his tail, lay down exactly between us."[72] Bates initially addresses Sigurd as an object in drawing on his name's legendary link to the "Gold of Ophir." But Sigurd defies characterization as a possession. In lying down "exactly between" Bates and Comen, he indicates that he is a third partner in their relationship. Inhabiting a double position as an anthropomorphized subject and a fetishized object, Sigurd exceeds both classifications.

The dog facilitates a newly intimate relationship between Bates and Comen, as the book's dedication demonstrates: the book is "inscribed to the one whom Sigurd loved best." Read in the context of the passage describing Sigurd's impartiality to the two women, that means the book is inscribed to both Bates herself and to Comen. The dog's love is in fact not preferential—there is no one person whom he loves best—but relational: he loves both Bates and Comen and inserts himself into their relationship. These passages indicate that Sigurd inhabits a position where the "encounter value" between the women and the dog is multiple: each has a relationship to the animal; they jointly share a bond with the dog and newly experience their bond to each other through the dog.

As "things" with which we engage affectively, pets suffer from a double animation—as commodities, as creatures—that situates them at the core of modern biopolitics. In fact, they become exemplary "things" in the sense that they realize the central fantasy of commodity culture, the fantasy that things have a life of their own beyond their relationship with the desiring subject. If object relations structure our sense of subjectivity, then the pet—as the ultimate, doubly animated thing—occupies a physical and figurative position beyond and at the very core of our subjectivity; it both exemplifies and unsettles liberal subject formation. Animal autobiographies make visible structures of biopolitical domination, and they enable us to recognize the mutual dependency of constructions of gender on constructions of species. Resisting the demarcation between subjects and objects, they explore alternative forms of being that hinge on relationships—that is, forms that do not exist a priori as stable categories, but that are themselves subject to change and development. Exploring structures of objectification, they are equally invested in examining how and whether representation functions as an exclusively human practice or as a shared site of cross-species encounter. Although we might object that animal autobiographies tell us nothing about "real" animals, they in fact complicate what we might mean by the terms *real* and *animals*. By tying the real to the symbolic, they highlight that our desire for "the real" is itself subject to representation. Nevertheless, they also open up a space for the entry of the "real" animal into our representational schemes. They enable us to recognize that our representational relationship to animals is itself always going to impact how we perceive of the real or the symbolic. Replacing the Cartesian subject with forms of agency based on relationships, animal autobiographies create a space for different forms of becoming. That becoming extends to the development of individual subjectivity, which undergoes perpetual change as its affective relationships shift, and to the emergence of new social possibilities, such as the queer family. It teaches us how to read Millie against the grain of her commercial exploitation and to see puppy love as a means of questioning the heteronormative and anthropocentric subject formation it aims to establish. Animal representations not only inhabit the interstitial site on which the biopolitical depends but also allow us to imagine an outside to the totalizing aspirations of biopower.

EPILOGUE

From many vantage points, "biopolitical subjectivity" is a contradiction in terms: in current critical accounts, biopolitics is about populations, sovereignty, and violence, but most often not about subjectivity. My book has tried to offer a corrective of this view in two senses: first, in linking the emergence of biopolitics historically to the emergence of liberal subjectivity and, second, by suggesting ways in which subjectivity is the battleground as well as the by-product of biopolitics. As its by-product, subjectivity both affirms and undermines biopolitics, just as biopolitics affirms and undermines certain notions of the subject. The end result of these deliberations is that we need to reconsider what we might mean by subjectivity not just as an object of critique, but also as a range of possibilities. As my book title announces, my focus of interest here is not biopolitical theory and its concerns with populations per se. Rather, I have examined the mediating role of "biopolitical subjectivity" in American literature and culture—and vice versa, the impact of animal representations on our understanding of biopolitics and subjectivity.

Margot Norris has pointed out that literary studies entered the interdisciplinary field of animal studies belatedly.[1] Although that belated arrival has recently been made up for by the wealth, in terms of quantity and quality, of publications in literary animal studies, my book has been suggesting ways in which literary animal studies not only contributes to but also critically intervenes in and reshapes the field of animal studies, first and foremost perhaps by challenging the field's sense of its own progressive telos. Literary—or, more broadly, cultural—animal studies challenges monolithic accounts by which the early modern period instated a human/animal divide that was unchallenged before Bentham's concern with suffering and Darwin's account of evolution. The narrative I have been mapping tracks an ongoing dialogue about interspecies relationships, where distinctions between as well as connections among species are a strategy for the exercise of biopower and a tactic for exercising other forms of biopolitics.

I have been suggesting that we might trace a set of relationships in which we do not know—a priori or, for that matter, a posteriori—what or who "the animal" or "the human" is because such definitions emerge in a complex matrix of intimacies and representations; that is, they enable us to abandon the realm of ontological difference and locate us productively in the terrain of epistemological uncertainty. To the three ways in which "recent histories of animals" have approached their enterprise—namely, "intellectual history, humane history, and holistic history"[2]—this book adds history of sexuality. Animal love forms an affective spectrum that connects bestiality with puppy love and presses us beyond the human–animal dyad in ways that encourage us to specify—though not, I would insist, to taxonomize—how we are seeing the partners of the relationship. Part of the issue here is that these partners are socially constructed: the structure of witnessing that is integral to bestiality makes these relationships public in that we are talking not only about the direct partners of the (sexual) relationship, but also about the witnesses to these affective encounters: the White House Press Corps' documentation of the new dog's arrival at the White House in 2009 is paradigmatic of the strange publics we construct around animal intimacies. That public dimension is an upshot not only of the legal cases, but also of animal representations more broadly speaking: we are implicated in these affective relationships.

Those affective relationships, as I have described them, branch into the ugly, in Sianne Ngai's sense of the term: they place us in a terrain of affective and political "equivocality." In fact, those ugly feelings are precisely the meeting ground between the political and the aesthetic: Ngai points out that, with the exception of "theories of modern sovereignty and the state, it is the discourse of philosophical aesthetics, rather than that of political philosophy or economy, in which emotions have traditionally played the most pivotal role." One of the examples she singles out for analysis is the "American cultural discourse that from the antebellum period forward has found it compelling to imagine the racialized subject as an excessively emotional and expressive subject (a situation in which the affect I call 'animatedness' becomes especially problematic)," particularly because that concept becomes the focus of "various kinds of symbolic struggle." For Ngai, a particular challenge lies in understanding "the politically charged predicament of suspended agency from which all those ugly feelings ensue."[3]

We need to rethink our practices of textual engagement if we are going to account for our affective relations, including our ugly feelings, with animals. This book has aimed to develop a theory of embodied reading that argues for the importance of animal representations in American literature. It also claims that the numerous and various presence of animals constitutes a way of negotiating the conditions of subjectivity under biopolitics. It offers a way to understand subjectivity in relation to embodiment and in relation to the discourse formations that abstract and concretize such embodiment. By "animal representations," then, I do not mean just instances in which an animal appears in a text. More important I mean that animals appear in texts as disruptive presences that challenge our understanding of textual significance and figuration. "Animal representations" are an interface where the literal and symbolic meet and unsettle the terrains of modern taxonimization. That is what my Latinate title *Animalia Americana* playfully wants to capture.

The *Oxford English Dictionary* defines *animalia* as "the kingdom of living organisms that comprises the animals, now usually including only metazoans but formerly also including protozoans."[4] But, of course, what has interested me is precisely the second element of this definition: that these classifications and categories are unstable and that literature marks and produces that instability. In developing that analysis, I have assembled a menagerie and written a bestiary. But we know that menageries grow unwieldy and that bestiaries always call for further additions. One recurrent call in animal studies is for the field to imagine itself beyond its current expanse: "Any attempts to wrestle with our questions of ethics and politics and animality will have to move beyond our comfortable companions of cats and dogs and contemplate what it means to become familiar with the full (or, at least, with an expanded) spectrum of *animot*," says Richard Nash.[5] I hope that my book opens up the possibility for such further engagements, but I also wonder about the sense that to talk about animals, one has to talk about a "full . . . spectrum." Although such a call is aimed at generating a sense of differentiation and diversity, it nevertheless seems in danger of replicating a universalizing impulse. It seems to me that the "spectrum" we should be after is understanding the complexities of intimacies, subjectivities, and encounters. That approach can remain attentive not just to its inclusions, but also to its exclusions, and it can leave open a space for alterity that is not violently abjected nor systemically incorporated, but viably "other."

As Jeffrey Cohen has suggested, animals "function as reference and reflection, insubstantial allegories in which we discover ourselves. Yet such a transformation of animal bodies into merely human semblance ignores what might occur *between* animals and humans, what processes, desires, identities might circulate in the interspace where animal and human differences come together or come apart."[6] In ignoring that interspace, we are missing a crucial part of our cultural history, its normative mechanisms as well as its more radical possibilities. But what are those possibilities? Gilles Deleuze and Félix Guattari differentiate between three types of animals: the "individuated animals, family pets, sentimental, Oedipal animals each with its own petty history," which they distinguish from "animals as they are treated in the great divine myths, in such a way as to extract from them series or structures, archetypes or models," and then finally the third kind, "demonic animals, pack or affect animals that form a multiplicity, a becoming, a population, a tale."[7] I worry that the celebratory strand in this approach misses some of the complexities of what it means to "become animal" when you are a slave and when "becoming a population" is a lived experience of biopower. Instead of seeing the becoming-animal as a telos, I have picked up on another suggestion that Deleuze and Guattari make: although they focus on this third category, the becoming-animal, they indicate that an animal can be "treated in all three ways."[8] That mobility of registers seems to me truest to Anat Pick's reminder that "championing ulterior subjectivities does not in itself generate a new ethics if the question of power is left unaddressed."[9]

This project, then, sets out to unsettle constructed divides that hold philosophy apart from embodied life, that support biopolitical systematization, and that reproduce normative categories of gender, family, and sexuality.[10]

The challenge of these constructions is subsumed under the diverse inter-disciplinary inquiries emerging as "animal studies" that question the separa-tion of humans from (other) animals. This order of things has had profound social consequences in terms of racial hierarchy, social discipline, human procreation, domestic arrangements, population management—that is, for the activities Foucault describes as "biopolitics." This book locates the intersections of these activities in the terrain of animal representation and meditates on the indebtedness of human feeling to animal embodiment. But that indebtedness is also a key biopolitical strategy dedicated to the stra-tegically incomplete expulsion of behaviors and affects that define human beings and animals. That double bind has significant consequences, rang-ing from the creation of the abject body to the generation of alternative subject formations.

NOTES

Introduction

1. Sandra Sobieraj Westfall, "Michelle Obama: White House Dog Coming Soon!" *People Magazine*, February 25, 2009.

2. See the blog on "Bo Obama" at http://obama-dog.com/blog/about-bo-obama.html, accessed August 1, 2011.

3. Christina Bellantoni, reporting for the *Washington Times*, "President Obama's New Dog—Bo Obama Arrives at White House," available on YouTube at http://www.youtube.com/watch?v=-YAVP7JseLQ, my transcription.

4. For recent articles that survey the larger field of animal studies, see Elisa Aaltola, "Philosophy and Animal Studies: Calarco, Castricano, and Diamond," *Society and Animals* 17 (2009): 279–286; Kenneth Shapiro and Margo DeMello, "The State of Human–Animal Studies," *Society and Animals* 18 (2010): 307–318.

5. I borrow the phrase "the question of the animal" from Paola Cavalieri, *The Animal Question: Why Nonhuman Animals Deserve Human Rights*, trans. Catherine Woollard (New York: Oxford University Press, 2001), and Cary Wolfe, ed., *Zootologies: The Question of the Animal* (Minneapolis: University of Minnesota Press, 2003). See also Matthew Calarco, "Thinking Through Animals: Reflections on the Ethical and Political Stakes of the Question of the Animal in Derrida," *Oxford Literary Review* 29, no. 1 (2007): 1–15; Timothy Clark, "The Challenge of the Meta-contextual: Henry Lawson's 'Telling Mrs Baker' (1901) and Some Animal Questions for Australia," *Oxford Literary Review* 29, no. 1 (2007): 16–36.

6. The two pieces that were immediately canonized are Jacques Derrida, "The Animal That Therefore I Am (More to Follow)," *Critical Inquiry* 28, no. 2 (2002): 369–418, and

Jacques Derrida, "And Say the Animal Responded?" in Wolfe, ed., *Zoontologies*, 121–146. See also the following works by Jacques Derrida: "L'animal que donc je suis (à suivre)," in Marie-Louise Mallet, ed., *L'animal autobiographique: Autour de Jacques Derrida*, 251–301 (Paris: Galilée, 1999); "Violence Against Animals," in *For What Tomorrow: A Dialogue*, 62–77 (Stanford: Stanford University Press, 2004); *The Animal That Therefore I Am*, trans. David Willis, ed. John D. Caputo (New York: Fordham University Press, 2008); and *The Beast & the Sovereign*, vol. 1 (Chicago: University of Chicago Press, 2009).

7. I am using the term *erasing* here in the post-structuralist sense of *sous rature*; I do not mean the more colloquial sense of "doing away with" the subject, although post-structuralism has certainly been read that way, as Rei Terada sums up: "Much of the secondary literature on poststructuralist theory assumes, first, that this theory does not have an account of emotion, and, second, that evidence of its own emotion implies its own nonbelief in the human subject" (Rei Terada, *Feeling in Theory: Emotion after the "Death of the Subject"* [Cambridge, Mass.: Harvard University Press, 2001], 3). Derrida makes clear that the subject he is taking issue with is the Cartesian subject, which uses logocentrism to articulate its cohesion and to posit an absolute distinction between "the" human and "the" animal. Derrida is not arguing for a dissolution of distinctions, but for their proliferation in order to create space for viable forms of alterity; see, for instance, Derrida, "Violence Against Animals."

8. Peter Singer, *Animal Liberation* (New York: Avon Books, 1977). Taking issue with Singer, John Simons has argued for the importance of emphasizing difference; see John Simons, *Animal Rights and the Politics of Literary Representation* (Houndmills, U.K.: Palgrave, 2002), 23.

9. Singer, *Animal Liberation*, 9. For a critique of the term *speciesism*, see Cora Diamond, *The Realistic Spirit: Wittgenstein, Philosophy, and the Mind* (Cambridge, Mass.: MIT Press, 1991), 319.

10. Jeremy Bentham, *Introduction to the Principles of Morals and Legislation*, ed. J. H. Burns and H. L. A. Hart (Oxford: Clarendon Press, 1996), 283. The issue of pain was central to Victorian animal activism. See Lucy Bending, *The Representation of Bodily Pain in Late Nineteenth-Century English Culture* (Oxford: Clarendon Press, 2000); Coral Lansbury, *Old Brown Dog* (Madison: University of Wisconsin Press, 1985); James Turner, *Reckoning with the Beast: Animals, Pain, and Humanity in the Victorian Mind* (Baltimore: Johns Hopkins University Press, 1980). Humane societies increasingly relied on accounts of animals as having feelings not only in physical ways, but also in emotional ways; they argued "that animals were subjects in their own right, capable of not only pain but also fear, misery, memory and mourning" (Teresa Mangum, "Dog Years, Human Fears," in Nigel Rothfels, ed., *Representing Animals* [Bloomington: Indiana University Press, 2002], 37).

11. It is important to note, as Lori Gruen points out, that Peter Singer is often thought of as the " 'father of the modern animal rights movement,' " but that his "preference utilitarian view," as she calls it, "applies to all beings who have preferences" but "actually has

nothing to do with animals 'rights' per se" (Lori Gruen, *Ethics and Animals: An Introduction* [Cambridge: Cambridge University Press, 2011], 34). The issue of animal rights took foreground with Tom Regan's work: see Tom Regan, *The Case for Animal Rights* (Berkeley: University of California Press, 1983).

12. Cass R. Sunstein and Martha C. Nussbaum, eds., *Animal Rights: Current Debates and New Directions* (Oxford: Oxford University Press, 2004).

13. Richard A. Epstein, "Animals as Objects, or Subjects, of Rights," in Sunstein and Nussbaum, eds., *Animal Rights*, 158.

14. Richard A. Posner, "Animal Rights: Legal, Philosophical, and Pragmatic Perspectives," in Sunstein and Nussbaum, eds., *Animal Rights*, 65. Epstein similarly "rejects the proposition that the creation of rights for animals is a logical extension of the creation of full rights for women and slaves" (Epstein, "Animals as Objects, or Subjects, of Rights," 143–144).

15. Epstein, "Animals as Objects, or Subjects, of Rights," 143.

16. Steven Wise, "Animal Rights, One Step at a Time," in Sunstein and Nussbaum, eds., *Animal Rights*, 25. As Simon Lumsden has argued, "Despite what are sometimes the good intentions of this type of theory, by for example extending rights to animals and demanding the acknowledgement of nonhuman animal interests, the way such theories conceive values, norms and human reason itself does little to undermine the ontological division between rational animals and natural animals," which Lumsden proposes to do by examining "habit" as challenging the spirit–nature division and the exclusivity of the space of reason as the determining domain of norms (Simon Lumsden, "Habit, Reason, and the Limits of Normativity," *SubStance* 37, no. 3 [2008], 189, 197).

17. Diana Fuss, "Introduction: Human, All Too Human," in Diana Fuss, ed., *Human, All Too Human* (New York: Routledge, 1996), 1.

18. Cary Wolfe, "Human, All Too Human: 'Animal Studies' and the Humanities," *PMLA* 124, no. 2 (2009), 568.

19. A particularly fruitful discussion has emerged around the question of vulnerability, which takes issue with an ethics- and rights-based approach to contractualism and reciprocity. See Judith Butler, *Precarious Life: The Powers of Mourning and Violence* (London: Verso, 2004); Cora Diamond, "The Difficulty of Reality and the Difficulty of Philosophy," in Stanley Cavell, Cora Diamond, John McDowell, Ian Hacking, and Cary Wolfe, *Philosophy and Animal Life*, 43–90 (New York: Columbia University Press, 2008); Anat Pick, *Creaturely Poetics: Animality and Vulnerability in Literature and Film* (New York: Columbia University Press, 2011).

20. Terada, *Feeling in Theory*, 4, 21, emphasis in original.

21. Ralph Acampora has criticized "a certain affective/somatic deficit in animal ethics" and has developed his model of intersomaticity in response. This model departs from the feminist care ethic envisioned by Josephine Donovan and Carol Adams in that it sees conviviality as a "(pre-)moral texture" (Ralph Acampora, *Corporal Compassion: Animal Ethics and Philosophy of Body* [Pittsburgh: University of Pittsburgh

Press, 2006], 74, 73). See also Josephine Donovan and Carol J. Adams, eds., *Beyond Animal Rights: A Feminist Caring Ethic for the Treatment of Animals* (New York: Continuum,1996).

22. Richard W. Bulliet, *Hunters, Herders, and Hamburgers: The Past and Future of Human–Animal Relationships* (New York: Columbia University Press, 2005), 3.

23. Gary Francione, "You Hypocrites!" *New Scientist Archive* 186, no. 2502 (2005), 52.

24. Kari Weil, "A Report on the Animal Turn," *differences* 21, no. 2 (2010), 4.

25. Ibid., 13.

26. Lorraine Daston and Gregg Mitman, "Introduction," in Lorraine Daston and Gregg Mitman, eds., *Thinking with Animals: New Perspectives on Anthropomorphism* (New York: Columbia University Press, 2005), 11.

27. Weil, "A Report on the Animal Turn," 16.

28. Cary Wolfe, *What Is Posthumanism?* (Minneapolis: University of Minnesota Press, 2010), 99.

29. Michael Lundblad, "From Animal Studies to Animality Studies," *PMLA* 124, no. 2 (2009), 498.

30. This notion of a separation or chasm between the human and the animal is pervasive and takes one of its many recent forms in Giorgio Agamben's sense that there is a "central emptiness, the hiatus that—within man—separates man and animal" (Giorgio Agamben, *The Open: Man and Animal* [Stanford: Stanford University Press, 2004], 93). Agamben's work in *The Open* participates in one strand of current theory in that it ultimately locates "the animal" within "the human," as does Gilles Deleuze and Félix Guattari's notion of a deterritorialization that amounts to a becoming aware of the animal within the human (Eric Santner's notion of the "creaturely" can be read along these lines as well). For this critique of Agamben, Deleuze, and Guattari, see Weil, "A Report on the Animal Turn," 12; Donna Haraway, *When Species Meet* (Minneapolis: University of Minnesota Press, 2008), 27–30.

31. In suggesting that posthumanism is emerging as an alternative to animal studies, I do not mean to overlook or obscure the fact that the two areas of inquiry have developed in relation to one another; an essay that is important for their shared and respective genealogies is Donna Haraway, "A Manifesto for Cyborgs: Science, Technology, and Socialist Feminism in the 1980s," *Socialist Review* 80 (1985): 65–108.

32. N. Katherine Hayles, *How We Became Posthuman: Virtual Bodies in Cybernetics, Literature, and Informatics* (Chicago: University of Chicago Press, 1999). Other important theorizations of the term *posthuman* around that time include Neil Badmington, *Posthumanism* (New York: Palgrave, 2000); Neil Badmington, "Theorizing Posthumanism," *Cultural Critique* 53 (2003): 10–27; and Elaine Graham, *Representations of the Post/Human: Monsters, Aliens, and Others in Popular Culture* (Manchester, U.K.: Manchester University Press, 2002). Marianne deKoven reads the current interest in animals as part of a posthumanist turn in the academy; see Marianne deKoven, "Guest Column: Why Animals Now?" *PMLA* 124, no. 2 (2009): 361–369.

33. Peter Stallybrass and Allon White, *The Politics and Poetics of Transgression* (Ithaca: Cornell University Press, 1986), 192.

34. Hayles, *How We Became Posthuman*, xiv.

35. I am not alone in that interest. There has been a turn to the animal in posthumanist scholarship—for instance, in books published in the Posthumanities series by the University of Minnesota Press; nevertheless, the technological strand remains a defining one in posthumanist inquiry. I am also persuaded by David Willis's argument that bodies are themselves a form of *techne* (David Wills, *Dorsality: Thinking Back Through Technology and Politics* [Minneapolis: University of Minnesota Press, 2008]), but I still want to differentiate them from the modern technologies on which much posthumanist analysis focuses

36. The *Oxford English Dictionary* defines the Latin prefix *inter-* as "denoting 'Between or among other things or persons; between the parts of, in the intervals of, or in the midst of, something; together *with*; between times or places, at intervals, here and there" (*OED Online*, June 2011, at http://www.oed.com/view/Entry/97516).

37. Pick, *Creaturely Poetics*, 2–3.

38. Ibid., 11, emphasis in original.

39. Michael Donnelly, "On Foucault's Uses of the Notion of 'Biopower,' " in T. J. Armstrong, ed., *Michel Foucault, Philosopher: International Conference in Paris, 9,10, 11 January 1988* (New York: Routledge, 1992), 199–200.

40. Michel Foucault, *The History of Sexuality*, trans. Robert Hurley, 1st American ed. (New York: Pantheon Books, 1978), 139, emphasis in original.

41. See Nancy Armstrong and Warren Montag, "The Future of the Human: An Introduction," *differences* 20, nos. 2–3 (2009), 4.

42. Nicole Shukin, *Animal Capital: Rendering Life in Biopolitical Times* (Minneapolis: University of Minnesota Press, 2009), 11.

43. Although affect and feeling have private dimensions, recent scholarship has emphasized their public functions; see, for example, Glenn Hendler, *Public Sentiments: Structures of Feeling in Nineteenth-Century American Literature* (Chapel Hill: University of North Carolina Press, 2001).

44. See Cary Wolfe's talk "Humans and Animals in a Biopolitical Frame," given at the University of North Carolina, Chapel Hill, April 11, 2011 (at http://englishcomplit.unc.edu/node/888), which is connected to his forthcoming book *Before the Law: Humans and Other Animals in a Biopolitical Frame* (Chicago: University of Chicago Press, 2012).

45. I do not make that comment in order to dismiss the work of Carol Adams and others working in a feminist care approach to animal studies, but to point to the ongoing marginalization of the questions and concerns they raise.

46. Only one other monograph—Nicole Shukin's *Animal Capital*—creates such an intersection between animal studies and biopolitical theory, but her focus on geographies of food production and consumption significantly differs from my emphasis on affect and subjectivity.

47. A brief sample of recent work on biopower and biopolitics includes: Donnelly, "On Foucault's Uses of the Notion of 'Biopower'"; Ellen K. Feder, "The Dangerous Individual('s) Mother: Biopower, Family, and the Production of Race," *Hypatia* 22, no. 2 (2007): 60–78; Real Fillion, "Moving Beyond Biopower: Hardt and Negri's Postfoucauldian Speculative Philosophy of History," *History and Theory* 44 (2005): 47–72; Bruce Jennings, "The Liberalism of Life: Bioethics in the Face of Biopower," *Raritan* 22, no. 4 (2003): 132–146; Brett Levinson, "Biopolitics and Duopolies," *diacritics* 35, no. 2 (2005): 65–75; Achille Mbembe, "Necropolitics," *Public Culture* 15, no. 1 (2003): 11–40; Ladelle McWhorter, "Sex, Race, and Biopower: A Foucauldian Genealogy," *Hypatia* 19, no. 3 (2004): 38–62; Andrew Norris, "Introduction: Giorgio Agamben and the Politics of the Living Dead," in Andrew Norris, ed., *Politics, Metaphysics, and Death: Essays on Giorgio Agamben's "Homo Sacer,"* 1–30 (Durham, N.C.: Duke University Press, 2005); Julian Reid, "Life Struggles: War, Discipline, and Biopolitics in the Thought of Michel Foucault," *Social Text* 86, no. 1 (2006): 127–152; Gregory Tomso, "Viral Sex and the Politics of Life," *South Atlantic Quarterly* 107, no. 2 (2008): 265–285; and Ewa Plonowska Ziarek, "Bare Life on Strike: Notes on the Biopolitics of Race and Gender," *South Atlantic Quarterly* 107, no. 1 (2008): 89–105. This list is meant to be suggestive and by no means exhaustive.

48. For historical overviews of American exceptionalism, see Jack P. Greene, *The Intellectual Construction of America: Exceptionalism and Identity from 1492 to 1800* (Chapel Hill: University of North Carolina Press, 1993), and Deborah L. Madsen, *American Exceptionalism* (Edinburgh: Edinburgh University Press, 1998). Celebratory accounts of American exceptionalism in its current form emerged in response to the Cold War and reached their heyday in the 1950s with the publication of works such as Daniel J. Boorstin, *The Genius of American Politics* (Chicago: University of Chicago Press, 1953); Louis Hartz, *The Liberal Tradition in America: An Interpretation of American Political Thought Since the Revolution* (New York: Harcourt Brace, 1955): David Morris Potter, *People of Plenty; Economic Abundance and the American Character* (Chicago: University of Chicago Press, 1954); and Frank Tannenbaum, *The American Tradition in Foreign Policy* (Norman: University of Oklahoma Press, 1955). After the Vietnam War, the close association between American exceptionalism and foreign policy sparked disagreement about the extent to which American scholarship needed to divest itself of its own exceptionalist bias. Gene Wise's essay "'Paradigm Dramas' in American Studies" brought American exceptionalism to the forefront of critical consciousness and changed it from an object of celebration to a category of critique. Writing in 1979, Wise observed that the symbol–myth–image school that had given American studies coherence since the 1940s was giving way as scholars challenged its all-male, all-white configuration (Gene Wise, "'Paradigm Dramas' in American Studies: A Cultural and Institutional History of the Movement," *American Quarterly* 31, no. 3 [1979]: 293–337). Although the national paradigm was still largely in tact at the time, Wise anticipated that the field would open up to transnational scholarship. Against opposition from social scientists David Bell, Seymour

Martin Lipset, and Byron Shafer, historians Carl Degler, Ian Tyrell, Sean Wilentz, Eric Foner, and Akira Iriye argued against exceptionalism and for a transnational approach to historiography. See Daniel Bell, "'American Exceptionalism' Revisited: The Role of Civil Society," *Public Interest* 95 (1989): 38–56; Carl N. Degler, "In Pursuit of American History," *American Historical Review* 92, no. 1 (February 1987): 1–12; Eric Foner, ed., *The New American History* (Philadelphia: Temple University Press, 1990); Akira Iriye and Warren I. Cohen, eds., *The United States and Japan in the Postwar World* (Lexington: University Press of Kentucky, 1989); Seymour Martin Lipset, "A Unique People in an Exceptional Country," *Society* 28 (1990): 4–13; Byron E. Shafer, *Is America Different? A New Look at American Exceptionalism* (Oxford: Clarendon Press, 1991); Ian Tyrell, "American Exceptionalism in an Age of International History," *American Historical Review* 96 (1991): 1031–1055; and Sean Wilentz, "Against Exceptionalism: Class Consciousness and the American Labor Movement, 1790–1920," *International Labor and Working Class History* 26 (1984): 1–24. The 1990–1991 Gulf War fueled discussions of exceptionalism as a political force; see, for instance, Robert Vitalis, "Black Gold, White Crude: An Essay on American Exceptionalism, Hierarchy, and Hegemony in the Gulf," *Diplomatic History* 26, no. 2 (2002): 185–213. Work such as the essays collected in Amy Kaplan and Donald E. Peace, eds., *Cultures of United States Imperialism* (Durham, N.C.: Duke University Press, 1993), highlighted the conjunction between U.S. exceptionalism and a particular model of U.S. transnationalism—namely, the imperialism manifested in the Gulf War, which more than ten years after the volume's publication was followed by the U.S.–Iraq War, sometimes referred to as the second Gulf War. Writing before the invasion of Iraq in 2003, David Noble argued that we are witnessing the "end of American exceptionalism" (David W. Noble, *Death of a Nation: American Culture and the End of Exceptionalism* [Minneapolis: University of Minnesota Press, 2002]). As a scholarly category, however, American exceptionalism remains alive and well, as demonstrated by recent publications such as Jonathan A. Glickstein, *American Exceptionalism, American Anxiety: Wages, Competition, and Degraded Labor in the Antebellum United States* (Charlottesville: University of Virginia Press, 2002); Michael Ignatieff, ed., *American Exceptionalism and Human Rights* (Princeton: Princeton University Press, 2005); Seymour Martin Lipset, *American Exceptionalism: A Double-Edged Sword* (New York: Norton, 1996); Madsen, *American Exceptionalism*; Siobhán McEvoy-Levy, *American Exceptionalism and U.S. Foreign Policy: Public Diplomacy at the End of the Cold War* (New York: Palgrave, 2001).

49. Susan McHugh, *Animal Stories: Narrating Across Species Lines* (Minneapolis: University of Minnesota Press, 2011), 161.

50. Shukin, *Animal Capital*, 7–8. Agamben's position differs from Hannah Arendt's reading of bare life as a life stripped of all *but* its humanity (Hannah Arendt, *The Origins of Totalitarianims* [New York: Harcourt Brace Jovanovich, 1973], 293–302).

51. Gary Steiner, *Anthropocentrism and Its Discontents: The Moral Status of Animals in the History of Western Philosophy* (Pittsburgh: University of Pittsburgh Press, 2005), 6.

52. Dominick LaCapra, *History and Its Limits: Human, Animal, Violence* (Ithaca: Cornell University Press, 2009), 170. Susan Buck-Morss similarly takes Agamben to task for using "history ahistorically, in order to abstract from it a timeless ontology of power" (Susan Buck-Morss, "Visual Empire," *Diacritics* 37, nos. 2–3 [2007], 171).

53. Mbembe, "Necropolitics." See also Patricia Ticineto Clough, "Introduction," in Patricia Ticineto Clough and Jean Halley, eds., *The Affective Turn: Theorizing the Social* (Durham, N.C.: Duke University Press, 2007), 26.

54. Russ Castronovo, *Necro Citizenship: Death, Eroticism, and the Public Sphere in the Nineteenth-Century United States* (Durham, N.C.: Duke University Press, 2001), 10, emphasis in original.

55. Ann Laura Stoler, *Haunted by Empire: Geographies of Intimacy in North American History* (Durham, N.C.: Duke University Press, 2006), 2.

56. Anthony Bogues, "Imagination, Politics, and Utopia: Confronting the Present," *boundary 2* 33, no. 3 (2006), 156.

57. Ibid., 159.

58. Because of my concern with racial formation, I find it important to maintain the terms *subject* and *subjectivity* throughout the book. I am persuaded by Susan McHugh's thoughtful suggestion that agency is an effective way of reshaping our understanding of animals and animality, but I ultimately agree more with her reluctance when she "hesitate[s] to claim that distinguishing agency from subjectivity simply resolves concerns about deconstructive and other refutations of the foundational discourses of the humanist subject. Agency may never be completely or purely represented apart from this peculiar subject form" (McHugh, *Animal Stories*, 2). I want to suggest that—at least when dealing with historical animal representations—there can be an urgency to maintaining the focus on subjectivity so as not to participate in the politics of negation.

59. Philippe Ariès, *The Hour of Our Death*, trans. Helen Weaver (New York: Knopf, 1981), 353–395.

60. Kelly Oliver, *Animal Lessons: How They Teach Us to Be Human* (New York: Columbia University Press, 2009), 5.

61. Eve Kosofsky Sedgwick, *Epistemology of the Closet* (Berkeley: University of California Press, 1990), 85, 45, 48.

62. Roberto Esposito and Timothy Campbell, "Interview," trans. Anna Paparcone, *Diacritics* 36, no. 2 (2006), 50.

63. Andrew Benjamin, "Another Naming, a Living Animal: Blanchot's Community," *SubStance* 37, no. 3 (2008), 207, 208, 212.

64. Ibid., 218–219.

65. Ibid., 219, 222. For a powerful critique of Adamic naming as gendered, see Ursula K. LeGuin, "She Unnames Them," in *Buffalo Gals and Other Animal Presences*, 194–196 (Santa Barbara, Calif.: Capra Press, 1987).

66. Benjamin, "Another Naming," 223–224.

67. Jacques Rancière, "Who Is the Subject of the Rights of Man?" *South Atlantic Quarterly* 103, nos. 2–3 (2004), 302.

68. Christine Kenyon-Jones, *Kindred Brutes: Animals in Romantic-Period Writing* (Aldershot, U.K.: Ashgate, 2001), 7.

69. Harriet Ritvo, *The Animal Estate: The English and Other Creatures in the Victorian Age* (Cambridge, Mass.: Harvard University Press, 1987), 4.

70. Erica Fudge, "A Left-Handed Blow: Writing the History of Animals," in Nigel Rothfels, ed., *Representing Animals*, 3–18 (Bloomington: Indiana University Press, 2002).

71. Laura Brown, *Homeless Dogs and Melancholy Apes: Humans and Other Animals in the Modern Literary Imagination* (Ithaca: Cornell University Press, 2010), ix, 2.

72. Susan McHugh, "One or Several Literary Animal Studies?" H-Animal, H-Net, July 17, 2006, at http://www.h-net.org/~animal/ruminations_mchugh.html.

73. Keith Thomas, *Man and the Natural World: A History of the Modern Sensibility* (New York: Pantheon Books, 1983).

74. Yi-Fu Tuan associates this shift with a demotion of animals "from powers to pets," as the subtitle for chapter 5 in his book *Dominance and Affection: The Making of Pets* (New Haven: Yale University Press, 1984) summarily puts it.

75. Thomas, *Man and the Natural World*, see esp. 58–69.

76. The idea that urbanization and the disappearance of animals from people's lives go hand in hand has been a matter of dispute; see, for instance, Hilda Kean, *Animal Rights: Political and Social Change in Britain Since 1800* (London: Reaktion, 1998). There are several histories of pets and pet keeping; see, for instance, Katherine Grier, *Pets in America: A History* (Chapel Hill: University of North Carolina Press, 2006).

77. Mary Allen, *Animals in American Literature* (Urbana: University of Illinois Press, 1983), 10.

78. Jennifer Mason, *Civilized Creatures: Urban Animals, Sentimental Culture, and American Literature, 1850–1900* (Baltimore: Johns Hopkins University Press, 2005), 3.

79. Steve Baker, *The Postmodern Animal* (London: Reaktion, 2000), 20. Like Mason, Susan McHugh argues that "these stories are significant partly because they contradict conventional assumptions about the displacement of animals by machines in the everyday life of modernity" (McHugh, *Animal Stories*, 4).

80. Mason, *Civilized Creatures*, 137.

81. John Berger, "Why Look at Animals?" in *About Looking* (New York: Pantheon Books, 1980), 3. For a cross-historical account of this seeming contradiction, see Katherine Wills Perlo, *Kinship and Killing: The Animal in World Religions* (New York: Columbia University Press, 2009).

82. Philip Armstrong, *What Animals Mean in the Fiction of Modernity* (London: Routledge, 2008), 37–38.

83. Jonathan Lamb, "Gulliver and the Lives of Animals," in Frank Palmeri, ed., *Humans and Other Animals in Eighteenth-Century British Culture* (Aldershot, U.K.: Ashgate, 2006), 171.

84. Brown, *Homeless Dogs and Melancholy Apes*, 20–21.

85. See Haraway, "A Manifesto for Cyborgs"; Donna Haraway, *Primate Visions: Gender, Race, and Nature in the World of Modern Science* (New York: Routledge, 1989); and Ritvo, *The Animal Estate*. The role of the animal in colonialism and domestic power relations has been a particular focus in more recent postcolonial theory and ecocriticism. For a discussion of their intersections, see Graham Huggan and Helen Tiffin, *Postcolonial Ecocriticism: Literature, Animals, Environment* (London: Routledge, 2010). For the American context, an animal–environmental approach can be found in Virginia DeJohn Anderson, *Creatures of Empire: How Domestic Animals Transformed Early America* (Oxford: Oxford University Press, 2004). The field of animal geography took shape in the mid-1990s; see, for instance, the special issue "Animals and Geography" of *Society and Animals* (1998) as well as edited collections such as Jennifer Wolch and Jody Emel, eds., *Animal Geographies: Place, Politics, and Identity in the Nature–Culture Borderlands* (London: Verso, 1998), and Chris Philo and Chris Wilbert, eds., *Animal Spaces, Beastly Places: New Geographies of Human–Animal Relations* (London: Routledge, 2000).

86. Huggan and Tiffin, *Postcolonial Ecocriticism*, 18.

87. Carrie Rohman, *Stalking the Subject: Modernism and the Animal* (New York: Columbia University Press, 2009), 30.

88. Weil, "A Report on the Animal Turn," 2. Derrida was sharply critical of the Great Ape Project's attempt to include certain animals in *human* rights and to neglect a call for the inclusion of animals more broadly in ethical considerations (see Derrida, "Violence Against Animals").

89. Paul Shepard, *The Others: How Animals Made Us Human* (Washington, D.C.: Island Press, 1996). Temple Grandin and Catherine Johnson, *Animals Make Us Human: Creating the Best Life for Animals* (Boston: Houghton Mifflin Harcourt, 2009).

90. For examples of analyses that use evolution as their central category for cultural analysis, see Gillian Beer, *Darwin's Plots: Evolutionary Narrative in Darwin, George Elliot, and Nineteenth-Century Fiction* (London: Routledge & Kegan Paul, 1983); Joseph Carroll, *Literary Darwinism: Evolution, Human Nature, and Literature* (New York: Routledge, 2004); J. A. V. Chapple, *Science and Literature in the Nineteenth Century* (Houndsmill, U.K.: Macmillan, 1986); Alvar Ellegard, *Darwin and the General Reader: The Reception of Darwin's Theory of Evolution* (Chicago: University of Chicago Press, 1958); Evelyn Fox Keller, "Language and Ideology in Evolutionary Theory: Reading Cultural Norms Into Natural Law," in James Sheehan and Morton Sosna, eds., *The Boundaries of Humanity: Humans, Animals, Machines*, 85–102 (Berkeley: University of California Press, 1991); Robert J. Richards, *Darwin and the Emergence of Evolutionary Theories of Mind and Behavior* (Chicago: University of Chicago Press, 1987); Robert J. Richards, *The Meaning of Evolution: The Morphological Construction and Ideological Reconstruction of Darwin's Theory* (Chicago: University of Chicago Press, 1992);

William Rossi, "Evolutionary Theory," in Joel Myerson, Sandra Harbert Petrulionis, and Laura Dassow Walls, eds., *The Oxford Handbook of Transcendentalism*, 583–613 (Oxford: Oxford University Press, 2010); Joan Roughgarden, *Evolution's Rainbow: Diversity, Gender, and Sexuality in Nature and People* (Berkeley: University of California Press, 2004); Elliott Sober, "Comparative Psychology Meets Evolutionary Biology: Morgan's Canon and Cladistic Parsimony," in Daston and Mitman, *Thinking with Animals*, 87–99; and Robert M. Young, *Darwin's Metaphor: Nature's Place in Victorian Culture* (Cambridge: Cambridge University Press, 1985). This line of inquiry goes back to the nineteenth century; see Nathaniel Southgate Shaler, *Domesticated Animals: Their Relation to Man and to His Advancement in Civilization* (New York: Charles Scribner's Sons, 1895). For one of the earliest analyses of connections between evolutionary theory and literature, see Lionel Stevenson, *Darwin Among the Poets* (Chicago: University of Chicago Press, 1932).

91. Ritvo, *The Animal Estate*, 39.

92. René Girard, *Violence and the Sacred*, trans. Patrick Gregory (Baltimore: Johns Hopkins University Press, 1972), 8.

93. Erica Fudge, *Brutal Reasoning: Animals, Rationality, and Humanity in Early Modern England* (Ithaca: Cornell University Press, 2006), 58.

94. Eileen Crist, *Images of Animals: Anthropomorphism and Animal Mind* (Philadelphia: Temple University Press, 1999), 1, 5.

95. Armstrong and Montag, "The Future of the Human."

96. See Eric Santner, *On Creaturely Life: Rilke, Benjamin, Sebald* (Chicago: University of Chicago Press, 2006); Beatrice Hanssen, *Walter Benjamin's Other History: Of Stones, Animals, Human Beings, and Angels* (Berkeley: University of California Press, 1998); Bruce Thomas Boehrer, *Animal Characters: Nonhuman Beings in Early Modern Literature* (Philadelphia: University of Pennsylvania Press, 2010); Bruce Thomas Boehrer, *Shakespeare Among the Animals: Nature and Society in the Drama of Early Modern England* (New York: Palgrave, 2002); Erica Fudge, "The Dog, the Home and the Human, and the Ancestry of Derrida's Cat," *Oxford Literary Review* 29, no. 1 (2007): 37–54; Erica Fudge, *Perceiving Animals: Humans and Beasts in Early Modern English Culture* (Urbana: University of Illinois Press, 2000); Erica Fudge, ed., *Renaissance Beasts: Of Animals, Humans, and Other Wonderful Creatures* (Urbana: University of Illinois Press, 2004); Laurie Shannon, "The Eight Animals in Shakespeare; or, Before the Human," *PMLA* 124, no. 2 (2009): 472–479.

97. Erica Fudge, "Introduction," in Fudge, ed., *Renaissance Beasts*, 9.

98. Bruno Latour, *We Have Never Been Modern*, trans. Catherine Porter (Cambridge, Mass.: Harvard University Press, 1993), 29.

99. Armstrong, *What Animals Mean in the Fiction of Modernity*, 3, 5, 7, 11, 20, 49, 61.

100. McHugh, *Animal Stories*, 217.

101. Donna Landry, *Noble Brutes: How Eastern Horses Transformed English Culture* (Baltimore: Johns Hopkins University Press, 2009), 13.

102. Andrew Parker, Mary Russo, Doris Sommer, and Patricia Yaeger, "Introduction," in Andrew Parker, Mary Russo, Doris Sommer, and Patricia Yaeger, eds., *Nationalisms and Sexualities* (New York and London: Routledge, 1991), 1.

103. Anne McClintock, "'No Longer in a Future Heaven': Women and Nationalism in South Africa," *Transition* 51 (1991), 105.

104. Walter Benjamin, "Franz Kafka: On the Tenth Anniversary of His Death," in Hannah Arendt, ed., *Illuminations* (New York: Harcourt Brace and World, 1968), 122.

105. Rohman, *Stalking the Subject*, 8.

106. Wolfe, *What Is Posthumanism?* xxix.

107. Mason, *Civilized Creatures*, 1, 173.

108. Barbara Herrnstein-Smith, "Animal Relatives, Difficult Relations," *differences* 15, no. 1 (2004): 1–23; Michael Lundblad, "Epistemology of the Jungle: Progressive-Era Sexuality and the Nature of the Beast," *American Literature* 81, no. 4 (2009): 747–773.

109. Allen, *Animals in American Literature*, 14–15.

110. Gieri Bolliger and Antoine F. Goetschel, "Sexual Relations with Animals (Zoophilia): An Unrecognized Problem in Animal Welfare Legislation," in Andrea M. Beetz and Anthony L. Podberscek, eds., *Bestiality and Zoophilia: Sexual Relations with Animals* (LaFayette, Ind.: Purdue University Press, 2005), 24–25.

111. Andrea M. Beetz, "New Insights Into Bestiality and Zoophilia," in Beetz and Podberscek, eds., *Bestiality and Zoophilia*, 99–100. Hani Miletski has noted that zoophilia and bestiality are not distinct categories but occur in combination or on a spectrum, and he has conducted research to define "zoosexuality" as a "sexual orientation" (Hani Miletski, "Is Zoophilia a Sexual Orientation? A Study," in Beetz and Podberscek, eds., *Bestiality and Zoophilia*, 82–97).

112. Beetz, "New Insights Into Bestiality and Zoophilia," 99.

113. Lundblad, "From Animal Studies to Animality Studies," 500.

114. Alice A. Kuzniar, *Melancholia's Dog* (Chicago: University of Chicago Press, 2006), 4, 109.

115. Alice A. Kuzniar, "'I Married My Dog': On Queer Canine Literature," in Noreen Giffney and Myra Hird, eds., *Queering the Non/Human* (Burlington, Vt.: Ashgate, 2008), 207.

116. Ibid., 206–207.

117. Ibid., 208.

118. The story of animals' relationship to the law has usually been told in relation to the rise of humane societies (see Mason, *Civilized Creatures*, and Fudge, "A Left-Handed Blow").

119. For a theorization of the species grid that I take up more fully in chapter 1, see Cary Wolfe and Jonathan Elmer, "Subject to Sacrifice: Ideology, Psychoanalysis, and the Discourse of Species in Jonathan Demme's *Silence of the Lambs*," *boundary 2* 22, no. 3 (1995): 141–170.

120. John Locke, *The Educational Writings of John Locke: A Critical Edition with Introduction and Notes*, ed. James L. Axtell (Cambridge: Cambridge University Press, 1968), 226.

121. The discussion of (anti)representationalism reaches back at least twenty years to the publication of Richard Rorty's *Objectivity, Relativism, Truth* (Cambridge: Cambridge University Press, 1991) and continues today; see, for instance, Michael Arnold, "Remembering Things," *Information Soceity* 24, no. 1 (2008): 47–53; Francisco Calvo Garzon, "Towards a General Theory of Antirepresentationalism," *British Journal for the Philosphy of Science* 59, no. 3 (2008): 258–292; and Michael P. Wolf, "Language, Mind, and World: Can't We All Just Get Along?" *Metaphilosophy* 39, no. 3 (2008): 363–380.

122. Latour, *We Have Never Been Modern*, 27.

123. Michael Hardt, "Foreword: What Affects Are Good For," in Clough and Halley, eds., *The Affective Turn*, x.

124. I borrow some of my phrasing here from Jonathan Elmer, *On Lingering and Being Last: Race and Sovereignty in the New World* (New York: Fordham University Press, 2008), 4.

1. American Bestiality: Sex, Animals, and the Construction of Subjectivity

1. Quoted in David Dishneau, "Dog Handler at Abu Ghraib Convicted of Tormenting Prisoners," Associated Press, Local Wire, July 6, 2006, at http://web.lexis-nexis.com/universe/document?_m=2b7815b13185d0b53f1ca4fb0cce7a4f&_docnum=5&wchp=dGLbVzz-zSkVA&_md5=7db9d4b3edce7c0360d33a0e470179c0.

2. Kay Anderson, "White Natures: Sydney's Royal Agricultural Show in Post-humanist Perspective," *Transactions, Institute of British Geographers* 28, no. 4 (2003), 426.

3. For a thoughtful and forceful articulation of these concerns in relation to the Holocaust, see Anat Pick, *Creaturely Poetics: Animality and Vulnerability in Literature and Film* (New York: Columbia University Press, 2011), 6.

4. Dominick LaCapra, *History and Its Limits: Human, Animal, Violence* (Ithaca: Cornell University Press, 2009), 151–154.

5. Giorgio Agamben, *Homo Sacer: Sovereign Power and Bare Life*, trans. Daniel Heller-Roazen (Stanford: Stanford University Press, 1998), 8.

6. Jacques Derrida has taken up this issue of (non)sacrifice in relation to the physical consumption that this logic legitimates. He coined the phrase *carnophallogocentrism* to describe a discourse that constructs *man*kind's subjectivity by allowing for the noncriminal putting to death of animals. See Jacques Derrida, "'Eating Well,' or the Calculation of the Subject: An Interview with Jacques Derrida," in Eduardo Cadava, Peter Connor, and Jean-Luc Nancy, eds., *Who Comes After the Subject?* (New York: Routledge, 1991), 113. Akira Lippit points out that in *Minima Moralia: Reflections from Damaged Life*

(London: Verso, 1974) Theodor Adorno raises similar concerns about the connections between violence against humans and violence against animals: "According to Adorno's transferential logic, violence originates in the encounter between human and nonhuman beings. . . . [T]he ethics of murder is made possible by seeing the animal first as nonhuman, then inhuman. If one's victim can be seen as inhuman, the aggressor reasons, one is then justified in performing acts of violence, even murder, upon that inhuman body, since those acts now fall beyond the jurisdiction of the anthropocentric law" (See Akira Mizuta Lippit, "Magnetic Animal: Derrida, Wildlife, Animetaphor," *MLN* 113, no. 5 [1998], 1119).

7. Agamben, *Homo Sacer*, 105. The figure of the wolf-man has also had an extensive presence in literature. For the early modern period, that interest revolved around feral children, such as "Peter the Wild Boy," who was found in the woods of Germany and became a salon sensation in London. See Michael Newton, "Bodies Without Souls: The Case of Peter the Wild Boy," in Erica Fudge, Ruth Gilbert, and Susan Wiseman, eds., *At the Borders of the Human: Beasts, Bodies, and Natural Philosophy in the Early Modern Period*, 196–214 (New York: Palgrave, 2002). In a full monograph on the figure of the wild boy, *homo ferus*, Richard Nash argues that "the wild man constitutes a complex *alter ego* to the idealized abstraction of 'the Citizen of Enlightenment,' and that following his movement through the public sphere helps illuminate the process by which that idealized abstraction is reified into a particular construction of what constitutes 'human nature' " (Richard Nash, *Wild Enlightenment: The Borders of Human Identity in the Eighteenth Century* [Charlottesville: University of Virginia Press, 2003], 4). For the Victorian period, much of the scholarly interest in the wolf-man has centered on the "wolfish man" Heathcliff in Emily Brontë's *Wuthering Heights*; see Stevie Davies, "Emily Brontë & the Animals," in *Emily Brontë: Heretic* (London: Women's Press, 1994), 118–119. Recent attempts to read Heathcliff in relation to Brontë's dog "Keeper" include Maureen Adams, "Emily Brontë and Keeper," in *Shaggy Muses: The Dogs Who Inspired Virginia Woolf, Emily Dickinson, Edith Wharton, Elizabeth Barret Browning, and Emily Brontë*, 49–96 (Chicago: University of Chicago Press, 2011). For a discussion of the violence and love being worked out in Brontë, see Ivan Kreilkamp, "Petted Things: *Wuthering Heights* and the Animal," *Yale Journal of Criticism* 18, no. 1 (2005): 81–110.

8. Agamben, *Homo Sacer*, 105.

9. Ibid.

10. Susan Wiseman proposes a culturally specific way of figuring the wolf-man in her readings of early modern werewolf texts: "Wildness exists in two ways. . . . [I]t can be read as signifying an uncompromised quality out of which the social and civil human can be built, but, equally, it might represent the failure of the civil community" Her claim that accounts of the werewolf "overlap with other ways of understanding this border creature, ways that are strongly tied to ideas and experiences of the social and the civic," aligns her text with Agamben's and, as we will see momentarily, John Winthrop's writings (Susan J. Wiseman, "Hairy on the Inside: Metamorphosis and Civility in English

Werewolf Texts," in Erica Fudge, ed., *Renaissance Beasts: Of Animals, Humans, and Other Wonderful Creatures* [Urbana: University of Illinois Press, 2004], 50, 51).

11. Jacques Derrida, *The Beast & the Sovereign*, vol. 1 (Chicago: University of Chicago Press, 2009), 14.

12. For discussions of bestiality from an animal rights perspective, see especially the work of Piers Beirne, "Rethinking Bestiality: Towards a Concept of Interspecies Sexual Assault," *Theoretical Criminology* 1, no. 3 (1997): 317–340; Piers Beirne, "On the Sexual Assault of Animals: A Sociological View," in Angela N. H. Creager and William Chester Jordan, eds., *The Animal/Human Boundary: Historical Perspectives*, 193–227 (Rochester, N.Y.: University of Rochester Press, 2002).

13. Jasbir K. Puar, *Terrorist Assemblages: Homonationalism in Queer Times* (Durham, N.C.: Duke University Press, 2007), 112, 87–88.

14. Ibid., 112, 113.

15. Alphonso Lingis, "Bestiality," in H. Peter Steeves, *Animal Others: On Ethics, Ontology, and Animal Life*, 37–54 (Albany: State University of New York Press, 1999); Midas Dekkers, *Dearest Pet: On Bestiality*, trans. Paul Vincent (London: Verso, 1992). Several recent literary works have imagined bestiality as a crucial way of interrogating subjectivity; see, for instance, Edward Albee, *The Goat; or, Who Is Sylvia? (Notes Toward a Definition of Tragedy)* (Woodstock, N.Y.: Overlook Press, 2003), and Marie Darrieussecq, *Pig Tales: A Novel of Lust and Transformation*, trans. Linda Coverdale (New York: New Press, 1996).

16. For an overview of the role that "animal lovers" play in Western literature from the myth of Leda and the Swan on, see Wendy Doniger, "The Mythology of Masquerading Animals, or, Bestiality," in Arien Mack, ed., *Humans and Other Animals*, 343–365 (Columbus: Ohio State University Press, 1995), quote on 343.

17. Richard W. Bulliet, *Hunters, Herders, and Hamburgers: The Past and Future of Human–Animal Relationships* (New York: Columbia University Press, 2005), 5, 6, 9–10.

18. Historians' analysis of the state's relationship to animals has usually focused on animal protection legislation; see, for instance, the discussion of animal welfare legislation's connection to theories of social stability in Brian Henderson, "Animals and the State in Nineteenth-Century England," in *Peacable Kingdom: Stability and Change in Modern Britain*, 82–122 (Oxford: Clarendon Press, 1982).

19. Janet Moore Lindman and Michele Lise Tarter, "Introduction," in Janet Moore Lindman and Michele Lise Tarter, eds., *A Centre of Wonders: The Body in Early America* (Ithaca: Cornell University Press, 2001), 2.

20. Judith Butler, *Bodies That Matter: On the Discursive Limits of "Sex"* (New York: Routledge, 1993), xi.

21. Ibid., ix.

22. Ibid., 23.

23. My focus here is on the American context; for an analysis that links early modern Puritanism with modern animal relations in the European context, see

Kathleen Kete, "Animals and Ideology: The Politics of Animal Protection in Europe," in Nigel Rothfels, ed., *Representing Animals*, 19–34 (Bloomington: Indiana University Press, 2002). What makes Kete's article particularly interesting is the way she links Puritan ideology and the logic of the camp to animal *protection* laws. For further discussions of the death camps in relation to animal protection laws, see Arnold Arluke and Boria Sax, "The Nazi Treatment of Animals and People," in Lynda Birke and Ruth Hubbard, eds., *Reinventing Biology: Respect for Life and the Creation of Knowledge*, 228–260 (Bloomington: Indiana University Press, 1995).

24. Patricia Williams, "In Kind," *The Nation*, May 31, 2004; Susan Sontag, "Regarding the Torture of Others," *New York Times*, May 23, 2004.

25. For an assessment of the disciplinary and methodological stakes involved in focusing on "animals" or "animality," see Michael Lundblad, "From Animal Studies to Animality Studies," *PMLA* 124, no. 2 (2009): 496–502.

26. LaCapra, *History and Its Limits*, 151–154.

27. Ann Kibbey, *The Interpretation of Material Shapes in Puritanism: A Study of Rhetoric, Prejudice, and Violence* (Cambridge: Cambridge University Press, 1986), 3. Wayne Franklin makes a similar point in relation to the earlier literature of "discovery" when he writes that, "from the start, language and event in America have been linked almost preternatually to each other," a link that he sees as carrying over into later forms of American writing (Wayne Franklin, *Discoverers, Explorers, Settlers: The Diligent Writers of Early America* [Chicago: University of Chicago Press, 1979], xi).

28. David Hackett Fischer, *Albion's Seed: Four British Folkways in America* (New York: Oxford University Press, 1989), 91–92.

29. Jens Rydström, *Sinners and Citizens: Bestiality and Homosexuality in Sweden, 1880–1950* (Chicago: University of Chicago Press, 2003), 78.

30. Nash, *Wild Enlightenment*, 9.

31. Bestiality had been a capital offense in England since the sixteenth century (John Canup, *Out of the Wilderness: The Emergence of an American Identity in Colonial New England* [Middletown, Conn.: Wesleyan University Press, 1990], 44–45). Sodomy remained punishable by death until 1805 (Thomas A. Foster, *Sex and the Eighteenth-Century Man* [Boston: Beacon Press, 2006], 212 n. 4). At the beginning of the seventeenth century, bestiality trials proliferated in other countries as well, making its criminalization a hallmark of the emergence of modern states (Jonas Liliequist, "Peasants Against Nature: Crossing the Boundaries Between Man and Animal in Seventeenth- and Eighteenth-Century Sweden," in *Forbidden History: The State, Society, and the Regulation of Sexuality in Modern Europe. Essays from the "Journal of the History of Sexuality"* [Chicago: University of Chicago Press, 1992], 58).

32. See Canup, *Out of the Wilderness*, 34–36.

33. Roger Thompson, *Sex in Middlesex: Popular Mores in a Massachusetts County, 1649–1699* (Amherst: University of Massachusetts Press, 1986), 75. Richard Godbeer

reads the evidence differently than Thompson: although Puritan ministers were particularly horrified by bestiality, he argues that the record points to an "underlying disjunction between official ideology and popular responses" to sexual behavior that "seems to have been widespread and commonplace" (Richard Godbeer, *Sexual Revolution in Early America* [Baltimore: Johns Hopkins University Press, 2002], 112).

34. Godbeer, *Sexual Revolution in Early America*, 112.

35. Ibid.

36. Hani Miletski, "A History of Bestiality," in Andrea M. Beetz and Anthony L. Podberscek, *Bestiality and Zoophilia: Sexual Relations with Animals* (LaFayette, Ind.: Purdue University Press, 2005), 6.

37. Jonathan Goldberg, "Bradford's 'Ancient Members' and 'a Case of Buggery . . . Amongst Them,'" in Andrew Parker, Mary Russo, Doris Sommer, and Patricia Yaeger, eds., *Nationalisms and Sexualities* (New York: Routledge, 1991), 61. See also Jonathan Ned Katz, *Gay American History: Lesbians and Gay Men in the U.S.A.* (New York: Meridian Books, 1992), and Jonathan Ned Katz, *Gay/Lesbian Almanac: A New Documentary* (New York: Carroll & Graf, 1982). Interestingly, though, bestiality also figures in regulations of heterosexual relations: a 1639 law at Plymouth Plantation listed it specifically as a reason for divorce (Miletski, "A History of Bestiality," 16). It continues to be the case to this day that bestiality is grounds for divorce; see Gieri Bolliger and Antoine F. Goetschel, "Sexual Relations with Animals (Zoophilia): An Unrecognized Problem in Animal Welfare Legislation," in Beetz and Podberscek, eds., *Bestiality and Zoophilia*, 35.

38. For the American context, the data regarding the frequency of bestiality among the population that usually gets cited is from the Kinsey report (and it might be worth remembering here that Alfred Kinsey himself was trained as a zoologist): "8% of the male and 3.5% of the female populations of the US had had at least one zoophilic encounter during their lives. Among the rural population, which had easy access to animals, 17% of the men surveyed gave accounts of intimate experiences with animals, leading to orgasm . . . in some communities, estimates of up to 65% were determined. . . . In the urban population, however, the percentage was much lower: up to 4% and zoophilic contacts took place mainly during temporary sojourns to the country" (quoted in Bolliger and Goetschel, "Sexual Relations with Animals [Zoophilia]," 26). It is reasonable to assume that the actual number is higher, given that bestiality was "an illegal, punishable offense at the time of the surveys" (ibid., 26).

39. Rydström, *Sinners and Citizens*, 2, 7, 9, 17, 12, 18, 29, 30, 54, 69.

40. Quoted in Katz, *Gay American History*, 406.

41. Katz, *Gay/Lesbian Almanac*, 56.

42. John Putnam Demos, *Entertaining Satan: Witchcraft and the Culture of Early New England* (New York: Oxford University Press, 1982), 181. Rydström takes issue with associations of bestiality with witchcraft in that "the longevity of the concern for bestiality" persisted "long after the witch trials had ceased to appear before the courts" (Rydström, *Sinners and Citizens*, 8).

43. William Bradford, *Of Plymouth Plantation 1620–1674*, ed. Francis Murphy (New York: Modern Library, 1981), 355. Murphy notes in his introduction that Bradford's text was "first printed in its entirety in 1856" (xxv).

44. Godbeer, *Sexual Revolution in Early America*, 105.

45. Ibid., 112, 102.

46. Bolliger and Goetschel, "Sexual Relations with Animals," 24.

47. For a compelling consideration of the intersections between religious beliefs and attitudes to animals, see Katherine Wills Perlo, *Kinship and Killing: The Animal in World Religions* (New York: Columbia University Press, 2009).

48. For a discussion of early modern attitudes toward food's influence on the body, see Trudy Eden, "Food, Assimilation, and the Malleability of the Human Body in Early Virginia," in Lindman and Tarter, eds., *A Centre of Wonders*, 29–42. For an analysis of the conjunction in early modern thought between the body and the body politic, see Jacquelyn Miller, "The Body Politic and the Body Somatic: Benjamin Rush's Fear of Social Disorder and His Treatment for Yellow Fever," in Lindman and Tarter, eds., *A Centre of Wonders*, 61–74.

49. Samuel Danforth, *The Cry of Sodom Enquired Into; Upon Occasion of the Arraignment and Condemnation of Benjamin Goad, for His Prodigious Villany: Together with a Solemn Exhortation to Tremble at Gods Judgements, and to Abandon Youthful Lusts. / by S. D.* (Cambridge: Marmaduke Johnson, 1674), 5, emphasis in original. Bestiality evidently remained an issue; see Cotton Mather, *Warnings from the Dead. Or Solemn Admonitions Unto All People; but Especially Unto Young Persons to Beware of Such Evils as Would Bring Them to the Dead. By Cotton Mather. In Two Discourses, Occasioned by a Sentence of Death, Executed on Some Unhappy Malefactors. Together with the Last Confession, Made by a Young Woman, Who Dyed on June 8. 1693. One of These Malefactors* (Boston: Bartholomew Green, for Samuel Phillips, 1693), 43–45. As John Canup points out, Cotton Mather recorded "with fastidious horror" the case of a man "confounding himself with a *bitch*" and "hideously conversing with a *sow*." Subsequently referring to the perpetrator as a "hell hound" and a "*bewitch'd beast*," Mather made clear that bestiality performed "the melding of what should have remained two distinct realms of creation" (quoted in Canup, *Out of the Wilderness*, 36, emphasis in original).

The literature condemning bestiality proliferated in both the colonies and England; see, for instance, Lancelot Andrewes, *The Pattern of Catechistical Doctrine at Large, or, a Learned and Pious Exposition of the Ten Commandments with an Introduction, Containing the Use and Benefit of Catechizing, the Generall Grounds of Religion, and the Truth of Christian Religion in Particular, Proved Against Atheists, Pagans, Jews, and Turks / by the Right Reverend Father in God Lancelot Andrews . . . ; Perfected According to the Authors Own Copy and Thereby Purged from Many Thousands of Errours, Defects, and Corruptions, Which Were in a Rude Imperfect Draught Formerly Published, as Appears in the Preface to the Reader* (n.p.: n.p., 1650). The language of bestiality as a sin has had lasting power: writing in 1955, Konrad Lorenz said that "anyone who, disappointed and embittered by human failings, denies his love to mankind in order to transfer it to a dog or a cat, is definitely committing a grave sin, social sodomy so to speak, which is as disgusting as the sexual kind" (quoted in Marjorie Garber, *Dog Love* [New York: Simon & Schuster, 1996], 123).

The reference to "prostitute" in the passage from Danforth given in the text makes sense in the context of another biblical passage, Deutoronomy 23:17–18, which links whoring and sodomy/bestiality: "17. There shall be no whore of the daughters of Israel, nor a sodomite of the sons of Israel. 18. Thou shalt not bring the hire of a whore, or the price of a dog, into the house of the Lord thy God for any vow; for even both these are abomination unto the Lord thy God." This association between bestiality and prostitution/whoring was widespread in the contemporary literature; see also Richard Allestree, *The Causes of the Decay of Christian Piety, or, an Impartial Survey of the Ruines of Christian Religion, Undermin'd by Unchristian Practice Written by the Author of the Whole Duty of Man* (London: R. Norton for T. Garthwait, 1667). The reference to prostitution suggests an inequality between the sexual partners. As Jens Rydström writes, "There is an extensive literature on the historical patterns of male same-sex relations, and most of these studies agree that the gay couple as a partnership between equals is a modern invention. Before the modernization of sexuality, a same-sex relationship almost invariably involved a difference, either in social status, in age, or in the masculinity or femininity of appearance, which today we call gender identity" (Rydström, *Sinners and Citizens*, 124–125). The reference also ties bestiality to extramarital sex, an association that had been prevalent since the sixteenth-century Reformation, when "many voices in the rising wave of publications on marriage relied on an implicit or explicit opposition between marriage and sodomy/Sodom" (Helmut Puff, *Sodomy in Reformation Germany and Switzerland, 1400–1600* [Chicago: University of Chicago Press, 2003], 170).

50. As John Murrin explains, "Bestiality lowered a man to the level of a beast, but it also left something human in the animal. To eat a defiled animal thus involved the danger of cannibalism" (John M. Murrin, " 'Things Fearful to Name': Bestiality in Early America," in Angela N. H. Creager and William Chester Jordan, eds., *The Animal/Human Boundary: Historical Perspectives* [Rochester, N.Y.: University of Rochester Press, 2002], 117).

51. My slippage between the specific law that condemned Granger to death and law in general is deliberate. I am using Agamben to argue that law establishes itself by a process of inclusive exclusion, a point that Derrida has made in relation to animals specifically when he examines how justice organizes itself around the violence of "a noncriminal putting to death" of animals, which he sees as a manipulable category (Derrida, " 'Eating Well,' or the Calculation of the Subject," 112). My reading of bestiality as an ongoing and structuring issue in biopower is in keeping with Jonathan Goldberg's analysis of current statutes: in "the 1986 Supreme Court decision in *Bowers v. Hardwick* (478 U.S. 186)," he states, justices drew on "biblical prohibitions and the sixteenth-century English law that lies behind the statues of the colonies" (Goldberg, "Bradford's 'Ancient Members,' " 61).

52. Susan M. Stabile, "A 'Doctrine of Signatures': The Epistolary Physicks of Esther Burr's Journal," in Lindman and Tarter, eds., *A Centre of Wonders*, 109.

53. David Hackett Fischer records what might be the most extreme case of this absolute division and its fungibility. In New Haven, a one-eyed servant named George Spencer was accused of bestiality when a sow gave birth to a deformed pig that also had one eye. Spencer was pressured into a confession, which he then recanted, only to confess and recant again. In the absence of the requisite two witnesses for the act to become legally actionable, the magistrates got creative: the "piglet was admitted as one witness, and the recanted confession was accepted as another. George Spencer was hanged for bestiality" (Fischer, *Albion's Seed*, 91–92). In her work on medieval attitudes toward animals, Joyce Salisbury documents that "we can see the early Christian paradigm of separation between humans and animals breaking down by the twelfth century" in the "sexual intercourse between human beings and animals" (Joyce E. Salisbury, *The Beast Within: Animals in the Middle Ages*, 2nd ed. [London: Routledge, 2011], 7).

54. Canup, *Out of the Wilderness*, 36.

55. The draconian regulation of bestiality lasted into the nineteenth century: "With the exception of Illinois . . . and New Hampshire, zoophilia was considered a severe crime in all the North American states well into the last century" (Bolliger and Goetschel, "Sexual Relations with Animals," 34). Current laws regarding bestiality have been in flux: "In 1962, Illinois became the first American state to revise its criminal code . . . and sexual acts with animals were no longer considered criminal offenses (L'Etalon Doux 1996). In 1997, twenty-five states, the District of Columbia, and the United States Government outlawed bestiality. The sentences ranged from a mere fine of not more than $500 in Tennessee to an indeterminate life sentence in Michigan (Miletski 2002). The laws in the United States have been changing, and . . . in 2001, three states—Iowa, Maine, and Oregon—passed laws criminalizing bestiality" (Miletski, "A History of Bestiality," 17). Roughly half the states still outlaw zoophilia but treat it as either a felony or a misdemeanor (ibid.). At least some of the colonial legislative ethos still seems current today: "Most of the current laws are part of legislation on sex offending, as in the US and the UK, implying that bestiality is not only a sexual offense but one that also needs to be addressed because of its potential danger to society and violation of religious and moral codes" (Andrea M. Beetz, "Bestiality and Zoophilia: Associations with Violence and Sex Offending," in Beetz and Podberscek, eds., *Bestiality and Zoophilia*, 66). Richard Posner and Katharine Silbaugh explain in their 1996 assessment of sex laws in the United States that "some of the early statutes remain in place today, and typically carry heavier penalties than sodomy statutes that have been modernized and focus on human conduct. . . . At early common law, there was no offense of cruelty to animals. However, such statutes have been in place in the United States for quite some time. The focus of such statutes is different from that of the traditional sodomy statute; anticruelty statutes are concerned both with the treatment of the animal and with the offense to community standards, while antibestiality provisions embodied in the sodomy statutes are

aimed only at offenses to community standards" (Richard A. Posner and Katharine B. Silbaugh, *A Guide to America's Sex Laws* [Chicago: University of Chicago Press, 1996], 207). Andrea Beetz has argued that "bestiality still remains largely a taboo subject. . . . [R]ather than considering bestiality as a problem of a single person, the involved animal, and its owner, it has been perceived as a violation of the whole community" (Andrea M. Beetz, "New Insights Into Bestiality and Zoophilia," in Beetz and Podberscek, eds., *Bestiality and Zoophilia*, 115).

56. Like Danforth, Samuel Willard, a leading minister in Boston at the end of the seventeenth century, distinguished between two categories of "unlawful and prohibited mixtures"—namely, the "natural" and "unnatural," with bestiality and sodomy falling into the second category because of "the species and sexes" involved. By contrast, fornication (which included adultery, polygamy, and incest) was more "natural" because it fell "within the compass of the species and sexes" (quoted in Canup, *Out of the Wilderness*, 66).

57. Godbeer, *Sexual Revolution in Early America*, 64–65.

58. David Halperin, *How to Do the History of Homosexuality* (Chicago: University of Chicago Press, 2002), 41. The view that sexual acts and sexual identities remained separate from one another until the nineteenth century has come under attack from other scholars as well; see Foster, *Sex and the Eighteenth-Century Man*.

59. Foucault himself has relatively little to say about animals in relation to the history of sexuality, but he does discuss them in conjunction with "the insane"; see chapter 3 in Michel Foucault, *Madness and Civilization: A History of Insanity in the Age of Reason*, trans. Richard Howard (New York: Vintage Books, 1965), 65–84. Recent discussions have asked whether zoophilia is a sexual orientation; see Hani Miletski, "Is Zoophilia a Sexual Orientation? A Study," in Beetz and Podberscek, eds., *Bestiality and Zoophilia*, 82–97.

60. See the earlier discussion regarding women's relation to bestiality; here again the fungibility of species becomes evident in that masculinity was requisite for sexual acts to count as bestiality, but that masculinity did not have to be tied to humanity.

61. Arnold Davidson, "The Horror of Monsters," in James Sheehan and Morton Sosna, eds., *The Boundaries of Humanity: Humans, Animals, Machines* (Berkeley: University of California Press, 1991), 42.

62. Sigmund Freud, *Totem and Taboo: Some Points of Agreement Between the Mental Lives of Savages and Neurotics* (1913 [1912–1913]), in *The Standard Edition of the Complete Psychological Works of Sigmund Freud*, vol. 13, ed. James Strachey (London: Hogarth Press, 1955), 2, 2 n. 2, 31–32, 129, 140–141. See also Sigmund Freud, *History of an Infantile Neurosis* (1918), in *The Standard Edition of the Complete Psychological Works of Sigmund Freud*, vol. 17, ed. James Strachey, 1–124 (London: Hogarth Press, 1955).

63. For ways in which structuralist anthropologists have analyzed the connections between sexuality, animals, symbols, and taboos (often with a focus on food taboos), see some of the founding texts: Mary Douglas, *Natural Symbols: Explorations in Cosmology*

(New York: Pantheon Books, 1970); Mary Douglas, *Purity and Danger: An Analysis of Concepts of Pollution and Taboo* (New York: Praeger, 1966); Edmund Leach, "Anthropological Aspects of Language: Animal Categories and Verbal Abuse," in Eric H. Lenneberg, ed., *New Directions in the Study of Language*, 23–63 (Cambridge, Mass.: MIT Press, 1964); Marshall David Sahlins, *Culture and Practical Reason* (Chicago: University of Chicago Press, 1976); Yi-fu Tuan, *Dominance and Affection: The Making of Pets* (New Haven: Yale University Press, 1984); and Roy G. Willis, *Man and Beast* (New York: Basic Books, 1974). Taking issue with Claude Lévi-Strauss's claim that totemism has retreated in contemporary society, Marshall Sahlins writes that "one must wonder whether it [the totemic operator] has not been replaced by species and varieties of manufactured objects, which like totemic categories have the power of making even the demarcation of their individual owners a procedure of social classification." Sahlins ties that insight to an account of commodification, suggesting that "the modern totemism is not contradicted by a market rationality. On the contrary, it is promoted precisely to the extent that exchange value and consumption depend on decisions of 'utility,' " thus bridging the use of animals for totemic and capitalist purposes. He concludes that "the bourgeois totemism, in other words, is potentially more elaborate than any 'wild' (*sauvage*) variety, not that it has been liberated from a natural–material basis, but precisely because nature has been domesticated" (Sahlins, *Culture and Practical Reason*, 176–177, 178).

64. Kalpana Shesadri-Crooks, "Being Human: Bestiality, Anthropophagy, and Law," *Umbr(a)* 3, no. 1 (2003), 102.

65. Judith Butler, "Critically Queer," *GLX* 1 (1993), 27.

66. Judith Butler, *Gender Trouble: Feminism and the Subversion of Identity* (New York: Routledge, 1999), 179.

67. Judith Butler, "Performative Acts and Gender Constitution: An Essay in Phenomenology and Feminist Theory," in Katie Conboy, Nadia Medina, and Sarah Stanbury, eds., *Writing on the Body: Female Embodiment and Feminist Theory*, 401–417 (New York: Columbia University Press, 1997).

68. Michael Warner, "New English Sodom," *American Literature* 64, no. 1 (1992), 20.

69. John Winthrop, *History of New England*, 2 vols. (Boston: Little, Brown, 1853), 2:280–281.

70. Philip Armstrong has documented that in contemporaneous British texts, "conventionally the term *inhuman* signifies a mode of behaviour that represents the negative of the Enlightenment paradigm of the human: brutal, primitive, ruthless, cruel and excessive as opposed to civil, advanced, just, compassionate and decorous. In the version of history that underwrites the imperial mission, this kind of inhumanity constitutes a premodern phase that humans occupy before they are trained out of it, which is what Crusoe aims to do with Friday" (Philip Armstrong, *What Animals Mean in the Fiction of Modernity* [London: Routledge, 2008], 23). See also John Simons, *Animal Rights and the Politics of Literary Representation* (Houndmills, U.K.: Palgrave, 2002), 125–127.

71. For the use to which wild animals specifically have been put "as a richly ambiguous symbol for American discourse about matters sexual" and as a means "to symbolize the 'alien other,'" see the collected volume Angus K. Gillespie and Jay Mechling, eds., *American Wildlife in Symbol and Story* (Knoxville: University of Tennessee Press, 1987); the quotes here are from Gillespie and Mechling's introduction to this volume, p. 4.

72. Native Americans' relationships to animals have their own rich genealogies; see, for instance, Calvin Luther Martin's works *In the Spirit of the Earth: Rethinking History and Time* (Baltimore: Johns Hopkins University Press, 1992) and *The Way of the Human Being* (New Haven: Yale University Press, 1999).

73. Winthrop, *History of New England*, 104–105. In reading this and other passages, *wilderness* has been the term privileged for scholarly analysis. Readings abound of early American literature's relations to the environment and figurations of that environment as a "wilderness." See, for instance, Canup, *Out of the Wilderness*; Peter N. Carroll, *Puritanism and the Wilderness: The Intellectual Significance of the New England Frontier 1629–1700* (New York: Columbia University Press, 1969); Martha L. Finch, "'Civilized' Bodies and the 'Savage' Environment of Early New Plymouth," in Lindman and Tarter, eds., *A Centre of Wonders*, 43–59; Roderick Nash, *Wilderness and the American Mind* (New Haven: Yale University Press, 1982); and, of course, the *locus classicus* Perry Miller, *Errand Into the Wilderness* (Cambridge, Mass.: Belknap Press of Harvard University Press, 1959). For a connection between myth, anthropology, and wilderness, see also Richard Slotkin, *Regeneration Through Violence: The Mythology of the American Frontier 1600–1860* (Norman: University of Oklahoma Press, 1973), 146–180; Roy Harvey Pearce, *Savagism and Civilization: A Study of the Indian and the American Mind* (Berkeley: University of California Press, 1988).

74. The argument has also been advanced that "because they so clearly defied the norm of reproductive sexuality, the crimes of sodomy, buggery, and bestiality carried the death penalty" (John D'Emilio and Estelle B. Freedman, *Intimate Matters: A History of Sexuality in America* [New York: Harper & Row, 1988], 30). The anxiety about bestiality seems tied to concerns about miscegenation; Bradley Chapin argues that bestiality raised the fear of monstrous offspring and was therefore punishable by death (Bradley Chapin, *Criminal Justice in Colonial America, 1606–1660* [Athens: University of Georgia Press, 1983], 127). For a historical text that makes this association, see *God's Judgments Against Whoring. Being an Essay Towards a General History of It, from the Creation of the World to the Reign of Augustulus (Which According to Common Computation Is 5190 Years) and from Thence Down to the Present Year 1697: Being a Collection of the Most Remarkable Instances of Uncleanness That Are to Be Found in Sacred or Prophane History During That Time, with Observations Thereon* (n.p.: n.p., 1697). David Cressy discusses a sixteenth-century case of reproductive bestiality in "Agnes Bowker's Cat: Childbirth, Seduction, Bestiality, and Lies," in *Travesties and Transgressions in Tudor and Stuart England: Tales of Discord and Dissension*, 9–28 (Oxford: Oxford University Press, 2000). Erica Fudge takes Cressy to task for failing to ask what the story might tell us about human–animal

relationships even though he links it usefully to the emergence of empirical science (Erica Fudge, "Introduction," in Fudge, ed., *Renaissance Beasts*, 5).

75. Cotton Mather, *Magnalia Christi Americana: Or, the Ecclesiastical History of New-England, from Its First Planting in the Year 1620. Unto the Year of Our Lord, 1698. In Seven Books. . . . by . . . Cotton Mather,* . . . (London: Thomas Parkhurst, 1702), 176, emphasis in original.

76. For a fuller discussion of how the literature of conquest represented Native Americans as beastlike, see chapter 3, "Bestiality," in Bernard W. Sheehan, *Savagism and Civility: Indians and Englishmen in Colonial Virginia*, 65–88 (Cambridge: Cambridge University Press, 1980).

77. Mather, *Magnalia Christi Americana*, 64, emphasis in original.

78. As John Canup has argued, "Mather seems to have been especially fascinated with this imagery . . . [of] canine appetites. . . . Citing a 'philosopher of old [who] called our passions by the just name of *unnurtured dogs*,' Mather lauded Samuel Whiting for keeping 'these dogs with a strong chain upon them'" (Canup, *Out of the Wilderness*, 31–32, emphasis in original).

79. Ibid., 40.

80. Timothy Campbell, "Introduction," in Timothy Campbell, ed., *Bios: Biopolitics and Philosophy* (Minneapolis: University of Minnesota Press, 2008), xxxviii.

81. Ibid., xxxviii–xxxix, xl.

82. Jeremy Bentham, *Introduction to the Principles of Morals and Legislation*, ed. J. H. Burns and H. L. A. Hart (Oxford: Clarendon Press, 1996), 283, emphasis in original.

83. Bentham was not the first philosopher to perform this shift: Michel de Montaigne had traversed similar philosophical ground two centuries earlier in his *Apology for Raymond Sebond* (1580); see Michel de Montaigne, "An Apology for Raymond Sebond," in Linda Kalof and Amy Fitzgerald, eds., *The Animals Reader: The Essential Classic and Contemporary Writings*, 57–59 (Oxford: Berg, 2007).

84. In characterizing bestiality, medieval theology drew on the "traditional etymology that makes 'Sodom' mean 'mute.' Those guilty of the sin that cannot be named, that makes them less than human, are rendered mute as animals before God" (Mark Jordan, *The Invention of Sodomy in Christian Theology* [Chicago: University of Chicago Press, 1997], 106).

85. Peter Singer, *Animal Liberation* (New York: Avon Books, 1977).

86. Cary Wolfe, *Animal Rites: American Culture, the Discourse of Species, and Posthumanist Theory* (Chicago: University of Chicago Press, 2003), 39, 42.

87. A growing body of work, especially in the social sciences, has questioned essentialist readings of animals and examined the extent to which the encounter between human beings and animals shapes both; for the most current scholarship, see the journals *Society and Animals* and *Anthrozoos.* Approaching animals from a constructionist viewpoint, historians Keith Thomas and Harriet Ritvo have documented how seemingly stable categories such as animal breeds emerged at specific historical moments

and reflected the changing relationships between human and nonhuman animals. See Keith Thomas, *Man and the Natural World: A History of the Modern Sensibility* (New York: Pantheon Books, 1983); Harriet Ritvo, "The Animal Connection," in Sheehan and Sosna, eds., *The Boundaries of Humanity*, 68–84; Harriet Ritvo, *The Animal Estate: The English and Other Creatures in the Victorian Age* (Cambridge, Mass.: Harvard University Press, 1987); Harriet Ritvo, "Animal Problems," *Science, Technology, & Human Values* 10, no. 3 (1985): 87–91; Harriet Ritvo, "Animals in Nineteenth-Century Britain: Complicated Attitudes and Competing Categories," in Aubrey Manning and James Serpell, eds., *Animals and Human Society: Changing Perspectives*, 106–126 (London: Routledge, 1994); and Harriet Ritvo, "Pride and Pedigree: The Evolution of the Victorian Dog Fancy," *Victorian Studies* 29, no. 2 (1986): 227–253. Inscribing animals not only within history but within a history of sexuality, feminist scholars such as Carol Adams have argued that the construction of women's and animals' embodiment mirror one another in that patriarchal Western society consistently abjects both. Pointing out that animals consumed for food disappear "both literally and figuratively" from cultural consciousness, Adams argues that women's sexualized bodies all too often stand in for the "absent [animal] referent" (Carol J. Adams, *Neither Man nor Beast: Feminism and the Defense of Animals* [New York: Continuum, 1994], 17). Opening positions of animality to discourse analysis, Adams argues that the boundary between human beings and animals is not stable, and she points to the gendering of that instability, demonstrating that sexual difference and species distinctions are the disavowed sites where patriarchy asserts the dominance of man and mankind while denying the claims of women and animals. She has developed a feminist care ethic in relation to these challenges, arguing that feminism and animal advocacy must go hand in hand. See also the following works by Carol Adams: "Bestiality, the Unmentioned Abuse," *The Animals' Agenda* 15, no. 6 (1995): 29–31; *The Feminist Care Tradition in Animal Ethics* (New York: Columbia University Press, 2007); *The Pornography of Meat* (New York: Continuum, 2003); and *The Sexual Politics of Meat: A Feminist–Vegetarian Critical Theory* (New York: Continuum, 1990), as well as *Ecofeminism and the Sacred* (New York: Continuum, 1993), the collected volume that she edited.

88. Donna Haraway, *The Companion Species Manifesto: Dogs, People, and Significant Otherness* (Chicago: Prickly Paradigm Press, 2003), 12.

89. Gilles Deleuze and Félix Guattari, "Becoming-Animal," in Peter Atterton and Matthew Calarco, eds., *Animal Philosophy: Essential Readings in Continental Thought* (London: Continuum, 2004), 89–90.

90. Haraway, *The Companion Species Manifesto*, 61.

91. St. Augustine links bestiality to soldiers' forced rape of their captives; see Augustine, "Of the Violent Lust of the Souldiers, Executed Vpon the Bodies of the Captiues; Against Their Consents," in *St. Augustine, of the Citie of God Vvith the Learned Comments of Io. Lod. Viues. Englished by I. H.* (London: George Eld, 1610), at http://eebo.chadwyck.com/search/fulltext?ACTION=ByID&ID=D2000099842

6060042&SOURCE=var_spell.cfg&DISPLAY=AUTHOR&WARN=N&FILE=../
session/1313415143_17959.

92. Bulliet, *Hunters, Herders, and Hamburgers*, 6.

93. Anne McClintock, "Paranoid Empire: Specters from Guantanamo and Abu Ghraib," *Small Axe* 13, no. 1 (2009), 59.

94. Ibid.

95. Dora Apel, "Torture Culture: Lynching Photographs and the Images of Abu Ghraib," *Art Journal* 64, no. 2 (2005), 88.

96. McClintock, "Paranoid Empire," 60.

97. W. J. T. Mitchell, "Echoes of a Christian Symbol," *Chicago Tribune*, June 27, 2004.

98. Slavoj Žižek, "Between Two Deaths: The Culture of Torture," *London Review of Books*, June 3, 2004; Frank Rich, "It Was the Porn That Made Them Do It," *New York Times*, May 30, 2004.

99. Apel, "Torture Culture," 89.

100. Max Gordon, "Abu Ghraib: Postcards from the Edge," *OpenDemocracy* 13 (October 2004), at http://www.opendemocracy.net/media-abu_ghraib/article_2146.jsp.

101. McClintock, "Paranoid Empire," 63.

102. See, for instance, Patricia Williams's association of photos depicting dead bodies at Abu Ghraib with the open casket of Emmet Till (Williams, "In Kind"). For a fuller discussion of the connection with lynching, see Apel, "Torture Culture."

103. Carrie Rohman, *Stalking the Subject: Modernism and the Animal* (New York: Columbia University Press, 2009), 12.

104. Shesadri-Crooks, "Being Human," 111.

105. McClintock, "Paranoid Empire," 63.

106. Andrew Buncombe, Justin Huggler, and Leonard Doyle, "Abu Ghraib: Inmates Raped, Ridden Like Animals, and Forced to Eat Pork," *Independent* (2004), at http://www.independent.co.uk/news/world/middle-east/abu-ghraib-inmates-raped-ridden-like-animals-and-forced-to-eat-pork-564296.html. See also Maureen Dowd, "Torture Chicks Gone Wild," *New York Times*, January 30, 2005.

107. Judith Butler, *Precarious Life: The Powers of Mourning and Violence* (London: Verso, 2004), 78.

108. Ibid., 33.

109. Deborah Denenholz Morse and Martin A. Danahay, "Introduction," in Deborah Denenholz Morse and Martin A. Danahay, eds., *Victorian Animal Dreams: Representations of Animals in Victorian Literature and Culture* (Burlington, Vt.: Ashgate, 2007), 5.

110. Reading the abuse of prisoners in conjunction with an antigay agenda, Erin Runions has argued that "in the US, within the rhetoric of family values, raw sex is like bare life in that it is excluded from the social order." She argues that "law is seen as the avenue by which desire will be regulated and brought into conformity with the eschatology of the nation. . . . By way of stark contrast, the inclusion of bare life through the opposite approach to law overseas (that is, contempt for it) is also necessary to ensure US apocalyptic,

nationalist eschatology. In the state of exception, forever occasioned by the war on terror, domestic and international law is waived aside and torture is permitted" (Erin Runions, "Queering the Beast: The Antichrist's Gay Wedding," in Noreen Giffney and Myra Hird, eds., *Queering the Non/Human* [Burlington, Vt.: Ashgate, 2008], 97, 99).

111. People for the Ethical Treatment of Animals quoted in Ward Harkavy, "Abu Ghraib: A Chicken in Every Plot," *Village Voice*, May 10, 2005, at http://blogs.village-voice.com/pressclips/archives/2005/05/a_chicken_in_ev.php. In a 2004 op-ed piece for the *Los Angeles Times*, Peter Singer and Karen Dawn drew an analogy between the exemption of chickens from the so-called Humane Methods of Slaughter Act, which Congress passed in 1978, and the exclusion of detainees from the rights conferred by the Geneva Convention (Peter Singer and Karen Dawn, "Echoes of Abu Ghraib in a Chicken Slaughterhouse," *Los Angeles Times*, July 25, 2004). Animals currently do have some legal protections even though they are not legal subjects; for a state-by-state account of laws, see the American Society for the Prevention of Cruelty to Animals accounting at http://www.aspca.org/Fight-Animal-Cruelty/Advocacy-Center/state-animal-cruelty-laws.aspx. Peter Singer stirred up controversy when he wrote a review that seemed to endorse acts of bestiality; see Peter Singer, "Heavy Petting" (review of *Dearest Pet* by Midas Dekkers), *Nerve* (March 2001), at http://www.nerve.com/Opinions/Singer/heavyPetting/main.asp, and *Prospect* (April 2001): 12–13.

112. For a fuller reading of the role gender plays in the image of England holding a detainee by a dog leash, see the essays collected in Tara McKelvey, ed., *One of the Guys: Women as Aggressors and Torturers* (Emeryville, Calif.: Avalon, 2007).

113. "Metaphor," in Christopher Baldick, ed., *The Concise Oxford Dictionary of Literary Terms* (Oxford: Oxford University Press, 2008), from *Oxford Reference Online*, Dartmouth College, May 3, 2012, at http://www.oxfordreference.com/views/ENTRY.html?subview=Main&entry=t56.e712.

114. Henry Louis Gates, *The Signifying Monkey: A Theory of African-American Literary Criticism* (New York: Oxford University Press, 1988).

115. Cary Wolfe and Jonathan Elmer, "Subject to Sacrifice: Ideology, Psychoanalysis, and the Poverty of Humanism," in Cary Wolfe, *Animal Rites: American Culture, the Discourse of Species, and Posthumanist Theory* (Chicago: University of Chicago Press, 2003), 100.

116. For a compelling history of Western assumptions about Muslim attitudes toward animals and of the disruptions of those assumptions, see Donna Landry, "English Brutes, Eastern Enlightenment," in "Animal, All Too Animal," special issue of *The Eighteenth Century* 52, no. 1 (2011): 11–30. For an in-depth analysis of Muslim attitudes toward animals, see Nadeem Haque and Basheer Ahmad Masri, "The Principles of Animal Advocacy in Islam: Four Integrated Ecognitions," *Society & Animals* 19 (2011): 279–290; and Richard Foltz, *Animals in Islamic Tradition and Muslim Cultures* (Oxford: Oneworld, 2006).

117. According to a press release from the U.S. Department of Defense, military working dogs are their handler's friend as well as "their trusted companion, loyal follower and

No. 1 teammate" (Omar Villarreal, "Military Working Dogs, Handlers Train for Mission Success," Federal Information and News Dispatch, Defense Department Documents and Publications, February 6, 2006, at http://web.lexis-nexis.com/universe/document?_ m=c1cf2b84e1b4627e10ce6bb1dd4cea42&_docnum=36&wchp=dGLbVzb-zSkVb&_ md5=5a19961a90dd3402b9d667ed553b613a). The same press release also describes them as "the finest tools the military has to offer." The dog's role as friend or tool depends on the military's convenience, though; if historic precedent is any indication, Marco will not meet with a happy end. When World War II ended, the army ordered that all dogs who had gone through military training be killed. Of the 4,000 dogs estimated to have served in Vietnam, "281 were killed in action and no more than 250 came home"; the rest were killed, turned over to the South Vietnamese army, or simply left behind when the troops withdrew, discarded along with other military "tools" (Jessica Ravitz, "They Saved Soldiers' Lives, and Were Often Left Behind," *Salt Lake Tribune*, May 29, 2006).

118. Louis Althusser, "Ideology and Ideological State Apparatuses," in *Lenin and Philosophy, and Other Essays* (London: New Left Books, 1971), 162–170.

119. The photo, of course, is silent. Seymour Hirsch has documented that dog barking was an important element of the abuse at Abu Ghraib. Discussing one of the other photos that featured a guard dog, he writes: "The dogs are barking at a man who is partly obscured from the camera's view by the smiling soldier. Another image shows that the man, an Iraqi prisoner, is naked. His hands are clasped behind his neck and he is leaning against the door to a cell, contorted with terror, as the dogs bark a few feet away" (Seymour Hirsch, "Chain of Command: How the Department of Defense Mishandled the Disaster at Abu Ghraib," *The New Yorker*, May 17, 2004). For discussion of Smith in particular, see "Abu Ghraib Dog Handler Sentenced to 6 Months: Army Sergeant Convicted of Using Canines to Scare Prisoners at Iraqi Prison," MSNBC, updated March 22, 2006, at http://www.msnbc.msn.com/id/11943182.

120. Shesadri-Crooks, "Being Human," 110–111.

121. Mladen Dolar, *A Voice and Nothing More* (Cambridge, Mass.: MIT Press, 2006), 120, 122–123.

122. Following Douglas Kahn, I use the term *sound* as an inclusive category: "By sound I mean sounds, voices, and aurality" (Douglas Kahn, *Noise, Water, Meat* [Cambridge, Mass.: MIT Press, 1999], 3).

2. Bestiality Revisited: The Primal Scene of Biopower

Many thanks to John Stauffer for his generosity in sharing with me his transcription of Douglass's "Pictures" speech and for helping me locate Douglass's description of his encounter with the dog in "Farewell to the British People."

1. Orlando Patterson, *Slavery and Social Death: A Comparative Study* (Cambridge, Mass.: Harvard University Press, 1982), 5. As Andrew Norris has pointed out, the notion

of the social death of the slave first emerges in Locke's second of the *Two Treatises of Government*, where he argues that someone becomes a slave by trying to take another's life because by that act he is in fact already socially dead (Andrew Norris, "The Exemplary Exception: Philosophical and Political Decisions in Giorgio Agamben's *Homo Sacer*," in Andrew Norris, ed., *Politics, Metaphysics, and Death: Essays on Giorgio Agamben's "Homo Sacer"* [Durham, N.C.: Duke University Press, 2005], 272–273).

2. Patterson, *Slavery and Social Death*, 5, 9, viii.

3. Michel Foucault, *The History of Sexuality*, vol. 1, trans. Robert Hurley (New York: Vintage, 1990); Michel Foucault, *"Society Must Be Defended": Lectures at the Collège de France 1975–1976*, trans. David Macey, ed. Mauro Bertani and Alessandro Fontana (New York: Picador, 2003); Michel Foucault, *The Birth of Biopolitics: Lectures at the Collège de France, 1978–79*, trans. Graham Burchell, ed. Michel Senellart (New York: Palgrave Macmillan, 2008).

4. Foucault, *The History of Sexuality*, 1:139.

5. Foucault, *"Society Must Be Defended,"* 35. Foucault makes a similar claim when he writes in *The History of Sexuality* that "the old power of death that symbolized sovereign power was now carefully supplanted by the administration of bodies and the calculated management of life" (1:139–140).

6. Foucault, *The History of Sexuality*, 1:148–149, emphasis in original.

7. Ibid., 1:139, 146.

8. Foucault, *The Birth of Biopolitics*, 271–272.

9. Ibid., 274, 292.

10. Foucault, *The History of Sexuality*, 1:140–141, emphasis added.

11. Foucault, *"Society Must Be Defended,"* 29–30.

12. Patricia Ticineto Clough, "Introduction," in Patricia Ticineto Clough and Jean Halley, eds., *The Affective Turn: Theorizing the Social* (Durham, N.C.: Duke University Press, 2007), 19.

13. Foucault, *"Society Must Be Defended,"* 254.

14. Nicole Shukin, *Animal Capital: Rendering Life in Biopolitical Times* (Minneapolis: University of Minnesota Press, 2009), 5, Bhabha's emphasis.

15. Lisa Brawley, "Frederick Douglass's *My Bondage and My Freedom* and the Fugitive Tourist Industry," *Novel: A Forum on Fiction* 30, no. 1 (1996), 120.

16. Ibid.

17. Frederick Douglass, *My Bondage and My Freedom* (New York: Miller, Orton & Mulligan, 1855), 41.

18. John Winthrop, *History of New England*, 2 vols. (Boston: Little, Brown, 1853), 2:280–281.

19. Alexis de Tocqueville, *Democracy in America*, trans. George Lawrence, ed. J. P. Mayer (New York: Harper & Row, 1969), 317.

20. For the school of ethnology's theories, see Samuel George Morton, *Crania Americana: Or, a Comparative View of the Skulls of Various Aboriginal Nations of North and*

South America to Which Is Prefixed an Essay on the Variety of the Human Species (Philadelphia: John Pennington; London: James Madden, 1839); Samuel George Morton, *Brief Remarks on the Diversities of the Human Species: And on Some Kindred Subjects: Being an Introductory Lecture Delivered Before the Class of Pennsylvania Medical College, in Philadelphia, November 1, 1842* (Philadelphia: Merrihew & Thompson, 1842); Samuel George Morton, *Crania Aegyptiaca: Or, Observations on Egyptian Ethnography, Derived from Anatomy, History, and the Monuments* (Philadelphia: J. Pennington, 1844); Josiah Clark Nott, *Types of Mankind: Or, Ethnological Researches, Based Upon the Ancient Monuments, Paintings, Sculptures, and Crania of Races, and Upon Their Natural, Geographical, Philological, and Biblical History: Illustrated by Selections from the Inedited Papers of Samuel George Morton . . . and by Additional Contributions from Prof. L. Agassiz, Ll.D., W. Usher, M.D., and Prof. H. S. Patterson, M.D. By J. C. Nott and Geo. R. Gliddon,* 7th ed. (Philadelphia: Lippincott Gramoo, 1855); Josiah Clark Nott, *Indigenous Races of the Earth; or, New Chapters of Ethnological Inquiry; Including Monographs on Special Departments . . . Contributed by Alfred Maury . . . Francis Pulszky . . . and J. Aitken Meigs . . . Presenting Fresh Investigations, Documents, and Materials. By J. C. Nott . . . and Geo. R. Gliddon* (Philadelphia: J. B. Lippincott, 1857). Richard Colfax's *Evidence Against the Views of the Abolitionists* argued that "the Negroes, whether physically or morally considered, are so inferior as to resemble the brute creation as nearly as they do the white species" (Richard Colfax, *Evidence Against the Views of the Abolitionists, Consisting of Physical and Moral Proofs of Inferiority of the Negroes* [New York: n.p., 1833], 9). Douglass explicitly engaged with and rejected these theories; see, for instance, Frederick Douglass, "The Claims of the Negro Ethnologically Considered: An Address Delivered in Hudson, Ohio, on July 12, 1854," in *The Frederick Douglass Papers,* 4 vols., ed. John W. Blassingame, 2:497–525 (New Haven: Yale University Press, 1982). For Douglass's engagement with Morton's work and his resistance against polygenesis, see Robert Levine, *Martin Delany, Frederick Douglass, and the Politics of Representative Identity* (Chapel Hill: University of North Carolina Press, 1997), 10.

21. Douglass was particularly upset about the publication of Josiah Clark Nott's *Types of Mankind* (1855) and responded in a speech that denounced the book, which showcased the American school of ethnology, for its attempt to "brand the negro with natural inferiority" (Douglass, "The Claims of the Negro Ethnologically Considered," 2:519).

22. Kay Anderson, "White Natures: Sydney's Royal Agricultural Show in Posthumanist Perspective," *Transactions, Institute of British Geographers* 28, no. 4 (2003), 426.

23. René Descartes, "Animals Are Machines," in Tom Regan and Peter Singer, eds., *Animal Rights and Human Obligations* (Englewood Cliffs, N.J.: Prentice-Hall, 1976), 66. Janet Moore Lindman and Michele Lise Tarter read Descartes and the European *philosophes* as developing "a hierarchical system that separated embodiment from reason" and that provided one of the intellectual underpinnings for phrenology (Janet Moore Lindman and Michele Lise Tarter, "Introduction," in Janet Moore Lindman and Michele

Lise Tarter, eds., *A Centre of Wonders: The Body in Early America* [Ithaca: Cornell University Press, 2001], 4).

24. *The Dred Scott Decision. Opinion of Chief Justice Taney, with an Introduction by Dr. J. H. Van Evrie. Also, an Appendix, Containing an Essay on the Natural History of the Prognathous Race of Mankind, Originally Written for the New York Day-Book, by Dr. S. A. Cartwright, of New Orleans* (New York: Van Evrie, Horton, 1863), 45.

25. Marjorie Spiegel, *The Dreaded Comparison: Human and Animal Slavery* (Philadelphia: New Society, 1988); see also Keith Bradley, "Animalizing the Slave: The Truth of Fiction," *Journal of Roman Studies* 90 (2000): 110–125.

26. Dwight A. McBride, *Impossible Witnesses: Truth, Abolitionism, and Slave Testimony* (New York: New York University Press, 2001), 12.

27. Frederick Douglass, *Narrative of the Life of Frederick Douglass, an American Slave, Written by Himself* (New Haven: Yale University Press, 2001), 48; Frederick Douglass, *My Bondage and My Freedom*, ed. William L. Andrews (Urbana: University of Illinois Press, 1987), 29. Harriet Ritvo has documented the invention of a new kind of property in the eighteenth century that we would now recognize as genetic property and see in the context of biotechnology (Harriet Ritvo, "Possessing Mother Nature: Genetic Capital in Eighteenth-Century Britain," in John Berwer and Susan Staves, eds., *Early Modern Conceptions of Property*, 413–426 [London: Routledge, 1995]).

28. Karl Jacoby, "Slaves by Nature? Domestic Animals and Human Slavery," *Slavery & Abolition* 15, no. 1 (1994), 95. For the way Aristotle's *Politics* in particular was used to justify slavery, see Caroline Winterer, *The Culture of Classicism* (Baltimore: Johns Hopkins University Press, 2002), 75. Aristotle's theories on slavery affected not only African Americans but also Native Americans; for the importance of these theories to sixteenth-century Spanish imperialism, see Lewis Hanke, *Aristotle and the American Indians: A Study in Race Prejudice in the Modern World* (London: Hollis & Carter, 1959).

29. Aristotle, *The Politics*, trans. Carnes Lord (Chicago: University of Chicago Press, 1984), 41, 36.

30. Separating Aristotle's biological works from his "moral and political works," Robert Mayhew examines Aristotle's understandings of women but makes only two passing references to the issue of slavery (Robert Mayhew, *The Female in Aristotle's Biology* [Chicago: University of Chicago Press, 2004], 1–2, 14 n. 17). Mayhew largely rejects feminist critiques of Aristotle. For further engagement with those critiques and for intersections between gender studies and science, see Ruth Bleier, *Science and Gender: A Critique of Biology and Its Theories on Women* (New York: Pergamon, 1984); Lesley Ann Dean-Jones, *Women's Bodies in Classical Greek Science* (Oxford: Clarendon Press, 1994); Cynthia Freeland, ed., *Feminist Interpretations of Aristotle* (University Park: Pennsylvania University Press,1998); Cynthia Freeland, "Nourishing Speculation: A Feminist Reading of Aristotelian Science," in Bat-Ami Bar On, ed., *Engendering Origins: Critical Feminist Readings in Plato and Aristotle*, 145–188 (Albany: State University of New York Press, 1994); Luce Irigaray, "Place, Interval: A Reading of Aristotle, *Physics* Iv," in Freeland,

ed., *Feminist Interpreations of Aristotle*, 41–58; Lynda Lange, "Woman Is Not a Rational Animal: On Aristotle's Biology of Reproduction," in Sandra Harding and Merrill B. Hintikka, eds., *Discovering Reality: Feminist Perspectives on Epistemology, Metaphysics, Methodology, and Philosophy of Science*, 1–16 (Boston: Reiderl, 1983); Martha Nussbaum, "Aristotle, Feminism, and Needs for Functioning," in Freeland, ed., *Feminist Interpretations of Aristotle*, 248–259; Sue Rosser, *Biology and Feminism: A Dynamic Interaction* (New York: Twayne, 1992); Nancy Tuana, "Aristotle and the Politics of Reproduction," in Bar On, *Engendering Origins*, 189–206; and the extensive writings of Evelyn Fox Keller, including most recently Evelyn Fox Keller, *The Mirage of a Space Between Nature and Nurture* (Durham, N.C.: Duke University Press, 2010).

31. Other critics who read Hester's whipping as a rape include Levine, *Martin Delany, Frederick Douglass*, 123, and Sadiya Hartman, *Scenes of Subjection: Terror, Slavery, and Self-Making in Nineteenth-Century America* (New York: Oxford University Press, 1997), 81. Sexual acts perpetrated by masters against slaves could not be recognized legally as rape because the act did not injure the master's own property rights; see Andrea Stone, "Interracial Sexual Abuse and Legal Subjectivity in Antebellum Law and Literature," *American Literature* 81, no. 1 (2009): 65–92.

32. Hartman, *Scenes of Subjection*, 79.

33. Sabine Sielke, *Reading Rape: The Rhetoric of Sexual Violence in American Literature and Culture, 1790–1990* (Princeton: Princeton University Press, 2002), 22, 26.

34. Douglass, *Narrative*, 16.

35. In the colonial context discussed in chapter 1, "Sodomy and buggery, when penetration can be proved, are capital sins; rape is 'uncleanness,' a lesser charge" (Jonathan Goldberg, "Bradford's 'Ancient Members' and 'a Case of Buggery . . . Amongst Them,'" in Andrew Parker, Mary Russo, Doris Sommer, and Patricia Yaeger, eds., *Nationalisms and Sexualities* [New York: Routledge, 1991], 69).

36. "Bestiality," *Oxford English Dictionary*, 2d ed. (*OED Online*, March 2012, at http://www.oed.com/view/Entry/18199).

37. Robert Levine has argued that "the whip can be taken as a metonymy for the phallus of the master or overseer" (Levine, *Martin Delany, Frederick Douglass*, 122).

38. Douglass, *Narrative*, 16.

39. This question of how being stripped of clothes returns people to a primal humanity is raised in a text published a decade before Douglass's *Narrative*: Thomas Carlyle, *Sartor Resartus: The Life and Opinions of Herr Teufelsdröckh* (1831), ed. Roger Tarr (Berkeley: University of California Press, 2000). See also Jacques Derrida, "The Animal That Therefore I Am (More to Follow)," *Critical Inquiry* 28, no. 2 (2002): 369–418.

40. Louis Marin, *Food for Thought* (Baltimore: Johns Hopkins University Press, 1989), 44.

41. Alice A. Kuzniar, *Melancholia's Dog* (Chicago: University of Chicago Press, 2006), 68.

42. Ibid., 93.

43. Anat Pick, *Creaturely Poetics: Animality and Vulnerability in Literature and Film* (New York: Columbia University Press, 2011), 16.

44. Douglass, *Narrative*, 15–16.

45. John Carlos Rowe, *At Emerson's Tomb: The Politics of Classic American Literature* (New York: Columbia University Press, 1997), 115.

46. Douglass, *Narrative*, 15.

47. Tobias Menely, "Animal Signs and Ethical Significance: Expressive Creatures in the British Georgic," *Mosaic* 39, no. 4 (2006), 122.

48. Douglass builds on the fact that the term *master* had a double resonance in slavery and animal husbandry: as Teresa Magnum points out, *masters* was "the term Victorian writers most commonly applied" when talking about what we would now refer to as "dog owners" (Teresa Mangum, "Dog Years, Human Fears," in Nigel Rothfels, ed., *Representing Animals* [Bloomington: Indiana University Press, 2002], 38).

49. I am not the first to describe Douglass's witnessing of Hester's whipping as a "primal scene"; see Hartman, *Scenes of Subjection*, 4.

50. The distinction between voice and speech dates back to Aristotle; see Aristotle, "Animals Are Not Political," in Andrew Linzey and Paul Barry Clarke, eds., *Animal Rights: A Historical Anthology* (New York: Columbia University Press, 2004), 6.

51. Fred Moten has argued that "passionate utterance and response together take the form of an encounter, the mutual, negative positioning of master and slave. . . . [Utterance and response, seen together as encounter, form a kind of call wherein Hester's shrieks improvise both speech and writing" (Fred Moten, *In the Break: The Aesthetics of the Black Radical Tradition* [Minneapolis: University of Minnesota Press, 2003], 21).

52. René Descartes, *The Philosophical Writings of Descartes* (Cambridge: Cambridge University Press, 1985), 139, 140.

53. Foucault, *The History of Sexuality*, 1:140–141, emphasis added.

54. Elaine Scarry, *The Body in Pain: The Making and Unmaking of the World* (New York: Oxford University Press, 1985), 4, 39. Arguing against Scarry, Lucy Bending writes: "It has become a commonplace that pain defies language . . . [but] pain can enter into language and be accommodated by its structures—whether descriptive or metaphorical—in the face of a paucity of directly expressive words for painful sensations." She insists that "problems caused by the scarcity of direct language for pain do not automatically mean that there is no viable mode of expression" and refutes "the claim that there is no language for pain," taking into account not only human suffering but also the discussions over vivisection (Lucy Bending, *The Representation of Bodily Pain in Late Nineteenth-Century English Culture* [Oxford: Clarendon Press, 2000], 82–83). Bending is particularly attentive to the way in which a discourse of "the imperviousness of the savage to pain" circulated as part of these debates (124–133).

55. Jacques Derrida, "And Say the Animal Responded?" in Cary Wolfe, ed., *Zoontologies: The Question of the Animal* (Minneapolis: University of Minnesota Press, 2003), 124, 137, emphasis in original.

56. Douglass, *Narrative*, 16, 15.

57. Descartes, *The Philosophical Writings of Descartes*, 140.

58. Douglass, *My Bondage and My Freedom* (1987 edition), 131.

59. Cary Wolfe and Jonathan Elmer, "Subject to Sacrifice: Ideology, Psychoanalysis, and the Discourse of Species in Jonathan Demme's *Silence of the Lambs*," *boundary 2* 22, no. 3 (1995), 144, emphasis omitted. Douglass's invocation of animals may also have been a strategy for mobilizing abolitionist resources. In Great Britain and the United States, abolition and animal welfare emerged in conjunction with each other; see Jacoby, "Slaves by Nature?" 96–97, and Moira Ferguson, *Animal Advocacy and Englishwomen, 1780–1900: Patriots, Nation, and Empire* (Ann Arbor: University of Michigan Press, 1998), 28, 32, 43.

60. Aristotle, *The Politics*, 41.

61. Aristotle, *De Anima*, trans. R. D. Hicks. (Cambridge: Cambridge University Press, 1907), 53, 59, 55, 59.

62. David Hume, "Of the Reason of Animals," in Regan and Singer, eds., *Animal Rights and Human Obligations*, 70.

63. Frederick Douglass, "Pictures" (1865?), holograph of a speech, Frederick Douglass Papers, Library of Congress, Washington, D.C., on microfilm at Yale University, transcribed by John Stauffer, August 1996.

64. Emmanuel Lévinas, "Name of a Dog, or Natural Rights," in *Difficult Freedom: Essays on Judaism*, trans. Seán Hand (Baltimore: Johns Hopkins University Press, 1990), 153.

65. Douglass, *Narrative*, 38.

66. Mladen Dolar, *A Voice and Nothing More* (Cambridge, Mass.: MIT Press, 2006), 4, 28, 32, 42, 59, 73, 106, 107.

67. Foucault, *The Birth of Biopolitics*, 274, 292.

68. Judith Butler, *Bodies That Matter: On the Discursive Limits of "Sex"* (New York: Routledge, 1993), 8.

69. Johann Gottfried Herder, "Essay on the Origin of Language," in *On the Origin of Language* (Chicago: University of Chicago Press, 1966), 94, 87, 88. The innate quality of the sympathizer led Adam Smith to exclude animals from his *Theory of Moral Sentiments* (1759). As Markman Ellis sums up, "Are animals appropriate objects of sympathy? The central problem posed by animals for Adam Smith's theory of sympathy is their liminal status as feelers. . . . [T]here is a problem with reciprocity, for in Smith's estimation it is not at all clear that animals are capable of feeling sympathy for humans in the same way that humans can feel sympathy for them. And this double sympathy—this potential for reciprocated sympathy—is central to Smith's theory of moral sentiments and the virtuous society it proposes" (Markman Ellis, "Suffering Things: Lapdogs, Slaves, and Counter-Sensibility," in Mark Blackwell, ed., *The Secret Life of Things: Animals, Objects, and It-Narratives in Eighteenth-Century England* [Lewisburg, Pa.: Bucknell University Press, 2007], 103).

70. Douglass, "Pictures."

71. Timothy Morton, *Shelley and the Revolution in Taste: The Body and the Natural World* (Cambridge: Cambridge University Press, 1994), 28.

72. Shukin, *Animal Capital*, 9.

73. Annabel M. Patterson, *Fables of Power: Aesopian Writing and Political History* (Durham, N.C.: Duke University Press, 1991), 3. For additional discussion of the Aesopian tradition, see Jayne Elizabeth Lewis, *The English Fable: Aesop and Literary Culture 1651–1740* (Cambridge: Cambridge University Press, 1996); Mark Lovering, *A History of Augustan Fable* (Cambridge: Cambridge University Press, 1998); and Frank Palmeri, "The History of Fables and Cultural History in Eighteenth-Century England," in Lorna Clymer and Robert Mayer, eds., *Historical Boundaries, Narrative Forms: Essays on British Literature in the Long Eighteenth Century in Honor of Everett Zimmerman*, 141–163 (Newark: University of Delaware Press, 2007). Louise Robbins links the fable tradition to natural history in *Elephant Slaves and Pampered Parrots: Exotic Animals in Eighteenth-Century Paris* (Baltimore: Johns Hopkins University Press, 2002).

74. Aesop, Samuel Croxall, Robert Aitken, and James Poupard, *Fables of Aesop and Others* (Philadelphia: R. Aitken, 1777). Although most American editions of the fables were printed in Boston, Philadelphia, and New York, several editions were printed in Baltimore, where Douglass lived for part of his childhood: Aesop and H. Clarke, *Fabulae Aesopi Selectae, or, Select Fables of Aesop: With an English Translation More Literal Than Any Yet Extant: Designed for the Readier Instruction of Beginners in the Latin Tongue* (Baltimore: Fielding Lucas Jr., 1817); Aesop, *Aesop's Fables* (Baltimore: Samuel Wood & Sons, 1821). Several editions were published especially for children: Aesop, *The Little Esop* (Philadelphia: Smith and Peck, 1843); Aesop, *Little Fables for Little Folks: Selected for Their Moral Tendency, and Re-written in Familiar Words, Not One of Which Exceeds Two Syllables* (New Haven: S. Babcock, 1835); Aesop, *Child's Own Fable Book* (New York: Leavitt & Allen, 1860); Aesop, *A Child's Version of Aesop's Fables; with a Supplement Containing Fables from La Fontaine and Krilof* (Boston: Ginn, 1886); Aesop, Alexander Greaves, William Thompson, and Mahlon Day, *Aesop, Junior, in America: Being a Series of Fables Written Especially for the People of the United States of North America* (New York: Mahlon Day, 1834); Aesop and Mara Pratt-Chadwick, *Aesop's Fables, Vol. 1. First Grade* (Boston: Educational Pub., 1892). These editions were apparently popular: *Little Esop* alone went through at least eight editions (1843, 1844, 1845, 1847, 1855, 1856, 1857, 1859). Aesop's fables were also used for purposes of linguistic instruction in editions such as: Aesop and H. Clarke, *Fabulae Aesopi Selectae*; Aesop, *Aesop's Fables in French: With a Description of Fifty Animals Mentioned Therein and a French and English Dictionary of the Words Contained in the Work* (Philadelphia: Lindsay and Blakiston, 1852). *Aesop's Fables in French* enjoyed particular popularity, with subsequent editions appearing in 1854, 1856, 1864, 1865, and 1869.

75. The *Life of Aesop* was first printed in Aesop and Robert L'Estrange, *A History of the Life of Aesop* (Philadelphia: Southwark Office, 1798). Frank Palmeri identifies a particular

eighteenth-century subgenre of the animal fable that seems in keeping with the bodily narration generated in the *Life of Aesop*; he describes a group of "anti-allegorical fables" in which animals "speak from the subject position of their species" to critique human "behavior and attitudes toward animals, including anthropomorphism, from within the anthropomorphic form of the fable itself" (Frank Palmeri, "The Autocritique of Fables," in Frank Palmeri, ed., *Humans and Other Animals in Eighteenth-Century British Culture: Representation, Hybridity, Ethics* [Burlington, Vt.: Ashgate, 2006], 84).

76. Samuel Goodrich, *Famous Men of Ancient Times* (Boston: J. E. Hickman, 1843). Goodrich's text was evidently popular: it had gone through at least four editions by 1852.

77. Butler, *Bodies That Matter*, 8.

78. Marin, *Food for Thought*, 49, 54.

79. Ibid., 51.

80. Bruce Thomas Boehrer, *Animal Characters: Nonhuman Beings in Early Modern Literature* (Philadelphia: University of Pennsylvania Press, 2010), 3, 17, 10, 12.

81. Winterer, *The Culture of Classicism*, 11–82; Lawrence Levine, "William Shakespeare in America," in *Highbrow Lowbrow: The Emergence of Cultural Hierarchy in America*, 11–82 (Cambridge, Mass.: Harvard University Press, 1988).

82. Boehrer, *Animal Characters*, 16. Boehrer distinguishes Aristotle from Descartes (*Animal Characters*, 16), but that distinction has recently been subject to reevalutions. Likewise arguing for the distinction between Aristotle and Descartes, Riccardo Pozzo draws on Ernst Cassirer's work and writes: "As long as the concept of substance and the idea that a property is predicated on an individual subject maintained scientific primacy, Aristotelianism was in great demand and was able to defeat threatening alternatives . . . ; but as soon as Descartes established the convenience of expressing all scientific problems in terms of function, i.e. in terms of the relation of two or more ideas or bodies in space and time, Aristotelianism began an inexorable descent" (Riccardo Pozzo, "Introduction," in Riccardo Pozzo, ed., *The Impact of Aristotelianism on Modern Philosophy* [Washington, D.C.: Catholic University of America Press, 2004], viii). One of the first works to look at animals as animals and not (just) as metaphors in literary representations also pitted Descartes and Aristotle against each other in order to suggest that Cartesian thought remained a contested theory and met with opposition, especially by people who disputed Descartes's notions of animals as machines; see A. Lytton Sells, *Animal Poetry in French & English Literature & the Greek Tradition* (Bloomington: Indiana University Press, 1955), xxiii–xxiv. Akira Lippit links Aristotle and Descartes in their disenfranchisement of animals, though he distinguishes between the ways in which they justify that shared dismissal of animals (Akira Mizuta Lippit, *Electric Animal: Toward a Rhetoric of Wildlife* [Minneapolis: University of Minnesota Press, 2000], 33).

83. Douglass, *Narrative*, 28.

84. Ibid., 20–21.

85. Michael Chaney, *Fugitive Vision: Slave Image and Black Identity in Antebellum Narrative* (Bloomington: Indiana University Press, 2008), 132.

86. This advertisement is included in Abraham Chapman, ed., *Steal Away: Stories of the Runaway Slaves* (New York: Praeger, 1971), 61.

87. For a reading of Lévinas's "Name of a Dog" in relation to coevolution, by which "dogs and humans, as Lévinas implies, are thoroughly enmeshed in a messy partnership which is not reducible to a straightforward tale of human agency and canine passivity," see Karalyn Kendall, "The Face of a Dog: Levinasian Ethics and Human/Dog Coevolution," in Noreen Giffney and Myra Hird, eds., *Queering the Non/Human* (Burlington, Vt.: Ashgate, 2008), 199.

88. Lévinas, "Name of a Dog, or Natural Rights," 153.

89. Martin Heidegger, *The Fundamental Concepts of Metaphysics: World, Finitude, Solitude*, trans. William McNeill and Nicholas Walker (Bloomington: Indiana University Press, 1995), 177.

90. Anat Pick argues that "while the Holocaust performed a violent unraveling of human identity, disclosing human contingency and the genocidal impulses inherent in striving for human perfection, much of the scholarly and popular legacy of the atrocity has been, oddly, the restitution and rehabilitation of humanism. A creaturely reading retrieves the Holocaust's disavowed animality as central to the ethics of memory" (Pick, *Creaturely Poetics*, 6).

91. Lévinas, "Name of a Dog, or Natural Rights," 153. In the reading that follows, I go against the grain of critical interpretations of Lévinas, which are summed up in Carrie Rohman's statement that "the ethical call cannot issue from the nonhuman face for Lévinas, who defines alterity as exclusively human in its inseparability from the linguistic exchange between interlocutors" and who ultimately sees alterity not as "the radical alterity of the animal other, but [as] the relative alterity of the human other" (Carrie Rohman, *Stalking the Subject: Modernism and the Animal* [New York: Columbia University Press, 2009], 10, 11).

92. David Clark, "On Being 'the Last Kantian in Germany': Dwelling with Animals After Lévinas," in Jennifer Ham and Matthew Senior, eds., *Animal Acts: Configuring the Human in Western History* (New York: Routledge, 1997), 197. Matthew Calarco similarly takes Lévinas to task for an anthropocentric view; see Matthew Calarco, *Zoographies: The Question of the Animal from Heidegger to Derrida* (New York: Columbia University Press, 2008).

93. Lévinas, "Name of a Dog, or Natural Rights," 153.

94. Kuzniar, *Melancholia's Dog*, 1.

95. Lévinas, "Name of a Dog, or Natural Rights," 151.

96. For an extended inquiry into this problem, see John Llewelyn, "Am I Obsessed by Bobby? (Humanism of the Other Animal)," in Robert Bernasconi and Simon Critchley, eds., *Re-reading Levinas*, 234–247 (Bloomington: Indiana University Press, 1991).

97. Emmanuel Lévinas, "Interview," in Peter Atterton and Matthew Calarco, eds., *Animal Philosophy: Essential Readings in Continental Thought* (London: Continuum, 2004), 49, 50.

98. Frederick Douglass, "Farewell to the British People: An Address Delivered in London, England, on 30 March 1847," in *The Frederick Douglass Papers*, 2:50. Douglass is staging a claim that he makes repeatedly; for instance, he gives the same point in "What to the Slave Is the Fourth of July?" when he writes: "When the dogs in your streets, when the fowls of the air, when the cattle on your hills, when the fish of the sea, and the reptiles that crawl, shall be unable to distinguish the slave from a brute, then will I argue with you that the slave is a man!" (in Douglass, *My Bondage and My Freedom* [1855 edition], appendix, 443).

99. Douglass makes a similar point when he writes: "The dog dances when he [man] comes home, and whines piteously when he is absent. All these know that the negro is a MAN" (Douglass, "The Claims of the Negro," 2:503, emphasis in original).

100. Lévinas, "Name of a Dog, or Natural Rights," 152.

3. Animals and the Letter of the Law

1. Rei Terada, *Feeling in Theory: Emotion After The "Death of the Subject"* (Cambridge, Mass.: Harvard University Press, 2001), 4, 21.

2. Bruno Latour, *We Have Never Been Modern*, trans. Catherine Porter (Cambridge, Mass.: Harvard University Press, 1993), 27.

3. Mark Seltzer, *True Crime: Observations on Violence and Modernity* (New York: Routledge, 2007), 8.

4. Franco Moretti, *Signs Taken for Wonders: Essays in the Sociology of Literary Forms*, trans. Susan Fischer, David Forgacs, and David Miller (London: Verso, 1983), 146.

5. In a wonderfully complex chapter entitled "Murder in the Kitchen" in her cookbook, Alice B. Toklas links crime fiction to cooking and specifically discusses murder as the inaugurating event of the text: "Cookbooks have always intrigued and seduced me. When I was still a dilettante in the kitchen they held my attention, even the dull ones, from cover to cover, the way crime and murder stories did Gertrude Stein. When we first began reading Dashiell Hammett, Gertrude Stein remarked that it was his modern note to have disposed of his victims before the story commenced. Goodness knows how many were required to follow as the result of the first crime. And so it is in the kitchen. Murder and sudden death seem as unnatural there as they should be anywhere else" (Alice B. Toklas, *The Alice B. Toklas Cookbook* [New York: Harper & Row, 1984], 37).

6. Moretti, *Signs Taken for Wonders*, 137, emphasis omitted

7. Ibid., 134, 135, 137, 142, emphasis in original.

8. Emphasis omitted in this repeated quotation from "Murders." For a fuller discussion of the animal as criminal and vice versa, see Grace Moore, "Beastly Criminals and

Criminal Beasts: Stray Women and Stray Dogs in *Oliver Twist*," in Deborah Denenholz Morse and Martin A. Danahay, eds., *Victorian Animal Dreams: Representations of Animals in Victorian Literature and Culture*, 201–214 (Burlington, Vt.: Ashgate, 2007).

9. Edgar Allan Poe, "The Murders in the Rue Morgue," in *The Selected Writings of Edgar Allan Poe*, ed. G. R. Thompson (New York: Norton, 2004), 251.

10. For a detailed discussion of the relation of "Murders in the Rue Morgue" to newspaper accounts of thieving apes, see Shawn J. Rosenheim, *The Cryptographic Imagination: Secret Writings from Edgar Allan Poe to the Internet* (Baltimore: Johns Hopkins University Press, 1997).

11. As the term *murder* is defined in the *Oxford English Dictionary* (*OED Online*, September 2011, at http://www.oed.com/view/Entry/123858?rskey=XVkRBn&result=1&isAdvanced=false).

12. Poe's story is often hailed as the first work of detective fiction; a precursor that Poe knew was Voltaire's *Zadig, or Destiny* (1748), in which much of the investigation revolves around reading animal tracks; see the preface to Poe, "The Murders in the Rue Morgue," 239.

13. Preface to Poe, "The Murders in the Rue Morgue," 239, 240.

14. Ibid., 242.

15. Edgar Allan Poe, "The Murders in the Rue Morgue," *Graham's Lady's and Gentleman's Magazine*, April 1841, 166.

16. Ibid., emphasis in original. Subsequent quotations from "Murders" come from the version in *The Selected Writings of Edgar Allan Poe* cited in note 9.

17. For instance, Dupin points to the woman "strangled to death by manual strength, and thrust up a chimney, head downward," and rhetorically asks, "How great must have been that strength which could have thrust the body *up* such an aperture so forcibly that the united vigor of several persons was found barely sufficient to drag it *down*!" (Poe, "The Murders in the Rue Morgue," 259, emphasis in the original).

18. From the definition of *orangutan* in the *Oxford English Dictionary* (*OED Online*, September 2011, http://www.oed.com/view/Entry/132186?redirectedFrom=orangutan).

19. Poe's work is very much in line with eighteenth-century engagements with the orangutan. As Laura Brown explains, the orangutan "generates an ontological shock, a kind of identity crisis, promulgating the idea of human–animal proximity, or the even more surprising notion that a nonhuman being might actually be indistinguishable from a human" (Laura Brown, *Homeless Dogs and Melancholy Apes: Humans and Other Animals in the Modern Literary Imagination* [Ithaca: Cornell University Press, 2010], 4, see also 27–63). See also Susan Wiseman, "Monstrous Perfectibility: Ape–Human Transformations in Hobbes, Bulwer, Tyson," in Erica Fudge, Ruth Gilbert, and Susan Wiseman, eds., *At the Borders of the Human: Beasts, Bodies, and Natural Philosophy in the Early Modern Period*, 215–239 (New York: Palgrave, 2002); and Harriet Ritvo, "Border Trouble: Shifting the Line Between People and Other Animals," in Arien Mack, ed., *Humans and Other Animals*, 67–86 (Columbus: Ohio State University Press, 1995). In

relation to the public discussion of the nature of man, "orang outangs and feral children" occupy an equally problematic liminal position between man and nature (Richard Nash, *Wild Enlightenment: The Borders of Human Identity in the Eighteenth Century* [Charlottesville: University of Virginia Press, 2003], 163).

20. Marie Bonaparte, *The Life and Works of Edgar Allan Poe*, trans. John Rodker (London: Hogarth Press, 1949). Bonaparte contributed to the genre of animal (auto) biography that I discuss in chapter 5: in 1937, she published the memoir *Topsy, Chow-Chow au poil d'or*, which appeared in English translation in 1945 as *Topsy: The Story of a Gold-Haired Chow* (Susan McHugh, *Animal Stories: Narrating Across Species Lines* [Minneapolis: University of Minnesota Press, 2011], 126).

21. Rosenheim, *The Cryptographic Imagination*, 80.

22. Jacques Lacan, "Seminar on 'The Purloined Letter,'" in John P. Muller and William J. Richardson, eds., *The Purloined Poe*, 28–55 (Baltimore: Johns Hopkins University Press, 1988).

23. On Poe's racial politics, see especially Toni Morrison, *Playing in the Dark: Whiteness and the Literary Imagination* (Cambridge, Mass.: Harvard University Press, 1992); J. Gerald Kennedy and Liliane Weissberg, eds., *Romancing the Shadow: Poe and Race* (New York: Oxford University Press, 2001); and Maurice Lee, *Slavery, Philosophy, and American Literature, 1830–1860* (Cambridge: Cambridge University Press, 2005).

24. For the latter reading, see Lyndon Barrett, "Presence of Mind: Detection and Racialization in 'The Murders in the Rue Morgue,'" in Kennedy and Weissberg, eds., *Romancing the Shadow*, 157–176; and Joan Dayan, "Amorous Bondage: Poe, Ladies, and Slaves," *American Literature* 66, no. 2 (1994): 239–273. The association of orangutans in particular with slaves was a well-established trope by the time of Poe's writing. In *Notes on the State of Virginia*, Thomas Jefferson had included in his remarks on the comparative beauty of the races a comment about "the preference of the Oranootan for the black women over those of his own species" (Thomas Jefferson, *Notes on the State of Virginia* [Philadelphia: Prichard and Hall, 1788], 148).

25. Edgar Allan Poe, "The Philosophy of Composition," in *The Selected Writings of Edgar Allan Poe*, 679.

26. T. S. Eliot, "From Poe to Valéry" (1948), in *To Criticize the Critic, and Other Writings* (Lincoln: University of Nebraska Press, 1992), 35.

27. Jonathan Elmer, *Reading at the Social Limit* (Stanford: Stanford University Press, 1995), 213.

28. Edgar Allan Poe, "The Black Cat," in *The Selected Writings of Edgar Allan Poe*, 349, emphasis in original.

29. For Poe's relationship to Locke, see Joan Dayan, *Fables of Mind: An Inquiry Into Poe's Fiction* (New York: Oxford University Press, 1987).

30. *The Fire, or, Never Despair. With the History and Adventures of a Cat* (New Haven: I. Cooke, 1812). Poe may also have gotten his idea for "The Black Cat" from the larger tradition of European literature in which he was versed; Robert Darnton has documented

that "the torture of animals, especially cats, was a popular amusement throughout early modern Europe. . . . Far from being a sadistic fantasy on the part of a few half-crazed authors, the literary versions of cruelty to animals expressed a deep current of popular culture, as Mikhail Bakhtin has shown in his study of Rabelais" (Robert Darnton, *The Great Cat Massacre and Other Episodes in French Cultural History* [New York: Basic Books, 1983], 90).

31. *The Hare; or, Hunting Incompatible with Humanity: Written as a Stimulus to Youth Towards a Proper Treatment of Animals* (Philadelphia: Benjamin Johnson, 1802), 141.

32. Dorothy Kilner, *The Rotchfords; or the Friendly Counsellor: Designed for the Instruction and Amusement of the Youth of Both Sexes*, 2 vols. in one book (Philadelphia: James Humphrey, 1801), iii–iv, 73, 74, 78, emphasis in original.

33. Marian Scholtmeijer argues that, "in a strange way, acts of violence in these stories acknowledge the reality of animals. The moment of enlightenment for the reader if not obviously for the character comes with the recognition of the similarity between the victimized person and the victimized animal. It appears paradoxically that, by means of aggressive acts, urban people can reach across the chasm separating urban and animal life. Indeed—and this is the most terrifying feature of urbanism—cruelty to animals in the urban setting muddles up sanity with madness. In the fiction that brings the urban person to the point of cruelty to animals, that cruelty can even signal the individual's genuine contact with his or her own humanity" (Marian Louise Scholtmeijer, *Animal Victims in Modern Fiction: From Sanctity to Sacrifice* [Toronto: University of Toronto Press, 1993], 145).

34. For a discussion of the strategic use to which the narrator puts this confession for an insanity plea and of the way the text undercuts that plea by instating an extrajudicial sense of moral right, see John Cleman, "Irresistible Impulses: Edgar Allan Poe and the Insanity Defense," *American Literature* 63, no. 4 (1991): 623–640.

35. Poe, "The Black Cat," 349.

36. This breakdown taps into a larger issue: "Representations of domestic animals acting violently in Victorian art bring into conjunction categories that were increasingly viewed as separate, and make the animal the vehicle for an exploration of conflicting ideological codes of domesticity and aggression." In particular, they show "how permeable this barrier was to the forces of violence, class conflict and sexual domination" (Martin A. Danahay, "Nature Red in Hoof and Paw: Domestic Animals and Violence in Victorian Art," in Morse and Danahay, eds., *Victorian Animal Dreams*, 97, 116).

37. Poe, "The Black Cat," 355.

38. As Joseph Moldenhauer has pointed out, several of Poe's tales and especially moments of confession end in a swoon (Joseph J. Moldenhauer, "Murder as Fine Art: Basic Connections Between Poe's Aesthetics, Psychology, and Moral Vision," *PMLA* 83, no. 2 [1968], 295).

39. For a fuller discussion of the somatic effect sensational literature has on the reader, see D. A. Miller, *The Novel and the Police* (Berkeley: University of California Press, 1988).

40. Dayan, "Amorous Bondage," 241.

41. Madeleine Stern, "Poe: 'The Mental Temperament' for Phrenologists," *American Literature* 40, no. 2 (1968), 161.

42. Ibid., 162.

43. Edgar Allan Poe, "Review of *Phrenology and the Moral Influence of Phrenology: Arranged for General Study, and the Purposes of Education, from the First Published Works of Gall and Spurzheim, to the Latest Discoveries of the Present Period.* By Mrs. L. Miles. Philadelphia: Carey, Lea, and Blanchard," in Edgar Allan Poe, *Essays and Reviews*, ed. G. R. Thompson (New York: Library of America, 1984), 329–330, emphasis in original.

44. Edgar Allan Poe, "Phrenology," *Southern Literary Messenger* 2, no. 4 (1836), 286, emphasis in original.

45. Ivan Hannaford, *Race: The History of an Idea in the West* (Baltimore: Johns Hopkins University Press, 1996), 258.

46. See, for instance, "The Negro and Caucasian Brain Compared," *American Phrenological Journal* 3, no. 6 (1841): 282–283.

47. L. N. F. [Lorenzo Niles Fowler], "Application of Phrenology to Criticism, and the Analysis of Character, in a Letter to the Editor," *American Phrenological Journal* 1, no. 3 (1838), 65–71, accessed through http://www.proquest.com (L. N. F., "Article 1").

48. Stern, "Poe."

49. As quoted in A. Wren, "Application of Phrenology to the Analysis of the Character of Shakespeare's Iago," *American Phrenological Journal* 1, no. 7 (1839), 220. Thanks to my research assistant, Aurora Wells, for locating this information. For a fuller discussion of animal images in Shakespeare, see Bruce Thomas Boehrer, *Shakespeare Among the Animals: Nature and Society in the Drama of Early Modern England* (New York: Palgrave, 2002).

50. Wren, "Application of Phrenology," 215.

51. Lorenzo Niles Fowler, "Thinkers, Authors, Speakers," in *Lectures on Man: Being a Series of Discourses on Phrenology and Physiology* (London: Fowler & Wells, 1886), 140.

52. Dayan, "Amorous Bondage," 244.

53. See Terence Whalen, "Average Racism," in Kennedy and Weissberg, eds., *Romancing the Shadow*, 3–40.

54. Edgar Allan Poe, "The Gold-Bug," in *The Selected Writings of Edgar Allan Poe*, 329, 333.

55. Dayan, "Amorous Bondage," 263.

56. Poe's relation to cryptography has generated much scholarly interest. See William F. Friedman, "Edgar Allan Poe, Cryptographer," *American Literature* 8, no. 3 (1936): 266–280; John Hodgson, "Decoding Poe? Poe, W. B. Tyler, and Cryptography," *Journal of English and Germanic Philology* 92, no. 4 (1993): 523–534; Louis Renza, "Poe's Secret Autobiography," in Walter Benn Michaels and Donald E. Pease, eds., *The American Renaissance Reconsidered: Selected Papers from the English Institute, 1982–1983*, 58–89

(Baltimore: Johns Hopkins University Press, 1985); Rosenheim, *The Cryptographic Imagination*; Terence Whalen, "The Code for Gold: Edgar Allan Poe and Cryptography," *Representations* 46 (1994): 35–57; and W. K. Wimsatt, "What Poe Knew About Cryptography," *PMLA* 56 (1943): 754–779.

57. Poe, "The Gold-Bug," 341.

58. See, for instance, Harriet Ritvo, "The Animal Connection," in James Sheehan and Morton Sosna, eds., *The Boundaries of Humanity: Humans, Animals, Machines*, 68–84 (Berkeley: University of California Press, 1991).

59. Bill Brown, "Thing Theory," *Critical Inquiry* 28, no. 1 (2001), 4.

60. Poe, "The Philosophy of Composition," 680.

61. Ibid., 676–679, emphasis in original. Parrots also figure in "Hop-Frog," where the parrot scrapes his beak on the cage, and in "The Fall of the House of Usher," where Roderick's library includes Louis Gressert's poem "Vert-Vert, the Parrot." In an earlier work, "Romance" (1829), Poe had written that "a painted paroquet . . . taught me my alphabet to say" (Edgar Allan Poe, "Romance," in *Edgar Allan Poe: Complete Poems*, ed. Thomas Ollive Mabbott [Urbana: University of Illinois Press, 2000], 353). Poe's poem gave rise to a full bestiary of parodies that included "The Black Cat," "The Turkey," "The Whippoorwill," "The Pole Cat," and "The Dove"; for a full list and a discussion of Poe's relationship to ravens, see *Edgar Allan Poe: Complete Poems*, 352. For my account of the animal's relation to alphabetic instruction, see chapter 4 in this volume.

62. Jean-Luc Nancy, *Corpus*, trans. Richard A. Rand (New York: Fordham University Press, 2008), 15–17, emphasis in original.

63. N. Katherine Hayles, *How We Became Posthuman: Virtual Bodies in Cybernetics, Literature, and Informatics* (Chicago: University of Chicago Press, 1999), 4.

64. James Berkley, "Post-human Mimesis and the Debunked Machine: Reading Environmental Appropriation in Poe's 'Maelzel's Chess-Player' and 'The Man That Was Used Up,'" *Comparative Literature Studies* 41, no. 3 (2004), 362, 372.

65. Matthew Taylor, "Edgar Allan Poe's (Meta-)Physics: A Pre-history of the Posthuman," *Nineteenth-Century Literature* 62, no. 2 (2007): 193–222.

66. For the fullest discussion of the practice of animal magnetism, see Alison Winter, *Mesmerized: Powers of Mind in Victorian Britain* (Chicago: University of Chicago Press, 1998).

67. Franz Anton Mesmer, *Précis historique des faits relatifs au magnétisme-animal jusques en avril 1781. Par M. Mesmer, . . . ouvrage traduit de l'allemand* (London: n.p., 1781), available in *Eighteenth Century Collections Online*, Dartmouth College, February 5, 2009, 83, at http://find.galegroup.com/ecco/infomark.do?&contentSet=ECCOArticles&type=multipage&tabID=T001&prodId=ECCO&docId=CW106570806&source=gale&userGroupName=dartmouth&version=1.0&docLevel=FASCIMILE.

68. Edgar Allan Poe, "The Raven," in *Edgar Allan Poe: Complete Poems*, 364.

69. Thomas Carl Wall's observation that "bare life has all the phenomenality of a dream" might be helpful to keep in mind here (Thomas Carl Wall, "Au Hasard," in

Andrew Norris, ed., *Politics, Metaphysics, and Death: Essays on Giorgio Agamben's "Homo Sacer"* [Durham, N.C.: Duke University Press, 2005], 32).

70. Nancy, *Corpus*, 69, emphasis in original.

71. Edgar Allan Poe, "The Poetic Principle," in *The Selected Writings of Edgar Allan Poe*, 701.

72. Poe, "The Philosophy of Composition," 680.

73. Poe, "The Poetic Principle," 700.

74. Edgar Allan Poe, "To Philip P. Cooke (Letter 240)," in *The Selected Writings of Edgar Allan Poe*, 684.

75. Doris V. Falk, "Poe and the Power of Animal Magnetism," *PMLA* 84, no. 3 (1969), 544.

76. See, for instance, Moldenhauer, "Murder as Fine Art."

77. Elmer, *Reading at the Social Limit*, 106. See also Robert Shulman, "Poe and the Powers of the Mind," *English Language History* 37, no. 2 (1970): 245–262.

78. Poe, "The Murders in the Rue Morgue," 243, 264.

79. Ibid., 264, 248, 243. For a useful rereading of Freud's dream work as not merely symbolic but as pointing to literal animal presence, see Akira Mizuta Lippit, "Magnetic Animal: Derrida, Wildlife, Animetaphor," *MLN* 113, no. 5 (1998): 1111–1125.

80. Poe, "The Murders in the Rue Morgue," 243, 241.

4. Animals, Affect, and the Formation of Liberal Subjectivity

1. For a recent overview of the "turn to affect," the larger field, and a particularly rich engagement with its relation to Deleuzian philosophy and neuroscience, see Ruth Leys, "The Turn to Affect: A Critique," *Critical Inquiry* 37, no. 3 (2011): 434–472.

2. Lionel Trilling, *The Liberal Imagination: Essays on Literature and Society* (New York: Viking Press, 1950), x–xi.

3. Trilling's work has been claimed by neoconservatives and dismissed by scholars eager to move beyond "the age of heroic criticism" (Louis Menand, "Regrets Only: Lionel Trilling and His Discontents," *The New Yorker*, September 29, 2008, at http://www.newyorker.com/arts/critics/atlarge/2008/09/29/080929crat_atlarge_menand); he has been faulted for being a naive "believer in Matthew Arnold's ideal of 'disinterestedness'" and for his exclusion of women from literature and criticism (Andrew Delbanco, "Night Vision," *New York Review of Books* 48, no. 1 [2001], 38). For other reassessments of Trilling, see Carolyn G. Heilbrun, "Men Were the Only Models I Had," *Chronicle of Higher Education* 48, no. 7 (2001): B7–B11, and Michael Kimmage, "Lionel Trilling's *The Middle of the Journey* and the Complicated Origins of the Neo-conservative Movement," *Shofar* 21, no. 3 (2003): 48–63. For an overview of critiques of scholarship based on paradigms of postwar American liberalism, see Chantal Mouffe, "American Liberalism and Its Communitarian Critics," in Chantal

Mouffe, ed., *The Return of the Practical*, 23–40 (New York: Verso, 1993). For feminist critiques of liberalism, see Carol Pateman, *The Problem of Political Obligation: A Critical Analysis of Liberal Theory* (New York: Wiley, 1979), and Catharine MacKinnon, *Toward a Feminist Theory of the State* (Cambridge, Mass.: Harvard University Press, 1989).

4. According to Ann Cvetkovich, scholars developed a theoretical interest in emotions because they were trying to understand the simultaneous cultural dismissal of the feminine as emotional and of the emotional as feminine. Interrogating this double devaluation, scholars asked when emotions functioned to perpetuate the social order that devalued women and whether emotions could be mustered as a politically liberating tool. To answer these questions, they turned to the historical archive because "the representation of social problems as affective dilemmas can be traced to its origins in eighteenth- and nineteenth-century culture" (Ann Cvetkovich, *Mixed Feeling: Feminism, Mass Culture, and Victorian Sensationalism* [New Brunswick, N.J. : Rutgers University Press, 1992], 2). Landmark publications that made sentiment a locus of sustained critical inquiry include Ann Douglas, *The Feminization of American Culture* (New York: Knopf, 1977); Shirley Samuels, ed., *The Culture of Sentiment: Race, Gender, and Sentimentality in Nineteenth-Century America* (New York: Oxford University Press,1992); and Jane P. Tompkins, *Sensational Designs: The Cultural Work of American Fiction, 1790–1860* (New York: Oxford University Press, 1985).

5. Patricia Ticineto Clough and Jean Halley, eds., *The Affective Turn: Theorizing the Social* (Durham, N.C.: Duke University Press, 2007).

6. Michael Hardt, "Foreword: What Affects Are Good For," in Clough and Halley, eds., *The Affective Turn*, x.

7. Trilling, *The Liberal Imagination*, xiv, xi, xi.

8. Rei Terada, *Feeling in Theory: Emotion After the "Death of the Subject"* (Cambridge, Mass.: Harvard University Press, 2001), 3, 4. Brian Matsumi undertakes a similar project, but it leads him to reject the term *emotion* and to privilege, in distinction, the term *affect* (Brian Matsumi, *Parables for the Virtual: Movement, Affect, Sensation* [Durham, N.C.: Duke University Press, 2002], 27). Ruth Leys has taken him—and more broadly the field of affect theory that emerged from an engagement with Deleuzian philosophy, on the one hand, and with neuroscience, on the other—to task for creating dualistic terms that privilege the body and its affects over the mind and its processes of cognition and symbolization (Leys, "The Turn to Affect," 468).

9. Terada, *Feeling in Theory*, 6.

10. Ibid., 17, 21. Cvetkovich similarly argues that, "like sexuality and other physical processes, affect is not a pre-discursive entity, a fact that is often obscured by the construction of affects or bodily sensations as natural. To study the politics of affect, then, is more broadly to study the politics of cathexis and to explore how meanings are given to the energy attached to particular events and representations" (Cvetkovich, *Mixed Feeling*, 24).

11. Terada, *Feeling in Theory*, 2.

12. Lauren Berlant, "Intimacy: A Special Issue," *Critical Inquiry* 24, no. 2 (1998), 281–286. Bruce Burgett credits this special issue with having launched the now decade-long interest in issues of intimacy (Bruce Burgett, "Sex, Panic, Nation," *American Literary History* 21, no. 1 [2008], 69). Works that examine the importance of sentiment/sentimentality and sympathy specifically for nineteenth-century literature's mediations between nominally private feeling and public structures of feeling include Elizabeth Barnes, *States of Sympathy: Seduction and Democracy in the American Novel* (New York: Columbia University Press, 1997); Julie Ellison, *Cato's Tears and the Making of Anglo-American Emotion* (Chicago: University of Chicago Press, 1999); and Julia A. Stern, *The Plight of Feeling: Sympathy and Dissent in the Early American Novel* (Chicago: University of Chicago Press, 1997). For a discussion of "the ambiguity between mind and matter, art and nature that Locke's *Essay* fosters" and of this ambiguity's impact on British poetry, see Jerome McGann, *The Poetics of Sensibility: A Revolution in Literary Style* (Oxford: Clarendon Press, 1996).

13. Christopher Peterson, "Of Canines and Queers: Review of *Melancholia's Dog*: Reflections on Our Animal Kinship," *GLQ* 15, no. 2 (2009), 354.

14. Gillian Brown, *The Consent of the Governed: The Lockean Legacy in Early American Culture* (Cambridge, Mass.: Harvard University Press, 2001), 17.

15. Jay Fliegelman, *Prodigals and Pilgrims: The American Revolution Against Patriarchal Authority, 1750–1800* (Cambridge: Cambridge University Press, 1982), 5. Jerome Huyler has documented that Locke's educational writings were "well advertised" in America by the middle of the eighteenth century, with "*Thoughts Concerning Education*, itself reprinted more than nineteen times before 1761." Moreover, the text's ideas were disseminated by the popularity of writings directly developing "avowedly Lockean" themes and ranging from educational tracts (Isaac Watts, Phillip Doddridge, James Burgh) to fictional texts (Samuel Richardson, Daniel Defoe, Oliver Goldsmith, and Lawrence Sterne) and popular guidebooks (Lord Chesterfield's *Letters to His Son*, John Gregory's *A Father's Legacy to His Daughter*) (Jerome Huyler, *Locke in America: The Moral Philosophy of the Founding Era* [Kansas City: University Press of Kansas, 1995], 201).

16. John Locke, *The Educational Writings of John Locke: A Critical Edition with Introduction and Notes*, ed. James L. Axtell (Cambridge: Cambridge University Press, 1968), 181; all italics in quotes from Locke are in the original. Because of this emphasis on self-discipline, Locke insisted that corporeal punishment should not form a part of children's rearing (150). There was one exception to this prohibition: children were to be punished physically in cases of "*Obstinacy* or *Rebellion*" (177) to make clear to them that they needed to submit to the laws of reason. The aim of such corporeal punishment was to induce in children a feeling of shame that was ultimately geared at reaffirming the social relationships into which they entered.

17. Ibid., 158.

18. Locke is often associated with the theory of the blank paper, or tabula rasa, but as Mary Midgley clarifies, "This theory, though first popularized by Locke, was brought

to its extreme form by John B. Watson, the founding father of behaviorism, and was a cornerstone of the original version of that doctrine. Locke himself had meant by it merely that we are born without *knowledge*" (Mary Midgley, *Beast and Man: The Roots of Human Nature* [Ithaca: Cornell University Press, 1978], 19, emphasis in original).

19. Another dimension of Locke's engagement with animals is his rhetoric of "good Breeding"—for instance, when he writes: "The next good Quality belonging to a Gentleman is *good Breeding*. There are Two Sorts of *ill Breeding*: The one a *sheepish Bashfulness*: And the other a *mis-becoming Negligence and Disrespect* in our Carriage; Both which are avoided by duly observing this one Rule, *Not to think meanly of our selves, and not to think meanly of others*" (Locke, *The Educational Writings of John Locke*, 245). This dimension of his work goes beyond my purposes here; for a discussion that links this rhetoric of breeding to practices of animal husbandry, see Jenny Davidson, *Breeding: A Partial History of the Eighteenth Century* (New York: Columbia University Press, 2009). The pioneering work on the relationship between animals, breeding, and class culture is Harriet Ritvo, "Pride and Pedigree: The Evolution of the Victorian Dog Fancy," *Victorian Studies* 29, no. 2 (1986): 227–253.

20. Locke, *The Educational Writings of John Locke*, 207.

21. The issue of what is natural in children lies at the core of Jean-Jacques Rousseau's educational philosophy, which was central to eighteenth- and nineteenth-century debates over education. I neglect Rousseau here because, as Christine Kenyon-Jones points out, "the application of this human or humane system to animals, as promulgated by Locke and his followers, is not found in Rousseau," and "the almost universal condemnation of cruelty to animals in late eighteenth-century" children's books "cannot be said, then, to owe much to Rousseau" (Christine Kenyon-Jones, *Kindred Brutes: Animals in Romantic-Period Writing* [Burlington Vt.: Ashgate, 2001], 59). A text that combined Locke's and Rousseau's approaches was *Practical Education* (1798), which the novelist Maria Edgeworth coauthored with her father, Richard Lovell Edgeworth. The first American edition of this work was published in 1801 (Maria Edgeworth and Richard Lovell Edgeworth, *Practical Education*, 2 vols. [New York: G. F. Hopkins, 1801]). The Edgeworths argued for the importance of "inducing useful and agreeable habits, well regulated sympathy and benevolent affections" in young children (vii). Key to that endeavor was the proper management of children's relationship to animals, to which the Edgeworths turned their attention in a section titled "Sympathy and Sensibility." Claiming that "the *humanity* of children cannot, perhaps, properly be said to be exercised upon animals," the Edgeworths explained that children's fondness for animals easily "degenerates into cruelty" (282, emphasis in original). Drawing a class-based comparison, they argued that a natural feeling of compassion needs to undergo the process of educational transformation: "We must not depend merely upon the natural feelings of compassion, as preservatives against cruelty; the *instinctive* feelings of compassion are strong amongst uneducated people, yet these do not restrain them from acts of cruelty. . . . It is the same with all persons, in all ranks of life, whose minds are uncultivated" (282–293, emphasis in original). The Edgeworths saw the emotional relationship to animals as one that calls for the differentiation

between instinctive and cultivated feelings of compassion: as an instinctual relationship, compassion can take on its proper moral function only through a process of education and cultivation—where the "minds'" (282) production of sympathy ensures the proper "education of the heart" (vii). This education also makes a material difference in the lives of the animals themselves. Transposing the discourse of captivity and liberation from the children they study to animals, the Edgeworths wrote that "until young people have fixed *habits* of benevolence, and a taste for occupation, perhaps it is not prudent to trust them with the care or protection of animals. Even when they are enthusiastically fond of them, they cannot by their utmost ingenuity make the animals so happy in a state of captivity, as they would be in a state of liberty. They are apt to insist upon doing animals good against their will, and they are often unjust in the defence of their favourites" (283, emphasis in original). Echoing an earlier expressed concern with children's preferential treatment of some animals over others and the insistence that such preference causes abuse, the Edgeworths clearly linked animals to a political and democratic agenda. They insisted that children should be taught to regard with benevolence those animals who are not "thought beautiful" in order to ensure that "their benevolence towards the animal world will not be illiberally confined to favourite lapdogs, and singing birds" (283). Insisting on an even-handedness with which all animals are to be regarded, they argued that only such egalitarianism can make the "state of captivity" as agreeable to animals as the "state of liberty." Indeed, this understanding will help children comprehend the regulatory regime in which they live: "Children, though they must perceive the necessity for destroying certain animals, need not be themselves executioners; they should not conquer the natural repugnance to the sight of the struggles of pain, and the convulsions of death; their aversion to being the cause of pain should be preserved both by principle and habit. Those who have not been habituated to the bloody form of cruelty, can never fix their eye upon her without shuddering" (285). This passage is particularly telling, for it suggests that the regulation of cruelty to animals is directly tied to a compliance with the state's arrogation of the power of violence to itself. It establishes a strange form of egalitarianism: it upholds a differentiation of animals, but a differentiation that is not based on an intrinsic natural hierarchy as much as on a notion of social necessity. Such social necessity similarly establishes differentiations among people charged with different relations to animals. For additional analysis of the Edgeworths' pedagogical writing in its relationship to science education, Rousseau's philosophy, and the natural world, see Julia Douthwaite, "Experimental Child-Rearing After Rousseau: Maria Edgeworth, *Practical Education*, and *Belinda*," *Irish Journal of Feminist Studies* 2, no. 2 (1997): 35–56, and Julia Douthwaite, *The Wild Girl, Natural Man, and the Monster: Dangerous Experiments in the Age of Enlightenment* (Chicago: University of Chicago Press, 2002).

22. Locke, *The Educational Writings of John Locke*, 207, 226. There has been some speculation on whether this exclusion of butchers from juries was historic fact; see Hibernicus, "Butchers on Juries," *Notes and Queries* 186, no. 11 (1944): 254, and Lloyd G.

Stevenson, "On the Supposed Exclusion of Butchers and Surgeons from Jury Duty," *Journal of the History of Medicine and Allied Sciences* 9, no. 2 (1954): 235–238.

23. Locke, *The Educational Writings of John Locke*, 226.

24. Ibid., 226–227, emphasis in original.

25. Ibid., 227.

26. Ibid., 256, 259.

27. Karen Sánchez-Eppler, *Touching Liberty: Abolition, Feminism, and the Politics of the Body* (Berkeley: University of California Press, 1993), 26–27.

28. Elizabeth Maddock Dillon, "Sentimental Aesthetics," *American Literature* 76, no. 3 (2004), 500.

29. Brown, *The Consent of the Governed*, 4.

30. Scholars have recently examined Dickinson's relationship to public discussions and her understanding of the role that affect plays in challenging our understanding of subjectivity. As Sarah Blackwood has argued, "Whereas American Renaissance writers such as Emerson and Thoreau and their later Cold War critical champions believed in a coherent interior that continually projected itself upon the world, indeed, that the world's meaning and logic emanated from such an individual self, Dickinson explored the possibility that a dialectical relationship exists between the self and the world" (Sarah Blackwood, "'The Inner Brand': Emily Dickinson, Portraiture, and the Narrative of Liberal Interiority," *Emily Dickinson Journal* 14, no. 2 [2005], 56).

31. Emily Dickinson, *The Letters of Emily Dickinson*, ed. Thomas H. Johnson, 3 vols. (Cambridge, Mass.: Belknap Press of Harvard University Press,1958), 2:449.

32. We might also think of the diminutive term *small* here in relation to Ivan Kreilkamp's observation that "pets in Victorian literature embody minorness in various and complex ways—one of which relates to genre. When pets and especially dogs feature as characters in Victorian narratives, those narratives tend to fall into the orbit of one of two minor generic categories, either children's literature or the anecdote" (Ivan Kreilkamp, "Dying Like a Dog in *Great Expectations*," in Deborah Denenholz Morse and Martin A. Danahay, eds., *Victorian Animal Dreams: Representations of Animals in Victorian Literature and Culture* [Burlington, Vt.: Ashgate, 2007], 83).

33. To a reader familiar with Dickinson's hand, the signature might not have that ability to play and ambiguate, but as Jeanne Holland has documented, Dickinson experimented with the material production of her texts to allow for that ambiguity (Jeanne Holland, "Scraps, Stamps, and Cutouts: Emily Dickinson's Domestic Technologies of Publication," in Margaret J. M. Ezell and Katherine O'Brien O'Keeffe, eds., *Cultural Artifacts and the Production of Meaning: The Page, the Image, and the Body* [Ann Arbor: University of Michigan Press, 1994], 146).

34. Dickinson, *The Letters of Emily Dickinson*, 2:403.

35. Ibid., 2:404.

36. Donna Haraway, *The Companion Species Manifesto: Dogs, People, and Significant Otherness* (Chicago: Prickly Paradigm Press, 2003), 12.

37. Ibid., 50.

38. Ibid., 3. This position is contested in feminist writings on animals, which often privilege a sense of the wild over the domesticated as liberating; see, for instance, Stacy Alaimo, *Undomesticated Ground: Recasting Nature as Feminist Space* (Ithaca: Cornell University Press, 2000).

39. Thomas Wentworth Higginson, "Women and Men; Children and Animals," *Harper's Bazaar*, July 30, 1887.

40. Arlo Bates, "Books and Authors," *Boston Sunday Courier* 96 (1890), 2.

41. Carlo was a Newfoundland dog; the breed is said to be particularly intelligent; see J. S. [John Selby] Watson, *Reasoning Power in Animals* (London: Reeve, 1867).

42. Jack L. Capps, *Emily Dickinson's Reading 1836–1886* (Cambridge, Mass.: Harvard University Press, 1966), 95; Jane Donahue Eberwein, *An Emily Dickinson Encyclopedia* (Westport, Conn.: Greenwood Press, 1998), 41, 192. There was also a children's book by Elizabeth Fenwick entitled *The Life of the Famous Dog Carlo* (1806; London: Tabart, 1812) (Laura Brown, *Homeless Dogs and Melancholy Apes: Humans and Other Animals in the Modern Literary Imagination* [Ithaca: Cornell University Press, 2010], 131). The inspiration for this animal autobiography was a performing dog, as Teresa Mangum documents: "Even as the wealthier classes took up breeding and training of show dogs, the early-nineteenth-century general public delighted in the spectacle of 'Carlo, the Performing Dog' on the London stage. . . . [I]n his daily performances, Carlo leapt from a high plank to drag a drowning young girl from a tub of water, a feat he describes in his alleged autobiography" (Teresa Mangum, "Dog Years, Human Fears," in Nigel Rothfels, ed., *Representing Animals* [Bloomington: Indiana University Press, 2002], 36).

43. Locke, *The Educational Writings of John Locke*, 298. As Samuel Pickering documents, "Before the reign of Queen Anne, the *Guardian of Education* stated in 1802, there were 'very few' books written for children. '*The first period of Infantine* [*sic*] *and Juvenile Literature*' began, the journal declared, after Mr. Locke popularized 'the idea of uniting amusement with instruction.'" Pickering points out that "one of the most important threads to be woven into the fabric of character, Locke taught in *Some Thoughts*, was kindness to animals. . . . Until the end of the eighteenth century, Locke's emphasis upon the danger of cruelty to animals influenced the depiction of animals in children's books. Drawing upon Locke's ideas, writers of children's books used animals as didactic devices to lead children away from cruelty and to benevolence" (Samuel F. Pickering, *John Locke and Children's Books in Eighteenth-Century England* [Knoxville: University of Tennessee Press, 1981], 7, 12). Margaret Blount traces the "history of animal stories through these three strains—folklore, fable and romance" (Margaret Joan Blount, *Animal Land: The Creatures of Children's Fiction* [New York: William Morrow, 1975], 26). For a complex account of both Locke's and Rousseau's impact on children's literature, understandings of child psychology, and theorizations of language, see Jacqueline Rose, *The Case of Peter Pan or the Impossibility of Children's Fiction* (London: Macmillan Press, 1984), esp. 44–65. For the impact of their theories on childhood education and on the status of

fantasy in children's literature, see Geoffrey Summerfield, *Fantasy and Reason: Children's Literature in the Eighteenth Century* (Athens: University of Georgia Press, 1985). Tess Cosslett traces the impact of Locke's work on the development of children's literature and the centrality of animal representations (Tess Cosslett, *Talking Animals in British Children's Fiction, 1786–1914* [Burlington, Vt.: Ashgate, 2006], esp. 9–36).

44. [Sarah] Trimmer, *Fabulous Histories: Designed for the Instruction of Children Respecting Their Treatment of Animals* (London: Printed for T. Longman, G. G. J. and J. Robinson, and J. Johnson, 1786), microform.

45. Aesop, *Aesop's Fables in French: With a Description of Fifty Animals Mentioned Therein and a French and English Dictionary of the Words Contained in the Work* (Philadelphia: Lindsay and Blakiston, 1852).

46. Asa Bullard, *Dog Stories*, His Sunnybank Stories (Boston: Lee & Shepard, 1863), 7–10, 64. For the sisterly warfare, see "Our Kitty and Carlo," 11–13; for the temptation of Carlo, see 25–27.

47. Ibid., 60.

48. Mary Allen reads Dickinson's interest in noise in relation to onomatopoeia, especially in the bee poems (Mary Allen, *Animals in American Literature* [Urbana: University of Illinois Press, 1983], 56).

49. Emily Dickinson, poem 1236, in *The Poems of Emily Dickinson: Reading Edition*, ed. R. W. Franklin (Cambridge, Mass.: Belknap Press of Harvard University Press, 1998), 485.

50. From Martha Dickinson Bianchi, "Selections from the Unpublished Letters of Emily Dickinson to Her Brother's Family; Chosen and Arranged by Her Niece Martha Dickinson Bianchi," *Atlantic Monthly* (January 1915), 37.

51. Ibid.

52. Dickinson, poem 334, in *The Poems of Emily Dickinson*, 149.

53. Dickinson, poem 333, in ibid., 149.

54. Akira Mizuta Lippit, "Magnetic Animal: Derrida, Wildlife, Animetaphor," *MLN* 113, no. 5 (1998), 1112. Mary Midgley makes a similar point when she writes: "I look at the traditional marks of man, such as speech, rationality and culture, and try to show how we might view them, not as alien or hostile to the underlying emotional structure in which we so much resemble other species, but as growing out of and completing it" (Midgley, *Beast and Man*, xxii).

55. Ibid., 1113, 1118.

56. The definition of *orthography* as given in the *Oxford English Dictionary*, 3rd ed. (*OED Online*, March 2012, at http://www.oed.com/view/Entry/132833).

57. Higginson, "Women and Men," 530.

58. Cousin Daisy, *The Picture Alphabet* (Philadelphia: J. B. Lippincott , 1879), n.p.

59. Patricia Crain, *The Story of A: The Alphabetization of America from the New England Primer to the Scarlet Letter* (Stanford: Stanford University Press, 2000), 5, 7, 36.

60. Dickinson, poem 591, in *The Poems of Emily Dickinson*, 265–266.

61. See Midori Asahina, "'"Fascination" Is Absolute of Clime': Reading Emily Dickinson's Correspondence with Higginson as Naturalist," *Emily Dickinson Journal* 14, no. 2 (2005): 103–119.

62. Higginson, "Women and Men."

5. Rethinking Liberal Subjectivity: The Biopolitics of Animal Autobiography

1. For an elaboration of this claim from the perspective of animal geography, see Heidi Nast's analysis of the link between conditions of modern commodification and affective pet relations in "Loving . . . Whatever: Alienation, Neoliberalism, and Pet-Love in the Twenty-First Century," *ACME* 5, no. 2 (2006): 300–327. Nast's work builds off two key texts in the analysis of how the pet has emerged as a link between structures of affect and domination: Yi-fu Tuan, *Dominance and Affection: The Making of Pets* (New Haven: Yale University Press, 1984), and Marc Shell, "The Family Pet," *Representations* 15 (1986): 121–153.

2. Laura Brown, *Homeless Dogs and Melancholy Apes: Humans and Other Animals in the Modern Literary Imagination* (Ithaca: Cornell University Press, 2010), 115, 29.

3. Because I am focusing here primarily on gender and not emphasizing race as much, I do not discuss what probably remains the most famous of animal biographies, Anna Sewell's *Black Beauty: The Autobiography of a Horse* (1877), which borrows heavily from the genre of slave autobiography. For a discussion of this novel, see Jennifer Mason, *Civilized Creatures: Urban Animals, Sentimental Culture, and American Literature, 1850–1900* (Baltimore: Johns Hopkins University Press, 2005), esp. 122–156. For feminist critiques of the connection between bestiality, pornography, and gender, see Margret Grebowicz, "When Species Meat: Confronting Bestiality Pornography," *Humanimalia* 1, no. 2 (2010): 1–17; Carol Adams, "Bestiality, the Unmentioned Abuse," *The Animals' Agenda* 15, no. 6 (1995): 29–31; and Carol J. Adams, *The Sexual Politics of Meat: A Feminist–Vegetarian Critical Theory* (New York: Continuum, 1990).

4. The photograph was taken by William Wegman, whose corpus of dog photography has recently met with critical analysis; see, for instance, Alice Kuzniar's discussion in *Melancholia's Dog* of Wegman's ability to reveal the complicated dynamics of shame and his interest in linking children and animals in his book publications (Alice A. Kuzniar, *Melancholia's Dog* [Chicago: University of Chicago Press, 2006], 83–100).

5. Kate Bonniwell, "Publisher's Note," *Life* (May 1989), 3.

6. The idea of Mother's Day and a women's peace movement came to Howe as she was reading about the Franco–Prussian War in 1870 and found herself wondering: "Why do not the mothers of mankind interfere in these matters, to prevent the waste of that human life of which they alone know and bear the cost?" Given the obstacles

she faced, she decided instead to hold an annual Mothers' Peace Day, which was to be celebrated on June 2; the first such celebration took place in Boston in 1873 (Deborah Pickman Clifford, *Mine Eyes Have Seen the Glory: A Biography of Julia Ward Howe* [Boston: Little, Brown, 1978], 185, 187). Howe's antiwar activism and her founding of Mother's Day became touchstones for the peace movement during World War I (Edwin Mead, "Woman and War: Julia Ward Howe's Peace Crusade," *World Peace Foundation Pamphlet Series* 4, no. 6 [1914]: 1–11). In 1873, "the first Mother's Day was celebrated in eighteen American cities, as well as in Rome and Constantinople, and friends of peace in Philadelphia continued to observe her mother's day for over fifty years, even forming a Julia Ward Howe Peace Band" (Valarie H. Ziegler, *Diva Julia: The Public Romance and Private Agony of Julia Ward Howe* [Harrisburg, Pa.: Trinity Press International, 2003], 117).

7. The proclamation was first published as a broadside under the title "Appeal to Womanhood Throughout the World" in Boston, September 1870; see http://memory.loc.gov/cgi-bin/query/h?ammem/rbpebib:@field(NUMBER+@band(rbpe+07400300)).

8. See Amy Swerdlow, "Woman's Peace Festival, June 2, 1873," in "Teaching About Peace, War, and Women in the Military," special issue of *Women's Studies Quarterly* 12, no. 2 (1984): 29. Mother's Day did not become an official holiday until 1914, but women's losses during the Civil War were commemorated by the annual Decoration Day (later Memorial Day) festivities (Alice Fahs, "The Feminized Civil War: Gender, Northern Popular Literature, and the Memory of the War, 1861–1900," *Journal of American History* 85, no. 4 [1999], 1483). For a history of the holiday's development in the Progressive Era and its ties to the Sunday school movement, see Kathleen W. Jones, "Mother's Day: The Creation, Promotion, and Meaning of a New Holiday in the Progressive Era," *Texas Studies in Literature and Language* 22, no. 2 (1980): 175–196. A longer history of such a day existed in Europe, where "Mothering Sunday" was observed on the fourth Sunday of Lent (Jones, "Mother's Day," 192).

9. Michel Foucault, *The History of Sexuality*, trans. Robert Hurley, 1st American ed. (New York: Pantheon Books, 1978), 139.

10. Gregory Tomso, "Viral Sex and the Politics of Life," *South Atlantic Quarterly* 107, no. 2 (2008), 275–276.

11. Foucault, *The History of Sexuality*, 140–141.

12. Eric Santner, *On Creaturely Life: Rilke, Benjamin, Sebald* (Chicago: University of Chicago Press, 2006), 12, 80.

13. Giorgio Agamben, *The Open: Man and Animal* (Stanford: Stanford University Press, 2004), 80, 83, 93. Although Julia Lupton is indebted to Agamben, she, by contrast, reads *The Tempest*'s "Creature Caliban" as a figure whose in-betweenness remains in excess of the different contexts in which he participates and unsettles "the false universalism of global capitalism" as well as "the drive to particularize him" (Julia Lupton, "Creature Caliban," *Shakespeare Quarterly* 51, no. 1 [2000], 21, 3).

14. Bill Brown, "Thing Theory," *Critical Inquiry* 28, no. 1 (2001), 4.

15. Bill Brown, "The Tyranny of Things (Trivia in Karl Marx and Mark Twain)," *Critical Inquiry* 28, no. 2 (2002), 446, 451.

16. Donna Haraway, *When Species Meet* (Minneapolis: University of Minnesota Press, 2008), 45, 47, 54, 60, 66–67. For a fuller discussion of this "biocapitalistic" conjunction, see Jenny Davidson, *Breeding: A Partial History of the Eighteenth Century* (New York: Columbia University Press, 2009).

17. For a reading of queer animal depictions in recent children's films, see Judith Halberstam, *The Queer Art of Failure* (Durham, N.C.: Duke University Press, 2011), 27–52.

18. Bill Brown, "Object Relations in an Expanded Field," *differences* 17, no. 3 (2006), 91, 93.

19. D. W. Winnicott, *Playing and Reality* (New York: Routledge, 1957), 2, 3, 6, 10, 6, 14. Jessica Benjamin takes issue with Lacan and Klein when she argues that a subject can "relate to the other without assimilating the other to the self through identification" (Jessica Benjamin, *Shadow of the Other: Intersubjectivity and Gender in Psychoanalysis* [New York: Routledge, 1998], 94).

20. One fascinating way to think in historic terms about animals as transitional objects that are never (fully) relinquished emerges in Jeffrey Cohen's discussion of medieval "Chevalerie," in which he notes: "Whereas contemporary biographies are apt to mark the entrance into adult identity through an epiphanal narration of the 'awakening to sexuality' . . . , the chivalric movement from youth (squiredom) to maturity (knighthood) is more likely to involve a lesson about horses." The lesson does not involve leaving the horse behind or creating a hierarchy of domination and submission but requires transforming one's relationship to that horse and apprenticing oneself into new forms of shared embodiment (Jeffrey J. Cohen, *Medieval Identity Machines* [Minneapolis: University of Minnesota Press, 2003], 52). For a reading of contemporary horse–human relations in literature, see Susan McHugh, *Animal Stories: Narrating Across Species Lines* (Minneapolis: University of Minnesota Press, 2011).

21. Kathryn Bond Stockton, *The Queer Child, or Growing Sideways in the Twentieth Century* (Durham, N.C.: Duke University Press, 2009).

22. Mother's Day was commoditized from the time it was officially recognized as a holiday by President Woodrow Wilson in 1914; see Leigh Eric Schmidt, "The Commercialization of the Calendar: American Holidays and the Culture of Consumption, 1870–1930," *Journal of American History* 78, no. 3 (1991): 887–916.

23. I borrow the term *heterosexual matrix* from Judith Butler, "Critically Queer," *GLX* 1 (1993), 27.

24. "Puppy love," *Oxford English Dictionary*, 2d ed. (Oxford: Oxford University Press, 1989): "puppy-love (*contemptuous*): cf. *calf-love*," "applied to a person as a term of contempt."

25. Early child psychologists attributed a tendency to anthropomorphize children and their relation with animals. For an account of the development of child psychology and its complex relation to Locke's, Rousseau's, and Darwin's theories of nature, see

Holly Blackford, "Child Consciousness in the American Novel: *Adventures of Huckleberry Finn* (1885), *What Maisie Knew* (1897), and the Birth of Child Psychology," in Monika Elbert, ed., *Children's Literature and Culture*, 245–258 (New York: Routledge, 2008); and John R. Morss, *The Biologising of Childhood: Developmental Psychology and the Darwinian Myth* (London: Lawrence Erlbaum, 1990).

26. Barbara Bush, "Millie's Six-Pack: Dog Days and Springer Fever at the White House," *Life* (May 1989), 33.

27. Responding to a reader's query regarding why Barbara Bush's book was listed as nonfiction, the *New York Times* weakly replied that "the publisher of Millie's Book, William Morrow & Company, lists it under 'nonfiction' and 'autobiography'" ("Talking Dogs," *New York Times*, February 3, 1991). For an account of the book's sales ranking, see "Book Review 100 Years," *New York Times*, October 6, 1996. For the sales figure listed, see "First Dog 'Millie' Dies," *Pittsburgh Post-Gazette*, May 21, 1997.

28. Michael Kranish, "White House's Top Dog; 'Millie' Royalties Eclipse the President's Wages," *Boston Globe*, April 16, 1992. Millie gained celebrity endorsements: Garfield (the cartoon cat created by Jim Davis) reviewed the book favorably (Garfield, "Not Bad for a Dog," *New York Times*, September 16, 1990).

29. Sidonie Smith and Julia Watson, "Introduction: Situating Subjectivity in Women's Autobiographical Practices," in Sidonie Smith and Julia Watson, eds., *Women, Autobiography, Theory: A Reader* (Madison: University of Wisconsin Press, 1998), 5.

30. Animal autobiography has been particularly popular with queer writers; a brief genealogy includes Michael Field, *Whym Chow, Flame of Love* (London: Eragny Press, 1914); Katharine Lee Bates, *Sigurd Our Golden Collie and Other Comrades of the Road* (New York: E. P. Dutton, 1919); Virginia Woolf, *Flush: A Biography* (London: Hogarth Press, 1933); J. R. Ackerley, *My Dog Tulip* (New York: New York Review of Books, 1999); and Mark Doty, *Dog Years: A Memoir*, 1st ed. (New York: HarperCollins, 2007). A brief and by no means conclusive history of the broader genre of animal biography, which has strong ties with children's literature and was particularly popular at the turn of the nineteenth to the twentieth century, includes titles such as *Stories About Dogs, for Our Boys and Girls* (Boston: Lee and Shepard, 1854); Asa Bullard, *Dog Stories*, His Sunnybank Stories (Boston: Lee & Shepard, 1863); George Ricks, *Object Lessons and How to Give Them* (Boston: D. C. Heath, 1893); Marshall Saunders, *Beautiful Joe: An Autobiography; with an Introduction by Hezekiah Butterworth* (Philadelphia: Charles H. Banes, 1894); Mary Eleanor Wilkins Freeman, *Understudies; Short Stories by Mary E. Wilkins* (New York: Harper & Bros., 1901); Ouida [Marie Louise de la Ramée], *A Dog of Flanders* (East Aurora, N.Y.: Roycrofters, 1906); Ethelbert Talbot, *Tim: The Autobiography of a Dog* (New York: Harper, 1914); John Muir, *Stickeen* (Boston: Houghton Mifflin, 1915); Ernest Harold Baynes, *Polaris: The Story of an Eskimo Dog* (New York: Macmillan, 1923); E. V. Lucas, *If Dogs Could Write: A Second Canine Miscellany*, 2nd ed. (London: Methuen, 1929); Eva Brunell Seeley, *Chinook and His Family, True Dog Stories* (Boston: Ginn, 1930); Moyra Charlton, *Patch: The Story of a Mongrel* (London: Methuen, 1931); H. J. Pickering,

Dog-Days on Trout Waters (New York: Derrydale Press, 1933); Albert Payson Terhune, *A Book of Famous Dogs*, 1st ed. (New York: Doubleday, Doran, 1937); Sir James Frazer and Lady Frazer, *Pasha the Pom: The Story of a Little Dog* (London: Blackie & Son, 1937); Robert J. May, *Winking Willie* (New York: Maxton, 1948); and Alastair McBain and Corey Ford, *A Man of His Own and Other Dog Stories* (New York: Whittlesey House, 1949). For British literature, Tess Cosslett has recently compiled a history of animal autobiography in chapter 3 of *Talking Animals in British Children's Fiction, 1786–1914* (Burlington, Vt.: Ashgate, 2006). Barbara T. Gates traces the rise of animal biography to its height of popularity in the 1890s; see Barbara T. Gates, *Kindred Nature* (Chicago: University of Chicago Press, 1998), 220–230. Deborah Morse and Martin Danahay point out that "countless imperial narratives were told by animals" (Deborah Denenholz Morse and Martin A. Danahay, "Introduction," in Deborah Denenholz Morse and Martin A. Danahay, eds., *Victorian Animal Dreams: Representations of Animals in Victorian Literature and Culture* [Burlington, Vt.: Ashgate, 2007], 6). For an account of the figure of the talking animal in relation to satire, see Kathryn Perry, "Unpicking the Seam: Talking Animals and Reader Pleasure in Early Modern Satire," in Erica Fudge, ed., *Renaissance Beasts: Of Animals, Humans, and Other Wonderful Creatures*, 19–36 (Urbana: University of Illinois Press, 2004).

31. Teresa Mangum, "Dog Years, Human Fears," in Nigel Rothfels, ed., *Representing Animals* (Bloomington: Indiana University Press, 2002), 43.

32. Barbara Bush, *Millie's Book: As Dictated to Barbara Bush* (New York: William Morrow, 1990), 10, 13.

33. Ibid.

34. Ibid., 29.

35. Ibid., 22.

36. Ibid., 61.

37. Ibid.

38. Ibid.

39. Ibid., 13, 19, 64.

40. Whether a signature establishes authorial subjectivity is a contested issue; see Jacques Derrida, "Interpreting Signatures (Nietzsche/Heidegger): Two Questions," *Philosophy and Literature* 10, no. 2 (1986): 246–262.

41. Bush, *Millie's Book*, 136.

42. Cohen, *Medieval Identity Machines*, 40. See also the essays collected in Noreen Giffney and Myra Hird, eds., *Queering the Non/Human* (Burlington, Vt.: Ashgate, 2008).

43. Brown, *Homeless Dogs and Melancholy Apes*, 67, 66; the lapdog also figured prominently in "antifemale satire" (76).

44. Mangum, "Dog Years, Human Fears," 43, 44.

45. Stockton, *The Queer Child*, 90.

46. Bush, "Millie's Six-Pack," 34.

47. Jacques Lacan, *The Seminar of Jacques Lacan*, trans. Sylvana Tomaselli, ed. Jacques-Alain Miller (New York: Norton, 1988), 50, 323. For a useful analysis of the role that

animals play in the interpretative schema Freud develops in *The Interpretation of Dreams*, see Akira Mizuta Lippit, "Magnetic Animal: Derrida, Wildlife, Animetaphor," *MLN* 113, no. 5 (1998): 1111–1125.

48. The full text of Derrida's animal project, which was originally given in lecture form, has only recently become available in English translation; see Jacques Derrida, *The Animal That Therefore I Am*, trans. David Willis, ed. John D. Caputo (New York: Fordham University Press, 2008).

49. Jacques Derrida, "The Animal That Therefore I Am (More to Follow)," *Critical Inquiry* 28, no. 2 (2002), 379–380. John Berger makes a similar point when he writes: "The eyes of an animal when they consider a man are attentive and wary. The same animal may well look at other species in the same way. He does not reserve a special look for man. But by no other species except man will the animal's look be recognized as familiar. Other animals are held by the look. Man becomes aware of himself returning the look" (John Berger, *About Looking* [New York: Pantheon Books, 1980], 2).

50. For animals, the importance of same-species mirroring was developed in the experiments with imprinting made famous by Konrad Lorenz; see, for instance, Konrad Lorenz and Paul Leyhausen, *Motivation of Human and Animal Behavior: An Ethological View* (New York: Van Nostrand Reinhold, 1973), 113–114.

51. Lacan, *The Seminar of Jacques Lacan*, 323.

52. Haraway, *When Species Meet*, 20, 22. Haraway borrows the term *autre-mondialisation* from Beatriz Preciado; see ibid., 3.

53. Tacitly agreeing with Virginia Woolf's own deprecating comments about her novel, Woolf criticism has by and large ignored *Flush*. The novel has only recently come under scrutiny and found critical acclaim in the context of literary animal studies; see, for instance, Alison Booth, "The Scent of a Narrative: Rank Discourse in *Flush* and Written on the Body," *Narrative* 8, no. 1 (2000): 3–22; Marjorie Garber, *Dog Love* (New York: Simon & Schuster, 1996); Jacqui Griffiths, "Almost Human: Intermediate Children and Dogs in *Flush* and *The Sound and the Fury*," *Yearbook of English Studies* 32 (2002): 163–176; Philip Howell, "Flush and the *Banditti*: Dog-Stealing in Victorian London," in Chris Philo and Chris Wilbert, eds., *Animal Spaces, Beastly Places: New Geographies of Human–Animal Relations*, 35–55 (London: Routledge, 2000); Jutta Ittner, "Part Spaniel, Part Canine Puzzle: Anthropomorphism in Woolf's *Flush* and Auster's *Timbuktu*," *Mosaic* 39, no. 4 (2006): 181–196; Kuzniar, *Melancholia's Dog*; Craig Smith, "Across the Widest Gulf: Nonhuman Subjectivity in Virginia Woolf's *Flush*," *Twentieth Century Literature* 48, no. 3 (2002): 348–361; and Dan Wylie, "The Anthropomorphic Ethic: Fiction and the Animal Mind in Virginia Woolf's *Flush* and Barbara Gowdy's *The White Bone*," *ISLE: Interdisciplinary Studies in Literature and Environment* 9, no. 2 (2002): 115–131. See also chapter 5 in Kari Weil's new book, *Thinking Animals: Why Animal Studies Now?* (New York: Columbia University Press, 2012). For a fuller discussion of Woolf's relation to animals and/as queer children, especially in relation to Mrs. Dalloway, see Stockton, *The Queer Child*. Alice Kuzniar writes of *Flush* that "one of the great

accomplishments of this novel is that it sensitively balances pet affection with a subtle ironization of it" and that "Woolf here raises the brilliant paradox that estrangement can also lead to intuitive comprehension—to intimacy"; "a cultural studies approach, however, that exposes the specular construction and bolstering of bourgeois subjectivity via the pet dog loses sight of what intimacy accomplishes for the invalid Miss Barrett" (Kuzniar, *Melancholia's Dog*, 121–123).

54. Woolf, *Flush*, 22–23.

55. Ivan Kreilkamp has recently argued that "animals in the Victorian period . . . are often treated as semi-human in the realm of culture and as semi-characters in the realm of literature. What I mean by this is that animals, or certain privileged domesticated animals, are given names and invested with personality and individual identity, that this status is unreliable and subject to sudden abrogation. One of the primary signs of the precariousness of pets' status as human-like characters is their troubled relationship to memory and memorializing, particularly in the form of writing or print" (Ivan Kreilkamp, "Dying Like a Dog in Great Expectations," in Morse and Danahay, eds., *Victorian Animal Dreams*, 82). For a reading of animals as characters, see Bruce Thomas Boehrer, *Animal Characters: Nonhuman Beings in Early Modern Literature* (Philadelphia: University of Pennsylvania Press, 2010).

56. Rei Terada, *Feeling in Theory: Emotion After The "Death of the Subject"* (Cambridge, Mass.: Harvard University Press, 2001), 4, 17–18.

57. Kuzniar, *Melancholia's Dog*, 117.

58. Jacques Derrida, "L'animal que donc je suis (à suivre)," in Marie-Louise Mallet, ed., *L'animal autobiographique: Autour de Jacques Derrida* (Paris: Galilée, 1999), 256.

59. Robert Darnton, *The Great Cat Massacre and Other Episodes in French Cultural History* (New York: Basic Books, 1983), 95.

60. Jonathan Lamb, "Modern Metamorphoses and Disgraceful Tales," *Critical Inquiry* 28, no. 1 (2001), 133. For Barbara Gates, the genre of animal autobiography "reached its zenith in the 1890s," and she sees the genre as encompassing "two shorter kinds of animal stories, the brief animal anecdote and the animal chronicle, which details a pet animals' life from birth to death or from acquisition to loss" (Gates, *Kindred Nature*, 220). For a fuller account of the genre of it-narratives, see the essays collected in Mark Blackwell, ed., *The Secret Life of Things: Animals, Objects, and It-Narratives in Eighteenth-Century England* (Lewisburg, Pa.: Bucknell University Press, 2007).

61. Derrida, "The Animal That Therefore I Am (More to Follow)," 390.

62. Derrida, *The Animal That Therefore I Am*, 22.

63. Linda Peterson, "Gender and Autobiographical Form," in James Olney, ed., *Studies in Autobiography* (New York: Oxford University Press, 1988), 212–213.

64. There has been a marked turn in recent years to the sacred as a terrain of inquiry, ranging from Slavoj Žižek's recent work to the inquiries by Alain Badiou and others, leading Anat Pick to conclude that "the task at hand, I would therefore argue, is not only posthumanist and postanthropocentric, but also, and no less significantly, postsecular"

(Anat Pick, *Creaturely Poetics: Animality and Vulnerability in Literature and Film* [New York: Columbia University Press, 2011], 18).

65. Smith and Watson, "Introduction," 5.

66. Mary G. Mason, "The Other Voice: Autobiographies of Women Writers," in Smith and Watson, eds., *Women, Autobiography, Theory*, 321.

67. Bates was also one of the first scholars to launch the field of American literary studies; see Katharine Lee Bates, *American Literature* (New York: Macmillan, 1898). To date, almost no scholarly work has been published on Bates.

68. Bates, *Sigurd Our Golden Collie*, 14, 30, 32.

69. Ibid., 43–46.

70. Bates's book was reviewed along these lines: "We like her writing best when it is most bookish. That is its note. We have other books on our shelves aplenty in which the canine hero plays a more tragic or pathetic or even humorous role, but none in which he is more humanly literate than Miss Bates's Sigurd of the golden fleece" ("Review of *Sigurd Our Golden Collie* by Katharine Lee Bates," *The Review* 2, no. 39 [1920], 135).

71. Bates, *Sigurd Our Golden Collie*, 89.

72. Ibid., 43.

Epilogue

1. Margot Norris, "The Human Animal in Fiction," *parallax* 12, no. 1 (2006): 4–20.

2. Erica Fudge, "A Left-Handed Blow: Writing the History of Animals," in Nigel Rothfels, ed., *Representing Animals* (Bloomington: Indiana University Press, 2002), 8.

3. Sianne Ngai, *Ugly Feelings* (Cambridge, Mass.: Harvard University Press, 2005), 1, 5, 7, 12.

4. "Animalia," *Oxford English Dictionary* (*OED Online*, September 2011, at http://www.oed.com/view/Entry/273491?redirectedFrom=animalia).

5. Richard Nash, "Joy and Pity: Reading Animal Bodies in Late Eighteenth-Century Culture," in "Animal, All Too Animal," special issue of *The Eighteenth Century* 52, no. 1 (2011), 53.

6. Jeffrey J. Cohen, *Medieval Identity Machines* (Minneapolis: University of Minnesota Press, 2003), 42, emphasis in original.

7. Gilles Deleuze and Félix Guattari, "Becoming-Animal," in Peter Atterton and Matthew Calarco, eds., *Animal Philosophy: Essential Readings in Continental Thought* (London: Continuum, 2004), 89–90.

8. Ibid.

9. Anat Pick, *Creaturely Poetics: Animality and Vulnerability in Literature and Film* (New York: Columbia University Press, 2011), 65.

10. For some of the formulations that follow, I am indebted and grateful to the Columbia University Press readers.

BIBLIOGRAPHY

Aaltola, Elisa. "Philosophy and Animal Studies: Calarco, Castricano, and Diamond." *Society and Animals* 17 (2009): 279–286.

"Abu Ghraib Dog Handler Sentenced to 6 Months: Army Sergeant Convicted of Using Canines to Scare Prisoners at Iraqi Prison." Associated Press, updated March 22, 2006. At http://www.msnbc.msn.com/id/11943182.

Acampora, Ralph. *Corporal Compassion: Animal Ethics and Philosophy of Body.* Pittsburgh: University of Pittsburgh Press, 2006.

Ackerley, J. R. *My Dog Tulip.* New York: New York Review of Books, 1999.

Adams, Carol. "Bestiality, the Unmentioned Abuse." *The Animals' Agenda* 15, no. 6 (1995): 29–31.

——, ed. *Ecofeminism and the Sacred.* New York: Continuum, 1993.

——. *The Feminist Care Tradition in Animal Ethics.* New York: Columbia University Press, 2007.

——. *Neither Man nor Beast: Feminism and the Defense of Animals.* New York: Continuum, 1994.

——. *The Pornography of Meat.* New York: Continuum, 2003.

——. *The Sexual Politics of Meat: A Feminist–Vegetarian Critical Theory.* New York: Continuum, 1990.

Adams, Maureen. "Emily Brontë and Keeper." In *Shaggy Muses: The Dogs Who Inspired Virginia Woolf, Emily Dickinson, Edith Wharton, Elizabeth Barret Browning, and Emily Brontë*, 49–96. Chicago: University of Chicago Press, 2011.

Adorno, Theodor. *Minima Moralia: Reflections from Damaged Life.* London: Verso, 1974.

Aesop. *Aesop's Fables.* Baltimore: Samuel Wood & Sons, 1821.

——. *Aesop's Fables in French: With a Description of Fifty Animals Mentioned Therein and a French and English Dictionary of the Words Contained in the Work*. Philadelphia: Lindsay and Blakiston, 1852.

——. *Child's Own Fable Book*. New York: Leavitt & Allen, 1860.

——. *A Child's Version of Aesop's Fables; with a Supplement Containing Fables from La Fontaine and Krilof*. Boston: Ginn, 1886.

——. *The Little Esop*. Philadelphia: Smith and Peck, 1843.

——. *Little Fables for Little Folks: Selected for Their Moral Tendency, and Re-written in Familiar Words, Not One of Which Exceeds Two Syllables*. New Haven: S. Babcock, 1835.

Aesop and H. Clarke. *Fabulae Aesopi Selectae, or, Select Fables of Aesop: With an English Translation More Literal Than Any Yet Extant: Designed for the Readier Instruction of Beginners in the Latin Tongue*. Baltimore: Fielding Lucas Jr., 1817.

Aesop, Samuel Croxall, Robert Aitken, and James Poupard. *Fables of Aesop and Others*. Philadelphia: R. Aitken, 1777.

Aesop, Alexander Greaves, William Thompson, and Mahlon Day. *Aesop, Junior, in America: Being a Series of Fables Written Especially for the People of the United States of North America*. New York: Mahlon Day, 1834.

Aesop and Robert L'Estrange. *A History of the Life of Aesop*. Philadelphia: Southwark Office, 1798.

Aesop and Mara Pratt-Chadwick. *Aesop's Fables: Vol. 1. First Grade*. Boston: Educational Pub., 1892.

Agamben, Giorgio. *Homo Sacer: Sovereign Power and Bare Life*. Trans. Daniel Heller-Roazen. Stanford: Stanford University Press, 1998.

——. *The Open: Man and Animal*. Stanford: Stanford University Press, 2004.

Alaimo, Stacy. *Undomesticated Ground: Recasting Nature as Feminist Space*. Ithaca: Cornell University Press, 2000.

Albee, Edward. *The Goat; or, Who Is Sylvia? (Notes Toward a Definition of Tragedy)*. Woodstock, N.Y.: Overlook Press, 2003.

Allen, Mary. *Animals in American Literature*. Urbana: University of Illinois Press, 1983.

Allestree, Richard. *The Causes of the Decay of Christian Piety, or, an Impartial Survey of the Ruines of Christian Religion, Undermin'd by Unchristian Practice Written by the Author of the Whole Duty of Man*. London: R. Norton for T. Garthwait, 1667.

Althusser, Louis. "Ideology and Ideological State Apparatuses." In *Lenin and Philosophy, and Other Essays*, 121–173. London: New Left Books, 1971.

Anderson, Kay. "White Natures: Sydney's Royal Agricultural Show in Post-humanist Perspective." *Transactions, Institute of British Geographers* 28, no. 4 (2003): 422–441.

Anderson, Virginia DeJohn. *Creatures of Empire: How Domestic Animals Transformed Early America*. Oxford: Oxford University Press, 2004.

Andrewes, Lancelot. *The Pattern of Catechistical Doctrine at Large, or, a Learned and Pious Exposition of the Ten Commandments with an Introduction, Containing the*

Use and Benefit of Catechizing, the Generall Grounds of Religion, and the Truth of Christian Religion in Particular, Proved Against Atheists, Pagans, Jews, and Turks / by the Right Reverend Father in God Lancelot Andrews . . . ; Perfected According to the Authors Own Copy and Thereby Purged from Many Thousands of Errours, Defects, and Corruptions, Which Were in a Rude Imperfect Draught Formerly Published, as Appears in the Preface to the Reader. N.p.: n.p., 1650.

Apel, Dora. "Torture Culture: Lynching Photographs and the Images of Abu Ghraib." *Art Journal* 64, no. 2 (2005): 88–100.

Arendt, Hannah. *The Origins of Totalitarianism.* New York: Harcourt Brace Jovanovich, 1973.

Ariès, Philippe. *The Hour of Our Death.* Trans. Helen Weaver. New York: Knopf, 1981.

Aristotle. "Animals Are Not Political." In Andrew Linzey and Paul Barry Clarke, eds., *Animal Rights: A Historical Anthology,* 6–7. New York: Columbia University Press, 2004.

——. *De Anima.* Trans. R. D. Hicks. Cambridge: Cambridge University Press, 1907.

——. *The Politics.* Trans. Carnes Lord. Chicago: University of Chicago Press, 1984.

Arluke, Arnold and Boria Sax. "The Nazi Treatment of Animals and People." In Lynda Birke and Ruth Hubbard, eds., *Reinventing Biology: Respect for Life and the Creation of Knowledge,* 228–260. Bloomington: Indiana University Press, 1995.

Armstrong, Nancy and Warren Montag. "The Future of the Human: An Introduction." *differences: a journal of feminist cultural studies* 20, nos. 2–3 (2009): 1–8.

Armstrong, Philip. *What Animals Mean in the Fiction of Modernity.* London: Routledge, 2008.

Arnold, Michael. "Remembering Things." *Information Society* 24, no. 1 (2008): 47–53.

Asahina, Midori. " '"Fascination" Is Absolute of Clime': Reading Emily Dickinson's Correspondence with Higginson as Naturalist." *Emily Dickinson Journal* 14, no. 2 (2005): 103–119.

Augustine. "Of the Violent Lust of the Souldiers, Executed Vpon the Bodies of the Captiues; Against Their Consents." In *St. Augustine, of the Citie of God Vvith the Learned Comments of Io. Lod. Viues. Englished by I. H.* London: George Eld, 1610. At http://eebo.chadwyck.com/search/fulltext?ACTION=ByID&ID=D20000998426060 042&SOURCE=var_spell.cfg&DISPLAY=AUTHOR&WARN=N&FILE=../ session/1313415143_17959.

Badmington, Neil. *Posthumanism.* New York: Palgrave, 2000.

——. "Theorizing Posthumanism." *Cultural Critique* 53 (2003): 10–27.

Baker, Steve. *The Postmodern Animal.* London: Reaktion, 2000.

Barnes, Elizabeth. *States of Sympathy: Seduction and Democracy in the American Novel.* New York: Columbia University Press, 1997.

Barrett, Lyndon. "Presence of Mind: Detection and Racialization in 'The Murders in the Rue Morgue.' " In J. Gerald Kennedy and Liliane Weissberg, eds., *Romancing the Shadow: Poe and Race,* 157–176. New York: Oxford University Press, 2001.

Bates, Arlo. "Books and Authors." *Boston Sunday Courier*, November 23, 1890.

Bates, Katharine Lee. *American Literature*. New York: Macmillan, 1898.

——. *Sigurd Our Golden Collie and Other Comrades of the Road*. New York: E. P. Dutton, 1919.

Baynes, Ernest Harold. *Polaris: The Story of an Eskimo Dog*. New York: Macmillan, 1923.

Beer, Gillian. *Darwin's Plots: Evolutionary Narrative in Darwin, George Elliot, and Nineteenth-Century Fiction*. London: Routledge & Kegan Paul, 1983.

Beetz, Andrea M. "Bestiality and Zoophilia: Associations with Violence and Sex Offending." In Andrea M. Beetz and Anthony L. Podberscek, eds., *Bestiality and Zoophilia: Sexual Relations with Animals*, 46–70. LaFayette, Ind.: Purdue University Press, 2005.

——. "New Insights Into Bestiality and Zoophilia." In Andrea M. Beetz and Anthony L. Podberscek, eds., *Bestiality and Zoophilia: Sexual Relations with Animals*, 98–119. LaFayette, Ind.: Purdue University Press, 2005.

Beirne, Piers. "On the Sexual Assault of Animals: A Sociological View." In Angela N. H. Creager and William Chester Jordan, eds., *The Animal/Human Boundary: Historical Perspectives*, 193–227. Rochester, N.Y.: University of Rochester Press, 2002.

——. "Rethinking Bestiality: Towards a Concept of Interspecies Sexual Assault." *Theoretical Criminology* 1, no. 3 (1997): 317–340.

Bell, Daniel. "'American Exceptionalism' Revisited: The Role of Civil Society." *Public Interest* 95 (1989): 38–56.

Bending, Lucy. *The Representation of Bodily Pain in Late Nineteenth-Century English Culture*. Oxford: Clarendon Press, 2000.

Benjamin, Andrew. "Another Naming, a Living Animal: Blanchot's Community." *SubStance* 37, no. 3 (2008): 207–227.

Benjamin, Jessica. *Shadow of the Other: Intersubjectivity and Gender in Psychoanalysis*. New York: Routledge, 1998.

Benjamin, Walter. "Franz Kafka: On the Tenth Anniversary of His Death." In Hannah Arendt, ed., *Illuminations*, 111–140. New York: Harcourt Brace and World, 1968.

Bentham, Jeremy. *Introduction to the Principles of Morals and Legislation*. Ed. J. H. Burns and H. L. A. Hart. Oxford: Clarendon Press, 1996.

Berger, John. *About Looking*. New York: Pantheon Books, 1980.

Berkley, James. "Post-human Mimesis and the Debunked Machine: Reading Environmental Appropriation in Poe's 'Maelzel's Chess-Player' and 'The Man That Was Used Up.'" *Comparative Literature Studies* 41, no. 3 (2004): 356–376.

Berlant, Lauren. "Intimacy: A Special Issue." *Critical Inquiry* 24, no. 2 (1998): 281–288.

Bianchi, Martha Dickinson. "Selections from the Unpublished Letters of Emily Dickinson to Her Brother's Family; Chosen and Arranged by Her Niece Martha Dickinson Bianchi." *Atlantic Monthly* (January 1915): 35–42.

Blackford, Holly. "Child Consciousness in the American Novel: *Adventures of Huckleberry Finn* (1885), *What Maisie Knew* (1897), and the Birth of Child Psychology." In Monika Elbert, ed., *Children's Literature and Culture*, 245–258. New York: Routledge, 2008.

Blackwell, Mark, ed. *The Secret Life of Things: Animals, Objects, and It-Narratives in Eighteenth-Century England*. Lewisburg, Pa.: Bucknell University Press, 2007.

Blackwood, Sarah. " 'The Inner Brand': Emily Dickinson, Portraiture, and the Narrative of Liberal Interiority." *Emily Dickinson Journal* 14, no. 2 (2005): 48–59.

Bleier, Ruth. *Science and Gender: A Critique of Biology and Its Theories on Women*. New York: Pergamon, 1984.

Blount, Margaret Joan. *Animal Land: The Creatures of Children's Fiction*. New York: William Morrow, 1975.

Boehrer, Bruce Thomas. *Animal Characters: Nonhuman Beings in Early Modern Literature*. Philadelphia: University of Pennsylvania Press, 2010.

——. *Shakespeare Among the Animals: Nature and Society in the Drama of Early Modern England*. New York: Palgrave, 2002.

Bogues, Anthony. "Imagination, Politics, and Utopia: Confronting the Present." *boundary 2* 33, no. 3 (2006): 151–159.

Bolliger, Gieri and Antoine F. Goetschel. "Sexual Relations with Animals (Zoophilia): An Unrecognized Problem in Animal Welfare Legislation." In Andrea M. Beetz and Anthony L. Podberscek, eds., *Bestiality and Zoophilia: Sexual Relations with Animals*, 23–45. LaFayette, Ind.: Purdue University Press, 2005.

Bonaparte, Marie. *The Life and Works of Edgar Allan Poe*. Trans. John Rodker. London: Hogarth Press, 1949.

Bonniwell, Kate. "Publisher's Note." *Life* (May 1989): 3.

"Book Review 100 Years." *New York Times*, October 6, 1996.

Boorstin, Daniel J. *The Genius of American Politics*. Chicago: University of Chicago Press, 1953.

Booth, Alison. "The Scent of a Narrative: Rank Discourse in *Flush* and *Written on the Body*." *Narrative* 8, no. 1 (2000): 3–22.

Bradford, William. *Of Plymouth Plantation 1620–1674*. Ed. Francis Murphy. New York: Modern Library, 1981.

Bradley, Keith. "Animalizing the Slave: The Truth of Fiction." *Journal of Roman Studies* 90, (2000): 110–125.

Brawley, Lisa. "Frederick Douglass's *My Bondage and My Freedom* and the Fugitive Tourist Industry." *Novel: A Forum on Fiction* 30, no. 1 (1996): 98–128.

Brown, Bill. "Object Relations in an Expanded Field." *differences* 17, no. 3 (2006): 88–106.

——. "Thing Theory." *Critical Inquiry* 28, no. 1 (2001): 1–16.

——. "The Tyranny of Things (Trivia in Karl Marx and Mark Twain)." *Critical Inquiry* 28, no. 2 (2002): 442–469.

Brown, Gillian. *The Consent of the Governed: The Lockean Legacy in Early American Culture*. Cambridge, Mass.: Harvard University Press, 2001.

Brown, Laura. *Homeless Dogs and Melancholy Apes: Humans and Other Animals in the Modern Literary Imagination*. Ithaca: Cornell University Press, 2010.

Buck-Morss, Susan. "Visual Empire." *Diacritics* 37, nos. 2–3 (2007): 171–198.

Bullard, Asa. *Dog Stories*. His Sunnybank Stories. Boston: Lee & Shepard, 1863.

Bulliet, Richard W. *Hunters, Herders, and Hamburgers: The Past and Future of Human–Animal Relationships*. New York: Columbia University Press, 2005.

Buncombe, Andrew, Justin Huggler, and Leonard Doyle. "Abu Ghraib: Inmates Raped, Ridden Like Animals, and Forced to Eat Pork." *Independent*, May 22, 2004. At http://proquest .umi.com/pqdlink?did=640116601&Fmt=2&clientId=4347&RQT=309- &VName=PQD.

Burgett, Bruce. "Sex, Panic, Nation." *American Literary History* 21, no. 1 (2008): 67–86.

Bush, Barbara. *Millie's Book: As Dictated to Barbara Bush*. New York: William Morrow, 1990.

——. "Millie's Six-Pack: Dog Days and Springer Fever at the White House." *Life* (May 1989): 32–36.

Butler, Judith. *Bodies That Matter: On the Discursive Limits of "Sex."* New York: Routledge, 1993.

——. "Critically Queer." *GLX* 1 (1993): 17–32.

——. *Gender Trouble: Feminism and the Subversion of Identity*. New York: Routledge, 1999.

——. "Performative Acts and Gender Constitution: An Essay in Phenomenology and Feminist Theory." In Katie Conboy, Nadia Medina, and Sarah Stanbury, eds., *Writing on the Body: Female Embodiment and Feminist Theory*, 401–417. New York: Columbia University Press, 1997.

——. *Precarious Life: The Powers of Mourning and Violence*. London: Verso, 2004.

Calarco, Matthew. "Thinking Through Animals: Reflections on the Ethical and Political Stakes of the Question of the Animal in Derrida." *Oxford Literary Review* 29, no. 1 (2007): 1–15.

——. *Zoographies: The Question of the Animal from Heidegger to Derrida*. New York: Columbia University Press, 2008.

Campbell, Timothy. "Introduction." In Timothy Campbell, ed., *Bios: Biopolitics and Philosophy*, vii–xlii. Minneapolis: University of Minnesota Press, 2008.

Canup, John. *Out of the Wilderness: The Emergence of an American Identity in Colonial New England*. Middletown, Conn.: Wesleyan University Press, 1990.

Capps, Jack L. *Emily Dickinson's Reading 1836–1886*. Cambridge, Mass.: Harvard University Press, 1966.

Carlyle, Thomas. *Sartor Resartus: The Life and Opinions of Herr Teufelsdröckh in Three Books*. 1831. Ed. Roger Tarr. Berkeley: University of California Press, 2000.

Carroll, Joseph. *Literary Darwinism: Evolution, Human Nature, and Literature*. New York: Routledge, 2004.

Carroll, Peter N. *Puritanism and the Wilderness: The Intellectual Significance of the New England Frontier 1629–1700*. New York: Columbia University Press, 1969.

Castronovo, Russ. *Necro Citizenship: Death, Eroticism, and the Public Sphere in the Nineteenth-Century United States*. Durham, N.C.: Duke University Press, 2001.

Cavalieri, Paola. *The Animal Question: Why Nonhuman Animals Deserve Human Rights*. Trans. Catherine Woollard. New York: Oxford University Press, 2001.

Chaney, Michael. *Fugitive Vision: Slave Image and Black Identity in Antebellum Narrative*. Bloomington: Indiana University Press, 2008.

Chapin, Bradley. *Criminal Justice in Colonial America, 1606–1660*. Athens: University of Georgia Press, 1983.

Chapman, Abraham, ed. *Steal Away: Stories of the Runaway Slaves*. New York: Praeger,1971.

Chapple, J. A. V. *Science and Literature in the Nineteenth Century*. Houndsmill, U.K.: Macmillan, 1986.

Charlton, Moyra. *Patch: The Story of a Mongrel*. London: Methuen, 1931.

Clark, David. "On Being 'the Last Kantian in Germany': Dwelling with Animals after Lévinas." In Jennifer Ham and Matthew Senior, eds., *Animal Acts: Configuring the Human in Western History*, 165–198. New York: Routledge, 1997.

Clark, Timothy. "The Challenge of the Meta-contextual: Henry Lawson's 'Telling Mrs Baker' (1901) and Some Animal Questions for Australia." *Oxford Literary Review* 29, no. 1 (2007): 16–36.

Cleman, John. "Irresistible Impulses: Edgar Allan Poe and the Insanity Defense." *American Literature* 63, no. 4 (1991): 623–640.

Clifford, Deborah Pickman. *Mine Eyes Have Seen the Glory: A Biography of Julia Ward Howe*. Boston: Little, Brown, 1978.

Clough, Patricia Ticineto. "Introduction." In Patricia Ticineto Clough and Jean Halley, eds., *The Affective Turn: Theorizing the Social*, 1–33. Durham, N.C.: Duke University Press, 2007.

Cohen, Jeffrey J. *Medieval Identity Machines*. Minneapolis: University of Minnesota Press, 2003.

Colfax, Richard. *Evidence Against the Views of the Abolitionists, Consisting of Physical and Moral Proofs of Inferiority of the Negroes*. New York: n.p., 1833.

Cosslett, Tess. *Talking Animals in British Children's Fiction, 1786–1914*. Burlington, Vt.: Ashgate, 2006.

Cousin Daisy. *The Picture Alphabet*. Philadelphia: Lippincott , 1879.

Crain, Patricia. *The Story of A: The Alphabetization of America from the New England Primer to the Scarlet Letter*. Stanford: Stanford University Press, 2000.

Cressy, David. "Agnes Bowker's Cat: Childbirth, Seduction, Bestiality, and Lies." In *Travesties and Transgressions in Tudor and Stuart England: Tales of Discord and Dissension*, 9–28. Oxford: Oxford University Press, 2000.

Crist, Eileen. *Images of Animals: Anthropomorphism and Animal Mind*. Philadelphia: Temple University Press, 1999.

Cvetkovich, Ann. *Mixed Feeling: Feminism, Mass Culture, and Victorian Sensationalism*. New Brunswick, N.J.: Rutgers University Press, 1992.

Danahay, Martin A. "Nature Red in Hoof and Paw: Domestic Animals and Violence in Victorian Art." In Deborah Denenholz Morse and Martin A. Danahay, eds., *Victorian Animal Dreams: Representations of Animals in Victorian Literature and Culture*, 97–119. Burlington, Vt.: Ashgate, 2007.

Danforth, Samuel. *The Cry of Sodom Enquired Into; Upon Occasion of the Arraignment and Condemnation of Benjamin Goad, for His Prodigious Villany: Together with a Solemn Exhortation to Tremble at Gods Judgements, and to Abandon Youthful Lusts. / by S. D.* Cambridge: Marmaduke Johnson, 1674.

Darnton, Robert. *The Great Cat Massacre and Other Episodes in French Cultural History*. New York: Basic Books, 1983.

Darrieussecq, Marie. *Pig Tales: A Novel of Lust and Transformation*. Trans. Linda Coverdale. New York: New Press, 1996.

Daston, Lorraine and Gregg Mitman. "Introduction." In Lorraine Daston and Gregg Mitman, eds., *Thinking with Animals: New Perspectives on Anthropomorphism*, 1–14. New York: Columbia University Press, 2005.

——, eds. *Thinking with Animals: New Perspectives on Anthropomorphism*. New York: Columbia University Press, 2005.

Davidson, Arnold. "The Horror of Monsters." In James Sheehan and Morton Sosna, eds., *The Boundaries of Humanity: Humans, Animals, Machines*, 36–67. Berkeley: University of California Press, 1991.

Davidson, Jenny. *Breeding: A Partial History of the Eighteenth Century*. New York: Columbia University Press, 2009.

Davies, Stevie. "Emily Brontë & the Animals." In *Emily Brontë: Heretic*, 102–137. London: Women's Press, 1994.

Dayan, Joan. "Amorous Bondage: Poe, Ladies, and Slaves." *American Literature* 66, no. 2 (1994): 239–273.

——. *Fables of Mind: An Inquiry Into Poe's Fiction*. New York: Oxford University Press, 1987.

Dean-Jones, Lesley Ann. *Women's Bodies in Classical Greek Science*. Oxford: Clarendon Press, 1994.

D'Emilio, John and Estelle B. Freedman. *Intimate Matters: A History of Sexuality in America*. New York: Harper & Row, 1988.

Degler, Carl N. "In Pursuit of American History." *American Historical Review* 92, no. 1 (February 1987): 1–12.

Dekkers, Midas. *Dearest Pet: On Bestiality*. Trans. Paul Vincent. London: Verso, 1992.

DeKoven, Marianne. "Guest Column: Why Animals Now?" *PMLA* 124, no. 2 (2009): 361–369.

Delbanco, Andrew. "Night Vision." *New York Review of Books* 48, no. 1 (2001): 38.

Deleuze, Gilles and Félix Guattari. "Becoming-Animal." In Peter Atterton and Matthew Calarco, eds., *Animal Philosophy: Essential Readings in Continental Thought*, 87–100. London: Continuum, 2004.

Demos, John Putnam. *Entertaining Satan: Witchcraft and the Culture of Early New England*. New York: Oxford University Press, 1982.

Derrida, Jacques. "And Say the Animal Responded?" In Cary Wolfe, ed., *Zoontologies: The Question of the Animal*, 121–146. Minneapolis: University of Minnesota Press, 2003.

——. "L'animal que donc je suis (à suivre)." In Marie-Louise Mallet, ed., *L'animal autobiographique: Autour de Jacques Derrida*, 251–301. Paris: Galilée, 1999.

——. *The Animal That Therefore I Am*. Trans. David Willis. Ed. John D. Caputo. New York: Fordham University Press, 2008.

——. "The Animal That Therefore I Am (More to Follow)." *Critical Inquiry* 28, no. 2 (2002): 369–418.

——. *The Beast & the Sovereign*. Vol. 1. Chicago: University of Chicago Press, 2009.

——. "'Eating Well,' or the Calculation of the Subject: An Interview with Jacques Derrida." In Eduardo Cadava, Peter Connor, and Jean-Luc Nancy, eds., *Who Comes After the Subject?* 96–119. New York: Routledge, 1991.

——. "Interpreting Signatures (Nietzsche/Heidegger): Two Questions." *Philosophy and Literature* 10, no. 2 (1986): 246–262.

——. "Violence Against Animals." In *For What Tomorrow: A Dialogue*, 62–77. Stanford: Stanford University Press, 2004.

Descartes, René. "Animals Are Machines." In Tom Regan and Peter Singer, eds., *Animal Rights and Human Obligations*, 60–66. Englewood Cliffs, N.J.: Prentice-Hall, 1976.

——. *The Philosophical Writings of Descartes*. Cambridge: Cambridge University Press, 1985.

De Tocqueville, Alexis. *Democracy in America*. Trans. George Lawrence. Ed. J. P. Mayer. New York: Harper & Row, 1969.

Diamond, Cora. "The Difficulty of Reality and the Difficulty of Philosophy." In Stanley Cavell, Cora Diamond, John McDowell, Ian Hacking, and Cary Wolfe, *Philosophy and Animal Life*, 43–90. New York: Columbia University Press, 2008.

——. *The Realistic Spirit: Wittgenstein, Philosophy, and the Mind*. Cambridge, Mass.: MIT Press, 1991.

Dickinson, Emily. *The Letters of Emily Dickinson*. Ed. Thomas H. Johnson. 3 vols. Cambridge, Mass.: Belknap Press of Harvard University Press, 1958.

——. *The Poems of Emily Dickinson: Reading Edition*. Ed. R. W. Franklin. Cambridge, Mass.: Belknap Press of Harvard University Press, 1998.

Dillon, Elizabeth Maddock. "Sentimental Aesthetics." *American Literature* 76, no. 3 (2004): 495–523.

Dishneau, David. "Dog Handler at Abu Ghraib Convicted of Tormenting Prisoners." Associated Press, Local Wire, July 6, 2006. At http://web.lexis-nexis.com/universe/document?_m=2 b7815b13185d0b53f1ca4fb0cce7a4f&_docnum=5&wchp=dGLbVzz-zSkVA&_md5=7 db9d4b3edce7c0360d33a0e470179c0.

Dolar, Mladen. *A Voice and Nothing More*. Cambridge, Mass.: MIT Press, 2006.

Doniger, Wendy. "The Mythology of Masquerading Animals, or, Bestiality." In Arien Mack, ed., *Humans and Other Animals*, 343–365. Columbus: Ohio State University Press, 1995.

Donnelly, Michael. "On Foucault's Uses of the Notion of 'Biopower.'" In T. J. Armstrong, ed., *Michel Foucault, Philosopher: International Conference in Paris, 9,10, 11 January 1988*, 199–203. New York: Routledge, 1992.

Donovan, Josephine and Carol J. Adams, eds. *Beyond Animal Rights: A Feminist Caring Ethic for the Treatment of Animals*. New York: Continuum, 1996.

Doty, Mark. *Dog Years: A Memoir*. New York: HarperCollins, 2007.

Douglas, Ann. *The Feminization of American Culture*. New York: Knopf, 1977.

Douglas, Mary. *Natural Symbols: Explorations in Cosmology*. New York: Pantheon Books, 1970.

——. *Purity and Danger: An Analysis of Concepts of Pollution and Taboo*. New York: Praeger, 1966.

Douglass, Frederick. "The Claims of the Negro Ethnologically Considered: An Address Delivered in Hudson, Ohio, on July 12, 1854." In *The Frederick Douglass Papers*, 4 vols., ed. John W. Blassingame, 2:497–525. New Haven: Yale University Press, 1982.

——. "Farewell to the British People: An Address Delivered in London, England, on 30 March 1847." In *The Frederick Douglass Papers*, 4 vols., ed. John Blassingame, 2:19–52. New Haven: Yale University Press, 1982.

——. *The Frederick Douglass Papers*. Ed. John W. Blassingame. 4 vols. New Haven: Yale University Press, 1982.

——. *My Bondage and My Freedom*. New York: Miller, Orton & Mulligan, 1855.

——. *My Bondage and My Freedom*. Ed. William L. Andrews. Urbana: University of Illinois Press, 1987.

——. *Narrative of the Life of Frederick Douglass, an American Slave, Written by Himself*. New Haven: Yale University Press, 2001.

——. "Pictures" (1865?), holograph of a speech. Frederick Douglass Papers, Library of Congress, Washington, D.C. On microfilm at Yale University, transcribed by John Stauffer, August 1996.

Douthwaite, Julia. "Experimental Child-Rearing After Rousseau: Maria Edgeworth, *Practical Education*, and *Belinda*." *Irish Journal of Feminist Studies* 2, no. 2 (1997): 35–56.

——. *The Wild Girl, Natural Man, and the Monster: Dangerous Experiments in the Age of Enlightenment*. Chicago: University of Chicago Press, 2002.

Dowd, Maureen. "Torture Chicks Gone Wild." *New York Times*, January 30, 2005.

The Dred Scott Decision. Opinion of Chief Justice Taney, with an Introduction by Dr. J. H. Van Evrie. Also, an Appendix, Containing an Essay on the Natural History of the Prognathous Race of Mankind, Originally Written for the New York Day-Book, by Dr. S. A. Cartwright, of New Orleans. New York: Van Evrie, Horton, 1863.

Eberwein, Jane Donahue. *An Emily Dickinson Encyclopedia*. Westport, Conn.: Greenwood Press, 1998.

Eden, Trudy. "Food, Assimilation, and the Malleability of the Human Body in Early Virginia." In Janet Moore Lindman and Michele Lise Tarter, eds., *A Centre of Wonders: The Body in Early America*, 29–42. Ithaca: Cornell University Press, 2001.

Edgeworth, Maria and Richard Lovell Edgeworth. *Practical Education*. 2 vols. New York: G. F. Hopkins, 1801.

Eliot, T. S. "From Poe to Valéry." 1948. In *To Criticize the Critic, and Other Writings*, 27–42. Lincoln: University of Nebraska Press, 1992.

Ellegard, Alvar. *Darwin and the General Reader: The Reception of Darwin's Theory of Evolution*. Chicago: University of Chicago Press, 1958.

Ellis, Markman. "Suffering Things: Lapdogs, Slaves, and Counter-Sensibility." In Mark Blackwell, ed., *The Secret Life of Things: Animals, Objects, and It-Narratives in Eighteenth-Century England*, 92–116. Lewisburg, Pa.: Bucknell University Press, 2007.

Ellison, Julie. *Cato's Tears and the Making of Anglo-American Emotion*. Chicago: University of Chicago Press, 1999.

Elmer, Jonathan. *On Lingering and Being Last: Race and Sovereignty in the New World*. New York: Fordham University Press, 2008.

——. *Reading at the Social Limit*. Stanford: Stanford University Press, 1995.

Epstein, Richard A. "Animals as Objects, or Subjects, of Rights." In Cass R. Sunstein and Martha C. Nussbaum, eds., *Animal Rights: Current Debates and New Directions*, 143–174. Oxford: Oxford University Press, 2004.

Esposito, Roberto and Timothy Campbell. "Interview." Trans. Anna Paparcone. *Diacritics* 36, no. 2 (2006): 49–56.

Fahs, Alice. "The Feminized Civil War: Gender, Northern Popular Literature, and the Memory of the War, 1861–1900." *Journal of American History* 85, no. 4 (1999): 1461–1494.

Falk, Doris V. "Poe and the Power of Animal Magnetism." *PMLA* 84, no. 3 (1969): 536–546.

Feder, Ellen K. "The Dangerous Individual('s) Mother: Biopower, Family, and the Production of Race." *Hypatia* 22, no. 2 (2007): 60–78.

Ferguson, Moira. *Animal Advocacy and Englishwomen, 1780–1900: Patriots, Nation, and Empire*. Ann Arbor: University of Michigan Press, 1998.

Field, Michael. *Whym Chow, Flame of Love*. London: Eragny Press, 1914.

Fillion, Real. "Moving Beyond Biopower: Hardt and Negri's Postfoucauldian Speculative Philosophy of History." *History and Theory* 44 (2005): 47–72.

Finch, Martha L. " 'Civilized' Bodies and the 'Savage' Environment of Early New Plymouth." In Janet Moore Lindman and Michele Lise Tarter, eds., *A Centre of Wonders: The Body in Early America*, 43–59. Ithaca: Cornell University Press, 2001.

The Fire, or, Never Despair. With the History and Adventures of a Cat. New Haven: I. Cooke, 1812.

"First Dog 'Millie' Dies." *Pittsburgh Post-Gazette*, May 21, 1997.

Fischer, David Hackett. *Albion's Seed: Four British Folkways in America.* New York: Oxford University Press, 1989.

Fliegelman, Jay. *Prodigals and Pilgrims: The American Revolution Against Patriarchal Authority, 1750–1800.* Cambridge: Cambridge University Press, 1982.

Foltz, Richard. *Animals in Islamic Tradition and Muslim Cultures.* Oxford: Oneworld, 2006.

Foner, Eric, ed. *The New American History.* Philadelphia: Temple University Press, 1990.

Foster, Thomas A. *Sex and the Eighteenth-Century Man.* Boston: Beacon Press, 2006.

Foucault, Michel. *The Birth of Biopolitics: Lectures at the Collège de France, 1978–79.* Trans. Graham Burchell. Ed. Michel Senellart. New York: Palgrave Macmillan, 2008.

——. *The History of Sexuality.* Vol. 1. Trans. Robert Hurley. New York: Vintage, 1990.

——. *The History of Sexuality.* Trans. Robert Hurley. 1st American ed. New York: Pantheon Books, 1978.

——. *Madness and Civilization: A History of Insanity in the Age of Reason.* Trans. Richard Howard. New York: Vintage Books, 1965.

——. *"Society Must Be Defended": Lectures at the Collège de France 1975–1976.* Trans. David Macey. Ed. Mauro Bertani and Alessandro Fontana. New York: Picador, 2003.

Fowler, Lorenzo Niles [as L. N. F.]. "Application of Phrenology to Criticism, and the Analysis of Character, in a Letter to the Editor." *American Phrenological Journal* 1, no. 3 (1838): 65–71. Accessed through http://www.proquest.com (L. N. F., "Article 1").

——. "Thinkers, Authors, Speakers." In *Lectures on Man: Being a Series of Discourses on Phrenology and Physiology*, 132–147. London: Fowler & Wells, 1886.

Francione, Gary. "You Hypocrites!" *New Scientist Archive* 186, no. 2502 (2005): 51–52.

Franklin, Wayne. *Discoverers, Explorers, Settlers: The Diligent Writers of Early America.* Chicago: University of Chicago Press, 1979.

Frazer, Sir James and Lady Frazer. *Pasha the Pom: The Story of a Little Dog.* London: Blackie & Son, 1937.

Freeland, Cynthia, ed. *Feminist Interpreations of Aristotle.* University Park: Pennsylvania University Press, 1998.

——. "Nourishing Speculation: A Feminist Reading of Aristotelian Science." In Bat-Ami Bar On, ed., *Engendering Origins: Critical Feminist Readings in Plato and Aristotle*, 145–188. Albany: State University of New York Press, 1994.

Freeman, Mary Eleanor Wilkins. *Understudies; Short Stories by Mary E. Wilkins.* New York: Harper & Bros., 1901.

Freud, Sigmund. *History of an Infantile Neurosis* (1918). In *The Standard Edition of the Complete Psychological Works of Sigmund Freud*, vol. 17, ed. James Strachey, 1–124. London: Hogarth, 1955.

——. *Totem and Taboo: Some Points of Agreement Between the Mental Lives of Savages and Neurotics* (1913 [1912–1913]). In *The Standard Edition of the Complete Psychological Works of Sigmund Freud*, vol. 13, ed. James Strachey, vii–162. London: Hogarth Press, 1955.

Friedman, William F. "Edgar Allan Poe, Cryptographer." *American Literature* 8, no. 3 (1936): 266–280.

Fudge, Erica. *Brutal Reasoning: Animals, Rationality, and Humanity in Early Modern England.* Ithaca: Cornell University Press, 2006.

——. "The Dog, the Home and the Human, and the Ancestry of Derrida's Cat." *Oxford Literary Review* 29, no. 1 (2007): 37–54.

——. "Introduction." In Erica Fudge, ed., *Renaissance Beasts: Of Animals, Humans, and Other Wonderful Creatures*, 1–17. Urbana: University of Illinois Press, 2004.

——. "A Left-Handed Blow: Writing the History of Animals." In Nigel Rothfels, eds., *Representing Animals*, 3–18. Bloomington: Indiana University Press, 2002.

——. *Perceiving Animals: Humans and Beasts in Early Modern English Culture.* Urbana: University of Illinois Press, 2000.

——, ed. *Renaissance Beasts: Of Animals, Humans, and Other Wonderful Creatures.* Urbana: University of Illinois Press, 2004.

Fuss, Diana. "Introduction: Human, All Too Human." In Diana Fuss, ed., *Human, All Too Human*, 1–7. New York: Routledge, 1996.

Garber, Marjorie. *Dog Love.* New York: Simon & Schuster, 1996.

Garfield. "Not Bad for a Dog." *New York Times*, September 16, 1990.

Garzon, Francisco Calvo. "Towards a General Theory of Antirepresentationalism." *British Journal for the Philosophy of Science* 59, no. 3 (2008): 259–292.

Gates, Barbara T. *Kindred Nature.* Chicago: University of Chicago Press, 1998.

Gates, Henry Louis. *The Signifying Monkey: A Theory of African-American Literary Criticism.* New York: Oxford University Press, 1988.

Giffney, Noreen and Myra Hird, eds. *Queering the Non/Human.* Burlington, Vt.: Ashgate, 2008.

Gillespie, Angus K. and Jay Mechling, eds. *American Wildlife in Symbol and Story.* Knoxville: University of Tennessee Press, 1987.

Gillespie, Angus K. and Jay Mechling. "Introduction." In Angus K. Gillespie and Jay Mechling, eds., *American Wildlife in Symbol and Story*, 1–14. Knoxville: University of Tennessee Press, 1987.

Girard, René. *Violence and the Sacred.* Trans. Patrick Gregory. Baltimore: Johns Hopkins University Press, 1972.

Glickstein, Jonathan A. *American Exceptionalism, American Anxiety: Wages, Competition, and Degraded Labor in the Antebellum United States.* Charlottesville: University of Virginia Press, 2002.

Godbeer, Richard. *Sexual Revolution in Early America.* Baltimore: Johns Hopkins University Press, 2002.

God's Judgments Against Whoring. Being an Essay Towards a General History of It, from the Creation of the World to the Reign of Augustulus (Which According to Common Computation Is 5190 Years) and from Thence Down to the Present Year 1697: Being a Collection of the Most Remarkable Instances of Uncleanness That Are to Be Found in Sacred or Prophane History During That Time, with Observations Thereon. N.p.: n.p., 1697.

Goldberg, Jonathan. "Bradford's 'Ancient Members' and 'a Case of Buggery . . . Amongst Them.'" In Andrew Parker, Mary Russo, Doris Sommer, and Patricia Yaeger, eds., *Nationalisms and Sexualities,* 60–76. New York: Routledge, 1991.

Goodrich, Samuel. *Famous Men of Ancient Times.* Boston: J. E. Hickman, 1843.

Gordon, Max. "Abu Ghraib: Postcards from the Edge." *OpenDemocracy* 13 (October 2004). At http://www.opendemocracy.net/media-abu_ghraib/article_2146.jsp.

Graham, Elaine. *Representations of the Post/Human: Monsters, Aliens, and Others in Popular Culture.* Manchester, U.K.: Manchester University Press, 2002.

Grandin, Temple and Catherine Johnson. *Animals Make Us Human: Creating the Best Life for Animals.* Boston: Houghton Mifflin Harcourt, 2009.

Grebowicz, Margret. "When Species Meat: Confronting Bestiality Pornography." *Humanimalia* 1, no. 2 (2010): 1–17.

Greene, Jack P. *The Intellectual Construction of America: Exceptionalism and Identity from 1492 to 1800.* Chapel Hill: University of North Carolina Press, 1993.

Grier, Katherine. *Pets in America: A History.* Chapel Hill: University of North Carolina Press, 2006.

Griffiths, Jacqui. "Almost Human: Intermediate Children and Dogs in *Flush* and *The Sound and the Fury.*" *Yearbook of English Studies* 32 (2002): 163–176.

Gruen, Lori. *Ethics and Animals: An Introduction.* Cambridge: Cambridge University Press, 2011.

Halberstam, Judith. *The Queer Art of Failure.* Durham, N.C.: Duke University Press, 2011.

Halperin, David. *How to Do the History of Homosexuality.* Chicago: University of Chicago Press, 2002.

Hanke, Lewis. *Aristotle and the American Indians: A Study in Race Prejudice in the Modern World.* London: Hollis & Carter, 1959.

Hannaford, Ivan. *Race: The History of an Idea in the West.* Baltimore: Johns Hopkins University Press, 1996.

Hanssen, Beatrice. *Walter Benjamin's Other History: Of Stones, Animals, Human Beings, and Angels.* Berkeley: University of California Press, 1998.

Haque, Nadeem and Basheer Ahmad Masri. "The Principles of Animal Advocacy in Islam: Four Integrated Ecognitions." *Society & Animals* 19 (2011): 279–290.

Haraway, Donna. *The Companion Species Manifesto: Dogs, People, and Significant Otherness.* Chicago: Prickly Paradigm Press, 2003.

——. "A Manifesto for Cyborgs: Science, Technology, and Socialist Feminism in the 1980s." *Socialist Review* 80 (1985): 65–108.

——. *Primate Visions: Gender, Race, and Nature in the World of Modern Science.* New York: Routledge, 1989.

——. *When Species Meet.* Minneapolis: University of Minnesota Press, 2008.

Hardt, Michael. "Foreword: What Affects Are Good For." In Patricia Ticineto Clough and Jean Halley, eds., *The Affective Turn: Theorizing the Social*, ix–xiii. Durham, N.C.: Duke University Press, 2007.

The Hare; or, Hunting Incompatible with Humanity: Written as a Stimulus to Youth Towards a Proper Treatment of Animals. Philadelphia: Benjamin Johnson, 1802.

Harkavy, Ward. "Abu Ghraib: A Chicken in Every Plot." *Village Voice*, May 10, 2005. At http://blogs.villagevoice.com/pressclips/archives/2005/05/a_chicken_in_ev.php.

Hartman, Sadiya. *Scenes of Subjection: Terror, Slavery, and Self-Making in Nineteenth-Century America.* New York: Oxford University Press, 1997.

Hartz, Louis. *The Liberal Tradition in America: An Interpretation of American Political Thought Since the Revolution.* New York: Harcourt Brace, 1955.

Hayles, N. Katherine. *How We Became Posthuman: Virtual Bodies in Cybernetics, Literature, and Informatics.* Chicago: University of Chicago Press, 1999.

Heidegger, Martin. *The Fundamental Concepts of Metaphysics: World, Finitude, Solitude.* Trans. William McNeill and Nicholas Walker. Bloomington: Indiana University Press, 1995.

Heilbrun, Carolyn G. "Men Were the Only Models I Had." *Chronicle of Higher Education* 48, no. 7 (2001): B7–B11.

Henderson, Brian. "Animals and the State in Nineteenth-Century England." In *Peacable Kingdom: Stability and Change in Modern Britain*, 82–122. Oxford: Clarendon Press, 1982.

Hendler, Glenn. *Public Sentiments: Structures of Feeling in Nineteenth-Century American Literature.* Chapel Hill: University of North Carolina Press, 2001.

Herder, Johann Gottfried. "Essay on the Origin of Language." In *On the Origin of Language*, 87–166. Chicago: University of Chicago Press, 1966.

Herrnstein-Smith, Barbara. "Animal Relatives, Difficult Relations." *differences* 15, no. 1 (2004): 1–23.

Hibernicus. "Butchers on Juries." *Notes and Queries* 186, no. 11 (1944): 254.

Higginson, Thomas Wentworth. "Women and Men; Children and Animals." *Harper's Bazaar*, July 30, 1887.

Hirsch, Seymour. "Chain of Command: How the Department of Defense Mishandled the Disaster at Abu Ghraib." *New Yorker*, May 17, 2004.

Hodgson, John. "Decoding Poe? Poe, W. B. Tyler, and Cryptography." *Journal of English and Germanic Philology* 92, no. 4 (1993): 523–534.

Holland, Jeanne. "Scraps, Stamps, and Cutouts: Emily Dickinson's Domestic Technologies of Publication." In Margaret J. M. Ezell and Katherine O'Brien O'Keeffe, eds., *Cultural Artifacts and the Production of Meaning: The Page, the Image, and the Body*, 139–182. Ann Arbor: University of Michigan Press, 1994.

Howell, Philip. "Flush and the *Banditti*: Dog-Stealing in Victorian London." In Chris Philo and Chris Wilbert, eds., *Animal Spaces, Beastly Places: New Geographies of Human–Animal Relations*, 35–55. London: Routledge, 2000.

Huggan, Graham and Helen Tiffin. *Postcolonial Ecocriticism: Literature, Animals, Environment*. London: Routledge, 2010.

Hume, David. "Of the Reason of Animals." In Tom Regan and Peter Singer, eds., *Animal Rights and Human Obligations*, 69–71. Englewood Cliffs, N.J.: Prentice-Hall, 1976.

Huyler, Jerome. *Locke in America: The Moral Philosophy of the Founding Era*. Kansas City: University Press of Kansas, 1995.

Ignatieff, Michael, ed. *American Exceptionalism and Human Rights*. Princeton: Princeton University Press, 2005.

Irigaray, Luce. "Place, Interval: A Reading of Aristotle, *Physics* Iv." In Cynthia Freeland, ed., *Feminist Interpreations of Aristotle*, 41–58. University Park: Pennsylvania University Press, 1998.

Iriye, Akira and Warren I. Cohen, eds. *The United States and Japan in the Postwar World*. Lexington: University Press of Kentucky, 1989.

Ittner, Jutta. "Part Spaniel, Part Canine Puzzle: Anthropomorphism in Woolf's *Flush* and Auster's *Timbuktu*." *Mosaic* 39, no. 4 (2006): 181–196.

Jacoby, Karl. "Slaves by Nature? Domestic Animals and Human Slavery." *Slavery & Abolition* 15, no. 1 (1994): 89–99.

Jefferson, Thomas. *Notes on the State of Virginia*. Philadelphia: Prichard and Hall, 1788.

Jennings, Bruce. "The Liberalism of Life: Bioethics in the Face of Biopower." *Raritan* 22, no. 4 (2003): 132–146.

Jones, Kathleen W. "Mother's Day: The Creation, Promotion, and Meaning of a New Holiday in the Progressive Era." *Texas Studies in Literature and Language* 22, no. 2 (1980): 175–196.

Jordan, Mark. *The Invention of Sodomy in Christian Theology*. Chicago: University of Chicago Press, 1997.

Kahn, Douglas. *Noise, Water, Meat*. Cambridge, Mass.: MIT Press, 1999.

Kaplan, Amy and Donald E. Pease, eds. *Cultures of United States Imperialism*. Durham, N.C.: Duke University Press, 1993.

Katz, Jonathan Ned. *Gay American History: Lesbians and Gay Men in the U.S.A.* New York: Meridian Books, 1992.

——. *Gay/Lesbian Almanac: A New Documentary*. New York: Carroll & Graf, 1982.

Kean, Hilda. *Animal Rights: Political and Social Change in Britain Since 1800*. London: Reaktion, 1998.

Keller, Evelyn Fox. "Language and Ideology in Evolutionary Theory: Reading Cultural Norms Into Natural Law." In James Sheehan and Morton Sosna, eds., *The Boundaries of Humanity: Humans, Animals, Machines*, 85–102. Berkeley: University of California Press, 1991.

——. *The Mirage of a Space Between Nature and Nurture*. Durham, N.C.: Duke University Press, 2010.

Kendall, Karalyn. "The Face of a Dog: Levinasian Ethics and Human/Dog Co-evolution." In Noreen Giffney and Myra Hird, eds., *Queering the Non/Human*, 185–204. Burlington, Vt.: Ashgate, 2008.

Kennedy, J. Gerald and Liliane Weissberg, eds. *Romancing the Shadow: Poe and Race*. New York: Oxford University Press, 2001.

Kenyon-Jones, Christine. *Kindred Brutes: Animals in Romantic-Period Writing*. Burlington Vt.: Ashgate, 2001.

Kete, Kathleen. "Animals and Ideology: The Politics of Animal Protection in Europe." In Nigel Rothfels, ed., *Representing Animals*, 19–34. Bloomington: Indiana University Press, 2002.

Kibbey, Ann. *The Interpretation of Material Shapes in Puritanism: A Study of Rhetoric, Prejudice, and Violence*. Cambridge: Cambridge University Press, 1986.

Kilner, Dorothy. *The Rotchfords; or the Friendly Counsellor: Designed for the Instruction and Amusement of the Youth of Both Sexes*. 2 vols. in one book. Philadelphia: James Humphrey, 1801.

Kimmage, Michael. "Lionel Trilling's *The Middle of the Journey* and the Complicated Origins of the Neo-conservative Movement." *Shofar* 21, no. 3 (2003): 48–63.

Kranish, Michael. "White House's Top Dog: 'Millie' Royalties Eclipse the President's Wages." *Boston Globe*, April 16, 1992.

Kreilkamp, Ivan. "Dying Like a Dog in *Great Expectations*." In Deborah Denenholz Morse and Martin A. Danahay, eds., *Victorian Animal Dreams: Representations of Animals in Victorian Literature and Culture*, 81–94. Burlington, Vt.: Ashgate, 2007.

——. "Petted Things: *Wuthering Heights* and the Animal." *Yale Journal of Criticism* 18, no. 1 (2005): 81–110.

Kuzniar, Alice A. " 'I Married My Dog': On Queer Canine Literature." In Noreen Giffney and Myra Hird, eds., *Queering the Non/Human*, 205–226. Burlington, Vt.: Ashgate, 2008.

——. *Melancholia's Dog*. Chicago: University of Chicago Press, 2006.

Lacan, Jacques. *The Seminar of Jacques Lacan*. Trans. Sylvana Tomaselli. Ed. Jacques-Alain Miller. New York: Norton, 1988.

——. "Seminar on 'The Purloined Letter.' " In John P. Muller and William J. Richardson, eds., *The Purloined Poe*, 28–55. Baltimore: Johns Hopkins University Press, 1988.

LaCapra, Dominick. *History and Its Limits: Human, Animal, Violence*. Ithaca: Cornell University Press, 2009.

Lamb, Jonathan. "Gulliver and the Lives of Animals." In Frank Palmeri, ed., *Humans and Other Animals in Eighteenth-Century British Culture*, 169–177. Aldershot, U.K.: Ashgate, 2006.

——. "Modern Metamorphoses and Disgraceful Tales." *Critical Inquiry* 28, no. 1 (2001): 133–166.

Landry, Donna. "English Brutes, Eastern Enlightenment." In "Animal, All Too Animal," special issue of *The Eighteenth Century* 52, no. 1 (2011): 11–30.

——. *Noble Brutes: How Eastern Horses Transformed English Culture*. Baltimore: Johns Hopkins University Press, 2009.

Lange, Lynda. "Woman Is Not a Rational Animal: On Aristotle's Biology of Reproduction." In Sandra Harding and Merrill B. Hintikka, eds., *Discovering Reality: Feminist Perspectives on Epistemology, Metaphysics, Methodology, and Philosophy of Science*, 1–16. Boston: Reiderl, 1983.

Lansbury, Coral. *Old Brown Dog*. Madison: University of Wisconsin Press, 1985.

Latour, Bruno. *We Have Never Been Modern*. Trans. Catherine Porter. Cambridge, Mass.: Harvard University Press, 1993.

Leach, Edmund. "Anthropological Aspects of Language: Animal Categories and Verbal Abuse." In Eric H. Lenneberg, ed., *New Directions in the Study of Language*, 23–63. Cambridge, Mass.: MIT Press, 1964.

Lee, Maurice. *Slavery, Philosophy, and American Literature, 1830–1860*. Cambridge: Cambridge University Press, 2005.

LeGuin, Ursula K. "She Unnames Them." In *Buffalo Gals and Other Animal Presences*, 194–196. Santa Barbara, Calif.: Capra Press, 1987.

Lévinas, Emmanuel. "Interview." In Matthew Calarco and Peter Atterton, eds., *Animal Philosophy: Essential Readings in Continental Thought*, 49–50. London: Continuum, 2004.

——. "Name of a Dog, or Natural Rights." In *Difficult Freedom: Essays on Judaism*, trans. Seán Hand, 151–153. Baltimore: Johns Hopkins University Press, 1990.

Levine, Lawrence. "William Shakespeare in America." In *Highbrow Lowbrow: The Emergence of Cultural Hierarchy in America*, 11–82. Cambridge, Mass.: Harvard University Press, 1988.

Levine, Robert. *Martin Delany, Frederick Douglass, and the Politics of Representative Identity*. Chapel Hill: University of North Carolina Press, 1997.

Levinson, Brett. "Biopolitics and Duopolies." *diacritics* 35, no. 2 (2005): 65–75.

Lewis, Jayne Elizabeth. *The English Fable: Aesop and Literary Culture 1651–1740*. Cambridge: Cambridge University Press, 1996.

Leys, Ruth. "The Turn to Affect: A Critique." *Critical Inquiry* 37, no. 3 (2011): 434–472.

Liliequist, Jonas. "Peasants Against Nature: Crossing the Boundaries Between Man and Animal in Seventeenth- and Eighteenth-Century Sweden." In *Forbidden History:*

The State, Society, and the Regulation of Sexuality in Modern Europe. Essays from the "Journal of the History of Sexuality," 57–89. Chicago: University of Chicago Press, 1992.

Lindman, Janet Moore and Michele Lise Tarter. "Introduction." In Janet Moore Lindman and Michele Lise Tarter, eds., *A Centre of Wonders: The Body in Early America,* 1–9. Ithaca: Cornell University Press, 2001.

Lingis, Alphonso. "Bestiality." In H. Peter Steeves, ed., *Animal Others: On Ethics, Ontology, and Animal Life,* 37–54. Albany: State University of New York Press, 1999.

Lippit, Akira Mizuta. *Electric Animal: Toward a Rhetoric of Wildlife.* Minneapolis: University of Minnesota Press, 2000.

——. "Magnetic Animal: Derrida, Wildlife, Animetaphor." *MLN* 113, no. 5 (1998): 1111–1125.

Lipset, Seymour Martin. *American Exceptionalism: A Double-Edged Sword.* New York: Norton, 1996.

——. "A Unique People in an Exceptional Country." *Society* 28 (1990): 4–13.

Llewelyn, John. "Am I Obsessed by Bobby? (Humanism of the Other Animal)." In Robert Bernasconi and Simon Critchley, eds., *Re-reading Levinas,* 234–247. Bloomington: Indiana University Press, 1991.

Locke, John. *The Educational Writings of John Locke: A Critical Edition with Introduction and Notes.* Ed. James L. Axtell. Cambridge: Cambridge University Press, 1968.

Lorenz, Konrad and Paul Leyhausen. *Motivation of Human and Animal Behavior: An Ethological View.* New York: Van Nostrand Reinhold, 1973.

Lovering, Mark. *A History of Augustan Fable.* Cambridge: Cambridge University Press, 1998.

Lucas, E. V. *If Dogs Could Write: A Second Canine Miscellany.* 2nd ed. London: Methuen, 1929.

Lumsden, Simon. "Habit, Reason, and the Limits of Normativity." *SubStance* 37, no. 3 (2008): 188–206.

Lundblad, Michael. "Epistemology of the Jungle: Progressive-Era Sexuality and the Nature of the Beast." *American Literature* 81, no. 4 (2009): 747–773.

——. "From Animal Studies to Animality Studies." *PMLA* 124, no. 2 (2009): 496–502.

Lupton, Julia. "Creature Caliban." *Shakespeare Quarterly* 51, no. 1 (2000): 1–23.

MacKinnon, Catharine. *Toward a Feminist Theory of the State.* Cambridge, Mass.: Harvard University Press, 1989.

Madsen, Deborah L. *American Exceptionalism.* Edinburgh: Edinburgh University Press, 1998.

Mangum, Teresa. "Dog Years, Human Fears." In Nigel Rothfels, ed., *Representing Animals,* 35–47. Bloomington: Indiana University Press, 2002.

Marin, Louis. *Food for Thought.* Baltimore: Johns Hopkins University Press, 1989.

Martin, Calvin Luther. *In the Spirit of the Earth: Rethinking History and Time.* Baltimore: Johns Hopkins University Press, 1992.

———. *The Way of the Human Being*. New Haven: Yale University Press, 1999.

Mason, Jennifer. *Civilized Creatures: Urban Animals, Sentimental Culture, and American Literature, 1850–1900*. Baltimore : Johns Hopkins University Press, 2005.

Mason, Mary G. "The Other Voice: Autobiographies of Women Writers." In Sidonie Smith and Julia Watson, eds., *Women, Autobiography, Theory: A Reader*, 321–324. Madison: University of Wisconsin Press, 1998.

Mather, Cotton. *Magnalia Christi Americana: Or, the Ecclesiastical History of New-England, from Its First Planting in the Year 1620. Unto the Year of Our Lord, 1698. In Seven Books. . . . by . . . Cotton Mather, . . .* London: Thomas Parkhurst, 1702.

———. *Warnings from the Dead. Or Solemn Admonitions Unto All People; but Especially Unto Young Persons to Beware of Such Evils as Would Bring Them to the Dead. By Cotton Mather. In Two Discourses, Occasioned by a Sentence of Death, Executed on Some Unhappy Malefactors. Together with the Last Confession, Made by a Young Woman, Who Dyed on June 8. 1693. One of These Malefactors*. Boston: Bartholomew Green for Samuel Phillips, 1693.

Matsumi, Brian. *Parables for the Virtual: Movement, Affect, Sensation*. Durham, N.C.: Duke University Press, 2002.

May, Robert J. *Winking Willie*. New York: Maxton, 1948.

Mayhew, Robert. *The Female in Aristotle's Biology*. Chicago: University of Chicago Press, 2004.

Mbembe, Achille. "Necropolitics." *Public Culture* 15, no. 1 (2003): 11–40.

McBain, Alastair and Corey Ford. *A Man of His Own and Other Dog Stories*. New York: Whittlesey House, 1949.

McBride, Dwight A. *Impossible Witnesses: Truth, Abolitionism, and Slave Testimony*. New York: New York University Press, 2001.

McClintock, Anne. " 'No Longer in a Future Heaven': Women and Nationalism in South Africa." *Transition* 51 (1991): 104–123.

———. "Paranoid Empire: Specters from Guantanamo and Abu Ghraib." *Small Axe* 13, no. 1 (2009): 50–74.

McEvoy-Levy, Siobhán. *American Exceptionalism and U.S. Foreign Policy: Public Diplomacy at the End of the Cold War*. New York: Palgrave, 2001.

McGann, Jerome. *The Poetics of Sensibility: A Revolution in Literary Style*. Oxford: Clarendon Press, 1996.

McHugh, Susan. *Animal Stories: Narrating Across Species Lines*. Minneapolis: University of Minnesota Press, 2011.

———. "One or Several Literary Animal Studies?" H-Animal, H-Net, July 17, 2006. At http://www.h-net.org/~animal/ruminations_mchugh.html.

McKelvey, Tara, ed. *One of the Guys: Women as Aggressors and Torturers*. Emeryville, Calif.: Avalon, 2007.

McWhorter, Ladelle. "Sex, Race, and Biopower: A Foucauldian Genealogy." *Hypatia* 19, no. 3 (2004): 38–62.

Mead, Edwin. "Woman and War: Julia Ward Howe's Peace Crusade." *World Peace Foundation Pamphlet Series* 4, no. 6 (1914): 1–11.

Menand, Louis. "Regrets Only: Lionel Trilling and His Discontents." *The New Yorker*, September 29, 2008. At http://www.newyorker.com/arts/critics/atlarge/2008/09/29/080929crat_atlarge_menand.

Menely, Tobias. "Animal Signs and Ethical Significance: Expressive Creatures in the British Georgic." *Mosaic* 39, no. 4 (2006): 111–128.

Mesmer, Franz Anton. *Précis historique des faits relatifs au magnétisme-animal jusques en avril 1781. Par M. Mesmer, . . . ouvrage traduit de l'allemand.* London: n.p., 1781.

"Metaphor." In Christopher Baldick, ed., *The Concise Oxford Dictionary of Literary Terms.* Oxford: Oxford University Press, 2008. From *Oxford Reference Online*, Dartmouth College, May 3, 2012. At http://www.oxfordreference.com/views/ENTRY.html?subview=Main&entry=t56.e712.

Midgley, Mary. *Beast and Man: The Roots of Human Nature.* Ithaca: Cornell University Press, 1978.

Miletski, Hani. "A History of Bestiality." In Andrea M. Beetz and Anthony L. Podberscek, eds., *Bestiality and Zoophilia: Sexual Relations with Animals*, 1–22. LaFayette, Ind.: Purdue University Press, 2005.

——. "Is Zoophilia a Sexual Orientation? A Study." In Andrea M. Beetz and Anthony L. Podberscek, eds., *Bestiality and Zoophilia: Sexual Relations with Animals*, 82–97. LaFayette, Ind.: Purdue University Press, 2005.

Miller, D. A. *The Novel and the Police.* Berkeley: University of California Press, 1988.

Miller, Jacquelyn. "The Body Politic and the Body Somatic: Benjamin Rush's Fear of Social Disorder and His Treatment for Yellow Fever." In Janet Moore Lindman and Michele Lise Tarter, eds., *A Centre of Wonders: The Body in Early America*, 61–74. Ithaca: Cornell University Press, 2001.

Miller, Perry. *Errand Into the Wilderness.* Cambridge, Mass.: Belknap Press of Harvard University Press, 1959.

Mitchell, W. J. T. "Echoes of a Christian Symbol." *Chicago Tribune*, June 27, 2004.

Moldenhauer, Joseph J. "Murder as Fine Art: Basic Connections Between Poe's Aesthetics, Psychology, and Moral Vision." *PMLA* 83, no. 2 (1968): 284–297.

Montaigne, Michel de. "An Apology for Raymond Sebond." In Linda Kalof and Amy Fitzgerald, eds., *The Animals Reader: The Essential Classic and Contemporary Writings*, 57–59. Oxford: Berg, 2007.

Moore, Grace. "Beastly Criminals and Criminal Beasts: Stray Women and Stray Dogs in *Oliver Twist*." In Deborah Denenholz Morse and Martin A. Danahay, eds., *Victorian Animal Dreams: Representations of Animals in Victorian Literature and Culture*, 201–214. Burlington, Vt.: Ashgate, 2007.

Moretti, Franco. *Signs Taken for Wonders: Essays in the Sociology of Literary Forms.* Trans. Susan Fischer, David Forgacs, and David Miller. London: Verso, 1983.

Morrison, Toni. *Playing in the Dark: Whiteness and the Literary Imagination.* Cambridge, Mass.: Harvard University Press, 1992.

Morse, Deborah Denenholz and Martin A. Danahay. "Introduction." In Deborah Denenholz Morse and Martin A. Danahay, eds., *Victorian Animal Dreams: Representations of Animals in Victorian Literature and Culture,* 1–12. Burlington, Vt.: Ashgate, 2007.

Morss, John R. *The Biologising of Childhood: Developmental Psychology and the Darwinian Myth.* London: Lawrence Erlbaum, 1990.

Morton, Samuel George. *Brief Remarks on the Diversities of the Human Species: And on Some Kindred Subjects: Being an Introductory Lecture Delivered Before the Class of Pennsylvania Medical College, in Philadelphia, November 1, 1842.* Philadelphia: Merrihew & Thompson, 1842.

——. *Crania Aegyptiaca: Or, Observations on Egyptian Ethnography, Derived from Anatomy, History, and the Monuments.* Philadelphia: J. Pennington, 1844.

——. *Crania Americana: Or, a Comparative View of the Skulls of Various Aboriginal Nations of North and South America to Which Is Prefixed an Essay on the Variety of the Human Species.* Philadelphia: John Pennington; London: James Madden, 1839.

Morton, Timothy. *Shelley and the Revolution in Taste: The Body and the Natural World.* Cambridge: Cambridge University Press, 1994.

Moten, Fred. *In the Break: The Aesthetics of the Black Radical Tradition.* Minneapolis: University of Minnesota Press, 2003.

Mouffe, Chantal. "American Liberalism and Its Communitarian Critics." In Chantal Mouffe, ed., *The Return of the Practical,* 23–40. New York: Verso, 1993.

Muir, John. *Stickeen.* Boston: Houghton Mifflin, 1915.

Murrin, John M. " 'Things Fearful to Name': Bestiality in Early America." In Angela N. H. Creager and William Chester Jordan, eds., *The Animal/Human Boundary: Historical Perspectives,* 115–156. Rochester, N.Y.: University of Rochester Press, 2002.

Nancy, Jean-Luc. *Corpus.* Trans. Richard A. Rand. New York: Fordham University Press, 2008.

Nash, Richard. "Joy and Pity: Reading Animal Bodies in Late Eighteenth-Century Culture." In "Animal, All Too Animal," special issue of *The Eighteenth Century* 52, no. 1 (2011): 47–67.

——. *Wild Enlightenment: The Borders of Human Identity in the Eighteenth Century.* Charlottesville: University of Virginia Press, 2003.

Nash, Roderick. *Wilderness and the American Mind.* New Haven: Yale University Press, 1982.

Nast, Heidi. "Loving . . . Whatever: Alienation, Neoliberalism, and Pet-Love in the Twenty-First Century." *ACME* 5, no. 2 (2006): 300–327.

"The Negro and Caucasian Brain Compared." *American Phrenological Journal* 3, no. 6 (1841): 282–283.

Newton, Michael. "Bodies Without Souls: The Case of Peter the Wild Boy." In Erica Fudge, Ruth Gilbert, and Susan Wiseman, eds., *At the Borders of the Human: Beasts, Bodies, and Natural Philosophy in the Early Modern Period*, 196–214. New York: Palgrave, 2002.

Ngai, Sianne. *Ugly Feelings*. Cambridge, Mass.: Harvard University Press, 2005.

Noble, David W. *Death of a Nation: American Culture and the End of Exceptionalism*. Minneapolis: University of Minnesota Press, 2002.

Norris, Andrew. "The Exemplary Exception: Philosophical and Political Decisions in Giorgio Agamben's *Homo Sacer*." In Andrew Norris, ed., *Politics, Metaphysics, and Death: Essays on Giorgio Agamben's "Homo Sacer,"* 262–283. Durham, N.C.: Duke University Press, 2005.

——. "Introduction: Giorgio Agamben and the Politics of the Living Dead." In Andrew Norris, ed., *Politics, Metaphysics, and Death: Essays on Giorgio Agamben's "Homo Sacer,"* 1–30. Durham, N.C.: Duke University Press, 2005.

Norris, Margot. "The Human Animal in Fiction." *parallax* 12, no. 1 (2006): 4–20.

Nott, Josiah Clark. *Indigenous Races of the Earth; or, New Chapters of Ethnological Inquiry; Including Monographs on Special Departments . . . Contributed by Alfred Maury . . . Francis Pulszky . . . and J. Aitken Meigs . . . Presenting Fresh Investigations, Documents, and Materials. By J. C. Nott . . . and Geo. R. Gliddon*. Philadelphia: J. B. Lippincott, 1857.

——. *Types of Mankind: Or, Ethnological Researches, Based Upon the Ancient Monuments, Paintings, Sculptures, and Crania of Races, and Upon Their Natural, Geographical, Philological, and Biblical History: Illustrated by Selections from the Inedited Papers of Samuel George Morton . . . and by Additional Contributions from Prof. L. Agassiz, Ll.D., W. Usher, M.D., and Prof. H. S. Patterson, M.D. By J. C. Nott and Geo. R. Gliddon*. 7th ed. Philadelphia: Lippincott Gramoo, 1855.

Nussbaum, Martha. "Aristotle, Feminism, and Needs for Functioning." In Cynthia Freeland, ed., *Feminist Interpretations of Aristotle*, 248–259. University Park: Pennsylvania University Press, 1998.

Oliver, Kelly. *Animal Lessons: How They Teach Us to Be Human*. New York: Columbia University Press, 2009.

Ouida [De La Ramée, Marie Louise]. *A Dog of Flanders*. East Aurora, N.Y.: Roycrofters, 1906.

Palmeri, Frank. "The Autocritique of Fables." In Frank Palmeri, ed., *Humans and Other Animals in Eighteenth-Century British Culture: Representation, Hybridity, Ethics*, 83–100. Burlington, Vt.: Ashgate, 2006.

——. "The History of Fables and Cultural History in Eighteenth-Century England." In Lorna Clymer and Robert Mayer, eds., *Historical Boundaries, Narrative Forms: Essays on British Literature in the Long Eighteenth Century in Honor of Everett Zimmerman*, 141–163. Newark: University of Delaware Press, 2007.

Parker, Andrew, Mary Russo, Doris Sommer, and Patricia Yaeger. "Introduction." In Andrew Parker, Mary Russo, Doris Sommer, and Patricia Yaeger, eds., *Nationalisms and Sexualities*, 1–18. New York: Routledge, 1991.

Pateman, Carol. *The Problem of Political Obligation: A Critical Analysis of Liberal Theory.* New York: Wiley, 1979.

Patterson, Annabel M. *Fables of Power: Aesopian Writing and Political History.* Durham, N.C.: Duke University Press, 1991.

Patterson, Orlando. *Slavery and Social Death: A Comparative Study.* Cambridge, Mass.: Harvard University Press, 1982.

Pearce, Roy Harvey. *Savagism and Civilization: A Study of the Indian and the American Mind.* Berkeley: University of California Press, 1988.

Perlo, Katherine Wills. *Kinship and Killing: The Animal in World Religions.* New York: Columbia University Press, 2009.

Perry, Kathryn. "Unpicking the Seam: Talking Animals and Reader Pleasure in Early Modern Satire." In Erica Fudge, ed., *Renaissance Beasts: Of Animals, Humans, and Other Wonderful Creatures*, 19–36. Urbana: University of Illinois Press, 2004.

Peterson, Christopher. "Of Canines and Queers: Review of *Melancholia's Dog*: Reflections on Our Animal Kinship." *GLQ* 15, no. 2 (2009): 352–354.

Peterson, Linda. "Gender and Autobiographical Form." In James Olney, ed., *Studies in Autobiography*, 211–222. New York: Oxford University Press, 1988.

Philo, Chris and Chris Wilbert, eds. *Animal Spaces, Beastly Places: New Geographies of Human–Animal Relations.* London: Routledge, 2000.

Pick, Anat. *Creaturely Poetics: Animality and Vulnerability in Literature and Film.* New York: Columbia University Press, 2011.

Pickering, H. J. *Dog-Days on Trout Waters.* New York: Derrydale Press, 1933.

Pickering, Samuel F. *John Locke and Children's Books in Eighteenth-Century England.* Knoxville: University of Tennessee Press, 1981.

Poe, Edgar Allan. "The Black Cat." In *The Selected Writings of Edgar Allan Poe*, ed. G. R. Thompson, 348–355. New York: Norton, 2004.

——. *Edgar Allan Poe: Complete Poems.* Ed. Thomas Ollive Mabbott. Urbana: University of Illinois Press, 2000.

——. "The Gold-Bug." In *The Selected Writings of Edgar Allan Poe*, ed. G. R. Thompson, 321–348. New York: Norton, 2004.

——. "The Murders in the Rue Morgue." *Graham's Lady's and Gentleman's Magazine* (April 1841): 166–180.

——. "The Murders in the Rue Morgue." In *The Selected Writings of Edgar Allan Poe*, ed. G. R. Thompson, 239–266. New York: Norton, 2004.

——. "The Philosophy of Composition." In *The Selected Writings of Edgar Allan Poe*, ed. G. R. Thompson, 675–684. New York: W. W. Norton, 2004.

——. "Phrenology." *Southern Literary Messenger* 2, no. 4 (1836): 286–287.

———. "The Poetic Principle." In *The Selected Writings of Edgar Allan Poe*, ed. G. R. Thompson, 698–704. New York: Norton, 2004.

———. "Review of *Phrenology and the Moral Influence of Phrenology: Arranged for General Study, and the Purposes of Education, from the First Published Works of Gall and Spurzheim, to the Latest Discoveries of the Present Period*. By Mrs. L. Miles. Philadelphia: Carey, Lea, and Blanchard." In Edgar Allan Poe, *Essays and Reviews*, ed., G. R. Thompson, 329–331. New York: Library of America, 1984.

———. "To Philip P. Cooke (Letter 240)." In *The Selected Writings of Edgar Allan Poe*, ed. G. R. Thompson, 684–685. New York: Norton, 2004.

Posner, Richard A. "Animal Rights: Legal, Philosophical, and Pragmatic Perspectives." In Cass R. Sunstein and Martha C. Nussbaum, eds., *Animal Rights: Current Debates and New Directions*, 51–77. Oxford: Oxford University Press, 2004.

Posner, Richard A. and Katharine B. Silbaugh. *A Guide to America's Sex Laws*. Chicago: University of Chicago Press, 1996.

Potter, David Morris. *People of Plenty: Economic Abundance and the American Character*. Chicago: University of Chicago Press, 1954.

Pozzo, Riccardo. "Introduction." In Riccardo Pozzo, ed., *The Impact of Aristotelianism on Modern Philosophy*, vii–xvi. Washington, D.C.: Catholic University of America Press, 2004.

Puar, Jasbir K. *Terrorist Assemblages: Homonationalism in Queer Times*. Durham, N.C.: Duke University Press, 2007.

Puff, Helmut. *Sodomy in Reformation Germany and Switzerland, 1400–1600*. Chicago: University of Chicago Press, 2003.

Rancière, Jacques. "Who Is the Subject of the Rights of Man?" *South Atlantic Quarterly* 103, nos. 2–3 (2004): 297–310.

Ravitz, Jessica. "They Saved Soldiers' Lives, and Were Often Left Behind." *Salt Lake Tribune*, May 29, 2006.

Regan, Tom. *The Case for Animal Rights*. Berkeley: University of California Press, 1983.

Reid, Julian. "Life Struggles: War, Discipline, and Biopolitics in the Thought of Michel Foucault." *Social Text* 86, no. 1 (2006): 127–152.

Renza, Louis. "Poe's Secret Autobiography." In Walter Benn Michaels and Donald E. Pease, eds., *The American Renaissance Reconsidered: Selected Papers from the English Institute, 1982–1983*, 58–89. Baltimore: Johns Hopkins University Press, 1985.

"Review of *Sigurd Our Golden Collie* by Katharine Lee Bates." *The Review* 2, no. 39 (1920): 135.

Rich, Frank. "It Was the Porn That Made Them Do It." *New York Times*, May 30, 2004.

Richards, Robert J. *Darwin and the Emergence of Evolutionary Theories of Mind and Behavior*. Chicago: University of Chicago Press, 1987.

———. *The Meaning of Evolution: The Morphological Construction and Ideological Reconstruction of Darwin's Theory*. Chicago: University of Chicago Press, 1992.

Ricks, George. *Object Lessons and How to Give Them*. Boston: D. C. Heath, 1893.

Ritvo, Harriet. "The Animal Connection." In James Sheehan and Morton Sosna, eds., *The Boundaries of Humanity: Humans, Animals, Machines*, 68–84. Berkeley: University of California Press, 1991.

——. *The Animal Estate: The English and Other Creatures in the Victorian Age*. Cambridge, Mass.: Harvard University Press, 1987.

——. "Animal Problems." *Science, Technology, & Human Values* 10, no. 3 (1985): 87–91.

——. "Animals in Nineteenth-Century Britain: Complicated Attitudes and Competing Categories." In Aubrey Manning and James Serpell, eds., *Animals and Human Society: Changing Perspectives*, 106–126. London: Routledge, 1994.

——. "Border Trouble: Shifting the Line Between People and Other Animals." In Arien Mack, ed., *Humans and Other Animals*, 67–86. Columbus: Ohio State University Press, 1995.

——. "Possessing Mother Nature: Genetic Capital in Eighteenth-Century Britain." In John Berwer and Susan Staves, eds., *Early Modern Conceptions of Property*, 413–426. London: Routledge, 1995.

——. "Pride and Pedigree: The Evolution of the Victorian Dog Fancy." *Victorian Studies* 29, no. 2 (1986): 227–253.

Robbins, Louise E. *Elephant Slaves and Pampered Parrots: Exotic Animals in Eighteenth-Century Paris*. Baltimore: Johns Hopkins University Press, 2002.

Rohman, Carrie. *Stalking the Subject: Modernism and the Animal*. New York: Columbia University Press, 2009.

Rorty, Richard. *Objectivity, Relativism, Truth*. Cambridge: Cambridge University Press, 1991.

Rose, Jacqueline. *The Case of Peter Pan or the Impossibility of Children's Fiction*. London: Macmillan, 1984.

Rosenheim, Shawn J. *The Cryptographic Imagination: Secret Writings from Edgar Allan Poe to the Internet*. Baltimore: Johns Hopkins University Press, 1997.

Rosser, Sue. *Biology and Feminism: A Dynamic Interaction*. New York: Twayne, 1992.

Rossi, William. "Evolutionary Theory." In Joel Myerson, Sandra Harbert Petrulionis, and Laura Dassow Walls, eds., *The Oxford Handbook of Transcendentalism*, 583–613. Oxford: Oxford University Press, 2010.

Roughgarden, Joan. *Evolution's Rainbow: Diversity, Gender, and Sexuality in Nature and People*. Berkeley: University of California Press, 2004.

Rowe, John Carlos. *At Emerson's Tomb: The Politics of Classic American Literature*. New York: Columbia University Press, 1997.

Runions, Erin. "Queering the Beast: The Antichrist's Gay Wedding." In Noreen Giffney and Myra Hird, ed., *Queering the Non/Human*, 79–110. Burlington, Vt.: Ashgate, 2008.

Rydström, Jens. *Sinners and Citizens: Bestiality and Homosexuality in Sweden, 1880–1950*. Chicago: University of Chicago Press, 2003.

Sahlins, Marshall David. *Culture and Practical Reason*. Chicago: University of Chicago Press, 1976.

Salisbury, Joyce E. *The Beast Within: Animals in the Middle Ages.* 2nd ed. London: Routledge, 2011.

Samuels, Shirley, ed. *The Culture of Sentiment: Race, Gender, and Sentimentality in Nineteenth-Century America.* New York: Oxford University Press, 1992.

Sánchez-Eppler, Karen. *Touching Liberty: Abolition, Feminism, and the Politics of the Body.* Berkeley: University of California Press, 1993.

Santner, Eric. *On Creaturely Life: Rilke, Benjamin, Sebald.* Chicago: University of Chicago Press, 2006.

Saunders, Marshall. *Beautiful Joe: An Autobiography; with an Introduction by Hezekiah Butterworth.* Philadelphia: Charles H. Banes, 1894.

Scarry, Elaine. *The Body in Pain: The Making and Unmaking of the World.* New York: Oxford University Press, 1985.

Schmidt, Leigh Eric. "The Commercialization of the Calendar: American Holidays and the Culture of Consumption, 1870–1930." *Journal of American History* 78, no. 3 (1991): 887–916.

Scholtmeijer, Marian Louise. *Animal Victims in Modern Fiction: From Sanctity to Sacrifice.* Toronto: University of Toronto Press, 1993.

Sedgwick, Eve Kosofsky. *Epistemology of the Closet.* Berkeley: University of California Press, 1990.

Seeley, Eva Brunell. *Chinook and His Family, True Dog Stories.* Boston: Ginn, 1930.

Sells, A. Lytton. *Animal Poetry in French & English Literature & the Greek Tradition.* Bloomington: Indiana University Press, 1955.

Seltzer, Mark. *True Crime: Observations on Violence and Modernity.* New York: Routledge, 2007.

Shafer, Byron E. *Is America Different? A New Look at American Exceptionalism.* Oxford: Clarendon Press, 1991.

Shaler, Nathaniel Southgate. *Domesticated Animals: Their Relation to Man and to His Advancement in Civilization.* New York: Charles Scribner's Sons, 1895.

Shannon, Laurie. "The Eight Animals in Shakespeare; or, Before the Human." *PMLA* 124, no. 2 (2009): 472–479.

Shapiro, Kenneth and Margo DeMello. "The State of Human–Animal Studies." *Society and Animals* 18 (2010): 307–318.

Sheehan, Bernard W. *Savagism and Civility: Indians and Englishmen in Colonial Virginia.* Cambridge: Cambridge University Press, 1980.

Shell, Marc. "The Family Pet." *Representations* 15 (1986): 121–153.

Shepard, Paul. *The Others: How Animals Made Us Human.* Washington, D.C.: Island Press, 1996.

Shesadri-Crooks, Kalpana. "Being Human: Bestiality, Anthropophagy, and Law." *Umbr(a)* 3, no. 1 (2003): 97–114.

Shukin, Nicole. *Animal Capital: Rendering Life in Biopolitical Times.* Minneapolis: University of Minnesota Press, 2009.

Shulman, Robert. "Poe and the Powers of the Mind." *English Literary History* 37, no. 2 (1970): 245–262.

Sielke, Sabine. *Reading Rape: The Rhetoric of Sexual Violence in American Literature and Culture, 1790–1990.* Princeton: Princeton University Press, 2002.

Simons, John. *Animal Rights and the Politics of Literary Representation.* Houndmills, U.K.: Palgrave, 2002.

Singer, Peter. *Animal Liberation.* New York: Avon Books, 1977.

——. "Heavy Petting" (review of *Dearest Pet* by Midas Dekkers). *Nerve* (March 2001), at http://www.nerve.com/Opinions/Singer/heavyPetting/main.asp, and *Prospect* (April 2001): 12–13.

Singer, Peter and Karen Dawn. "Echoes of Abu Ghraib in a Chicken Slaughterhouse." *Los Angeles Times,* July 25, 2004.

Slotkin, Richard. *Regeneration Through Violence: The Mythology of the American Frontier 1600–1860.* Norman: University of Oklahoma Press, 1973.

Smith, Craig. "Across the Widest Gulf: Nonhuman Subjectivity in Virginia Woolf's *Flush.*" *Twentieth Century Literature* 48, no. 3 (2002): 348–361.

Smith, Sidonie and Julia Watson. "Introduction: Situating Subjectivity in Women's Autobiographical Practices." In Sidonie Smith and Julia Watson, eds., *Women, Autobiography, Theory: A Reader,* 3–56. Madison: University of Wisconsin Press, 1998.

Sober, Elliott. "Comparative Psychology Meets Evolutionary Biology: Morgan's Canon and Cladistic Parsimony." In Lorraine Daston and Gregg Mitman, eds., *Thinking with Animals: New Perspectives on Anthropomorphism,* 87–99. New York: Columbia University Press, 2005.

Sontag, Susan. "Regarding the Torture of Others." *New York Times,* May 23, 2004.

Spiegel, Marjorie. *The Dreaded Comparison: Human and Animal Slavery.* Philadelphia: New Society, 1988.

Stabile, Susan M. "A 'Doctrine of Signatures': The Epistolary Physicks of Esther Burr's Journal." In Janet Moore Lindman and Michele Lise Tarter, eds., *A Centre of Wonders: The Body in Early America,* 109–126. Ithaca: Cornell University Press, 2001.

Stallybrass, Peter and Allon White. *The Politics and Poetics of Transgression.* Ithaca: Cornell University Press, 1986.

Steiner, Gary. *Anthropocentrism and Its Discontents: The Moral Status of Animals in the History of Western Philosophy.* Pittsburgh: University of Pittsburgh Press, 2005.

Stern, Julia A. *The Plight of Feeling: Sympathy and Dissent in the Early American Novel.* Chicago: University of Chicago Press, 1997.

Stern, Madeleine. "Poe: 'The Mental Temperament' for Phrenologists." *American Literature* 40, no. 2 (1968): 155–163.

Stevenson, Lionel. *Darwin Among the Poets.* Chicago: University of Chicago Press, 1932.

Stevenson, Lloyd G. "On the Supposed Exclusion of Butchers and Surgeons from Jury Duty." *Journal of the History of Medicine and Allied Sciences* 9, no. 2 (1954): 235–238.

Stockton, Kathryn Bond. *The Queer Child or Growing Sideways in the Twentieth Century*. Durham, N.C.: Duke University Press, 2009.

Stoler, Ann Laura. *Haunted by Empire: Geographies of Intimacy in North American History*. Durham, N.C.: Duke University Press, 2006.

Stone, Andrea. "Interracial Sexual Abuse and Legal Subjectivity in Antebellum Law and Literature." *American Literature* 81, no. 1 (2009): 65–92.

Stories About Dogs, for Our Boys and Girls. Boston: Lee and Shepard, 1854.

Summerfield, Geoffrey. *Fantasy and Reason: Children's Literature in the Eighteenth Century*. Athens: University of Georgia Press, 1985.

Sunstein, Cass R. and Martha C. Nussbaum, eds. *Animal Rights: Current Debates and New Directions*. Oxford: Oxford University Press, 2004.

Swerdlow, Amy. "Woman's Peace Festival, June 2, 1873." In "Teaching about Peace, War, and Women in the Military," special issue of *Women's Studies Quarterly* 12, no. 2 (1984): 29.

Talbot, Ethelbert. *Tim: The Autobiography of a Dog*. New York: Harper, 1914.

"Talking Dogs." *New York Times*, February 3, 1991.

Tannenbaum, Frank. *The American Tradition in Foreign Policy*. Norman: University of Oklahoma Press, 1955.

Taylor, Matthew. "Edgar Allan Poe's (Meta-)Physics: A Pre-history of the Post-human." *Nineteenth-Century Literature* 62, no. 2 (2007): 193–222.

Terada, Rei. *Feeling in Theory: Emotion After the "Death of the Subject."* Cambridge, Mass.: Harvard University Press, 2001.

Terhune, Albert Payson. *A Book of Famous Dogs*. 1st ed. New York: Doubleday, Doran, 1937.

Thomas, Keith. *Man and the Natural World: A History of the Modern Sensibility*. New York: Pantheon Books, 1983.

Thompson, Roger. *Sex in Middlesex: Popular Mores in a Massachusetts County, 1649–1699*. Amherst: University of Massachusetts Press, 1986.

Toklas, Alice B. *The Alice B. Toklas Cookbook*. New York: Harper & Row, 1984.

Tompkins, Jane P. *Sensational Designs: The Cultural Work of American Fiction, 1790–1860*. New York: Oxford University Press, 1985.

Tomso, Gregory. "Viral Sex and the Politics of Life." *South Atlantic Quarterly* 107, no. 2 (2008): 265–285.

Trilling, Lionel. *The Liberal Imagination: Essays on Literature and Society*. New York: Viking Press, 1950.

Trimmer, [Sarah]. *Fabulous Histories: Designed for the Instruction of Children Respecting Their Treatment of Animals*. London: T. Longman, G. G. J. and J. Robinson, and J. Johnson, 1786. Microform.

Tuan, Yi-fu. *Dominance and Affection: The Making of Pets*. New Haven: Yale University Press, 1984.

Tuana, Nancy. "Aristotle and the Politics of Reproduction." In Bat-Ami Bar On, ed., *Engendering Origins: Critical Feminist Readings in Plato and Aristotle*, 189–206. Albany: State University of New York Press, 1994.

Turner, James. *Reckoning with the Beast: Animals, Pain, and Humanity in the Victorian Mind*. Baltimore: Johns Hopkins University Press, 1980.

Tyrell, Ian. "American Exceptionalism in an Age of International History." *American Historical Review* 96 no. 4 (1991): 1031–1055.

Villarreal, Omar. "Military Working Dogs, Handlers Train for Mission Success." Federal Information and News Dispatch, Defense Department Documents and Publications, February 6, 2006. At http://web.lexis-nexis.com/universe/document?_m=c1cf2b8 4e1b4627e10ce6bb1dd4cea42&_docnum=36&wchp=dGLbVzb-zSkVb&_md5= 5a19961a90dd3402b9d667ed553b613a.

Vitalis, Robert. "Black Gold, White Crude: An Essay on American Exceptionalism, Hierarchy, and Hegemony in the Gulf." *Diplomatic History* 26, no. 2 (2002): 185–213.

Wall, Thomas Carl. "Au Hasard." In Andrew Norris, ed., *Politics, Metaphysics, and Death: Essays on Giorgio Agamben's "Homo Sacer,"* 31–48. Durham, N.C.: Duke University Press, 2005.

Warner, Michael. "New English Sodom." *American Literature* 64, no. 1 (1992): 19–47.

Watson, J. S. [John Selby]. *Reasoning Power in Animals*. London: Reeve, 1867.

Weil, Kari. "A Report on the Animal Turn." *differences* 21, no. 2 (2010): 1–23.

——. *Thinking Animals: Why Animal Studies Now?* New York: Columbia University Press, 2012.

Westfall, Sandra Sobieraj. "Michelle Obama: White House Dog Coming Soon!" *People Magazine*, February 25, 2009.

Whalen, Terence. "Average Racism." In J. Gerald Kennedy and Liliane Weissberg, eds., *Romancing the Shadow: Poe and Race*, 3–40. New York: Oxford University Press, 2001.

——. "The Code for Gold: Edgar Allan Poe and Cryptography." *Representations* 46 (1994): 35–57.

Wilentz, Sean. "Against Exceptionalism: Class Consciousness and the American Labor Movement, 1790–1920." *International Labor and Working Class History* 26 (1984): 1–24.

Williams, Patricia. "In Kind." *The Nation*, May 31, 2004.

Willis, Roy G. *Man and Beast*. New York: Basic Books, 1974.

Wills, David. *Dorsality: Thinking Back Through Technology and Politics*. Minneapolis: University of Minnesota Press, 2008.

Wimsatt, W. K. "What Poe Knew About Cryptography." *PMLA* 56 (1943): 754–779.

Winnicott, D. W. *Playing and Reality*. New York: Routledge, 1957.

Winter, Alison. *Mesmerized: Powers of Mind in Victorian Britain*. Chicago: University of Chicago Press, 1998.

Winterer, Caroline. *The Culture of Classicism*. Baltimore: Johns Hopkins University Press, 2002.

Winthrop, John. *History of New England*. 2 vols. Boston: Little, Brown, 1853.

Wise, Gene. " 'Paradigm Dramas' in American Studies: A Cultural and Institutional History of the Movement." *American Quarterly* 31, no. 3 (1979): 293–337.

Wise, Steven. "Animal Rights, One Step at a Time." In Cass R. Sunstein and Martha C. Nussbaum, eds., *Animal Rights: Current Debates and New Directions*, 19–50. Oxford: Oxford University Press, 2004.

Wiseman, Susan J. "Hairy on the Inside: Metamorphosis and Civility in English Werewolf Texts." In Erica Fudge, ed., *Renaissance Beasts: Of Animals, Humans, and Other Wonderful Creatures*, 50–69. Urbana: University of Illinois Press, 2004.

——. "Monstrous Perfectibility: Ape–Human Transformations in Hobbes, Bulwer, Tyson." In Erica Fudge, Ruth Gilbert, and Susan Wiseman, eds., *At the Borders of the Human: Beasts, Bodies, and Natural Philosophy in the Early Modern Period*, 215–239. New York: Palgrave, 2002.

Wolch, Jennifer and Jody Emel, eds. *Animal Geographies: Place, Politics, and Identity in the Nature–Culture Borderlands*. London: Verso, 1998.

Wolf, Michael P. "Language, Mind, and World: Can't We All Just Get Along?" *Metaphilosophy* 39, no. 3 (2008): 363–380.

Wolfe, Cary. *Animal Rites: American Culture, the Discourse of Species, and Posthumanist Theory*. Chicago: University of Chicago Press, 2003.

——. *Before the Law: Humans and Other Animals in a Biopolitical Frame*. Chicago: University of Chicago Press, 2012.

——. "Human, All Too Human: 'Animal Studies' and the Humanities." *PMLA* 124, no. 2 (2009): 564–575.

——. *What Is Posthumanism?* Minneapolis: University of Minnesota Press, 2010.

——, ed. *Zoontologies: The Question of the Animal*. Minneapolis: University of Minnesota Press, 2003.

Wolfe, Cary and Jonathan Elmer. "Subject to Sacrifice: Ideology, Psychoanalysis, and the Discourse of Species in Jonathan Demme's *Silence of the Lambs*." *boundary 2* 22, no. 3 (1995): 141–170.

——. "Subject to Sacrifice: Ideology, Psychoanalysis, and the Poverty of Humanism." In *Animal Rites: American Culture, the Discourse of Species, and Posthumanist Theory*, 97–121. Chicago: University of Chicago Press, 2003.

Woolf, Virginia. *Flush: A Biography*. London: Hogarth Press, 1933.

Wren, A. "Application of Phrenology to the Analysis of the Character of Shakespeare's Iago." *American Phrenological Journal* 1, no. 7 (1839): 212–228.

Wylie, Dan. "The Anthropomorphic Ethic: Fiction and the Animal Mind in Virginia Woolf's *Flush* and Barbara Gowdy's *The White Bone*." *ISLE: Interdisciplinary Studies in Literature and Environment* 9, no. 2 (2002): 115–131.

Young, Robert M. *Darwin's Metaphor: Nature's Place in Victorian Culture*. Cambridge: Cambridge University Press, 1985.

Ziarek, Ewa Plonowska. "Bare Life on Strike: Notes on the Biopolitics of Race and Gender." *South Atlantic Quarterly* 107, no. 1 (2008): 89–105.

Ziegler, Valarie H. *Diva Julia: The Public Romance and Private Agony of Julia Ward Howe.* Harrisburg, Pa.: Trinity Press International, 2003.

Žižek, Slavoj. "Between Two Deaths: The Culture of Torture." *London Review of Books*, June 3, 2004.

INDEX